An Introduction to Chinese Philosophy

This comprehensive introduction to early Chinese philosophy covers a range of philosophical traditions which arose during the Spring and Autumn (722–476 BCE) and Warring States (475–221 BCE) periods in China, including Confucianism, Mohism, Daoism and Legalism. It considers concepts, themes and argumentative methods of early Chinese philosophy and follows the development of some ideas in subsequent periods, including the introduction of Buddhism into China. The book examines key issues and debates in early Chinese philosophy, cross-influences between its traditions and interpretations by scholars up to the present day. The discussion draws upon both primary texts and secondary sources, and there are suggestions for further reading. This will be an invaluable guide for all who are interested in the foundations of Chinese philosophy and its richness and continuing relevance.

KARYN L. LAI is Senior Lecturer in the School of History and Philosophy, University of New South Wales, Australia. She is the author of *Learning from Chinese Philosophies: Ethics of Interdependent and Contextualised Self* (2006).

An Introduction to Chinese Philosophy

KARYN L. LAI
University of New South Wales

CAMBRIDGE UNIVERSITY PRESS
Cambridge, New York, Melbourne, Madrid, Cape Town,
Singapore, São Paulo, Delhi

Cambridge University Press
The Edinburgh Building, Cambridge CB2 8RU, UK

Published in the United States of America by Cambridge
University Press, New York

www.cambridge.org
Information on this title: www.cambridge.org/9780521608923

First published 2008

Printed in the United Kingdom at the University Press, Cambridge

A catalogue record for this publication is available from the British Library

Library of Congress Cataloguing in Publication data
Lai, Karyn, 1964–
An introduction to Chinese philosophy / Karyn L. Lai.
p. cm.
Includes bibliographical references and index.
ISBN 978-0-521-84646-2 (hardback) – ISBN 978-0-521-60892-3 (pbk.)
1. Philosophy, Chinese. I. Title.

B5231.L34 2008
181′.11–dc22

2008015650

ISBN 978-0-521-84646-2 hardback
ISBN 978-0-521-60892-3 paperback

For Sophie, Toby and Michael

Contents

Preface

This book covers the different philosophical traditions in early Chinese philosophy, focusing on their concepts, themes, reasoning and argumentative methods. It introduces readers to fundamental ideas in the different traditions, debates among thinkers, cross-influences between traditions, as well as interpretive theories about these ideas, including those of contemporary scholars. The chapters are organised to reflect the chronological development of Chinese philosophies, as far as this is possible. **A List of Dates** is provided at the outset to set out important chronological information about selected thinkers and how they are placed in relation to other thinkers. This list is selective and brief, listing only those thinkers and periods that are discussed in the book. The at-a-glance table should help the reader place thinkers in their historical context in relation to other thinkers. Dates are also included in the text in places where they are integral to the specific point being made.

A short list of **Suggestions for Further Reading** is provided at the end of each chapter. These are the most important primary and secondary sources for a student in Chinese philosophy to be familiar with. A more extended **Bibliography** is included at the end of the book. The items here, set out in two separate lists, *Primary Texts* and *Secondary Sources*, provide a more extended reading list. The **Glossary** at the end of the book is set out in three sections comprising *Texts*, *Names* and *Concepts and Themes*. The lists are alphabetically arranged in *Pinyin* transliteration, and, where possible, an English translation is provided.

It is advisable to read the chapters in the order in which they appear as each chapter builds upon the preceding ones. Chapter One is an important chapter that presents key themes and argumentative methods in Chinese philosophy which are developed in subsequent chapters. Readers might find it beneficial to revisit some of the discussions in Chapter One at appropriate points.

I conclude the book with a **Postscript** designed to give readers a sense of ongoing studies in Chinese philosophy, as well as to suggest a number of interesting areas for further exploration.

List of Dates (in Chronological Order)

Periods in Chinese History	Thinkers	Dates
Xia dynasty		ca. 2070 BCE–1600 BCE
Shang dynasty		ca. 1600 BCE–1046 BCE
Zhou dynasty		1122 BCE–221 BCE
Spring and Autumn period (*Chunqiu*)		722 BCE–476 BCE
	Guan Zhong	683 BCE–642 BCE
	Confucius (Kongzi)	551 BCE–479 BCE
	Deng Xi	d. 501 BCE
	Zisi	483? BCE–402? BCE
	Mozi	480? BCE–390? BCE
Warring States period (*Zhanguo*)		475 BCE–221 BCE
	Gaozi	420? BCE–350 BCE
	Zhuangzi	399? BCE–295? BCE
	Mencius	385? BCE–312? BCE
	Gongsun Long	b. 380? BCE
	Hui Shi	370? BCE–310? BCE
	Yang Zhu	ca. 350 BCE
	Shang Yang	d. 338 BCE
	Shen Dao	350? BCE–275? BCE
	Shen Buhai	d. 337 BCE
	Xunzi	310? BCE–219? BCE
	Zou Yan	305? BCE–240? BCE
	Lü Buwei	291? BCE–235? BCE
	Han Fei	280? BCE–233 BCE
	Li Si	280? BCE–208? BCE
Qin dynasty		221 BCE–206 BCE
Han dynasty		206 BCE–220 CE
	Jia Yi	201 BCE–168? BCE

Periods in Chinese History	Thinkers	Dates
	Dong Zhongshu	195? BCE–115? BCE
	Liu An	180? BCE–122? BCE
	Sima Tan	d. 110 BCE
	Sima Qian	145 BCE–86? BCE
	Ban Biao	3 CE–54 CE
	Ban Gu	32–92
	Ban Zhao	35–100
Three Kingdoms (*Sanguo*)		220–280
	Wang Bi	226–249
Jin dynasty		260–420
	Guo Xiang	d. 312
	Dao-an	312–385
	Hui Yuan	334–416
	Kumarajiva (*Jiumoluoshi*)	344–413
	Dao Sheng	360?–434?
Northern Wei dynasty		386–534
Southern and Northern dynasties		420–589
	Bodhidharma	470–543
	Zhi Yi	538–597
	Ji Zang	540–623
	Du Shun	557–640
Sui dynasty		581–618
	Xuan Zang	596–664
	Hong Ren	601–674
	Shen Xiu	605?–706?
Tang dynasty		618–907
	Hui Neng	638–713
	Fa Zang	643–712
	Shen Hui	670–762
	Han Yu	768–824
	Li Ao	d. ca. 844
Five dynasties and Ten Kingdoms		907–960
Song dynasty		960–1260
Yuan dynasty		1271–1368
Ming dynasty		1368–1644
Qing dynasty		1644–1911

1 Chinese Philosophy

An Introduction to Chinese Philosophy examines the major philosophical concepts, themes and texts in early Chinese philosophy, roughly from the time of Confucius in the sixth century BCE to the Han period (206 BCE–220 CE). This is the period of the origins of Chinese philosophy insofar as the extant texts reveal elements of reflective and systematic thinking. The philosophies discussed here are a representative selection of intellectual debates of early China. The aim is not to present a comprehensive and exhaustive survey of Chinese philosophical themes and texts, an encyclopaedic task. Rather, the topics covered in this book are selective and representative of the field. In this way, we may engage at a deeper level with a number of prominent issues debated by thinkers of the time, and which have continuing relevance today.

This book attempts to achieve a balance between articulating the general spirit and style of Chinese philosophy as a disciplinary field, and identifying the more distinctive features of each of the philosophies. The doctrines discussed include Confucianism, Mohism, Daoism, Legalism, Theory of Names (by the Mingjia and Dialecticians) and Buddhism. Discussions will focus on concepts, themes, conceptual frameworks, elements of philosophical reasoning, argumentative devices in the selected traditions, and on debates and disagreements between them. Understanding the disagreements is at least as important as recognising the distinctive ideas of each tradition, as it draws attention both to contrasts and common elements of those traditions as they evolved alongside others.

Although Buddhism was introduced into China toward the end of the period of our concern, it would be remiss not to include some discussion of its key concepts. Buddhism went through various transformations from the time it was introduced into China and gradually began to take on a distinctive character, that of *Chinese* Buddhism, from around the sixth century. It also became an influential doctrine and shaped the subsequent development of Chinese philosophy. Many of its features found their way into existing Chinese traditions, especially Daoism and Neo-Confucianism. However, in order to keep the volume to a manageable size, it has not been possible to include a discussion of Neo-Confucianism. Neo-Confucianism was a development of Confucian doctrines and was a prominent philosophical movement from the tenth century, although some of its origins may be traced as far back as Han Confucianism. Many of the discussions by Neo-Confucian thinkers focus on metaphysical and meta-philosophical issues and it is unfortunate that these cannot be included. In order to include discussions of Neo-Confucianism we would have had to cover at least another eleven centuries of Chinese philosophy. Hopefully, the discussions in this volume will provide readers with a good understanding of the fundamental conceptual frameworks and concerns of Chinese philosophy and thereby equip readers to understand later developments in Chinese philosophy.

A second objective of this volume is to capture a sense of intellectual debt and cross-influences between the traditions. While some attention has been given to chronology, the primary concern is the coherent presentation of philosophical themes. In other words, thematic coherence takes priority over chronological order. For instance, the *Yijing* (*The Book of Changes*) is discussed relatively late in the volume because of the influential interpretations of it by thinkers during the Han Dynasty. Yet, many of the ideas were nascent in earlier discussions.

Some attempt is made to compare the features of Chinese philosophy with parallel aspects of western philosophy. However, the aim of such comparisons is to elucidate the characteristics of Chinese philosophy rather than to present and account for differences in the two fields as such. Attention is also given to contemporary debates in the field of Chinese philosophy by modern and contemporary scholars who work in China and beyond. Many of these scholars are enthused by insights in the different philosophies and committed to demonstrating their relevance to the contemporary world. Their interest in Chinese philosophy extends beyond the study of the texts themselves, and toward issues of pragmatic import. These scholars are both inheritors of these traditions and contributors to them.

This book should be read in conjunction with a close reading of the primary texts. If it is not possible to read more complete versions of the texts, readers should at least obtain a reliable compendium of primary sources such as Wm Theodore de Bary and Irene Bloom's *Sources of Chinese Tradition* (Vol. 1: 1999) or Wing-tsit Chan's *A Source Book in Chinese Philosophy* (1963a).

Origins of Chinese Philosophy

Prolonged unrest in China during the Spring and Autumn (*Chunqiu*) period (722–476 BCE) and the Warring States (*Zhanguo*) period (475–221 BCE) brought an end to the feudalistic Zhou dynasty (1122–221 BCE). During this extended period of turmoil, many men who had previously lived in privileged circumstances were displaced and forced to seek alternative means of living. Many of them had views about the causes of the unrest and proposed solutions for rectifying it. The Spring and Autumn period saw the rise of scholar-officials (*shi*), men who gave advice to those in power and who were identified by loyalty to their ministers (Hsu 1965). Confucius and many of his pupils were part of this phenomenon (Hsu 1965: 34–7). Although the *shi* had been displaced from their previous privileged positions, they had rapidly regained social status and established themselves as a distinct social and cultural elite. Those who were capable made themselves indispensable to their ministers and began to play more active roles than the ministers (Hsu 1965: 8). As a result, there was much competition among those in power to attract the most capable advisers (Hsu 1999: 572–83).

It was in this climate of widespread patronage of ideas and learning that we see the beginnings of systematic inquiry in China. The scholar-officials offered their visions for rectifying society. The urgency of the political situation shaped the theories of this period; many of the discussions focused on morality, political society and good governance. The *Zhuangzi*, a Daoist text composed between the fourth and third centuries BCE, describes the proliferation of ideas at that time:

> The empire is in utter confusion, sagehood and excellence are not clarified, we do not have the one Way and Power…There is an analogy in the ears, eyes, nose and mouth; all have something they illuminate but they cannot exchange their functions, just as the various specialities of the Hundred Schools all have their strong points and at times turn out useful. However, they are not inclusive, not comprehensive; these are men each of whom has his own little corner. (*Zhuangzi*, Chapter 33, trans. Graham 2001: 275)

Scholars have adopted the phrase *baijia zhi xue* (Hundred Schools of Learning) to characterise the diversity of ideas and the spirit of debate of the time.[1] The term '*jia*' (literally 'house'; meaning 'group') referred to the doctrinal groups the early thinkers identified with. However, the classifications of doctrine (*xue*) were largely unsystematic during the early period of Chinese intellectual history. Sima Tan (died 110 BCE), a historian, was among the first to categorise the different lines of thought in early China. He simplified their doctrines under six categories:

(1) *Yin-Yang school*: grounded in a belief in two major principles *yin* (female) and *yang* (male) and applied in particular to cosmology;
(2) *Ru school*: the school of the literati, the scholars. Confucians were included in this group;
(3) *Mo school*: the Mohist school, a close-knit organisation of soldiers and craftsmen with strict discipline, founded by Mozi;
(4) *Ming school*: the Mingjia. Thinkers categorised in this group discussed topics relating to the correspondence between language and reality;
(5) *Fa school*: comprised by the Legalists, emphasised punishments (*fa*) as a primary instrument of social control;
(6) *Dao-De school*: comprised by thinkers who emphasised the way (*dao*) and power (*de*) in debates in metaphysics and political and social philosophy. (Fung 1948: 30–1)

Sima Tan's classification of the six schools of thought was rather haphazard. He identified three of them (*yin-yang*, *fa* and *dao-de*) according to their doctrinal commitments, one according to the social profile of its adherents (*ru*, the literati), one according to the name the group had given itself (*mo*, following the name of their founder), and one according to the area of inquiry (*ming*: names). This complexity, present from the beginning, remains an important feature of Chinese intellectual debate. Against the background of many competing views, argumentation and justification of ideas were important, as was thinking that synthesised a range of perspectives. In the following section, we attend to a number of distinctive features of Chinese philosophy.

Features of Chinese Philosophy

Self Cultivation

The early Chinese thinkers believed the purpose of learning was to better oneself and society. They discussed different concepts of self cultivation (*xiushen*). The Confucians believed that learning and the cultivation of virtue were aspects of the same process. For them, the cultivated person was a person who could legitimately lead the people. This belief has had a broad influence in Chinese society. An important and lasting legacy of this belief is the institution of the Civil Service Examinations, a system for the recruitment of top scholars for the civil service. This system was founded on the belief that scholars of the classical texts will also be adept practitioners of good government and was in place for over 1300 years, from the Sui Dynasty (581–618 CE) to the Qing (1644–1911 CE).

While belief in the unity of wisdom and virtue has strong Confucian overtones, thinkers of the other schools also deliberated on the topic of *xiushen*. In the *Mozi* text, associated with Mohism, there is an entire chapter devoted to *xiushen*. There, its author discusses the development of a commitment to benefit the world (Schwartz 1985: 158). Philosophical Daoism, associated with the texts *Daodejing*, *Zhuangzi* and *Liezi*, advocated intuitive and experiential grasp of *dao*, leading to a way of life unsullied by conventional practices, beliefs and expectations. Self cultivation in this tradition involves undoing many of the effects of socialisation and nurturing one's life according to the axioms of non-conditioned action (*wuwei*) and spontaneity (*ziran*). There were also religious Daoists, especially during the Han Dynasty, who were preoccupied with attaining immortality; they interpreted *dao* in religious and mystical terms. For them, *xiushen* involved esoteric practices, rigorous discipline of the body and explorations in alchemy (Robinet 1997; Kohn 1993). Yang Zhu (c. 350 BCE) who is often described as an 'egoist', promoted a philosophy of 'each for himself' (*weiwo*). His idea of nurturing the self, which included attention to the body, was to keep the self unadulterated from corrupting influences in society.[2] Even the Dialecticians, who debated seemingly abstract topics relating to language and its connection with reality, were concerned to provide practical advice to those in power (Graham 1989: 75–95).

For the early thinkers, it was not simply that intellectual inquiry had to have practical outcomes. More importantly, the pursuit of learning incorporated a sense of morality. This meant that conceptions of morality were often articulated in dynamic and situational terms in order to capture the developmental nature of self cultivation. As we will see in the following chapters, discussions of ethics in Chinese philosophy almost always engage with issues at the level of practical application; these may differ from stage to stage or vary from person to person according to ability. This does not mean that Chinese philosophers did not consider abstract matters. There was much speculative thought, including the contemplation of logical puzzles (especially by the Dialecticians), metaphors, analogies and suggestive imagery. Overall, however, less attention was paid to discussions about universal or normative standards and principles. The overwhelming emphasis on experience and practice in discussions of ethics may have instigated Immanuel Kant's disparaging view of Chinese philosophy:

> Philosophy is not to be found in the whole Orient . . . Their teacher Confucius teaches in his writings nothing outside a moral doctrine designed for the princes . . . and offers examples of former Chinese princes . . . But a concept of virtue and morality never entered the heads of the Chinese . . . In order to arrive at an idea . . . of the good [certain] studies would be required, of which [the Chinese] know nothing.[3]

But we must understand that the approach to ethics in Chinese philosophy does not begin with the task of deciding on right or good moral principles, in Kant's words, 'to arrive at an idea of the good'. From the perspective of self cultivation, an 'idea of the good' is a static concept and therefore inadequate to capture the needs of people at different developmental phases.[4] Furthermore, individuals develop their moral capacities at different rates and to different extents. The early Chinese thinkers recognised that while there are norms of action and behaviour, these must invariably be adapted to their contexts of application by particular individuals. For them, the basic problem was not to devise norms or standards for action but how these could be applied by different people in different situations. The primary moral question in Chinese philosophy is not, What ought I to do? but What is the best way to live?

Understanding the Self: Relationships and Contexts

In Chinese philosophy, an individual is essentially a relationally constituted and situated self. This means that there are many factors that shape the self, including its relationships with significant others and its experiences within its historical, cultural, social and political contexts. Rarely, if ever, is an individual expected to act as an independent, detached moral agent, or judged according to an idealised paradigm of independent selfhood. According to the picture of self in Chinese philosophy, relationships and environments largely determine an individual's values, thoughts, beliefs, motivations, behaviours and actions.

In a brief survey of the different doctrinal groups in Chinese philosophy, we see that this general feature is embodied in the different philosophies. Pre-Confucian discussions focused on the responsibilities of the ruler, the Son of Heaven (*tianzi*), who was the authoritative representative of Heaven (*tian*) to the people. Early Confucian and Mohist debates focused primarily on human relationships in the socio-political context. Later Confucians (during the Warring States and Han periods) also discussed the relationship between Heaven (*tian*), Earth (*di*) and humanity. Daoist thinkers looked beyond human relationships in their consideration of *dao*. Discussions in the *Daodejing* and *Zhuangzi*, two major Daoist texts, drew on analogies between the human and natural worlds. The texts emphasise the importance of understanding all entities, processes, events, causation and energies in their contexts. In the Han dynasty, cosmological thinking, which holds that there are connections between the cosmic and human realms, was a popular theme expounded on by both Confucians and Daoists. The *Book of Changes*, a text used for divination and whose composition is dated at around the ninth century BCE, was reinterpreted during this time to reinforce claims about continuities and correspondences in the human, natural and cosmic worlds (Schwartz 1985: 358–70). As we shall see, the pictures of self-realisation in the different philosophies are dramatically different and often the cause of deep disagreement. Nevertheless, they share a similar fundamental picture of life and existence. This is the view that individuals are inextricably relational and are contextually situated. In the chapters that follow, we examine the manifestations of this conception of life: good relationships are central to a good life, as is a stable society within which the individual negotiates his relationships with others.

From a contemporary perspective, the concept of self as primarily related to others and embedded in its environment raises concerns about the status of the individual. For instance, would a self conceived in this way be overwhelmed by its relationships: the aim in one's life might become an unbearable juggling task of being a mother, a daughter, an employee, a teacher, an aunt, a niece, and a wife? This is a picture of self created and determined almost entirely by its roles.[5] Similar concerns are raised in conjunction with Confucian or Chinese societies embodying a collectivist outlook, as contrasted with the situation in individualist societies which allow for and encourage responsibility, creativity and other expressions of the self (see the discussion in Tu 1972: 192–3). There is some basis for the concern that Chinese philosophy in general tends to focus on collective interests rather than individual interests, although we must resist the tendency to characterise ideologies in a dichotomous way, either as individualist or collectivist. It is inaccurate to say that the different Chinese philosophies do not attend to matters relating to the interests of individuals. They do consider details pertaining to particular individuals and events, but there is often a sense that it is exceedingly difficult to isolate matters that pertain only to one individual's interests.

We will see in the discussions that follow that instead of either 'collectivist' or 'individualist' Chinese philosophy tends to assume interdependence between entities or individuals. There are many discussions about the overlaps between individual interests and common interests, reminding us that it is artificial to think solely in terms of either self-interest or servitude to others. This applies to relationships among humans, human relationships with natural entities, and the place of humanity in its social and natural environments. It is not that Chinese philosophy does not have a conception of individual achievement. Rather, an individual's achievements, ingenuity, resourcefulness, as well as malfunctions and deficiencies, are only properly understood in light of a person's place in the conditioning environment. However, this is not to say that the environment takes precedence over individuals, as individuals may alter their contexts. In this way, neither the individual nor the whole has primacy over the other.

Conceptions of Harmony

Social harmony and stability were critical issues for the early thinkers in China. The period of the 'Hundred Schools', when Chinese philosophy first flourished in China, was a period of social unrest that lasted for over five centuries. The thinkers deliberated on the institutions, methods and processes that could ensure a more stable and peaceful existence. The Confucian vision of an ideal society sees good relationships as fundamental to social stability. The family was a microcosm of the state, which was the macrocosm encompassing edifying human interrelations, guided by institutions and governed by a benevolent (*ren*) sage king. The Mohists disagreed with the Confucian vision. They were worried that the Confucian focus on close relationships would inculcate partiality rather than altruism. They argued that, from the state's point of view, it was necessary to nurture general concern of each person for everyone else. The Confucian approach, which advocated the cultivation of special relationships, is effectively a system that fosters particular loyalties. According to the Mohists, the outcome, writ large, is war between families and states. The Mohists were convinced that the means to achieve harmony was through standardisation. They believed that it was important to have standards (*fa*) in order to ensure consistency in the way people were treated. In other words, standards were important institutions that contributed to socio-political stability. The Legalists shared these views about standards although they had very different conceptions of their purpose and implementation. While the Mohists sought to 'standardise' or normalise altruism, the Legalists conceived of it as an instrument by which to control the people. Their ultimate commitment was to maintain the power of the ruler. Uniformity was also important in the project of the Dialecticians, which grew out of early Mohist concerns. The Dialecticians aimed to ensure unity of doctrines and beliefs by settling disagreements. They believed that the root of disputes lay in improperly defined concepts and their applications, and that disputes would be settled if the connections between terms and their referents were clarified.

Among the early thinkers, the Daoists stand apart in their hesitancy about social order and uniformity. Daoist philosophy embraces multiplicity and plurality, often reflecting on natural kinds and events in the natural world in order to cast doubt on anthropocentric and reductive interpretations of events and processes. The Daoist philosophical texts express a sense of chaotic unpredictability in phenomena; numerous events defy attempts by humans to classify, control and manipulate. The *Zhuangzi* even seems to celebrate the messy cacophony of differences between individuals and views. Nevertheless, harmony remains an important end in Daoist philosophy. However, unlike the other philosophies, it does not hold that the elimination of individual differences is a prerequisite for harmony within the whole. According to the Daoist picture, attempts by other thinkers to systematise and unify difference actually caused fragmentation and dislocation. By contrast, the Daoists viewed harmony as a lively interchange between different points of view. In spite of its fundamental divergences from the other schools of thought, Daoist philosophy seeks an eventual coming-together in plurality. Passages in the *Daodejing* make frequent references to the all-embracing perspective of *dao*. In the *Zhuangzi*, there is also a particular concern that attempted solutions do not impose a false unity of multiplicities. There are many philosophically significant features of the holistic point of view in Chinese philosophy. From the perspective of the whole, relationships between individuals, beings and groups are not reducible. That is, the whole is not merely the sum of its parts; a proper account of it must include consideration of individuals, their relationships with others, and their place in the whole.

Conceptions of Change

Chinese philosophy posits continuities and correspondences between individual entities. This approach is articulated to different extents within the different schools. We see its clearest manifestation in the debates during the late Warring States and Han dynasties, when much effort was put into articulating systems of correspondences between cosmic and natural events (such as eclipses, earthquakes, positions of the planets, climate, weather and seasons), and events in the human world including those relating to human health, social institutions and political leadership. *The Book of Changes* was re-interpreted during this period and its assumptions associated with divinatory practices were explored. *The Book of Changes*, as its name implies, focuses on change and how its effects can extend across different realms. It holds that change is not a discontinuous, isolable phenomenon. Whether directly or indirectly, individuals may be affected by changes in their environments. This means that individuals are exposed to much that is beyond their immediate control. Likewise, their impact and influence on others can extend beyond what is immediately obvious or directly quantifiable. This is the theory of *ganying*, mutual resonance. The notion of mutual resonance crystallises the concept of interdependent selfhood, capturing the susceptibility of individuals to factors external to their being and beyond their immediate control, as well as their power to affect others. But the apparent fragility of the individual must not be interpreted solely in negative terms. Effects of change may also be positive. Furthermore, because of the myriad possibilities in mutual transformation, individuals should not merely seek what is only in their self-interest. The well-being of others whom they stand in relation to, and the robustness of their wider environment, are very likely to be constitutive of the good of individuals.

The concept of change is very closely linked to that of harmony. As we have discussed in the previous section, harmony may be thought of in different ways in Chinese philosophies: conformity, unity in purpose, cooperation, integration, order, stability and balance. Of course, these approaches capture very different pictures of the whole and the dynamics within. In Chinese philosophy, much effort is placed on understanding mutual influences, connections and change, and how these impact on harmony. It is wise to anticipate change, and to know how to respond to it optimally in order to attain a beneficial outcome.

The Philosophy of the *Yijing* (*The Book of Changes*)

The Book of Changes, as its title implies, attends to the changing situations in life, how these impact on individuals and their environments, and how one might respond to those changes, at least to minimise harms, if not to maximise benefits. In this regard, it embodies the practical orientation of Chinese philosophy. Not all of the *Yijing* is philosophical in nature. Its oldest sections, written in the ninth century BCE, were intended for divination purposes and its applications in actual divinatory practices were haphazard and lacking in systematic rigour. Yet, what is interesting about this text are its implicit assumptions about the world, the connections between its different parts, the relationships between entities, the complexity of causes and effects, the place of humanity in a constantly transforming world, and the importance of individual actions and responses.

During the Warring States and Han periods, thinkers turned their attention to the *Yijing* to plumb its insights and hidden assumptions. Commentaries were appended to the *Yijing* and these were deeply introspective about the project of the *Yijing* and its methods and applications. These commentaries are now included as part of the extant text. They are discussed in greater detail in Chapter Ten, with particular focus on the development of Chinese philosophy after the Qin period. The ideas and themes in the *Yijing* and other seminal texts of the period were instrumental in the development of Neo-Confucianism and in the reception of Buddhist thought and its subsequent evolution.

It is important here also to discuss some of the themes embedded in the *Yijing* for two reasons: these themes are manifest more broadly across the range of Chinese philosophical doctrines, and they are constitutive of the distinctive characteristics of Chinese philosophy. In fact, the *Yijing* is the one text that brings together most comprehensively the elements and conceptual frameworks of Chinese philosophical thinking. Hence, an awareness of these elements will enhance our appreciation of debates in Chinese philosophy. Here, I pre-empt the more detailed discussions in Chapter Ten by briefly describing some of the key features of the philosophy of the *Yijing*. The seven features discussed here mirror those set out in Chapter Ten.

(1) *The primacy of observation*. The *Yijing* emphasises observation as a critical element in reflective thinking, and perhaps procedurally prior to it. The predictions and prescriptions in the text are founded on observations of connections, movements and transformations in the world. From these observations, one perceives patterns, regularities and correlations. In an approach similar to that embodied in the *Yijing*, thinkers of different persuasions took observation as their respective starting points. For example, in their deliberations on social, political and ethical life, the thinkers were reacting to the corruption and selfishness in society. On the basis of their experiences, they offered different ideals and solutions. In the case of their ruminations about language and its connections with reality, the thinkers, especially the later Mohists, were preoccupied with how language, an artefact of civilisation, could reflect the diversity and plurality in the world. In sum, in these and other areas of concern, early Chinese philosophy has a palpably empirical character, deriving from observations and experiences of the world.

(2) *A holistic, all-encompassing perspective*. The *Yijing* divination statements are interpreted in order to draw out their application to specific cases. However, these statements inevitably place specific events within a larger environmental context. This awareness of a larger context is a manifest feature more generally of Chinese philosophy. In the different philosophical doctrines, there is attention to the whole, be it human society, *dao*, heaven and earth, or the cosmos. In Chinese philosophy, while it is recognised that individuals are the subjects of their experiences, it is also important to understand that experiences are only fully understood within a backgrounding environment. In this regard, it holds a conception of self as a contextually embedded being that is in part constituted by elements of its specific cultural and historical tradition; this is a picture of selfhood shared across the different doctrinal groups. Another important manifestation of a more inclusive, holistic perspective is the noticeable lack of (postulations of) entirely independent or transcendent entities or beings, over and above life in the world. However the whole is conceived – whether in terms of human society or cosmos – we do not find in Chinese philosophy engagement with abstract theoretical absolutes or

universals that set out or control the order of the world. Even the concept *dao*, sometimes described as transcendent, is not discontinuous from or independent of life in the world. Because Chinese philosophy holds a broad, all-encompassing perspective, it also tends to think of holism in inclusive terms.

(3) *A dialectical and complementary approach to dualisms.* The *Yijing* sets up complementary opposites in its conceptual framework with contrastive concepts such as high and low, action and repose, and hard and soft. These paired concepts are part of the explanatory framework of change, perhaps in seasonal or cyclic fashion, one phase replacing another and being replaced by it in due course. This binary complementation is most pronounced in, though not restricted to, Daoist philosophy. (For example, Confucianism emphasises reciprocity in relationships.) Daoist philosophy articulates binary pairs of evaluative concepts, hence casting doubt on conventional markers of success and well-being. Binary complementation also figures significantly in the Daoist approach to argumentation, especially in Zhuangzi's disagreements with the disputers (Bianzhe)[6], who sought to settle disputes by fixing names to their referents (objects and events) in the real world. Zhuangzi rejected their logic that things had to be either so or not-so (that is, according to the law of the excluded middle) and instead suggested that more could be gained from a dialectical approach that valued contrasts between perspectives.

(4) *Correlative thinking and resonance.* Correlative thinking is the broad view that events and situations in one realm are parallel to, or help to explain, those in another. An example from early Chinese philosophy would be the correlations drawn between a dysfunctional state and a diseased body, both lacking in alignment between parts and hence disharmonious. Resonances are more specific correspondences that actually postulate some causal connection. Both these themes are integral features of Han thought, and only fully developed then. Yet, there are suggestions of correlative thinking before this period, as for instance, in the cooperation, collusion or simpler correspondences between Heaven and Earth, on the one hand, and the socio-political realm, on the other, in both Confucian and Daoist philosophies. In Confucian philosophy, we also find more specific correspondences between harmony at state and family levels. We also know that beliefs in correspondences between cosmic phenomena and human well-being were widespread because Xunzi during the Warring

States period felt the need to dispel beliefs in cosmic phenomena, such as eclipses, as portents of forthcoming events in the human domain.

(5) *An interpretive approach to the meanings of the hexagrams and correspondences.* While this point relates specifically to the application of the *Yijing* in divination, we can also see the importance of the interpretive approach in Chinese philosophy more generally. For example, we will see in the course of this book that Chinese philosophy is averse to working primarily with universally applicable norms or truths. This is not to say that it does not uphold principles or values, but rather that it sees them has having *prima facie* status, and open to modification or adaptation according to relevant circumstantial factors. What is *relevant* in particular circumstances is at times open to interpretation. In the range of texts associated with the different thinkers, there is attention to the concrete, circumstantial and practical concerns of everyday life. This brings to mind a particular feature of reflection and scholarship in Chinese philosophy that ruminates on and interprets the insights of various thinkers, and applies them to situations at hand. Indeed, this method of appropriating insights is very much in use, and debated, in contemporary studies in Chinese philosophy.

(6) *Constant movement marked by the inevitability of change.* This feature is connected with the previous one, which emphasises openness to interpretation according to circumstantial factors. Here, the emphasis is on the inevitability of change, and perhaps its imminence. The *Yijing* embodies an attitude that is expectant of change and that seeks ways to prepare for it and deal with it. The early thinkers were acutely aware of constant changes in society brought about by socio-political unrest. In the debates among the different doctrinal groups, there was some consensus that the norms and ideals for the rectification of society had to adapt to the different needs brought about by new situations. Among these groups, it was only the earlier Confucians (excluding Xunzi although he was Confucianist) who were keen to rely on the ideas of antiquity.

(7) *The action-guiding nature of the judgements.* The task of divination is of course motivated by a desire to formulate courses of action that are effective and fruitful. This pragmatic orientation is conspicuous not only in the *Yijing* but in Chinese philosophy more generally. The early thinkers deliberated extensively on topics pertaining to ethics and government in order to improve their situation. In many ways, early Chinese philosophy

was driven by this urgent need to rectify society. In this regard, there was an ongoing criticism of the Bianzhe (the disputers) on the basis that they were engaged in sophistry for its own sake and did not make any practical difference to the way life was to be lived. However, as we will see in our discussion, even the Bianzhe's debates about language and meanings of terms and compound terms stemmed from practical concerns. The clearest indication of a concern with practical issues is in the discussion of strategies across the different doctrinal groups. In Confucianism, there are strategies to deal with relational others and the cultivation of skills to live meaningfully as a person in society. Daoists emphasised *wuwei*, a method that favours acquiescence and non-coercion; there were some others of Daoist persuasion who were keen to cultivate religious and alchemic techniques to prolong life. Legalists explicitly articulated a political strategy that allowed the ruler to control both the people and his administrative advisers. Finally, there were also texts on military strategy, such as the *Bingfa* (*Art of War*). Chinese philosophy is also noted for its focus on self cultivation, articulated by a wide range of thinkers who focused on moral cultivation, physical health, superhuman techniques, spiritual satisfaction and psychological well-being.

These seven elements of the philosophy of the *Yijing* outlined here will emerge again in our more detailed discussions in the book. We now turn our attention to a number of features of philosophical thinking in the Chinese tradition.

Thinking Philosophically

Debate and argumentation are prominent features of Chinese philosophy. From its beginnings during the Spring and Autumn period, thinkers have had to grapple with a difference and a plurality of viewpoints. J. J. Clarke, who investigates the reception and interpretation of Daoist ideas through periods in western intellectual history, argues that this context of plurality, and its implications, should not go unnoticed:

> Such debates must . . . be seen in the wider environment of an attitude of toleration and pluralism that has long been endemic at certain levels of Chinese cultural life, a cultural attitude which has not until relatively recently become acceptable in the West. (Clarke 2000: 27)

Clarke is referring to debates between rival Daoist and Buddhist thinkers from the fourth century CE. But there were earlier debates between Confucians, Daoists and Mohists, each set of thinkers rejecting the doctrines of others. From the third century BCE, there were gatherings of thinkers who debated issues. There was a notable assembly of thinkers of different persuasions under the auspices of Jixia, the Ji Gate in the capital of Qi during the Warring States period.[7] King Wei of Qi (357–320 BCE) was associated with this collection of thinkers. The proliferation of views and the gathering of thinkers in situations like the one at Jixia catalysed the development of the method of synthesis, which was a defining feature of philosophy in the Han period. This method of drawing insightful views from any number of different doctrines and integrating them into a viable theory continues to be a central feature of Chinese philosophy down to the present. The syncretic approach is markedly different from analysis, which involves understanding the assumptions that lie behind particular theories, and the justification of basic concepts and ideas. While analysis seeks to distinguish and isolate basic components of an argument, the syncretic approach integrates ideas from doctrines that are discrete and perhaps even oppositional. As a result of the widespread application of syncretic thinking, many Chinese philosophies have come to include elements from traditions other than their own. Thomé Fang, a Chinese philosopher, captures the syncretic spirit in this way: 'I am a Confucian by family tradition; a Taoist by temperament; a Buddhist by religion and inspiration' (Fang 1981: 525).

This makes it critical, in the study of Chinese philosophy, to acquire a sense of intellectual history in order to grasp the influences across the different traditions. The idea of tradition looms large in understanding Chinese philosophy partly because of the continuing use of synthesis even up to the present day. Ideas are built upon, re-interpreted, applied to different debates, and appropriated. The effect of these approaches on the different Chinese philosophies is an ongoing layering of themes, concepts and ideas. It is therefore immensely difficult clearly to distinguish specific characteristics of each of the original schools of thought associated with its founding thinker or thinkers. Thus, it makes more sense to speak of the different philosophical *traditions* rather than the philosophy of each specific 'school' as distinctive and clearly defined.

Another prominent feature of argumentation in Chinese philosophy is its preference for suggestive and evocative imagery, examples, analogies, metaphors and illustrations. The aim in using these argumentative devices is not to achieve precision in descriptions and explanations or clarity in expression.

The use of suggestive and illustrative tools in argumentation reflects a concern to illuminate ideas, explore their implications and ascertain their applications. This issue of argumentative methods is integrally connected to the question of the purpose of intellectual enquiry. The frequent use of suggestive methods points to an approach that places the onus of interpretation and understanding on the reader. Without doubt, readers will bring their perspectives to bear on their reading of texts in general. But there is an encouragement of, and perhaps even a requirement for, personal reflection when the text engages in metaphors, analogies and the like. It is therefore unsurprising when readers of the *Zhuangzi* comment on the power of the text to draw its readers into its discussions and to encourage reflective thinking. But it is not only the Daoist texts that embody this feature, however. The Confucian *Analects* also prompts readers to ask questions, consider different approaches and answers to these questions, imagine the contexts of the conversations, and reflect on reasons for belief and action. Reading these texts is primarily a reflective activity for the individual reader.

This is not to say that the articulation of theoretical foundations or philosophical truth is not a concern in Chinese philosophy. However, it certainly was not the only concern in the Chinese intellectual traditions, and not an important objective in some of them. The first chapter of the *Zhuangzi*, for example, is entitled "Going Rambling Without a Destination" (Graham 2001: 43–7). It communicates a belief in the value of reflective activity – of contemplation and reflection – as an end-in-itself. It is non-committal about its destination, if there is one.[8] That reflective activity is valued as an end rather than simply a means to truth generates important questions about the nature of philosophical thinking and the place of philosophy in human life. Not only does it challenge a particular conception of the end of philosophy in terms of truth, it also highlights the centrality of critical reflection in human development. In this spirit, the reader is encouraged to reflect on the elements of Chinese philosophy and perhaps, in the style of Chinese philosophy, to use them to acquire a deeper understanding both of Chinese philosophy and one's personal beliefs and commitments.

Suggestions for Further Reading

Fang, Thomé H. (1981) *Chinese Philosophy: Its Spirit and Its Development*, 2nd edn, Taipei: Linking Publishing.

Fung, Yu-Lan (1947) *The Spirit of Chinese Philosophy,* translated by E. R. Hughes, London: Routledge and Kegan Paul.

Fung, Yu-Lan (1948) *A Short History of Chinese Philosophy,* edited by Derk Bodde, New York: Free Press.

Notes

1. See Fung 1952: 132–69.
2. Yang Zhu's doctrine was interpreted by Mencius, the Confucian, as selfishness. Mencius was a harsh critic of Yang Zhu, noting the latter's unwillingness to shoulder social and civic responsibilities. See the discussion in Graham 1989: 53–64.
3. Helmuth von Glasenapp, *Kant und die Religionen des Osten*. Beihefte zum Jahrbuch der Albertus-Universität, Königsberg/Pr. (Kitzingen-Main: Holzner Verlag, 1954), pp. 105–6, translated by Julia Ching and quoted in 'Chinese Ethics and Kant', *Philosophy East and West*, Vol. 28, no. 2, April 1978. Ching focuses on fundamental differences in the structures and dynamics of early Chinese philosophy and Kantian philosophy.
4. The substantive issues, including such topics as the aims of social and individual lives, and measures of development in a person's character, vary from doctrine to doctrine. In the chapters that follow, these are discussed in detail with respect to the philosophies in the different schools.
5. Tu Weiming discusses this aspect of Confucian thought and rejects its assumptions about Confucianism as simplistic. Refer to Tu's 'A Confucian Perspective on Learning to be Human' in (1985) *Confucian Thought: Selfhood as Creative Transformation*, Albany: State University of New York Press, pp. 51–66. The discussion of roles in Confucian ethics is found at p. 58ff.
6. Their philosophy is discussed in Chapter Seven.
7. There is some debate, however, regarding the organisation at Jixia. Some scholars, such as Nivison, believe that Jixia was an institution (1999: 769–70). They also hold that many influential thinkers including Xunzi (310?–219? BCE) and Shen Dao (350?–275 BCE) were at this Academy. Nivison also notes that the scholars at the Academy were forbidden to take on political roles; they held only advisory capacities. However, Sivin argues that evidence on Jixia as a formally organised *academy* is very thin (1995b: 19–26).
8. This may be attributed to lack of interest in metaphysical issues, namely, those matters pertaining to an underlying truth or reality. Alternatively, the reason may be an epistemological one, that even if there were an underlying reality, it is impossible to know what it is like.

2 Confucius and the Confucian Concepts *Ren* and *Li*

Troubled by the unrest of the Spring and Autumn period, Confucius (Kongzi) (551–479 BCE) proposed the ethical reform of society. His proposal involved the elimination of the power-mongering and exploitative behaviours of those in power. The process was to be initiated and led by leaders of society who were paradigmatic men of broad education and ethical insight.

As the instigator of these ideas, Confucius is recognised as the founder of the *Ru-jia* doctrine (School of Literati), what we call the Confucian tradition in the west. The *Ru*-ists were educated men who sought to share and realise their insights on the ethical administration of government. Historically, the *Ru*-ists were part of a larger movement of educated scholar-officials (*shi*) appointed as advisers to those in power.[1]

Ru-ist education consisted in the cultivation of an ethically and ritually disciplined life. Some *Ru*-ists extended the rigours of ceremonial court ritual to the social and domestic arenas. Due to this phenomenon, Confucians have sometimes been thought of as traditionalists advocating traditional ritual court behaviours. It is interesting that Confucius in the *Analects* (7:1) notes that he is a transmitter, not a creator. But did he see himself primarily as a proponent of traditional ceremonial ritual?

Reading the *Analects*

The key text for Confucius' ideas is *The Analects of Confucius* (*Lunyu*). The text consists of fragments not written by Confucius himself but compiled by his disciples and second-generation disciples and collated over a period of time approximately seventy years after his death. The surviving text was probably formalised at around the Western Han period (206 BCE–9 CE).[2] More recently, scholars have also turned their attention to another unearthed version believed to pre-date the received version.[3]

The 499 short passages in the *Analects* are not systematically organised and repetitions and inconsistencies are common. Because it was written by a number of authors, there are several different interpretations of the key concepts in the *Analects*. It is possible to see differences between passages that are more or less authentic (reflecting Confucius' ideas) and others which have been modified or inserted at a later time.[4] We may also treat the text as a repository of insights into the intellectual history of Confucianism and of China more generally. Yet again, a good number of contemporary scholars – philosophers in particular – take the *Analects* as a text that is open-ended. These scholars continue to work on fresh commentaries and contemporary applications of ideas in the *Analects* text.

Confucius emerges from the *Analects* as a committed, conscientious and skilful thinker. In many passages a range of people, including dukes and governors of villages, consult him on issues relating to good government and, more broadly, the good life, and passages show how Confucius takes various factors into consideration and how he balances them to arrive at a decision. Many first-time readers of the *Analects* are struck by the lack of basic normative principles or criteria upon which Confucius bases his decisions. For instance, in *Analects* 13:18, he expects sons and fathers to cover up for each other's misdeeds:

> The Governor of She in conversation with Confucius said, "In our village there is someone called 'True Person.' When his father took a sheep on the sly, he reported him to the authorities."
>
> Confucius replied, "Those who are true in my village conduct themselves differently. A father covers for his son, and a son covers for his father. And being true lies in this." (trans. Ames and Rosemont Jr 1998a: 166–7)

Some people feel at a loss to explain how Confucius, known widely as the founder of Confucian ethics, could make such *im*moral prescriptions, and *Analects* 13:18 is often viewed with moral distaste because it endorses lying. But if we continue to reflect on this passage, there are more questions we want to ask. These include, What were the punishments, if any, for theft? What was the worth of a sheep? How was the neighbour affected? What are the consequences for the child, if he reveals his father's theft, and if he doesn't? The situation of this child is a uniquely difficult one and presents no easy solution. It is futile to speculate on the 'correct' answers to these questions. We should focus on more pertinent issues as, for instance, those at the meta-ethical level of enquiry. These issues include the place of family and loyalty in ethical life, the ethical significance of relationships, the requirement to cover up for another, Confucius' method of moral deliberation and its criteria.

Realistically, what Confucius is meant to have said to a duke about running a state, or how Confucius seats himself while eating, will have little relevance for us today. Perhaps we should not expect the *Analects* to provide normative answers to our ethical dilemmas. Instead, we might read it in order to understand the complexities associated with the process of moral reasoning as the early Confucians understood it. If this is correct, we may gain an understanding of how the Confucians studied the ancient texts (*Analects* 8:8, 1:15; 7:18; 8:3) and learnt from experiences of enlightened people in the past, that is, understanding how others may have acted admirably or fallen short of particular requirements (*Analects* 7:22). Seen in this light, the *Analects* is a collection of diary entries of other people's behaviours rather than a book of authoritative sayings or a comprehensive and systematic philosophical treatise. As a *manual of appropriate action and behaviour*, it can be used to generate and encourage reflective thinking about our own actions and commitments.

With this methodology in mind, let us proceed to examine two foundational concepts in Confucianism, *ren* (humaneness) and *li* (behavioural propriety). Together, they crystallise the Confucian ideal of cultivated humanism. Any understanding of Confucian philosophy rests on how we understand these two concepts and the interplay between them.

Ren: Humaneness

Ren is mentioned only occasionally in texts pre-dating Confucius.[5] In its earlier usage, the term referred to some manly or virile quality, particularly that of a king. For example, in two hunting poems in the *Book of Poetry* (*Shi Jing*), *ren* refers to two huntsmen who are 'handsome and *ren*' (Schwartz 1985: 51). In the *Book of History* (*Shu Jing*), *ren* refers to the benevolent attitude of the ruler to his subjects. In the hands of the Confucians, however, the term gradually came to denote a moral quality characteristic of humanity. Hence, it is not surprising to find some variation in its use in early Confucian philosophy, to denote humanity in general, humaneness as a distinguishing characteristic of humanity, or the primary human virtue of compassion. This characteristic was referred to in many ways, but most commonly as an inborn disposition or a feature of collective socio-political life. The meaning of the concept is also revealed in its Chinese character: *ren* (仁) is comprised by two characters, the left signifying humanity (人) and the right, two (二). This suggests that the concept pertains to human relatedness. Hence, the term has been variously translated into English as benevolence, love, humaneness, humanity, human-heartedness, compassion and sympathy.[6] Nevertheless, its meaning in the *Analects* is multifaceted and some more recent translations of *ren* avoid its identification with any one English term. Aspects of *ren* are considered in the following sections.

Ren as Love

Ren is 'to love all humanity', so says Confucius in *Analects* 12:22. James Legge (1815–97), a Christian missionary to China and an early translator of the classical Chinese texts into English, looked for opportunities to identify Confucian *ren* with Christian love (Legge 1893–5, vol. 1). Confucius' remark, which identifies *ren* with a general, indiscriminating love would have served Legge's purposes well. However, in *Analects* 4:3 it is said that 'only the man of *ren* knows how to like and dislike others', which suggests that the person of *ren* is discriminating in his assessment of others. Furthermore, in *Analects* 17:24, Confucius is explicit about the kinds of people he dislikes. Is there a tension between the two ideas, one that proclaims a general love for all and the other a discriminating appraisal of people's qualities? There is also a sense of a rather judgemental sternness in Confucius' recommendation that harm should be requited with justice, not kindness:

> Someone said, "What do you say concerning the principle that injury should be recompensed with kindness?" The master said, "With what then will you recompense kindness? Recompense injury with justice, and recompense kindness with kindness." (*Analects* 14:34, trans. Legge 1991: 288)

This unambiguous statement brings out an even-handed approach to what is just or right. The idea of undiscriminating love seems to be tempered by Confucius' critical assessments of people's moral qualities.

Ren, the Confucian Golden Rule

The golden rule takes the (moral) person as its starting point. It operates on the assumption that there is general agreement between people about desires and interests. In the *Analects*, the concept *shu*, translated as reciprocity or mutuality, captures the essence of the golden rule: there is much give-and-take in relationships (*Analects* 15:24). In *Analects* 4:15, *shu* is also accorded fundamental significance, this time in conjunction with another concept, *zhong*:

> The Master said, "Zeng, my friend! My way (*dao* 道) is bound together with one continuous strand." ...
>
> Master Zeng said, "The way of the Master is doing one's utmost (*zhong* 忠) and putting oneself in the other's place (*shu* 恕), nothing more." (trans. Ames and Rosemont Jr 1998a: 92)

Zhong is commonly translated as 'conscientiousness' or 'doing one's best'. However, these translations do not help us to understand why *zhong* should be coupled with *shu*. Perhaps a translation of *zhong* not in terms of action (*doing* one's best) but commitment (*being* one's best) will help us see their correlation better. In a nutshell, to *be* one's best (*zhong*) – so as to optimise one's achievements – involves the fostering of mutually benefiting relationships (*shu*). If we follow this line of reasoning, we might say that the self is enhanced and extended by relationships that enrich it. In this light, *zhong* and *shu* may be understood as two dimensions of the same process, hence the reference to 'one continuous strand' (*yiguan*).

The *Analects* presents a version of the golden rule: 'do not do to others what you do not wish to be done to yourself' (12:2; 15:24). This negative formulation of the golden rule is sometimes dubbed the 'silver rule' because it has a more passive approach: it does not require good or moral action but only ones that do not bring about harm (Allinson 1985: 305–15). In Confucian philosophy, the cultivation of mutually satisfying and beneficial relationships is an integral component of the good life. Self and society are symbiotic rather than mutually exclusive: the paradigmatic self benefits others in society (*Analects* 6:30). The Confucian ideal society is the ideal family writ large: the sage king is the benevolent father of the nation-family (*Analects* 8:6). The family environment is the first context where one learns to put oneself in the other's place.

Ren and the Cultivation of Special Relationships

The cultivation of *ren* begins with the development of family relationships with their correlative emotions and special obligations. In other words, one first learns about human attachment through interaction with family members. Hence it is said that filial piety (*xiao*) and brotherly respect (*di*) are the root of *ren* (*Analects* 1:2). This characterisation of *ren* which emphasises different emotional attachments (*Analects* 2:24) is sharply distinguished from *ren* as indiscriminating love, as considered above.

We might pause at this point to question the meaning of the 'root' of *ren*. It may mean that caring affection – especially the kinds of emotional attachment we have to family members – is a basic, defining trait of all humanity. This interpretation takes filial piety and, by extension, other familial ties as a primary fact of human existence. Alternatively, 'root' may indicate that the family context provides the first environment for moral development. Within this environment, one learns to be loyal, to empathise, negotiate, love, care, gain sympathy, express regret, balance competing loyalties and prioritise obligations (*Analects* 4:18). The skills learnt in the family environment are vital for a person's interactions with others in later life. If the *Analects* is correct that family relationships play a dominant role in one's formative years – that they shape the person in many important and subtle ways – it follows that contemporary moral philosophers should give serious consideration to these primary sources of influence in the moral life of the agent.

Ren as Ethical Wisdom

The *Analects* offers many examples of how *ren* shows itself in the life of the Confucian paradigmatic individual. For example, it is associated with five attitudes: deference, tolerance, making good on one's word, diligence and generosity (*Analects* 17:6). It is one of six desirable qualities of character (together with wisdom, making good on one's word, uprightness, courage and resoluteness (*Analects* 17:8)). It is realised in different contexts: domestic, public and social (*Analects* 13:19). One's commitment to *ren* must be manifest in both word and deed; Confucius intensely disliked glib talkers (*Analects* 12:3; 13:27; 4:22; 14:27). Realising *ren* in one's life is an overwhelmingly difficult task (*Analects* 15:10, 15:9). In taking up the challenge, one must learn widely yet reflect on what is close at hand (*Analects* 19:6; see also *Analects* 2:11). This captures the essence of practical wisdom: an ability to learn from others *in order to* reflect on one's own situation, and to apply these insights to one's actions. The person of *ren* is confident in his dealings:

> The Master said, "The wise (*zhi* 知) are not in a quandary; the authoritative (*ren* 仁) are not anxious; the courageous are not timid." (*Analects* 9:29; trans. Ames and Rosemont Jr 1998a: 132)

The simplicity of the statement highlights the calmness of the *ren*-person. Confucian scholar Antonio Cua aptly describes the enviable disposition of the man of *ren*: '[h]is *easeful* life is more a matter of attitude and confidence in his ability to deal with difficult and varying situations, rather than an exemplification of his infallible judgement and authority' (Cua 1971: 47). A more thorough reading of the *Analects* will allow readers to acquire a sense of the depth and breadth of *ren*, perhaps as the ultimate moral achievement in life. A fuller understanding of the concept requires an examination of other key concepts in the text.

Li: Behavioural Propriety

The concept '*li*' is also one of considerable elasticity. The term can refer to the normative codes of conduct in ancient or modern Chinese society, to the concrete instantiations of these codes in daily life, or to a concept. It was used in pre-Confucian texts to denote ritualistic religious behaviour for the purpose of inducing supernatural protection and blessing. It was believed that the will of the spirits could be influenced through ritual sacrifice (Skaja 1984). Many of the rituals, such as harvest and thanksgiving ones, were conducted only by the emperor, also referred to as the 'Son of Heaven'. However, during the Spring and Autumn and Warring States periods, the scope of the concept was gradually extended. For instance, it was also used to refer to ceremonial ritual in the petty courts (Dubs 1966: 116).

We can detect some of these variations in the scope of *li* in the *Analects* itself, which at times uses it to refer to religious ritual (*Analects* 3:17) and at others to the comportment of the cultivated person (*Analects* 12:1). Yet another usage in the *Analects* refers to behavioural propriety in the ordinary interactions of the common people (*Analects* 2:3). Partly because of its association with ancient behavioural norms, the concept *li* evokes a sense of conservatism. However, its employment in the *Analects* is not always consistent: at some points it appears to be rather inflexible (*Analects* 3:17), yet at some others amendable (*Analects* 9:3).

Standards of behavioural propriety served as guides for correct behaviour in a range of relational contexts: between children and parents (*Analects*

2:5), subject and ruler (*Analects* 3:18) and prince and minister (*Analects* 3:19). *Li* mapped out different standards for appropriate behaviour according to one's place in a particular relationship. In this way, individuals are familiarised with the different obligations and emotions that are appropriate in specific relationships. Ideally, continued *li*-practice fosters a deeper appreciation of human relationships. In addition, *li* also have an aesthetic dimension as they introduce a level of decorum in one's interactions with others (*Analects* 8:2). We should also note the anti-conformism which comes across in *Analects* 2:3:

> The Master said, "Lead the people with administrative injunctions (*zheng* 政) and keep them orderly with penal law (*xing* 刑), and they will avoid punishments but will be without a sense of shame. Lead them with excellence (*de* 德) and keep them orderly through observing ritual propriety (*li* 禮) and they will develop a sense of shame, and moreover, will order themselves." (trans. Ames and Rosemont Jr 1998a: 76)

This passage draws a sharp contrast between *li* and penal law (*fa*) as instruments of government. According to this passage, the motivational drive associated with the avoidance of punishment is an inferior one. The culture of penal law made people 'clever' and glib in order to evade punishment.[7] In contrast, Confucian *li* must be manifest in action (*Analects* 1:3, 4:24; 14:20; 14:27). Added to these concerns was the issue of penal law being overly general and universalistic.[8]

A number of the passages in the *Analects* emphasise that *li* must be practised with reverence (*Analects* 3:26; 17:21). In 17:11, the practice of both *li* and music is grounded in the sincere intentions and emotions of the gift-giver and the performer respectively:

> The Master said, 'Surely when one says "The rites, the rites," it is not enough merely to mean presents of jade and silk. Surely when one says "Music, music," it is not enough merely to mean bells and drums.' (trans. Lau, 1979a: 145)

The presentation of gifts – even expensive ones such as jade and silk – is an act devoid of significance if it is not accompanied by the appropriate underlying emotions. The analogy with music is informative too: clanging bells and beating drums do not constitute music. Meaningful performances of music are always accompanied by appropriate emotions. Are these appropriate emotions in effect expressions of *ren* itself?

Many of the passages in the *Analects* suggest a deep connection between *ren* and *li*: one's concern for humanity must be expressed intelligibly in lived contexts. In the words of the scholar Tu Weiming, Confucian self cultivation is about 'Learning to be Human' (1985: pp. 51–66). Here, it is important to reflect on the normative force of *li*, as inflexible norms of conduct may stifle individuality. Is there room in Confucian philosophy for the individual to challenge the status quo? This depends on how the relation between *ren* and *li* is understood, and which of the two concepts is thought to have precedence.

Ren and *Li*

In the *Analects* there is divided opinion regarding the relative priority of *ren* and *li*. Conversations associated with the disciples Ziyou and Zixia usually emphasise the greater significance of *li* while those involving Zengzi, Zizhang and Yanhui show a greater commitment to *ren* (Schwartz 1985: 130–4). This disagreement was later characterised as the '*nei-wai*' (inner-outer) debate. *Nei* captures the essence of the concept *ren*; it refers to the internal, perhaps innate, moral sense of humanity. By contrast, *wai* captures the spirit of *li*, the externally imposed, socially constructed norms which guide and in some ways limit the inner self. This debate approximates the nature-nurture question within the western tradition and its implications for moral cultivation. Which is more fundamental to the Confucian programme, natural (inner) moral inclination or its (outer) cultivation? *Analects* 6:18 makes it clear that both basic disposition (*zhi*) and refinement (*wen*) are necessary. Confucius here wittily rejects overemphasis on either:

> The Master said, "When one's basic disposition (*zhi* 質) overwhelms refinement (*wen* 文), the person is boorish; when refinement overwhelms one's basic disposition, the person is an officious scribe. It is only when one's basic disposition and refinement are in appropriate balance that you have the exemplary person (*junzi* 君子)." (trans. Ames and Rosemont Jr 1998a: 107–8)

There is no unqualified support in the *Analects* either for an 'inner' or 'outer' morality. Nevertheless, it is worth examining more of its passages to gain a better understanding of *ren* and *li* and their implications for contemporary debates.

Ren is Fundamental

Analects 3:3 asserts the priority of *ren* over *li*:

> The Master said, "What has a person who is not authoritative (*ren* 仁) got to do with observing ritual propriety (*li* 禮)? What has a person who is not authoritative got to do with the playing of music (*yue* 樂)?" (trans. Ames and Rosemont Jr 1998a: 82)

Music has two dimensions, one being the performative and the other its underlying emotion (*ren*). By analogy, the practice of *li* encompasses both performative know-how and the expression of human feeling. Neither *li* nor music are meaningful if they are not accompanied by the appropriate human sentiments (*ren*). In this passage and a number of others (2:8, 3:3; 3:12, 3:26; 17:17; 17:21; 19:14), *ren* is the ethical and motivational basis of *li* acts. In *Analects* 3:26, Confucius effectively sums up the futility of mechanical compliance:

> "What could I see in a person who in holding a position of influence is not tolerant, who in observing ritual propriety (*li* 禮) is not respectful, and who in overseeing the mourning rites does not grieve?" (trans. Ames and Rosemont Jr 1998a: 88)

In western moral philosophy, the intentions of the moral agent are often considered more ethically significant than behavioural compliance. Some contemporary Confucian scholars, perhaps influenced by this, seek to parallel this preference by placing emphasis on *ren*, the 'inner' commitment of the moral agent. Tu Weiming is a notable proponent of this view. He argues that commitment to human well-being (which he identifies with *ren*) is the foundation of Confucian ethics. As such, it cannot be overridden by behavioural norms which are contingent on historical and social factors. He provides an anecdote, citing the comments of the modern Chinese writer and critic, Lu Xun (1881–1936):

> During the Ming-Ch'ing [Ming-Qing] period, quite a number of widows committed suicide hoping to show that their acts were in conformity with the *li* of chastity. In view of such stupidity, Lu Hsün [Lu Xun] was quite justified in calling this type of *li* "eating man" (*ch'ih-jen*) [*chiren*]. (Tu 1968: 37)

For Tu, *ren* comes to the rescue of *li*. In cases where *li*-practices are no longer acceptable or detrimental to humanity, *ren* has the role of upholding a commitment to humanity. *Ren* is fundamental and therefore dubbed the higher order concept: '...*ren* as an inner morality is not caused by the mechanism of *li* from outside. It is higher-order concept which gives meaning to *li*' (1968: 33). In other words, *ren* provides the criteria for assessing *li*-practices. Tu seeks to establish the relevance of Confucian philosophy in contemporary debates. However, although his presentation of Confucian thought is enlightening, his understanding of *ren* as 'inner morality' requires more thought as it may generate the impression that *ren*-cultivation is a process directed by an autonomous, free-willing agent. Additionally, the scope of *ren* might be reduced if it is identified with 'morality'.[9] Finally, the description of *ren* as a higher order concept might downplay the significance of *li* within the Confucian tradition in a way that is misleading.

Li is Fundamental

We could also argue that *li* is the primary concept in Confucianism. Unlike *ren*, *li*-practices are more readily observable and can be regulated. From the practical point of view, it is through observing and practising *li*-behaviours that one learns about *ren* (cf. *Analects* 12:1). Henry Skaja (1984) believes that *li* is the fundamental concept in Confucianism. In his account, *li* fulfil spiritual, educative and governing functions. This means that *li* have an educational and civilising effect on individuals as they instil restraint and observation of propriety. Accordingly, a society of people guided by *li* will be orderly (*Analects* 1:2). But most importantly for Skaja, *li* are the conduit for human feeling, an 'objectification of the spirit of man' (1984: 49–50). According to Skaja, the process of self cultivation is seen primarily in terms of socialisation:

> Confucius...*transformed* and *generalized* the meaning of *li* from mere "rite" or "ritual sacrifice" to the necessary educative and self-reflective socialization process, itself, whereby man becomes humanized, i.e. socialized. (1984: 62–3)

However, we should perhaps be concerned that, if *li* have a basic place in Confucianism, then Confucian self cultivation may be reduced to a socialisation process. This is in fact a common criticism of Confucianism, that it advocates the subjugation of individuals to society. For instance, *Analects* 1:2 may be used to justify the conditioning of people's minds in order to establish an orderly, submissive society:

> Master You said, "It is a rare thing for someone who has a sense of filial and fraternal responsibility (*xiaodi* 孝弟) to have a taste for defying authority. And it is unheard of for those who have no taste for defying authority to be keen on initiating rebellion . . ." (trans. Ames and Rosemont Jr 1998a: 71)

The view that *li* is primal would give force to the portrayal of Confucianism as conservative traditionalism.

Ren and *Li* are Interdependent Concepts

The most persuasive view of *li* and *ren* is that *ren* and *li* are inextricably interdependent concepts. This means that either of the two concepts is meaningless on its own. According to this view, *ren* is manifest only in *li*-practices. *Ren-li* interdependence has been most clearly articulated by Shun Kwong-Loi.[10] Shun explains their interdependence by analogy with the use of language. For example, to understand the concept of tense *is* to be able to use its various forms effectively. Conversely, the effective use of grammatical structures associated with tense is an indication of a person's grasp of the concept. Analogously, to understand the depth of human feeling is to be able to express it appropriately; and one's ability to express human feeling is an indication of one's emotional maturity. Hence, in the case of language, Shun suggests that mastery of the usage of tense is *both* necessary and sufficient for the mastery of the concept within the linguistic community. One cannot plausibly claim to have mastered one but not the other. Similarly, one cannot claim to have fully mastered *li* without also understanding the human feeling it conveys; nor can one claim to be a person of *ren* if one is repeatedly unable to convey that to others. Shun's analysis of the *ren-li* connection is a creative and philosophically satisfying one as it raises other important issues, including the criteria or basis for modifying *li*. It is a good example of contemporary scholarship in the field that both critically analyses ideas in Chinese philosophy and enlivens them in contemporary debate.

Ren and *Li* in Contemporary Philosophical Debates

Although we might wish to introduce an element of creativity in the textual interpretation of the *Analects*, we must also balance that with the maintenance of its integrity as a text of the Warring States period. While the tendency is to emphasise *ren*, for a number of obvious reasons, we should also keep in mind that the concept *li* plays a significant role in the philosophy of the *Analects* and that *li*-practices have been the dominant face of Confucianism in the Chinese historical context. To put it slightly differently, perceptions of Confucianism have very much been shaped by understandings of *li* in the lived Chinese context.

Nevertheless, there have been interesting and insightful developments of *li* and *ren* by contemporary scholars in the English-speaking world. Some scholars employ the tools of an analytic approach in order to critically scrutinise the concepts and to assert their continuing significance.[11] Recently, a number of scholars have turned their attention to the concept *yi* (appropriateness) in the *Analects*.[12] They argue that *yi* adds another layer to moral reasoning in Confucianism. Identified as 'appropriateness' or 'right', *yi* plays a particular role in practical deliberation as it reflects the Confucian concern for ethical appropriateness rather than normativity. That is, there is emphasis on doing the 'right' thing in a particular context, rather than merely following a rule or norm. Comparative ethical analyses such as this have immense benefits for philosophical inquiry and dialogue across different philosophical traditions. Especially in ethics and moral philosophy, scholars note that Confucian philosophy attends to the contexts of social engagement and focuses on concrete moral practice in a much greater way than traditional western moral philosophy does. Other recent examples of productive encounters include the comparisons of Confucian *ren* and the feminist ethic of care, and discussions of environmental and ecological thinking in the Chinese philosophical traditions.[13]

Another contemporary rendition of *ren* and *li* is to emphasise their significance in self cultivation in contemporary socio-political contexts. Discussions by David Hall and Roger Ames have led the debates in this area. Their interpretation of *ren* as 'person-making' – though sometimes criticised as rather too post-modern – has been influential in discussions of Confucianism in a democratic context.[14] Another significant discussion in socio-political philosophy concerns the status of *ren* and *li* in the continuing development of culture and society in East Asian countries. A good example is the issue of the place and continuing significance of Confucian philosophy in a global context in which human rights are deemed fundamental. There is also the question of how Confucian philosophy might have shaped the discourse and ideas of the Asian values debate.[15]

Together, *ren* and *li* comprise the core of Confucian philosophy and an in-depth understanding of their interplay reveals many fundamental elements of Confucian thought. The study of *ren* and *li* prompts further enquiry into issues associated with the moral cultivation of the self in a relational, socio-political context. One important issue concerns the concept of self and relationality. In Confucian thought, the cultivation of mutually enriching relationships is integral to the self and its identity. This concept of an interdependent self generates a view of morality that defies normativity and generalisation, and focuses on the practical realisation of human goodness in lived contexts. Confucian philosophy highlights the need for moral philosophers carefully to consider the concept of the interdependent self and how it is constituted by its relationality.

Another issue associated with self-definition relates to the impact of social and ethical norms on individuals. From a Confucian point of view, it is critical to understand the criteria for decision-making which will, if necessary, override outdated or even harmful *li*-practices. How does the developing moral individual acquire a critical distance from social norms? What kinds of skills are necessary for an intelligent assessment of the continuing relevance and applicability of existing norms? These in turn raise further questions regarding how moral norms are decided upon and by whom, and how they are instituted in particular societies. Of course, these questions are important in contemporary contexts as well.

Finally, whether Confucian philosophy embodies or engenders a 'collectivist' ideology is a topic worthy of further consideration. The collectivist point of view is contrasted with an 'individualist' philosophy that is a defining characteristic of liberal democratic societies. But a more thorough understanding of Confucianism actually challenges the collectivist – individualist characterisation of socio-political organisations. In fact, the Confucian concept of the interdependent self, which sits at the crossroads of *ren* and *li*, cannot simply be characterised as embodying a collectivist approach to socio-political organisation. The cultivation of particular relationships is critical to the well-being of both society and the individual. The measures of personal well-being are linked to one's successes in negotiating relationships and balancing competing demands and obligations. The Confucian account of the interdependent self sets it within a rich tapestry of relationships; hence, Confucian philosophy offers a complex, realistic picture of self-in-community.

Suggestions for Further Reading

Confucius: The Analects, translated by Dim-Cheuk Lau (1979), Harmondsworth: Penguin Books.

The Analects of Confucius: A Philosophical Translation, translated by Roger Ames and Henry Rosemont Jr (1998a), New York: Ballantine Books.

Chan, Wing-tsit (1975) 'Chinese and Western Interpretations of *Jen* (Humanity)', *Journal of Chinese Philosophy*, vol. 2, no. 2: 107–29.

Fingarette, Herbert (1972) *Confucius: The Secular as Sacred*, New York: Harper and Row.

Tu, Weiming (1985) *Confucian Thought: Selfhood as Creative Transformation*, Albany: State University of New York Press.

Notes

1. The social mobility of a group of scholar-officials, the *shi*, rapidly increased during the Warring States period. Particularly during 512–464 BCE, the *shi*, having established themselves in their learning, began to play more active roles than rulers (Hsu 1965: 8). It has been suggested that Confucius and many of his pupils belonged to this *shi* class (Hsu 1965: 34–7). Competition between the many warring states necessitated the selection of capable functionaries by those in power (Hsu 1999: 572–83).
2. The text would have been read, memorised and re-written from memory by scholars in the era prior to print. It is therefore reasonable to expect a number of slightly different versions of the text. The received version of the *Analects* is known as the Marquis Zhang *Analects*.
3. In 1999, a collection of bamboo slips, believed to be the earliest known version of the *Analects*, was unearthed. This was from a 2000-year-old tomb (of an Emperor of the Han Dynasty) at Shijiazhuang, Hebei Province. The tomb and its contents are dated to around 55 BCE.
4. See, for example, Brooks and Brooks (1998), *The Original Analects: Sayings of Confucius and His Successors*.
5. Wing-tsit Chan presents a comprehensive discussion of the pre-Confucian usage of *ren* (1955: 295–319).
6. Chan suggests that Confucius was the first to have conceived of *ren* as the general virtue (1975: 107).
7. Hansen convincingly juxtaposes punishment as self-preserving, against *li* as other-regarding. Hansen provides an insightful analysis of the role of words in litigation (1992: 64–5).

8. The theme that relational attachment must be recognised in legal institutions has persisted through Chinese history, even up until the Ming (1368–1644) and Qin (1644–1911) dynasties; some scholars dub this phenomenon the 'Confucianisation of law'. Refer to Ch'u (1965: 267–79).
9. In a later article, Tu seems to move away from the characterisation of *ren* as 'personal morality' and a higher-order concept, independent of *li* (1972: 187–201). Here, he states that 'although *jen*, especially when used as a comprehensive virtue, gives meaning to *li*, *jen* without the manifestation of *li* is also inconceivable' (p. 188).
10. Shun (1993).
11. See, for example, Kwong-loi Shun (1993), Antonio Cua (1971, 1973, 1979, 1989, 1996a, 1996b), Philip Ivanhoe (1990), Benjamin Schwartz (1985), Angus C. Graham (1989), Karyn Lai (1995). Schwartz's and Graham's anthologies articulate Chinese philosophical ideas in the context of Chinese intellectual history. Both are excellent introductions to the field.
12. Refer to David Hall and Roger Ames (1997), Kim-Chong Chong (1998) and Karyn Lai (2003b).
13. See, for example, the collection of papers on feminism edited by Li Chenyang (2000), and an anthology which discusses ecological ideas in Confucianism edited by Mary E. Tucker and John Berthrong (1998).
14. Refer to Hall and Ames (1998, 1999), Sor-Hoon Tan (2004) and Joseph Grange (2004).
15. Refer to De Bary (1991, 1998), De Bary and Tu Weiming (eds.) (1998).

3 The Cultivation of Humanity in Confucian Philosophy: Mencius and Xunzi

Confucius' vision for rectifying society was a simple and idealistic one: good government begins in the moral self cultivation of able leaders. At times, the *Analects* acknowledges that the chances of such rectification were minimal (*Analects* 7:26; 9:13). Nevertheless, the ideology of self cultivation (*xiushen*) has had far-reaching effects in Chinese society and culture. The ideology that education begets moral wisdom was articulated in the Chinese Civil Service Examination system. The system, which ran from the Han dynasty (206 BCE–206 CE) up until 1905, recruited men who performed well in examinations based on Confucian texts. It was believed that scholars of the classical texts would also be ethically adept practitioners of good government.

The Confucian theme of self cultivation continues to have contemporary relevance for several reasons. First, it emphasises ethical merit as the basis of government. This is important because it requires government to be accountable. It was a positive change from hereditary leadership which did not ensure competent or ethical leaders. Secondly, it highlights the place of education in social development. Finally, Confucian moral philosophy has vital implications for contemporary moral philosophy due to a number of its key features: attention to character development, centrality of relationships in moral life, the progressive nature of moral development (that is, a focus on different elements of moral reasoning that are cultivated at different stages in a person's moral life), and the integrated nature of personal development and socio-political progress.

The Confucians were optimistic, yet pragmatic, in their assessment of human moral capacities and how these could be shaped to produce more fruitful outcomes for society. The theory of self cultivation played a central role in the Confucian hope for a better, more ethically focused society. Both Mencius (385?–312? BCE) and Xunzi (310?–219? BCE), thinkers belonging to the Confucian school, had to defend Confucian thought as different schools of thought emerged and evolved during the Warring States period. As a result, they sought ways to justify this vision, mainly by constructing an account of original human nature that required further development.

Mencius, one of the prominent early second-generation disciples of Confucius, argued that human nature is originally good. According to Mencius, malevolence was due to various extraneous factors that had led humans astray from their original natures. Hence, rectification was required to recover the lost originally good nature. Xunzi countered that human nature was morally bad to begin with and that it needed to be corrected to avoid the further disintegration of the human condition. The debate on the original state of human nature and its cultivation developed much further both within and outside the Confucian school. The disagreements between Mencius and Xunzi shaped the early development of Confucian philosophy after Confucius.

Mencius: The Cultivation of Human Nature

Mencius is thought to have studied with a pupil of Confucius' grandson, Zisi (483?–402? BCE).[1] He is the author of the second set of books in the Confucian canon, the *Four Books* (*Si Shu*).[2] His philosophy is optimistically humanistic as he believed that humans had inherent goodness. On this thesis, he built his theory of compassionate government (*ren zheng*). A famous story attributes Mencius' optimistic philosophy to his overwhelmingly positive experience of motherly love. The short, cryptic phrase captures his philosophy of human goodness: "human nature is good" (*xing shan*) (*Books of Mencius* 6A:6). Mencius dismisses other views on the connection between morality and human nature (*xing*):

> Kung-tu Tzu [Gongduzi] said, 'Kao Tzu [Gaozi] said, "There is neither good nor bad in human nature," but others say, "Human nature can become good or it can become bad, and that is why with the rise of King Wen [Wan] and King Wu, the people were given to goodness, while with the rise of King Yu and King Li, they were given to cruelty." Then there are others who say, "There are those who are good by nature, and there are those who are bad by nature. For this reason, Hsiang [Xiang] could have Yao as Prince, and Shun could have the Blind Man [Gu Sou] as father, and Ch'i [Qi], Viscount of Wei and Prince Pi Kan [Bi Gan] could have Tchou [Zhou] as nephew as well as sovereign." Now you say human nature is good. Does this mean that all the others are mistaken?' (*Books of Mencius* 6A:6, trans. Lau 1979b: 247)

The different conceptions of human nature that stand in contrast to Mencius' include:

(a) Morality is not an intrinsic part of human nature.
(b) Humans are born as a blank slate, a *tabula rasa*. They become good or bad depending on the influences around them.
(c) Some humans are born intrinsically good and others intrinsically bad.

The differences between the views in (a) and (b) are subtle: (a) emphatically dissociates morality from human nature while (b) focuses on the malleability and vulnerability of humans to external influences. The view in (c) expressly denies Mencius' assertion that goodness is a universal characteristic of humanity. When asked to clarify his position that human nature is good, Mencius begins with the refutation of Gaozi's (ca. 420–350 BCE) view that morality is not inherent in human nature.[3] In his extended responses, Mencius provides various analogies for an inborn moral nature – such as, for instance, that the flow of water from a higher level to a lower one is the inherent nature of water (*Books of Mencius* 6A:2). Mencius seems to assume that these analogies are adequate for the purpose, although they are merely an extended elaboration of his view.

The view (c), that innate moral characteristics or propensities are variable across individuals, also poses a problem for Mencius' theory. For Mencius, it is important that intrinsic goodness is universal because he also wants to maintain that all humans are potentially perfectible, regardless of hereditary status[4]: 'The sage and I are of the same kind', Mencius boldly proclaims (*Books of Mencius* 6A:7; trans. Lau 1979b: 249). He provides analogies of common human experiences – a liking for good flavours, sounds and sights – to support his argument that goodness is also a shared characteristic. The *irrelevance* of hereditary status to moral cultivation (and, ultimately, to involvement in good government) was an important underlying theme in Confucius' and Mencius' philosophies as it was in their personal lives. As common men without noble birthright, it is not surprising that they should assert this.

Mencius also attempted to provide a transcendent basis for a moral human nature. He identified that as the source of human goodness and asserted a unity between heaven and humanity[5]:

> For a man to give full realization to his heart [*xin*] is for him to understand his own nature, and a man who knows his own nature will know Heaven [*tian*]. By

> retaining his heart and nurturing his nature he is serving Heaven...(*Books of Mencius* 7A:1, trans. Lau 1979b: 287).

Mencius' aim was not to explore cosmic or spiritual concepts but simply to use the notion of heaven as a transcendent basis of human capacities and potential. However, we need to be careful in applying the term 'transcendent' to Mencius' concept of human nature. Mencius sought to locate the source of human goodness in *tian*, a source *more* fundamental than humanity itself; in that sense we may say that *tian* is the transcendent basis for human goodness. Yet, in another sense, the relation between *tian* and human nature is a closely intertwined one, interdependent rather than independent: the person who preserves (the goodness of) his heart–mind, *xin*, and who cultivates his nature is engaged *in one and the same process* of serving *tian*. As this passage reveals *xin*, the heart–mind, is the clue to understanding Mencius' conception of human nature. *Xin* in Mencius' philosophy is commonly translated 'heart', although the concept covers a set of capacities rather than an organ.[6] The set of capacities is both an intrinsic and a distinctive feature of humanity (*Books of Mencius* 2A:6; 4B:19; 6A:8). We should also note that Mencius did not distinguish deliberative morality from emotion (in the way we might find, say, in Plato's philosophy); hence the term *xin* is best translated as heart–mind. *Xin* is the seat of intellect, cognition, emotion and affection. It seemed to him both commonsensical and profound that the child who appreciated and understood her parents' love would reciprocate that concern and eventually extend it to others (*Books of Mencius* 7A:15). Emotion and moral sensitivity were, for him, deeply connected with moral deliberation. For Mencius, the task of moral cultivation was to re-ignite the lost heart–mind.

Mencius set out four basic manifestations of *xin*: *ren* (sympathy and compassion), *yi* (moral sense or rightness), *li* (respect resulting from recognising different relations and hierarchies) and *zhi* (wisdom) (*Books of Mencius* 2A:6). In characteristic style, Mencius does not provide justification for his selection of the four basic characteristics. Chad Hansen suggests that one problem in Mencius' theory of human nature is not that the four shoots of goodness are not universal features of the human psyche, but, rather, that they are far too *specific*: Mencius has not provided adequate justification for his selection of these traits as innately human.[7]

There is considerable co-referencing between *xin* and *xing* (human nature) in *Books of Mencius* so that it is at times difficult to articulate the difference between them.[8] This laxity in part reflects that Mencius believes *xin* is at the core of humanity. However, what is philosophically significant is whether Mencius' 'original' goodness is to be understood as an innate disposition toward goodness or the possession of a capacity that may be developed.

The first assertion, that goodness is an innate disposition, is the stronger one. Mencius' example of how *any* person would feel distress at seeing a child about to fall into a well and spontaneously attempt to save the child captures the essence of this view (*Books of Mencius* 2A:6. See also 6A:10). That there is a spontaneous desire to do what is good suggests a naturalistic and deterministic account of human goodness.[9] Defenders of this interpretation of human nature would be hard-pressed to provide reasons for greed, selfishness and evil. On the other hand, it is difficult fully to dismiss this interpretation because there are hints of this view in some of Mencius' discussions.

The second, weaker, interpretation holds that humans possess a *capacity* for developing a sense of goodness. If this capacity – or capacities, as the case may be – is not properly cultivated, it will easily be overcome by the adverse influences in society. In the famous discussion of the trees of the Niu Mountain, Mencius draws an analogy between the nourishment and care that trees should have and the moral cultivation of human nature (*Books of Mencius* 6A:8). A critical point of the analogy is the necessity of consistent and continual cultivation.

As there is support in the *Books of Mencius* text for both interpretations, some scholars take the middle ground and contend that *xing* embodies a dual meaning.[10] According to this view, *xing* refers *both* to an incipient capacity *and* its continuing cultivation. A. C. Graham explains the meaning of *xing* with reference to its etymology. Its right half consists of the character *sheng*, which means both birth and growth. Graham also refers to a general imprecision of Chinese concepts in order to explain *xing*:

> Mencius in particular seems never to be looking back towards birth, always forward to the maturation of a continuing growth. This accords with one's general impression when groping towards an understanding of early Chinese concepts, that often they tend to be more dynamic than their nearest Western equivalents, and that English translation freezes them into immobility.[11]

Mencius' theory of human nature begins positively in a universal incipient goodness; it culminates in an optimistic vision of an ethical, well-governed society. Although many aspects of Mencius' philosophy are riddled with questionable analogies, the tenor of his ideas and the aspiration toward a humane, benevolent government would have had much popular appeal in the climate of war and terror then. Additionally, his writings provide rich material for debates in philosophy, anthropology and moral psychology.

Xunzi: The Regulation of Human Behaviour

Xunzi is often hailed as the most scrupulous of the early Confucian philosophers because of the rigour in his argumentation. Recognition of Xunzi's intellectual prowess extended well beyond the Confucian school. He was well regarded at Jixia, where thinkers of different persuasions congregated to debate issues. In his authored work, the thirty-two-chapter *Works of Hsun Tzu* [*Xunzi*] text, Xunzi argued against the views of Legalist thinkers such as Shen Buhai and Shen Dao, the Daoist thinker Zhuangzi, the Mohist Mozi and the dialecticians, notably, Gongsun Long. However, Xunzi did not simply reject each of these views. Instead, he synthesised what he believed were important elements from these different philosophies with his personal Confucian convictions.

For example, Confucius rejected penal law (*fa*) as an instrument of cultivation (*Analects* 2:3; 12:13). But Xunzi was more realistic in endorsing the deterrent effects of *fa* as he believed that the method of positive reinforcement alone was inadequate for transforming society. In contrast to Mencius' positive assessment of human nature, Xunzi's views are notably pessimistic. His treatise on *xing* is entitled 'Xing E', that is, 'Human Nature is Evil' or 'Human Nature is Base'. Xunzi poses a counter-example to Mencius' child-about-to-fall-into-a-well example. He visualises two brothers vying for property, each of whom is self-serving at best. Xunzi notes that such selfishness is pervasive and argues for reform through a highly regulated socio-political context. He begins with a bleak postulation about the severe lack of moral goodness in original human nature:

> Man's nature (*xing*) is evil; goodness is the result of conscious activity. The nature of man is such that he is born with a fondness for profit... He is born with feelings of envy and hate... Hence, any man who follows his nature and indulges his emotions will inevitably become involved in wrangling and strife, will violate the forms and rules of society, and will end as a criminal. (*Works of Hsun Tzu* 23: 'The Nature of Man is Evil' trans. Watson 1963: 157)

Xunzi is not merely claiming that human nature is non-moral. He emphasises the *actively* selfish character of *xing* and its antisocial effects. Xunzi is often criticised for holding the view that human nature is 'evil' – and indeed, conventional translations of his theory of human nature interpret '*e*' as *evil*. Xunzi's philosophy, however, does not incorporate the elements of degenerateness or depravity we commonly associate with the concept of evil that has arisen from the Judaeo-Christian tradition. If we look carefully at this passage, it suggests that what Xunzi is concerned about is not inherent evil as such, but selfishness. Here, he seems to be saying that human nature is inherently selfish, and selfishness has undesirable outcomes. Selfishness results in strife and hatred and creates negative consequences not only for society but for the selfish person himself. This is detrimental and has negative consequences for society.

The disagreements between Mencius and Xunzi generate important philosophical and ethical questions. The difference in the views may be attributed to differences in the respective notions of *xing*.[12] There are also differences in their methods of moral cultivation. Mencius advocates the nurturing of socially positive behaviours while Xunzi believes primarily in instituting deterrents against antisocial behaviours. Moral cultivation in Mencius' view for the most part involves understanding the problem of the lost *xin* (mind–heart) and how it might be restored (*Books of Mencius* 6A:11, 12). Hence, Mencius states explicitly that the office of *xin* is to reflect and contemplate (*si*) (*Books of Mencius* 6A:15).[13] On the other hand, Xunzi advocates a more extensive program which underlines arduous practice and learning from external sources: goodness is the result of coordinated social regulation (*Works of Hsun Tzu* 23: 'The Nature of Man is Evil'). Xunzi believes that moral cultivation consists essentially in compliance with standards for behaviour such as *li* and *fa*. While a benevolent government is critical in Mencius' philosophy, Xunzi's system calls for an ethical regulator.

Li (Appropriate Behaviour) and *Fa* (Standards and Penal Law)

Xunzi argues against a programme that relies solely on eliciting other-regarding behaviour and feelings:

> Now the nature of man is evil. It must depend on teachers and laws (*fa*) to become correct and achieve propriety (*li*) and righteousness (*yi*)...The sage-kings of antiquity, knowing that the nature of man is evil, and

> that it is unbalanced, off the track, incorrect, rebellious, disorderly, and undisciplined, created the rules of propriety and righteousness and instituted laws and systems in order to correct man's feelings, transform them, and direct them…(*Works of Hsun Tzu* 23: 'The Nature of Man is Evil' trans. Chan 1963a: 128)

Li encourages positive (altruistic) behaviours while *fa*, the system of penal law enforced through punishment, discourages negative behaviours. *Li* and *fa* are *complementary* instruments for socio-political order (*Works of Hsun Tzu* 9: 'The Regulations of a King'). They work in tandem, *li* to encourage altruistic tendencies and *fa* to curb selfish ones. Xunzi meticulously investigates the origins of *li* and its applications; he eloquently expresses the sense of proportion and restraint brought about by implementing *li*:

> Rites [*li*] trim what is too long and stretch out what is too short, eliminate surplus and repair deficiency, extend the forms of love and reverence, and step by step bring to fulfilment the beauties of proper conduct. Beauty and ugliness, music and weeping, joy and sorrow are opposites, and yet rites make use of them all, bringing forth and employing each in its turn. (*Works of Hsun Tzu* 19: 'A Discussion of Ritual' trans. Watson 1963: 100)

Li is instrumental in the realisation of social harmony as it helps to mark each person's place within networks of relationships (*Works of Hsun Tzu* 14). Homer Dubs, who was a Chinese intellectual historian, captures the breadth of scope and versatility of Xunzi's *li*:

> *Li* is human emotion expressed, harmonized, and beautified so as to become a pattern for all. It uses the features, the voice, food, garments, and dwellings, and gives each their appropriate means of expressing emotion. As a pattern, *Li* aids those whose expression of sorrow would be too little, and those whose expression of sorrow would be too violent, alike to reach a golden mean. By means of *Li*, the degenerate son is kept from becoming worse than a beast, and the over-sensitive man is prevented from injuring himself. *Li* is the beautifying of man's original nature by means of acquired characteristics which could not be acquired of themselves. (trans. Dubs 1966: 146–7)

Dubs's description of *li* in Xunzi's philosophy captures Xunzi's idea of regulation. This conception of *li* is subtly different from its use both in the *Analects* and *Books of Mencius*. The *Analects* maintains a connection between *ren* (human feeling) and *li* (its expression), while the *Books of Mencius* unifies *ren* and *li* with moral discrimination and practical wisdom. In both these texts, *li* is primarily aligned with the cultivation of human moral sentiment. But Xunzi links *li* with *fa* and imputes the former with a stronger sense of compliance. This was a major point of departure from Confucius' thinking: Confucius understood *li* and *fa* to be based in fundamentally different conceptions of human good and social development. He claimed to be good at litigation while using it only as a last resort (*Analects* 12:13). A.C. Graham expresses Confucius' sentiments succinctly: 'Confucius accepts law as belonging to government, but measures success in ruling by how little it is necessary to apply it' (1989: 14). In comparison, Xunzi's approach to moral order is both more comprehensive and more cautious in its assumptions about human nature. His proposal for external regulation of behaviours appears to be a more viable system as contrasted with the naïveté in Mencius' idealistic humanism.

Zhengming: Regulating Society with Prescribed Titles

Another aspect of Xunzi's proposal relates to his debates with the dialecticians about names and their connection with reality. As we will see in a later chapter, the dialectician Gongsun Long emphasised the absolute nature of titles, assigning them a status akin to Platonic universals.[14] This debate on names and their connection with the world was a major issue that preoccupied thinkers from the fourth century BCE. The discussions covered topics in metaphysics, epistemology, philosophy of language and ethics. Confucius was engrossed with the use of titles to establish normative relationship obligations (*Analects* 12:11; 12:19; 13:3). For Confucius, *zhengming* is not primarily concerned with abstract, theoretical issues pertaining to the connection between names and reality nor is it about the modification of titles, as its common translation 'rectification of names' suggests. *Zhengming* in Confucian philosophy is an ethical theory concerning the appropriate conduct of those who bear particular titles.[15] Confucius seems to subscribe to a fundamental normative reality that language-terms must correspond with, and further propagate. But Xunzi rejects this assumption and contends that there is no mystery associated with the origin of names as their meanings are merely customary:

> Names have no intrinsic appropriateness. One agrees to use a certain name and issues an order to that effect, and if the agreement is abided by and

> becomes a matter of custom, then the name may be said to be appropriate, but if people do not abide by the agreement, then the name ceases to be appropriate. Names have no intrinsic reality. One agrees to use a certain name and issues an order that it shall be applied to a certain reality, and if the agreement is abided by and becomes a matter of custom, then it may be said to be a real name. (*Works of Hsun Tzu* 22: 'The Rectification of Names', trans. Watson 1963: 138)

In Xunzi's account, there is more responsibility attributed to the ruler and the leaders in society for the education of the people.[16] He is deeply conscious of the extent of influence wielded by those in power. The creation of standards through the determination of word-meanings is a powerful instrument with which entire populations may be swayed and managed. Xunzi astutely suggests that the role of government is not to encourage people not to have desires[17] but rather to manage the people's expectations such that '[although] one may not be able to enjoy all the most beautiful things in the world...yet he can still increase his joy...This is what it means to value the self and make other things work for you' (*ibid.*: 155–6).

In their responses to the socio-political unrest, Mencius and Xunzi begin from opposing assumptions. Mencius seeks to build upon an embryonic assumption, shared by the early Confucian disciples, of goodness inherent in humanity. He optimistically projects that human society will flourish if these sprouts of goodness are nurtured. Xunzi, on the other hand, postulates original selfishness to justify his recommendation for standards and measures such as *li* and *fa* to be enforced. Nevertheless he makes propitious projections for a society of people tempered by socio-political institutions: moral training and development can effectively overcome tendencies toward selfish indulgence. Burton Watson comments on the contrast between Xunzi's original nature and its subsequent development: 'To this dark initial thesis Hsün Tzu [Xunzi] contraposes the almost unlimitedly bright possibilities for improvement through study and moral training' (*ibid.*: 5). The early Confucians believed that all humans were morally perfectible and Xunzi was no exception in that regard. He states, unambiguously, that self cultivation is a real possibility for all humans. His statement is filled with conviction:

> The man in the street can become a Yu. What does this mean? What made the sage emperor Yu a Yu, I would reply, was the fact that he practiced

> benevolence and righteousness and abided by the proper rules and standards...Any man in the street has the essential faculties needed to understand benevolence, righteousness, and proper standards, and the potential ability to put them into practice. (*Works of Hsun Tzu* 23 'Human Nature is Evil', trans. Watson 1963: 166–7).

Both Mencius' and Xunzi's commitment to the perfectibility of the common man would have been radical within a social environment that was highly conscious of rank and status. Both blatantly assert the equality of all human beings. The notion of equality held by Mencius and Xunzi not only discredits the belief in *natural* inequality (that is, inequalities due to birthright or nobility) but also attacks existing inequalities. They challenge hereditary authority and replace it with an ethical meritocracy. Many of the chapters in the *Analects*, the *Books of Mencius* and the *Works of Hsun Tzu* are explicitly critical of existing socio-political structures and of those in power then. The model of government they propose involves an extensive engineering of human community.

The Way of Heaven and the Way of Humanity

The early Confucian thinkers did not provide a thorough justification for their vision of good government. More specifically, the rationale for its programme, including for the installation of *li* and *zhengming*, is not clearly articulated in the early texts. In the case of Mencius, we know that the basis of benevolent government lies in the abilities and intuitions of the benevolent ruler, but little more than that. Ultimately, these intuitions are grounded in heaven, as we have seen in *Books of Mencius* 7A:1. Mencius believed it was important to locate the ground of human well-being in a fundamental source. In expounding on the necessity for self cultivation, he needed to draw together these two elements: heaven and humanity. His method was to identify heaven as the source of human goodness (specifically, *xin*, the mind–heart). The task in self cultivation was to draw on this endowment in order to improve on human well-being.

In the seminal Confucian text the *Doctrine of the Mean* (*Zhongyong*), we see further development of the theme of cooperation between heaven and humanity.[18] The *Zhongyong* is a treatise on human and cosmic harmony, dealing with how equilibrium (*zhong*) and commonality (*yong*) are attained. The fundamental value in the *Zhongyong* is sincerity (*xin*), which is heaven's way. The practice of perfect sincerity by humans brings together a tripartite unity of heaven, earth and humanity. The comprehensiveness of this doctrine can only be understood when we view *Zhongyong* chapter 22 in its entirety:

> Only that one in the world who is most perfectly sincere is able to give full development to his nature. Being able to give full development to his nature, he is able to give full development to the nature of other human beings and, being able to give full development to the nature of other human beings, he is able to give full development to the natures of other living things. Being able to give full development to the natures of other living things, he can assist in the transforming and nourishing powers of Heaven and Earth; being able to assist in the transforming and nourishing powers of Heaven and Earth; he can form a triad with Heaven and Earth. (De Bary and Bloom 1999: 338)

We will understand more fully the early Confucian debate about human nature if we also examine Yang Zhu's doctrine of *xing*. Mencius is adamant that Yang Zhu's egoism is detrimental to society because he renounces the authority of the ruler in favour of looking after oneself (*Books of Mencius* 3B:9). Yang Zhu is described in the *Liezi* (c. 300 CE) as utterly selfish, unable directly to answer the question, 'If you could help the whole world at the cost of one hair of your body, would you do it?' (Graham 1978: 16; *Books of Mencius* 7A:26). Due to this representation, Yang Zhu's theory has often been ignored in serious scholarship. However, Graham points out the probable misrepresentation of the theory and how Yang Zhu's ideas are in fact important in understanding the twin issues of human nature and self cultivation. According to Graham, an earlier text, the *Lüshi Chunqiu* (*Master Lü's Spring and Autumn Annals*; c. 240 BCE), presents a different account of individualist thought (Graham 1978: 16–7). The main strands of this doctrine include keeping intact what heaven has bestowed, nourishing it and not interfering with it. This does not necessarily imply excessive selfishness but rather advocates 'nurturing and harmonising the vital tendencies and spontaneous inclinations which Heaven instilled in us when we were born' (*ibid.*: 17).

If Graham is correct, Yang Zhu's doctrine espouses a much closer connection between heaven and humanity than we see in the early Confucian theories. For Yang Zhu, one must be watchful that external factors are prevented from interfering with this original nature. In Mencius' philosophy, external factors are more differentiated: there are those which are detrimental to human well-being and others, such as benevolent leadership, which foster harmony and human development. The latter, positive, elements must be encouraged and individuals must be receptive to the guiding influences of the benevolent ruler. Graham presents the Yang Zhu–early Confucian debate thus:

> It had never been questioned that Heaven, the power responsible for all things being as they are, for the uncontrollable accidents of fortune and misfortune, for whatever in man is innate and independent of his will, has also ordained the principles by which we should live.... Now for the first time [in Confucian and Mohist thought] a metaphysical doubt enters Chinese thought, and a rift opens between Heaven and man, between what is and what should be. If Heaven is on the side of Yang Chu [Yang Zhu], on what is the morality of Confucians and Mohists to rest? (Graham 1978: 17)

The rift between heaven and humanity is even wider in Xunzi's philosophy. Xunzi devotes a chapter in his text to the discussion of heaven (Chapter 17, 'Discourse on Heaven' (*tianlun*)). There, he limits the jurisdiction of heaven to a natural order that does not intervene in human affairs. Also in the same chapter, he takes care to dispel superstitions – for instance, about eclipses and climate changes – in order to promote active responsibility of humans for socio-political affairs. As with the other Confucians, Xunzi emphasises the unity between heaven, earth and humanity. However, it is a rather detached version of the tripartite relationship in that the domains of the three are clearly defined, rather than overlapping. We see especially in Xunzi's philosophy an emphasis on human initiative in planning for and structuring a nation.

Personal Cultivation and Social Development

The early Confucian thinkers were working toward a humanistic government that looked upon the needs of the people as its first priority. Unfortunately, this important theme is often ignored in many popular renditions of Confucianism, where the focus is on leadership without mention of moral accountability. The Confucians were devoted to learning and cultivation, and committed to optimising the human condition through socio-political infrastructure. The ideal society was built upon the exemplary and paradigmatic commitment of the government to the people, especially in Mencius' philosophy.

In early Confucian philosophy, the cultivation of the self is primarily a directed process, coordinated by those with moral and political authority. In fact, for Confucius, moral and political capability are two integrated aspects of those in government. In this regard, one concern often articulated by critics is the collectivist nature of Confucian ideology. The worry is that the priority given to collective (for example, national or familial) well-being will always override individual interests and needs. This concern is not insignificant in the light of events in Chinese history – if indeed the cause may at least in part be attributed to Confucianism. The important question for contemporary Confucian scholars is whether there are elements in Confucian philosophy that uphold the basic integrity of the self. Some scholars such as Tu Weiming have sought the answer in a broader adapted understanding of self cultivation.[19] He argues that the cultivation of the self is not merely to blend into one's relational roles:

> The self as the center of relationships has always been the focus of Confucian learning. One's ability to harmonize human relations does indeed indicate one's self-cultivation, but the priority is clearly set. Self-cultivation is a precondition for harmonizing human relations; if human relations are superficially harmonized without the necessary ingredients of self-cultivation, it is practically unworkable and teleologically misdirected. (1985: 55–6)

Tu attempts to alleviate the concern that Confucian self cultivation is merely an acculturation process. Yet, we must be careful not to fragment the concept of self cultivation by identifying first- and second-order priorities or prerequisites: first the self, then its relationships. It is more accurate to characterise the Confucian concept of self as primarily a related self; this means that cultivation of good relationships will ultimately benefit the self. Indeed, Tu himself breaks the self–other and the individual–collective dichotomy in another essay:

> ...Confucian self-transformation is based on neither isolated self-control nor collective social sanction. It is in what may be called the "between" that its basis really lies...the main issue in Confucianism is never conceived of in terms of an "either-or" proposition. Rather, to be an authentic man is to be truthful to *both* one's selfhood and one's sociality. (1972: 192–3)

In Confucian philosophy, relationships are integral to and constitutive of a person's identity. This concept of self is essentially as a related entity that thrives on mutually beneficial relationships. It stands in contrast to those accounts of self that value detached impartiality or stoical, self-denying altruism. Confucian philosophy emphasises the basic interrelatedness of persons as a central feature of its account of morality. According to this view, self cultivation is the ethico-social realisation of individuals within their networks of relationships. The success of the Confucian vision relies on the interest of individuals in their shared well-being. The nature of cooperation and collaboration within Confucian society has been likened to musicians playing in concert. Every member of the ensemble has an important role to play, and a good performance is assessed not merely with reference to the ability of each of the players with respect to their roles, but also to how well the musicians play together.[20] The Confucian interdependent self deserves serious consideration as it provides rich insights into the centrality of human interaction and relationships in the lives of individuals. The concept of the interdependent self is a realistic account of self and one that has important implications for notions of action, intentionality, responsibility, accountability, choice and morality.

Character Development and the Cultivation of Skills

The person who has advanced a fair way into the self cultivation process will have developed inner resources that are independent of contemporary norms. *Analects* 13:23 notes that the *junzi*, the Confucian paradigmatic person,[21] does not seek to be similar to other people, although he aims to be harmonious with them:

> The *chun tzu* [*junzi*] seeks to be harmonious (*he*) but does not attempt to be similar (*tong*). The small man, by contrast, seeks to be similar and is not harmonious (trans. Lau 1979a: 122).

Both in the description of Confucius' developmental path (*Analects* 2:4) and the *junzi*'s achievements (*Analects* 15:21; 15:22), there is a sense of the paradigmatic person's detachment from conventional norms and expectations:

> The Master said, "You can study with some, and yet not necessarily walk the same path (*dao* 道); you can walk the same path as some, and yet not necessarily take your stand with them; you can take your stand with them,

> and yet not necessarily weigh things up in the same way." (*Analects* 9:30; trans. Ames and Rosemont, Jr 1998a: 133)

The paradigmatic person is a discriminating thinker who critically evaluates the beliefs, norms and practices of his society. He is a creator of standards rather than a follower (*Analects* 2:1; 12:19) and he possesses a keen sense of moral discrimination (*Analects* 4:3). For the *junzi*,

> [m]oral life is displayed not as a set of court-judgments on specifiable actions but rather as the development of relationships, skills, and ongoing virtues that make it possible to affect things for the better at the right time and in the right way. The power of this point derives from its contrast to the usual Western mode of moral thinking. Perhaps because of the pervasiveness of the juridical model, Western philosophers have looked at the judgeable action as the proper unit of moral worth. (Neville 1986: 191)

The training required to attain the skills of moral deliberation is extensive. It involves the cultivation of a range of capacities with the following features:

(1) Reading and reflecting to arouse one's sensibilities and sharpen critical skills (*Analects* 17:9).
(2) Reflective self-examination (*Analects* 15:6) of one's dealings with others (*Analects* 1:4) as well as a mindful attitude toward all matters (19:6; 16:10).
(3) Observation of the practices and conduct of others. Confucius was a keen observer of others' behaviours (*Analects* 2:10) and he learnt from both the good and the bad (*Analects* 7:22).
(4) Commitment to constant practice (*Analects* 19:5; 12:1) with a view to making manifest one's fundamental principles. This idea is captured in the concept *xin*, often translated 'sincerity' or 'trustworthiness'. *Xin* is an integral component in Confucian self cultivation (*Analects* 1:4–8; 9:24–25; 12:10; 14:37), once being described as the pin of a yoke that enables a carriage to be drawn (*Analects* 2:22).

We must not overstate the case for the independence of the paradigmatic person from his or her traditional culture. The paradigmatic person is attuned to the norms within her community (*Analects* 14:29), sensitive to others and aware of morally significant contextual factors. Hence, moral development includes the inculcation of a sense of shame (primarily, *xiu* and *chi* in the early Confucian texts), an internal consciousness that is uneasy when one has done bad things especially in the 'eyes of others'.[22] She also has a broad knowledge and understanding of situations in life, a depth of experience including learning from the experiences of others, and the deliberative skills required in making moral judgments. David Nivison, a contemporary scholar, argues that the question of self cultivation centres on the inculcation of moral sensitivity, which he terms *de* (virtue):

> ...the focus (in Confucian ethics) is not on how to define the good or the right, or to determine what is good or right; these things will seem unproblematic. The real problem seems to be how one becomes a person who has *de*; and this means that the moral tradition is centered from the start on self-cultivation and on how one conveys insight to a student or gets the student to change. (1999: 750)

Just as one might learn from the *Book of Odes* (also known as the *Book of Poetry*) during Confucius' time, the contemporary reader of the *Analects* may reflect on a range of skills as they are played out in its different passages. The passages provide a sense of the complexity and immediacy of different moral dilemmas. Each situation presents issues with different moral weights and competing obligations to be fulfilled. These insights familiarise the reader with an understanding of different obligations, loyalties and relational distance in his relationships with others. Especially in a harsh social environment, loyalties and support networks are an integral part of good relationships and are instrumental in pulling individuals through difficult moments. The application of these insights could assist in the cultivation of some fundamental skills in ethical reflection and deliberation.

Suggestions for Further Reading

Mencius, translated by Dim-Cheuk Lau (1979), revised edition, Hong Kong: The Chinese University Press.

Hsün Tzu: Basic Writings, translated by Burton Watson (1963), New York: Columbia University Press.

Xunzi: A Translation and Study of the Complete Works, translated by John Knoblock, vols. 1–3. vol. 1 (1988) books 1–6; vol. 2 (1990) books 7–16; vol. 3 (1994) books 17–32, Stanford: Stanford University Press.

Chan, Alan (editor) (2002) *Mencius: Contexts and Interpretations*, Honolulu: University of Hawai'i Press.

Cua, Antonio (2005) *Human Nature, Ritual, and History: Studies in Xunzi and Chinese Philosophy* (Studies in Philosophy and the History of Philosophy), Washington, D.C.: Catholic University of America Press.

Shun, Kwong-Loi (1997) *Mencius and Early Chinese Thought*, Stanford: Stanford University Press.

Notes

1. Refer to Wing-tsit Chan 1963a: 49.
2. The Confucian canon, the *Four Books* (*Si Shu*), were codified by the Neo-Confucian Zhu Xi (1130–1200). These four books (the *Great Learning* (*Daxue*), the *Analects* (*Lunyu*), the *Books of Mencius* and the *Doctrine of the Mean* (*Zhongyong*)) comprised the core of the official curriculum of the civil service examinations during the Yuan (1279–1368) and Ming (1368–1644) dynasties.
3. Kwong-Loi Shun presents a detailed analysis of Mencius' discussions with Gaozi, including philosophical details of their debates (1997: 87–94). Little is known of Gaozi's background and associations. Shun discusses a number of theses regarding his philosophical affiliations at pp. 123ff.
4. Chad Hansen notes that Mencius' view of human nature is far more optimistic than that set out in the *Analects* (Hansen 1992: 71ff.).
5. Mencius' strategy of grounding *xing* in *tian* resonates with the themes espoused in the *Zhongyong*. The *Zhongyong* is a classical Confucian text, also one of the Confucian *Four Books*, reputedly written by Confucius' grandson, Zisi, although some of it appears to have earlier origins, while other parts date from as late as the early Han period. Tu Weiming presents a metaphysical and religious interpretation of Confucian self cultivation based on the *Zhongyong* (Tu 1976).
6. In contemporary Chinese it can refer both to intellectual–moral capacity, the mind, as well as the physical organ, the heart.
7. Hansen writes, 'The empirical problem is not that his theory is implausibly *optimistic* as much as that it is implausibly *specific* about the *innate judgments of what counts as good*.' (1992: 168).
8. Benjamin Schwartz notes that 'the center of Mencius' problematique in dealing with man is really *not* the nature [*xing*] but the heart/mind [*xin*]' (1985: 266). See also Schwartz 1985: 288ff.; Ch'en, 1953; Ahern 1980: 183; and Graham 1967.
9. See, for example, Creel 1953: 88.
10. Schwartz 1985: 266 and Ho Hwang 1979: 201–9.

11. A. C. Graham (1990b) *Studies in Chinese Philosophy and Philosophical Literature*, 7. The *Shuowen Jiezi* also emphasises the derivative meaning of *xing* from *sheng*, growth. Further, it states that the term derives from *xin*, the heart–mind (at p. 502). These derivatives taken together suggest cultivation, a continual growth, of the *xin*. This could indicate the influence of Mencian philosophy in the *Shuowen*'s explication of *xing*.
12. Ch'en 1953, Ahern 1980, Munro 1969 and A. C. Graham (1967; and 1989: 250ff).
13. Philip Ivanhoe points out the different learning strategies implicated in each philosophy (Ivanhoe 1990). The philosophical distance between the two positions has persisted through developments in Chinese intellectual history and is manifest especially in Neo-Confucian thought (see Hansen 1992: 380 at note 16).
14. Gongsun Long emphasised the absoluteness of titles, assigning them a status that further perpetuated the underlying assumptions of the Confucian rectification of names (aligning names with reality), and also arguing for clear distinctions to be made. Refer to Y. P. Mei (1953) for a translation of the text.
15. There is no clear distinction between those roles within the socio-political and others in personal or private domains. *Zhengming* applies not only to the obligations of those who take on the more 'public' socio-political roles, but to obligations in relationships which have a distinctly more personal and private aspect as well. These discussions on the moral demands arising from relationships provide interesting grounds for comparison with the relatively recent interest in similar issues in contemporary western moral philosophy.
16. The potential for an inept or immoral ruler to manipulate the common people utilising this formulation of *zhengming* is not insignificant. It is a possibility that Xunzi considers only briefly, arguing that those who exploit the tool by recklessly making up new names and casting out the old – hence causing people to be deluded and confused – 'is a terrible evil and should be punished' (*Works of Hsun Tzu* 22: 'The Rectification of Names', trans. Watson 1963: 140).
17. Xunzi writes, 'All those who maintain that desires must be gotten rid of before there can be orderly government fail to consider whether desires can be guided, but merely deplore the fact that they exist at all. All those who maintain that desires must be lessened before there can be orderly government fail to consider whether desires can be controlled, but merely deplore the fact that they are so numerous . . . the possession or

nonpossession of desires has nothing to do with good government or bad' (*ibid*: 150).

18. The *Zhongyong* had traditionally been attributed to Confucius' grandson, Zisi. However, more recent scholarship dates it as a text of the Qin or early Han, though with some sections of much earlier origin. De Bary and Bloom's compilation of texts includes translated sections of the text as well as commentary on them (1999: 333–9).
19. Antonio Cua is perhaps the most insightful and prolific contemporary philosopher on the topic of moral theory and ethical cultivation in Confucian thought (in English-language publications). Herbert Fingarette's explanations of Confucian thought (1972, 1979, 1983) also present another interesting way of revitalising Confucian *li*.
20. Sartwell 1993, Fingarette 1983 and Lai 2003b.
21. Traditionally, *junzi* is a term applied to achievements available only to men: social and political status and ethical cultivation. In Confucius' time, the term *junzi* by definition excluded women. But here, I have translated *junzi* as 'paradigmatic person' in order to be gender neutral; after all, not all of the ideals associated with the Confucian *junzi* are out of reach of women today.
22. The distinction between the terms in the early Confucian texts is less than clear and, while there are subtle differences between the two concepts, both relate to shame: *xiu* seems to incorporate the idea of an internal moral-regulatory capacity while *chi* seems to capture the sense of embarrassment associated with being 'caught out'. However, this sense of embarrassment may also be internalised such that one may feel *chi* even in the absence of observers. The predominant concept in the *Analects* is *chi* while Mencius discusses *xiu* especially in connection with *wu*, aversion to evil (Lai 2006: 74–6). Xunzi by contrast does not seem to focus on shame as 'internal' regulation although, for him, shame stands in contrast to the concept of honour (*rong*), a concept closely related to a person's integrity (Cua 2005: 205–43).

4 Early Mohist Philosophy

Mozi's (480? BCE–390? BCE) criticisms of Ruist (Confucian) teachings and practice were incisive. It is likely that he had studied Confucian philosophy and interacted with a particular group of Ruist scholar-officials associated with the disciples Zixia and Ziyou. These disciples were preoccupied with the study of texts, ceremonial ritual and the cultivation of a privileged lifestyle. Mozi reacted to these aspects of Ruist doctrine and is said to have praised Confucius but rejected the Ruists he had met.[1] Mozi also rejected a number of Confucian doctrines. He singled out their reliance on paradigmatic men to bring about socio-political well-being and argued for a more participatory approach to maximising collective welfare: everyone must practise *jianai*, impartial and mutual concern for everyone. Mozi believed that the root cause of socio-political unrest was the selfishness of individuals; the majority of people lacked genuine concern for others not immediately connected with them. To make matters worse, the Confucians were propagating a culture of divisiveness and factionalism by encouraging people to give priority to family relationships.

Up until relatively recently, scholarship in Mohist philosophy has been fairly disparaging of its ideas and influence. For instance, Wing-tsit Chan, an influential Chinese philosopher, noted that 'philosophically Mohism is shallow and unimportant'.[2] The tendency was to interpret Mohism as a reaction against Confucianism, and a fairly weak attempt at that. But scholars including Schwartz, Graham and Hansen have more comprehensively outlined the aspects of Mozi's philosophy that were influential in shaping the subsequent development of Chinese philosophy.[3] Hansen considers Mozi to be the 'most important philosopher in the early half of the classical period'.[4] Mozi rejected Confucian traditionalism – the institution of *li*-practices – and assessed Confucian doctrines according to their efficacy in bringing about an improved human condition. He engaged critically with Confucian ideas, requiring from defenders of the tradition proper justification for their claims. He insisted on reasoned arguments according to a set of criteria. Mozi was instrumental in establishing the idea of argumentation in debate, *bian*. He set out three standards (*fa*) according to which all ethical actions or practices should be assessed: precedent (past practices), empirical veracity (experiences of the people) and utility. Mozi applied these criteria primarily to ethical issues, though his discussions on verifiability and justification were critical in setting the path for later developments especially in epistemology and philosophy of language. Prior to Mozi, debates in ancient China had focused almost entirely on ethical, political and metaphysical issues. Later Mohist thinkers extended Mozi's ideas in their influential discussions of language and logic. These Mohists introduced a number of key elements in philosophical enquiry to early Chinese philosophical debate, in particular, critical and objective assessment. Hence some scholars note with regret the overshadowing – for whatever reason – of Mohist philosophy in the subsequent development of Chinese philosophy.

Texts and Themes

Although fragments of Mohist writings have been lost, the remaining sections present a reasonably coherent picture of early Mohist philosophy. The writings, collected as an anthology entitled *Mozi* (or *Mo Tzu*), were written by Mozi's disciples and others influenced by his thought. The writing in this collection of essays is repetitious and ponderous. Some scholars suggest that this is due to the lesser educational and social status of the Mohists compared with the Confucians.[5] Of its remaining fifty-three chapters (originally eighty-three), the core of early Mohist philosophy is captured in a set of essays (chapters 8–39) covering ten doctrines. An eleventh topic, 'Against Confucianism', is not considered part of the ten doctrines. The ten topics are: (1) 'Elevating the Worthy', (2) 'Identifying with the Superior's Standard', (3) 'Impartial Concern', (4) 'Against Aggressive Warfare', (5) 'Economy in Expenditure', (6) 'Economy in Funerals', (7) 'Heaven's Intention', (8) 'Explaining Ghosts', (9) 'Rejecting Music' and (10) 'Rejecting Belief in Fate'.

Interestingly, there are three versions of essays on each of these doctrines. It is likely that these versions were written by thinkers belonging to three different Mohist sects. They may have been recollections of Mozi's speeches; this may also account for the repetitious elements, devices used more extensively in speeches than writing.[6]

The Essays

The essays which discuss the ten doctrines provide a reasonably clear picture of Mozi's ideas. The doctrines are paired according to their common themes:

(1) and (2) 'Elevating the Worthy' and 'Identifying with the Superior's Standard': Mozi expresses concern at the unbridled plurality of values. He views plurality as the cause of discord and suggests the implementation of a single criterion, *yi* (rightness), as the solution to the unrest. The basic measure of *yi* lies in benefit (*li*) to society. Mozi identifies three collective goods: wealth, high population and socio-political order. Men whose acts exemplify a commitment to *yi* should be appointed to lead the nation ('elevating the worthy'). Mozi also outlines an elaborate hierarchical system with rewards and punishments for implementing *yi*. When common people emulate the worthy, that is, when they identify with the vision and commitment of their superiors, clarity of right (*shi*) and wrong (*fei*) will prevail. The end-result of this is socio-political order.

(3) and (4) 'Impartial Concern' and 'Against Aggressive Warfare': Mozi upholds impartial concern of each person for everyone else as the essential antidote to aggression and opportunism at the expense of others. Some of the arguments in these essays are persuasive not least because they appear to stem from Mozi's personal commitment to collective well-being. In his clearly reasoned argument, he impartially weighs the gains from aggressive war against the loss of life, which is too high a price to pay. He attributes selfishness to an attitude, *bie*, the drawing of a sharp distinction between self and other. He urges the practice of *jianai*, expressed simply, though significantly, as 'valuing others as one values oneself' (*ai ren ruo ai qishen*) (Chapter 14: 'Impartial Concern').

(5) and (6) 'Economy in Expenditure' and 'Economy in Funerals': Mozi applies one of his basic criteria, utility, to evaluate these two (Confucian) practices. According to his assessment, expensive and elaborate funeral rituals and extended prescribed mourning periods are unjustified. (The mourning period for one's parents included three years' withdrawal from participation in ordinary activities, including work.) Mozi acknowledges that these rituals are widely accepted and practised, though he also notes their customary origin: 'they confuse what is habitual with what is proper, and

what is customary with what is right' (Chapter 25: 'Moderation in Funerals', trans. Watson 1963: 75). The disutility of these practices outweighs the fact that they have been accepted and in use for a long time.

(7) and (8) 'Heaven's Intention' and 'Explaining Ghosts': Mozi argues that heaven, *tian*, is the source and origin of *yi*. Evidence for heaven's *yi* is manifest in the socio-political order. Mozi provides many examples of heaven's *yi* to demonstrate its beneficence in its treatment of others. Mozi's *tian* is the paradigmatic impartial agent concerned for the well-being of all. The beneficent commitment of heaven is an objective and verifiable standard of measurement; it is comparable to the compass of a wheelwright and the square of a carpenter. All human actions and utterances must be measured against this objective standard set by *tian*. In this initiative, Mozi not only moves away from the traditional reliance on authority figures, he introduces the notions of impartiality and objectivity to early Chinese philosophy.

(9) and (10) 'Rejecting Music' and 'Rejecting Belief in Fate': Mozi rejects these practices as resource-intensive and indulgent. Although music is enjoyable, it distracts from more essential, life-sustaining activities. As with funeral practices, music is customary though of little utility. Music is a luxury for a few at the expense of the common people. In these thoughts Mozi expresses little thought for the place of aesthetic and cultural pursuits in human well-being. He presents a thin picture of social and community life, pared down to its essentials. Of course, this may be understandable in a situation of war. In his arguments against belief in fate, we also sense his abhorrence toward any activities that work against economic productivity. Mozi spurns belief in fate as it encourages resignation to one's situation and does not promote the maximisation of benefits. These writings encapsulate a thrifty, relentless work ethic, one that is more apparent here than in the early Confucian texts, although the phenomenon of parsimonious and hardworking Chinese populations is often attributed to the Confucian work ethic.

The remaining chapters of the *Mozi* are often grouped into four parts: the Epitomes (1–7), Logical Chapters (40–45: comprising the Canons and their exposition), Dialogues (46–50) and Military Chapters (51–71). These are written by later Mohist thinkers and hence often referred to as the later Mohist or Neo-Mohist Canon. The topics covered in these chapters include epistemology, ethics, logic, philosophy of language, geometry, military tactics and mechanics. The significant chapters in this collated set are the Canons and their exposition. The Canons deal in extended fashion with the issues of language, its meaning and its connection with epistemology. Later Mohist philosophy is discussed in Chapter Seven.

Maximising the Collective Good

Mozi is concerned about the selfish motives of those wanting to annex other states. For him, it is clear that the loss of lives at war is a tragic evil and far outweighs the gains acquired in the spoils of war. Mozi's argument is grounded in the assumption that correct ethical assessment must take into account the sum total of good and evil for all concerned: although a number of individuals stand to gain in war, a greater number will be affected negatively. To Mozi, it was clear that partiality – selfishness – was the root cause of sociopolitical disorder:

> When we inquire into the cause of these various harms, what do we find has produced them? Do they come about from loving others and trying to benefit them? Surely not! They come rather from hating others and trying to injure them. And when we set out to classify and describe those men who hate and injure others, shall we say that their actions are motivated by universality or partiality? Surely we must answer, by partiality, and it is this partiality in their dealings with one another that gives rise to all the great harms in the world. Therefore we know that partiality is wrong. (Chapter 16: 'Impartial Concern', trans. Watson 1963: 39)

Mozi's concern to maximise the collective good is an early and simple version of utilitarian theory; the welfare of all concerned is the primary driving force of his ethical philosophy. The concept *jianai* provides the basic ethical principle for the realisation of collective good. It is more profound than its common translation 'Universal Love' suggests. There is consensus among scholars that the term *ai* in the phrase *jianai* does not refer to the affectionate feeling commonly associated with love. Graham argues that the Mohist *ai* is an unemotional will and that the translation 'Universal Love' is both too warm and too vague. It is too warm because *jianai* is not about emotional love and too vague because it does not capture the sense of impartiality implied in the term *jian*.[7] A translation of the concept must capture Mozi's commitment to impartiality in order to attain collective well-being: Graham suggests 'concern for everyone' (Graham 1989: 41–2). In his deliberations on *jianai*, we see plenty of evidence that Mozi was a critical thinker who engaged at a metaethical level with his own theory. He identifies impartiality as the key to understanding and implementing a utilitarian ethic. While the Confucian relational ethic had its roots in the cultivation of particular attachments, *jianai* expresses the essence of an impartial approach that requires some detachment from one's interests and personal affiliations. It was not that the Confucians were not also concerned about social order and collective good. But from Mozi's perspective, their solution was headed in the wrong direction. To focus on cultivating particular relationships *as the avenue* to realising collective good simply would not work.

This disagreement is most pronounced when we contrast Mozi's ideas with those of Mencius. As we have seen in Chapter Three, Mencius emphasised the centrality and significance of particular human feelings – initially in terms of a child's affection for its parents – to a cultivated concern for humanity in general. Mencius uses the term *tui* (push, extend) explicitly to suggest the extension of the scope of human fellow-feeling. He cites the example of King Wan who extended his concern for his family to the common people:

> Treat with the reverence due to age the elders in your own family, so that the elders in the families of others shall be similarly treated…do this, and the kingdom may be made to go round in your palm. It is said in the Book of Poetry, "His example affected his wife. It reached to his brothers, and his family of the State was governed by it." – The language shows how king Wan simply took his kindly heart, and exercised it towards those parties. Therefore the carrying out [*tui*: extension of] his kindness of heart by a prince will suffice for the love and protection of all within the four seas…The way in which the ancients came greatly to surpass other men, was no other but this: – simply that they knew well how to carry out, so as to affect others, what they themselves did. (*Books of Mencius*, 1A:7:12, trans. Legge 1893–5: 143)

But Mozi is sceptical about this approach that relies on cultivating concern for others by the extension of one's particular relational attachments. *Tui* was an argument strategy in Chinese philosophy not unlike reasoning by analogy: one applies an established argument or practice to a relevantly similar scenario. But Mozi does not believe *tui* will work in this particular case: the two situations, one of specially cultivated affection and the other of generalised concern, are *relevantly dissimilar*. Would not the cultivation of particular relationships breed partiality (*bie*)? Aggressive war, in Mozi's eyes, is the manifestation of partiality writ large:

> When the emperor loves only himself and not his minister, he benefits himself to the disadvantage of the minister...As he loves only his own family and not other families, the thief steals from other families to profit his family...As he loves only his own state and not the others, the feudal lord attacks the other states to profit his own. These instances exhaust the confusion in the world. And when we look into the causes we find they all arise from want of mutual love. (Chapter 14: 'Impartial Concern', trans. Mei 1929: 79)

Although Mozi allows *ren* a part in his philosophy ('Impartial Concern'; 'Heaven's Intention'), the concept is relegated from its central position in Confucianism to denote benevolence in a very general sense. For the Confucians, *ren* is a dynamic concept that denotes both specific relational attachment (*ren*^{kinship}) and compassion for others (*ren*^{compassion}). Confucian philosophy regards *ren*^{compassion} as the fruition of *ren*^{kinship}. Indeed, the cultivation process is a continuous development of widening circles of mutually beneficial relationships (*Analects* 6:30). While Mozi accepts the instrumentality of *ren*^{compassion} in attaining social order, he disagrees that the path to achieve that is through the cultivation of special attachments. In particular, those manifest forms of *ren*, filial piety (*xiao*) and brotherly submission (*di*), teach people to discriminate against non-family. Mozi is not convinced that *ren*^{kinship} will successfully develop into *ren*^{compassion}. In other words, partiality is simply not universalisable:

> The Confucians say: "There are degrees to be observed in treating relatives as relatives, and gradations to be observed in honoring the worthy." They prescribe differences to be observed between close and distant relatives and between the honored and the humble. (Chapter 39: 'Against Confucians', trans. Watson 1963: 124)

Mozi's argument against *tui* in Confucianism is persuasive. On the other hand, Mencius is correct that the affective bonds especially between parent and child are foundational in human life and should be encouraged (*Books of Mencius* 7A:15). There is explicit recognition of the tension in the *Ru-Mo* (Confucianist-Mohist) debates in the *Books of Mencius*. In *Mencius* 3A:5, the Mohist Yi Zhi notes the implausibility of developing *ren*^{kinship} into *ren*^{compassion} as well as their basic incompatibility. In response, Mencius makes the point that there is really only one 'root' (*ben*: basis) of human compassion, but that Yi Zhi makes it two. Mencius' 'one root' is, presumably, *xin*, the mind–heart,[8] while Yi Zhi's 'two roots' are the mind–heart as well as utility. From Mencius' point of view, the Mohist interest in the utility of *ren*^{compassion} is misplaced. However, if we proceed to question *why* the Mohist is incorrect in considering the utility of *ren*^{compassion}, Mencius' reply must appeal to something else other than utility. In other words, Mencius could contend that the Mohist emphasis on the utility of *ren*^{compassion} is wrong because it is detrimental to society, or because it is less effective than Confucian *ren*^{kinship} in attaining social order. In making this claim, however, Mencius is himself subscribing to the notion of utility, of what is beneficial or harmful to society. Mozi's consideration of utility forces a critical analysis of Confucian commitments and their approaches to socio-political order. *Ren*^{kinship} fails the test of utility. Mozi puts up two candidates for consideration, one partial (that is, the basic principle of *ren*^{kinship}) and the other impartial:

> Suppose there are two men, one of them holding to partiality, the other to universality. The believer in partiality says, "How could I possibly regard my friend the same as myself, or my friend's father the same as my own?"...[The believer in universality] would say, "I have heard that the truly superior man of the world regards his friend the same as himself, and his friend's father the same as his own...Now let us ask, to whom would he entrust the support of his parents and the care of his wife and children? Would it be to the universal-minded man, or to the partial man? It seems to me that, on occasions like these, there are no fools in the world. Though one may disapprove of universality himself, he would surely think it best to entrust his family to the universal-minded man. (Chapter 16: 'Universal Love', trans. Watson 1963: 41–2)

Mozi puts up a compelling argument for the utility of *ren*^{compassion} and the potential disutility of *ren*^{kinship} on a large scale. Yet, although the Mohist focus on utility is persuasive, Mozi was not unaware of the fragility of his concept *jianai*. He was conscious of the unrealistic expectations in requiring people to think and act impartially. He deals with this concern in a rather weak statement that one's concern for others should incite similar responses from others: if one is impartial to others, it will inspire others to act in an equally impartial manner (Chapter 16: 'Impartial Concern').

The comparative discussion about *ren* is important as it sheds light on a critical concept in Chinese philosophy. *Ren* plays a key role in Confucian philosophy, in articulating its picture of humanity and the good life. In Mohism, the role is of *ren* is somewhat diminished though still a part of its theory of collective well-being. Both visions were optimistic in recommending moral guidance as one of the tasks of government. This accounts for why the Confucians and Mohists have sometimes been grouped together and their debate labelled *Ru-Mo*. But we should not let this obscure the significant differences in their respective conceptions of *ren*. Mozi holds a vision of human existence that is pared down to essentials. He has a list of social goods that does not include aesthetic and cultural pursuits and he judges behavioural ritual (*li*) and music purely in economic terms. Even the institution of *jianai* seems rather cold and calculated as it is underpinned by a standard set by the superiors. As we have seen earlier in Mozi's discussion of 'Identifying with the Superior's Standard', difference of opinion is to be eliminated by having only one standard, that which is set by the superior. The Mohist superior person is ultimately committed to social benefit and will implement a system of rewards and punishments to ensure the maximisation of utility. There is little consideration for the welfare of individuals because it is assumed that collective welfare will also benefit the individual. Yet, simplistic as this thesis may seem, Mozi's focus on collective good deserves serious consideration. The doctrine of *jianai* requires not simply ambivalent non-violence but active assistance of others and concern for their welfare. The term *li* (profit) in Mozi's philosophy is rightly translated 'benefit', while the Confucians had greatly narrowed its meaning to mean 'individual profit' – and hence were quick to reject it (*Analects* 9:1; 16:10). But Mozi's emphasis on utility is compelling, as is his discussion of standards of evaluation.

Working with Standards

Mozi sets out a Hobbesian-style hypothetical state of nature wherein a chaotic plurality of views precipitates disagreement and hostility between people in society. He argues that plurality is the primary cause of socio-political unrest:

> Why are the superiors now unable to govern their subordinates, and the subordinates unwilling to serve their superiors? It is because of a mutual

> disregard. What is the reason for this? The reason is a difference in standards. Whenever standards differ there will be opposition. (Chapter 13: 'Identification with the Superior's Standard', trans. Mei 1929: 72)

For Mozi, the fundamental cause of unrest is the proliferation of values. As we shall see later, Zhuangzi also worries about the same issue, although his remedy focuses on how we might embrace plurality. In contrast, Mozi believes that the function of government is to 'unify and assimilate morality throughout the Empire' (Graham 1978:13). Mozi seeks to replace different values with a single standard that will unify the nation. Mozi refers to the unifying code as a standard, *fa*. The concept *fa* in early Chinese philosophy has a range of meanings including normative standard or principle, a model or instance of the standard or even a paradigmatic person who realises it. In Mohist philosophy, *fa* has a pragmatic aspect and is most often used to refer to a model or paradigm. The paradigmatic person in Mohist philosophy *realises* different instantiations of rightness, *yi*. One might at this point be tempted to draw a Platonic distinction between the ideal (form) and its instantiations, although for Mozi the instantiations are fundamentally important. Instantiations of *yi* are beneficial (benefit, utility: *li*). When the people are united in their commitment to social utility, clarity (of right and wrong) is achieved. The wise ruler determines standards of right (*shi*) and wrong (*fei*) and the common people are to follow:

> ...all you people of the state shall identify yourselves with the emperor and shall not unite with the subordinates. What the emperor thinks to be right all shall think to be right; what he thinks to be wrong all shall think to be wrong. (Chapter 12, 'Identification with the Superior's Standard', trans. Mei 1929: 62)

But Mozi is aware that such homogeneity is not easy to attain – indeed, there is a need for its dictatorial implementation.[9] The common people are not expected to engage in or contribute to decisions about the standards. Mozi also outlines an elaborate system for maintaining uniformity: the common people are responsible for the everyday maintenance of these standards; they are required to inform the appropriate higher-level authority about exemplary instantiations of the standards, or breaches of it. Accordingly there would be rewards or punishments meted out in order to encourage adherence to the standard (the system of punishments and rewards was also adopted by the Legalist thinkers and became a prominent feature of Legalist philosophy). Both the denial of the common people's ability to make independent judgements and the reliance on external motivation for ethical behaviour are incompatible with contemporary liberal notions of selfhood and citizenship. Mozi justifies his totalitarian impositions by anchoring the standard in heaven's intention. The authority for the standard lies in a transcendent source, even beyond the decisions of the emperor: 'it is Heaven that decides what is right for the Son of Heaven' (Chapter 26: 'The Will of Heaven', trans. Watson 1963: 80). At times, Mozi takes a more humanistic approach and appeals to the concern of heaven for all humanity. In this argument, the profile of heaven changes accordingly, from a transcendental moral authority to a loving agent that cares for the personal welfare of each human being: 'Now Heaven loves the world universally and seeks to bring mutual benefit to all creatures. There is not so much as the tip of a hair which is not the work of Heaven' (Chapter 27: 'The Will of Heaven', trans. Watson 1963: 88).

It appears that Mozi's primary concern is not to specify the nature of heaven but simply to present an ultimate authority for the standard, *yi*. And because heaven desires *yi*, humans by implication should too: 'And Mo-tzu said: Be obedient. Be careful. Be sure to do what Heaven desires and avoid what Heaven abominates' (Chapter 28: 'Heaven's Intention', trans. Mei 1929: 151). The rationale for *yi* (here translated 'righteousness') as the standard is its efficacy in bringing about good order: 'When there is righteousness in the world, then the world is well ordered, but when there is no righteousness, then it is in disorder' (Chapter 27: 'The Will of Heaven', trans. Watson 1963: 84). In brief, *yi* is valued as a means to an end; it helps in the realisation of socio-political order. Heaven is the paradigmatic *fa*, the agent that realises *yi*. The singular characteristic of *tian* is its impartial concern for all: 'To obey the will of Heaven is to be universal and to oppose the will of Heaven is to be partial (in love)' (Chapter 28: 'Heaven's Intention', trans. Mei 1929: 155). Here, another aspect of Mozi's *tian* emerges: heaven, the paradigmatic agent, is in effect the ideal observer. Heaven sees everything impartially and acts on that basis. For humans to keep to the standard is to adopt heaven's perspective of impartiality.

The other significant application of standards, *fa*, figures in Mozi's discussion of the criteria for assessment. There are three criteria (*san fa*) according to which all assertions, practices and actions must be assessed. However, it is difficult to specify exactly the field of application of these tests as Mozi seems to apply the three criteria to arguments as well as actions and deeds. The three *fa* are *precedent, empirical veracity* and *utility*:

(1) *Precedent* – Mozi frequently discusses the actions of previous sage kings and the outcomes of their actions. Two important aspects of this criterion should be noted. First, the discussion of precedent very often turns into a discussion about the outcomes of the sage kings' actions. This means that this test is effectively subsumed under the third, that of utility. Secondly, this criterion seems fairly arbitrary, as we see in Mozi's selective use of examples to prove a particular point: this particular king implemented *x* and that had good outcomes; another king implemented *y* and that had negative outcomes. On the other hand, we should note that the selective use of examples is a standard strategy when arguing with precedents.

(2) *Empirical veracity* – the saying or action is checked against the experiences of the common people, 'the eyes and ears of the multitude' (Chapter 37: 'Belief in Fate'). This criterion weighs far less for Mozi than the first and third criteria.

(3) *Utility* – this is by far the most important consideration for Mozi. If an item did not satisfy this test, even though it did the first two, Mozi would reject it (for example, in the case of music, which satisfies the first two criteria but not the third). The rejection of fatalism is the clearest example of how this criterion is applied: fatalism has many disutilities, amongst them a lack of commitment to economic productivity. Mozi's appeal to this criterion was an innovation in early Chinese philosophy. In setting up utility as a fundamental criterion, it would override consideration of the first two criteria, precedent and empirical veracity, especially if there is some inconsistency between utility and the other two criteria. Most importantly, however, in emphasising utility as basic, Mozi was rejecting the appeals to tradition and authority that were common argumentation strategies in early Chinese philosophy.

Mozi's discussion of funeral ritual reflects just how committed he is to the criterion of utility. He even derives other values from utility (in this case, the traditional Confucian virtues *ren*, *yi* and *xiao*):

> In my opinion, if by following the principles and adopting the instructions of those who advocate elaborate funerals and lengthy

> mourning one can actually enrich the poor, increase the population, and bring stability and order to the state, then such principles are in accordance with benevolence [*ren*] and righteousness [*yi*] and are the duty of a filial son [*xiao*]. Those who lay plans for the state cannot but recommend them, and the benevolent man seeking to promote what is beneficial to the world cannot but adopt them and cause the people to praise and follow them all their lives. (Chapter 25: 'Moderation in Funerals', trans. Watson 1963: 66)

For Mozi, to say that something is useful in itself simply does not make sense. In an interesting discussion of this issue, he refers to a Confucian perspective on the topic. The Confucian argues that music is pursued for its own sake; this relies on a *double entendre* as both 'music' and 'joy' are designated by the same Chinese character. The Confucian is saying 'music is music' and 'music is joy'. Mozi argues specifically that one cannot appeal to a thing itself in order to provide its justification:

> Mozi asked a Confucianist why the Confucianists pursued music. He replied, music is pursued for music's sake. Mozi said: You have not yet answered me. Suppose I asked, why build houses. And you answered, it is to keep off the cold in winter, and the heat in summer, and to separate men from women. Then you would have told me the reason for building houses. Now I am asking why pursue music. And you answer music is pursued for music's sake. This is comparable to: "Why build houses?" "Houses are built for houses' sakes." (Chapter 48: 'Gong Meng', trans. Mei 1929: 237)

The three tests constitute the underlying argumentation structure of Mozi's entire philosophy; all of his ten topics have in fact been subject to these three tests. For example, in rejecting elaborate and extended funeral rituals, Mozi argues that, while there were precedents for such (as well as precedents for frugal practices), it is clearly not to the benefit of society if the former were encouraged and practised (Chapter 25: 'Economy in Funerals'). Hence, elaborate and extended funeral rituals, as advocated by the Confucians, should be prohibited.

The strategy of applying these tests is simply to measure items against certain benchmarks. The process of measuring aids one's discrimination (*bian*) between, for example, what is useful and what is not. The different areas of enquiry for Mozi – ranging from the ethical to the technical – require the same methods of verification. His epistemology is a simple and undifferentiated one between the different types of knowledge – as indeed he compares heaven's will with the compass of the wheelwright and the square of the carpenter. (Chapter 27: 'Heaven's Will'). The three tests Mozi specifically likens to a gnomon, the astronomer's post of standard height for measuring the sun's shadows (Chapter 35: 'Rejecting Belief in Fate').

These analogies reflect Mozi's conception of ethical deliberation. His picture of humanity is very much reduced from the Confucian vision of moral cultivation and self development. It appears that Mozi has, rather simply, extrapolated moral reasoning from craftsmanship. The major implication of this is that morality becomes a skill of recognising patterns and fit. Accordingly, the Mohist conception of knowledge is not about the accumulation of information but the practical applications of things and ideas. To know something is to be able to distinguish it – to pick it out – from others (*bian*). Interestingly, the Chinese terms *bian* (辯: dispute, disagreement) and *bian* (辨: distinguish, differentiate) are homophones. Mozi resorts to *bian* (distinguish) to resolve the problems of *bian* (disagreement). This concept *bian* (distinguish) captures the essence of Mohist epistemology. In this respect, to know is to have a skill to make distinctions.[10] Investigation of a particular concept would consist in investigating its applications. It is of course on these epistemological grounds that Mozi's three criteria are set up.

Here, we should note that Mencius recognises the key elements of Mohist philosophy and in 7B:5 seems to be addressing Mozi's reliance on skill. Mencius criticises the apparent simplicity of Mozi's *bian*, that it is merely the application of a standard to a problem or issue. There is much more than meets the eye in applying the standard (*fa*) because only a skilful (paradigmatic) person can do it properly. Mencius argues that 'A carpenter or a carriage-maker may give a man the circle and square, but cannot make him skilful in the use of them' (trans. Legge 1893–5: 480).

It is perhaps this passage that most clearly articulates the fundamental *Ru-Mo* disagreement about the significance of paradigmatic persons. The Confucians were concerned with cultivating learned individuals who would in turn teach others. But the Mohists were interested in standard measures of right action. In this light, it may be that the thin picture of humanity upheld by Mozi is partly the cause of Mohism's disfavour with other schools of thought and later scholars. To some extent this also reflects the affinity of the Chinese psyche with a richer picture of human community, engagement and learning.

Notwithstanding its eventual failure as a school, especially as compared with Confucian philosophy, we must not overlook the implications of Mohist philosophy on philosophical argumentation in Chinese philosophy. The tests introduce a new, important element of philosophical argumentation to early Chinese philosophy: that of consistency or constancy.[11] According to this principle, whether a claim is made by a king or a commoner is inconsequential to its validity; personal authority is not a criterion of Mozi's tests. The idea of personal authority is different from the merit-based authority identified in the section 'Identification with the Superior's Standard'. The superior's authority comes about not by virtue of his status or some other contingent factor but because he is committed to maximising social benefit. Mozi's support of merit-based authority is similar to Confucius' insistence that those who are not committed to the people should not be in office, and as well to Mencius' point that an evil ruler was not a king (*Mencius* 1B:8). Another reason why constancy (of criteria) is important is because the tests can be applied by *anyone* to yield the same result. There is a striking example of how Mozi quoted some of Confucius' ideas even though Confucius was his intellectual rival. The interchange unequivocally brings out the Mohist emphasis on the value of an idea being dissociated from its advocate:

> Mo-tzŭ [Mozi], when disputing with Ch'eng-tzŭ [Chengzi], cited something from Confucius. Ch'eng-tzŭ said: 'You are no Confucian, why do you cite Confucius'? Mo-tzŭ said: 'This is something of his which is dead right and for which there is no substitute . . . ' (*Mo-tzŭ*; cited in Graham 1978: 25)

The Mohist discussions on *bian* had a major impact on the thinking of the then contemporary and later thinkers including Mencius, the Daoists, Yang Zhu and Zhuangzi.[12] It would not be implausible to suggest that, had Mozi's philosophy not been eclipsed by Confucian themes, Chinese philosophical debate would have advanced much more significantly in the areas of philosophical argumentation and reasoning, epistemology and philosophy of science.

Suggestions for Further Reading

Mo Tzu: Basic Writings, translated by Burton Watson (1963), New York: Columbia University Press.

The Ethical and Political Works of Mo Tzu, translated by Yi-pao Mei (1929), London: Arthur Probsthain.

Graham, Angus C. (1989) 'A Radical Reaction: Mo-Tzu', in *Disputers of the Tao: Philosophical Argument in Ancient China,* La Salle: Open Court, pp. 33–53.

Hansen, Chad (1992) 'Mozi: Setting the Philosophical Agenda', in *A Daoist Theory of Chinese Thought*, New York: Oxford University Press, pp. 95–152.

Nivison, David (1980) 'Two Roots or One?', *Proceedings and Addresses of the American Philosophical Association*, 53:6 (August 1980), pp. 739–61.

Schwartz, Benjamin (1985) *The World of Thought in Ancient China*, Cambridge: Belknap Press of Harvard University Press.

Notes

1. Refer to Schwartz 1985: 133; 138–9.
2. Chan 1963b (*The way of Lao Tzu*): 212, cited and discussed by Hansen (1992: 95–6). Fung Yu-lan in his famous *Short History of Chinese Philosophy* (1948) suggests that Mohist philosophy is an extension of the lifestyle of the knights-errant and hence reflects aspects of the tight-knit organisational life of these knights (at p. 50).
3. Schwartz 1985, Graham 1978 and 1989, and Hansen 1992.
4. Hansen 1992: 95.
5. Refer to Hansen 1992: 95–8.
6. Graham suggests a classification of these texts into 'purist', 'compromising' and 'reactionary' according to the agendas of the sects (1989: 36; 51–2).
7. Graham 1989: 41. Schwartz also discusses the debate about the translation of *jianai* (1985: 148–50).
8. David Nivison (1980) suggests that Mencius' 'one root' is the heart, which is the seat of both 'what we really want to do [motivation]' and 'what we ought to do and can rightly recognize we ought to do [recognised obligation]' (p. 742).
9. We must of course question the value of such a goal.
10. Hansen (1992) discusses at length the skill of pattern recognition and making distinctions in Mohist philosophy (pp. 104ff.).
11. Hansen (1992) sees constancy as a most important contribution of Mohist philosophy; in fact 'constancy' is the term he selects to depict this feature of Mohist philosophy. Hansen discusses its philosophical implications in detail (pp. 110–15).
12. Refer to Schwartz (1985) for a detailed discussion of the influences of Mohist philosophy on other thinkers (at pp. 169–70).

5 Early Daoist Philosophy: The *Dao De Jing* as a Metaphysical Treatise

The philosophy of the *Daodejing* is discussed in this chapter and the next. A key concept of this text is *dao*, commonly translated 'path' or 'way'. *Dao* is a notoriously difficult concept, arguably the most complex, in Chinese philosophy because of its use in both generic and specific terms and its applications in a wide range of domains including the religious, humanistic and naturalistic. The discussions in these two chapters will clarify some of the conceptions of *dao* in the context of the *Daodejing*. Yet, as we will see, the text itself, being a composite text that was not compiled according to a particular 'school' or doctrine, is also notoriously cryptic. Hence, the philosophy of the text is at some level an interpretive matter. However, significant modern and contemporary scholarship focuses on textual and philological study of how particular sections of the text, or its key concepts, relate to other doctrines and texts of the same period. Scholarship on the *Daodejing* has intensified as older versions of the text have been discovered at Manwangdui (in 1973) and Guodian (in 1993). The extant text, annotated by Wang Bi (226–249 CE), has been ascribed an earliest composition date of ca. 250 BCE. However, the Guodian bamboo slips have been dated at approximately 300 BCE and the Mawangdui silk scrolls at 200 BCE or earlier. These discoveries have added to issues of textual complexity as well as scholarly interest.[1]

This chapter explores a range of themes associated with a metaphysical understanding of *dao*, that is, a concept of *dao* as the ultimate reality that stands in stark contrast with the human, the everyday and the conventional. The conception of *dao* as denoting reality that transcends ordinary life – not unlike the reality-appearance distinction in Plato's metaphysics – is the dominant interpretation of the concept *dao* in Daoist philosophy, especially in most English translations of the text. Two of the reasons for this are associated with its interpretation in terms of ideas that were dominant and readily available during the time in question. The first is Wang Bi's exposition of the philosophy of the *Daodejing*, which emphasised *dao* as a metaphysical concept; Wang Bi's interpretation was influential during the Warring States period and thereafter.[2] The second concerns the interpretation of *dao* in modern scholarship. Scholars such as Feng Youlan (Fung Yu-lan; 1895–1990), who had studied western philosophy, defined *dao* in metaphysical terms (Fung 1952: 177). Such pioneering work as Fung's established the groundwork for western scholars interested in Chinese philosophy, and for comparative philosophy more generally.

The following chapter deals with a different interpretation of the concept *dao*. It understands *dao*, together with other concepts in the *Daodejing* including especially *wuwei* (non-action), as ethical concepts. According to this analysis, the *Daodejing* is engaged in a meta-ethical analysis of existing values and practices. Both interpretations of *dao*, the metaphysical and the ethical, involve critical rejections of ideals and pursuits in human life as it was then conceived. The interpretations are not mutually exclusive and each may be seen in light of the other in order to generate a broader understanding of the philosophy of the *Daodejing* and its place in debates in early Chinese philosophy.

The Origins of Daoist Philosophy and the Early Daoist Texts

The early Daoist thinkers proposed radical changes to the ideals and practices of contemporary society. They rejected the narrowly human concerns of the philosophies of the other schools, their views on government and their unrelenting conventionality. The hostility of Daoist philosophy to the existing norms and practices led the modern Chinese thinker Hu Shih (1891–1962) to label Laozi, the alleged founder of Daoism, a rebel.[3] Wing-tsit Chan claims that 'Chinese civilization and the Chinese character would have been utterly different if the book *Lao Tzu* had never been written.'[4] In terms of its philosophical impact, Daoist philosophy accentuated the weaknesses of Confucian, Mohist and Legalist philosophies and prompted more thorough investigation of their fundamental ideas and values. It also influenced the nature of Chinese philosophical argumentation in its use of metaphor and suggestive imagery. But perhaps the most significant feature of Daoist philosophy is its distinctive conception of opposition and dialectical reasoning.

The two pre-Qin (prior to 221 BCE) texts that have received the most scholarly attention are the *Daodejing* and the *Zhuangzi*. There are other Daoist texts originating around the same period; the *Liezi* is thought to be easily accessible though not as representative of Daoist philosophy, or philosophically as interesting.[5] Regarding the dating of the *Daodejing* and *Zhuangzi*, the orthodox view is that the former predates the latter. However, there is a possibility that the *Daodejing* or at least some of its sections were written after the *Zhuangzi* was compiled.[6] The dating of these texts is difficult because there is scant evidence of a school of thinkers of the *dao* who gathered to discuss a common ideology, as with the Confucians. The early Daoist thinkers were a much more amorphous group.[7] Indeed, the phrase *dao*-school (*daojia*) was only used in the first century BCE by the Historian Sima Qian (145 BCE–86? BCE).[8] It was also traditionally held that the two texts belong to one continuous institution: the *Daodejing* represents Daoism in its early formative stages while the *Zhuangzi* captures the tenor of a developed, more mature Daoist philosophy.[9] This view was instigated by Han thinkers who classified the *Daodejing* and *Zhuangzi* as the two definitive texts of the early Daoist philosophical tradition (*daojia*). But most contemporary scholars now believe that the philosophy of the *Zhuangzi* is critically different from, and not merely a further development of, the *Daodejing*. The tendency to treat the two texts as espousing a homogeneous and continuous point of view should be avoided as there are important differences in their subject matter, treatment of issues and methods of argumentation. Some care must also be taken to distinguish philosophical Daoism from the later development of a religious branch of it during the Han dynasty, '*daojiao*' (*dao* religion/teaching). *Daojiao* incorporated elements of religious belief including revelation to celestial masters, 'doctrines, rituals, gods, and the ultimate goal of ascension to the heavens of the immortals'.[10]

The *Daodejing* was traditionally associated with the figure Laozi, an older contemporary of Confucius.[11] But contemporary scholars agree that its pieces are too diverse in topic and style to have been written by one person.[12] Linguistic and philological analyses demonstrate that the *Daodejing* was most probably a text compiled over a significant period of time during the pre-Qin period. The unorganised compilation of short pieces in the *Daodejing* reflects the diversity in interpretations of the concept *dao*. It was applied to a range of different debates relating to mysticism, health and longevity, statecraft, government, metaphysics, epistemology and ethics.

Dao as Reality: the Search for a New Reality

The opening phrase of the *Daodejing*, 'The Tao that can be told of is not the eternal Tao' (trans. Chan 1963b: 97), expresses the Daoist yearning for what is eternal and real:

道	可	道	非	常	道
dao	*ke*	*dao*	*fei*	*chang*	*dao*

There are three occurrences of the character '*dao*' but all of them have different meanings. The second *dao* is a verb, meaning to transmit or communicate. The first *dao*, a noun, is the ordinary, communicated *dao*. The third *dao*, also a noun, is qualified by *chang*. *Chang* has a number of possible meanings including lasting, unchanging, real and absolute. This third *dao* is beyond the reach of the ordinary *dao*, that which *can* be told. According to this interpretation, *dao* is the underlying reality that evades transmission and perhaps even comprehension.

The common translation of the phrase into English also encourages a metaphysical understanding of the concept *dao*. To satisfy the grammatical requirements of English, translators are required to insert a definite article – either 'a' or 'the' – before *chang dao*. If we qualify *chang dao* with 'the', we imply that there is only one reality. Alternatively, if we qualify it with 'a', we mean that there is at least one reality.[13] It is especially the translation of *dao* as '*the dao*' that asserts the singularity of *dao* as a term denoting reality. This makes a profound philosophical difference in terms of the doctrine of the *Daodejing*, for it may be construed either as supporting monism (in the case of 'the *dao*') or pluralism (in the case of 'a *dao*'). In either case, the result is to objectify the concept *dao*. The scholar Wing-tsit Chan notes that '[w]hereas in other schools Tao [*dao*] means a system or moral truth, in this school it is the One, which is natural, eternal spontaneous, nameless and indescribable' (1963a: 136).[14]

The ineffability of *dao* also frustrates attempts to understand the concept. Charles Fu identifies six dimensions of *dao*: material reality ('reality and manifestation'), origin, principle, function, virtue and technique (1973). These six dimensions are, effectively, different ways of conceptualising *dao*; they are not mutually exclusive categories. But why is it that *dao* cannot be communicated? We are also told in *Daodejing* 1 that *dao* is nameless (*wu ming*): 'The Nameless is the origin of Heaven and Earth' (trans. Chan 1963b: 97). In the *Daodejing*, the namelessness of *dao* is associated with its mystery (*xuan*; chapters 1, 51). The *Daodejing* does not explicitly offer reasons for the mystery of *dao*, for that would entail an undoing of its own assertion in *Daodejing* 1. Reality as we *do not know it* is vague and unpolished, likened to an uncarved block of wood (chapters 15, 19, 28, 33, 37, 57). According to *Daodejing* 1, there are two *daos*, one real (*chang dao*) and the other apparent, superficial or impermanent (the *dao* that *can* be told). Passages in the *Daodejing* suggest that *chang dao*, conceived of as the entirety of reality, is greater than the sum of its individual parts (chapter 14). This is because the relationships between the individual entities are also an important part of *dao*. Individual entities inevitably act on and mutually influence others; the resulting whole is dynamic and ceaselessly transforming. The dynamic interactions and mutual influences among all things comprising *dao* contribute to its ineffability and mystery (chapters 14, 16, 39, 42). In the *Daodejing*, there is a fine (unspoken) line between metaphysics and epistemology: *dao* (reality) is intricate and comprehensive, and therefore beyond human understanding. The epistemic feature of *dao*, its *unnameability*, derives from its metaphysical condition, its *namelessness*. Charles Fu describes the connection between the indescribable *dao* and what that means for (human) knowledge: '[*dao* is] ontologically non-differentiated and epistemologically non-differentiatable [sic]'.[15]

Dao as ultimate reality is at times characterised as the origin and source of all things; *dao* is the mother (*mu*) and ancestor (*zong*) of all (chapters 52, 4; see also chapters 1, 25), even prior to heaven and earth (chapters 14, 25). *Daodejing* 42 tells a story of this origin:

> Tao [Dao] produced [*sheng*] the One.
> The One produced the two.
> The two produced the three.
> And the three produced the ten thousand things...
>
> (trans. Chan 1963b: 176)

The concept *sheng* denotes both birth and growth. The biological–generative motif implies that *dao* produces or evolves into manifold things, the 'ten thousand things' (*wanwu*). As a concept signifying growth, *dao* provides sustenance: '[*dao*] is to the world as the River and the Sea are to rivulets and streams' (trans. Lau 1963: 91). This imagery creates a sense of dependence of all things on *dao*. In this regard, the *Daodejing* advocates reunion (*fu*; chapters 28, 64) of all things with *dao* or return (*fan*; chapters 25, 65) to it.

But we must also note that the account in the *Daodejing* of origination and source is at best vague. It is unclear whether *dao* is to be understood as the *material* source of all things, or whether it is a common *principle* inherent in all things or, indeed, whether it might be both. The first understanding, that *dao* is the material source of all things, is essentially a nature philosophy about some fundamental primary matter. There is, however, little else in early Chinese philosophy that suggests deliberations of this kind, even in discussions of the concept *qi* (energy, spirit).[16] The understanding of *dao* as the principle associated with origination is more philosophically profound and is associated with notions of dependence and sustenance. The production and sustenance of all things is articulated in a metaphor of bellows in *Daodejing* 5, though in this passage it is heaven and earth that are likened to the bellows:

> Heaven and Earth are not humane.
> They regard all things as straw dogs...
> ...How Heaven and Earth are like a bellows.
> While vacuous, it is never exhausted.
> When active, it produces even more...
>
> (trans. Chan 1963b: 107)

Wang Bi describes the features of the bellows and injects it with a sense of enduring sustenance:

> The inside of the bellows is empty, without feeling and without action. Therefore, while vacuous, it can never be exhausted, and when moved (used) will never be spent. In the vast and extensive space between heaven and earth they [the myriad things] are left alone. Therefore they [heaven and earth], like a bellows, cannot be exhausted. (trans. Rump 1979: 18; translator's annotations).

There is a paradoxical contrast between vacuity (*xu*) and yet never being exhausted (see also chapters 1, 45). The idea of vacuity is often associated with the concept *wu*, commonly translated as 'non-being' or 'nothing' (chapters 1, 40). But the translation of *wu* as non-being may be misleading because the latter has a range of established meanings in western philosophy and especially in continental philosophy. It may be mistakenly conceived to refer to non-existence, and antithetical to the concept 'being' (*you*). As with the story of origination, there are limitations if we interpret *wu* and *you* solely in material terms. *Wu* will simply mean 'does not exist' and *you* 'exists'; this is little more than naïve realism. In Daoist philosophy, *wu* and *you* are dialectical and interdependent opposites, perhaps best understood as aspects of *dao*:

> Lao Tzu's [Laozi's] non-being and being are likened to the great ocean and the totality of waves; they are two ways of looking at one and the same ontologically non-differentiated 'Tao' [*Dao*]. (Fu 1973: 374)

Charles Fu notes that *you* and *wu* are interdependent in the same way that reality and its manifestation are interdependent: the ocean is inseparable from its waves and vice versa. This analysis avoids a simple understanding of the concepts solely in terms of material existence. Fu highlights the ethical implications of Daoist *wu–you* in terms of how humans perceive their world: *either* to see the forest *or* the flora and fauna, but not both. In *Daodejing* 11, *wu* refers to what is not valued by the human eye: it is 'nothing' or 'vacuous' because it is seen as useless. But the chapter challenges this phenomenon by emphasising *wu*:

> Thirty spokes are united around the hub to make a wheel,
> But it is on its [*wu*] that the utility of the carriage depends.
> Clay is molded to form a utensil,
> But it is on its [*wu*] that the utility of the utensil depends.
> Doors and windows are cut out to make a room,
> But it is on its [*wu*] that the utility of the room depends.
> Therefore turn [*yu*] into advantage, and turn [*wu*] into utility.
> (trans. Chan 1963b: 119)

Both *wu* and *you* are aspects of *dao* that we must learn to see. Here, another integral aspect of Daoist philosophy emerges. Even as a metaphysical concept, *dao* embodies paradigmatic, action-guiding content. This appears to be a standard feature of early Chinese philosophy. We have already encountered this conceptual blurring between a paradigmatic entity and its normative standard (the ideal mode of its existence) both in Confucian and Mohist thought. The debating thinkers were aware of this assumption as evidenced in their debates about the correct use of names (*zhengming*). In Daoism, the blurring between a paradigmatic entity and its normative standard would mean that *dao* is both the ultimate reality and the paradigmatic principle for life. We have discussed how we might think about *dao* as metaphysical reality, but how are we to understand *dao* as a principle in human life? In other words, what are the practical consequences of paradigmatic *dao*? According to Wang Bi, the approach of heaven and earth is all-embracing, yet non-intrusive:

> Heaven and Earth leave what is natural (Tzu-jan [*ziran*], Self-so) alone. They do nothing and create nothing. The myriad things manage and order themselves. Therefore they are not benevolent. One who is benevolent will create things, set things up, bestow benefits on them and influence them. He gives favors and does something. When he creates, sets things up, bestows benefits on things and influences them, then things will lose their true being…Animals eat straw, though the earth does not reproduce it for them. Men eat dogs, though (heaven) does not produce dogs for them. If nothing is done to the myriad things, each will accord with its function, and everything is then self-sufficient. (trans. Rump 1979: 17)

Wang Bi has no doubt that the ways of heaven and earth are action-guiding. In this commentary on *Daodejing* 5, we are to take lessons from events in the natural world. These lessons articulate the contrast between projects in the human world and spontaneous events in the world of nature. There is a phrase in the passage that heaven and earth treat all things as straw dogs. Wang Bi translates the phrase 'straw dogs' as 'straw and dogs' to denote the different kinds in the natural world and their fragility. Nothing is immune from the forces of external change, including humanity. In this sense, *wanwu*, all things (literally, the ten thousand things) are at par. D. C. Lau has a different understanding of straw dogs. According to him, 'In the *T'ien yun* chapter in the *Chuang tzu* it is said that straw dogs were treated with the greatest deference before they were used as an offering, only to be discarded and trampled upon as soon as they had served their purpose' (1963: 61). For Lau, the fate of the straw dogs is understood in the context of the unfolding of natural events whereby all things have their moment and pass on when their moment passes. In the cycles of nature, nothing is eternal or preferred.[17] It is interesting that the two different conceptions of 'straw dogs' yield similar conclusions: the allegory exposes the unjustified assumption of human priority and its disastrous consequences.

Both analyses couple together a wariness of anthropocentrism with an appreciation of the natural world. The Daoist concept *ziran* is often translated as 'nature' and used to signify aspects of the natural world. This sense of *ziran* is not different from the Greek *phusis* which refers to natural kinds and the relations that obtain between them. *Ziran* as 'nature' emphasises a naturalistic perspective. According to this understanding, *dao* is more closely aligned with the (seemingly) spontaneous events in the natural world than the artificial contrivances in the human world:

> Nature [*ziran*] says few words.
> For the same reason a whirlwind does not last a whole morning.
> Nor does a rainstorm last a whole day.
> What causes them?
> It is Heaven and Earth (Nature).
> If even Heaven and Earth cannot make them last long, How much less can man?...
>
> (Chapter 23, trans. Chan 1963b: 141)

To model oneself on these ways, in other words, to mimic nature, is to reduce elements of artifice and contrivance in human life. Are we asked to replicate the ways of nature? Such nature-consciousness may at first appear predisposed toward the natural environment. However, there are a number of difficulties associated with this assumption. First the view of the *Daodejing*, expressed in terms of the 'heaven and earth' metaphor, does not explicitly value the natural environment. Rather, it seems to be a philosophy of indifference. For example, *Daodejing* 5 expresses the indifference of heaven and earth to all things. Benjamin Schwartz discusses this tension in the *Daodejing* as it relates to the study of nature:

> One may, in fact, point to commonalities between Lao-tzu's [Laozi's] nature and certain aspects of eighteenth- and nineteenth-century Western "scientific" naturalism. The processes of nature are not guided by a teleological consciousness and despite the pathos suggested by the use of the image of the mother with its nurturant associations, the *tao* [*dao*] is not consciously providential. (1985: 201)

The second problem concerns how we are to interpret the term 'nature'. This is because there is no indication in the *Daodejing* regarding which features of nature are to be modelled. Some difficult questions arise from this interpretation of *ziran* as nature, or a concern for it. They include:

(1) Which aspects of nature should human society be modelled upon? The *Daodejing* identifies quietude (*jing*), softness (*rou*), acquiescence (*ruo*),

non-assertiveness (*buzhen*) and simplicity (*pu*) (chapters 8, 16, 19, 22, 28, 31, 32, 36, 37, 43, 45, 64, 66, 76, 78). But how do we know to derive this particular set of characteristics rather than those pertaining to growth, decay or predation?

(2) Which naturalistic perspective are we to adopt? Biocentric (life-centred), eco-centric (centring on ecology), or holistic conceptual schemes, to name a few, have significantly different ultimate concerns.

(3) Which aspects of human life are 'natural' and which 'artificial'? Is reproduction 'natural'? Are built environments 'natural'? Is social and political organisation 'natural'?

The maxim to observe and mimic nature is very vague; which aspects of nature are to be mimicked is a moot point. Nevertheless, the presence of the phrase *ziran* in the *Daodejing* has prompted some scholars to draw on it in support of an environmental consciousness.[18] This is the third problem, the hasty application of *ziran* to discussions of the natural environment. Ramachandra Guha in 'Radical American Environmentalism and Wilderness Preservation: A Third World Critique' reminds us that:

> The detection of a 'love of wilderness' and of the 'first stirrings of an ecological sensibility' in Daoist thought reflect a selective reading of the Daoist texts as well as conjecture regarding the intention and attitudes of the early Daoists toward environmental concerns…such utopic renditions of Daoist thought need further to be justified in the face of ecological disasters in Chinese history.[19]

Further to that, Randall Peerenboom cautions against simplistic interpretations of what is natural. According to Peerenboom (1991), the interpretation of the message of the *Daodejing* as being supportive of naturalistic primitivism leads to triviality: either human beings belong to the realm of the natural – in which case the dictum to be natural, like *dao*, is superfluous – or they do not – in which case the dictum to be natural is a misdirected aim.

But we should keep in mind that Daoist philosophy can be read at different levels, literal as well as suggestive. The suggestive mode is more philosophically interesting. We may understand the overarching view of *dao* not in terms of a naturalistic order, but as recommending a different, perhaps more inclusive, way of understanding the world. This notion of *dao* will be explored in the following chapter. The next section examines the view of opposition in the *Daodejing*. The distinctive Daoist notions of contrast and complementation constitute the basic framework of Daoist philosophy.

Opposites: Contrast and Complementation

The *Daodejing* presents a large list of opposites including long/short, high/low, sound/voice, front/behind, use/wear out, being/non-being, good/evil, brilliant/dull, clear-cut/without distinction, bent/straight, empty/full, worn out/renewed, heavy/light, tranquil/hasty, male/female, white/black, hot/cold, strong/weak, contract/expand, destroy/promote, grasp/give, soft/hard, perfect/incomplete, skill/clumsiness, eloquence/stutter, act/without action, do/without ado, big/small, many/few and difficult/easy (chapters 2, 6, 11, 20, 22, 26, 28, 29, 36, 43, 45, 63). It calls attention to both terms of the contrastive pairs. In each case, there is an overturning of existing norms and values (strength, power and skill). However, these are not abandoned. The opposite terms are often poised in delicate balance as, for instance, in *Daodejing* 28, 'know the male but abide by the female' (trans. mine). While each term bears its own significance, it is also defined by the other:

> In order to contract, it is necessary first to expand.
> In order to weaken, it is necessary first to strengthen.
> In order to destroy, it is necessary first to promote.
> In order to grasp, it is necessary first to give.
> This is called subtle light.
> The weak and the tender overcome the hard and the strong…
>
> (*Daodejing* 36, trans. Chan 1963b: 164)

There is a sense of flux between the two extremes, first contracting, then expanding, then back to contracting again. There are different ways to understand the interplay between the terms of each contrastive pair (see chapters 7, 22, 26, 36, 40, 41, 45, 58, 63, 66). The interplay may be described as a to-and-fro swing, seesaw action, cyclical change or a cycle of development and decline. The concept of reversion, *fan* (for example, chapter 40), is also important in understanding the Daoist notion of contrast and complementation:

> Reversion is the opposition of the opposite: it is the derivation of opposite from an overexerted position. (Cheng 1977: 216)

According to this view, understanding its contrastive opposites helps in the definition of a term. In other words, comparisons reveal the distinctive characteristics of a concept or entity. For instance, the meaning of the term 'cold' is intensified when it is understood in contrast with its opposites: not merely 'hot', but also to different degrees, 'freezing', 'tepid' and 'boiling'. That the meaning of a particular term is deepened in relation to its opposite is an interesting assertion. For it is commonly assumed that more of the same of one thing – rather than its opposites – will enhance it. For the sake of argument, let us consider the height of a person: the common assumption is that the taller a person, the more prominent his height. According to the Daoist conception of opposites, it is when a tall person is contrasted with shorter people that his height is accentuated. A. C. Graham's portrayal of reversal in the *Daodejing* highlights the necessity of both the contrastive terms:

> For *Lao-tzu* [Laozi]... reversal is *not* a switch from preferring A to preferring B, aiming to become weak, soft, below instead of strong, hard and above. Since all human effort is against a downward pull toward B, that direction is a first approximation to the Way of spontaneous process, to be adjusted next to the upward impulse after renewal from the fecund bottom of B. *The reversal smashes the dichotomy of A and B*; in preferring to be submissive the sage does not cease to be oriented towards strength, for he recognises that surviving by yielding to a rising power is the road to victory over it when its climax is past. (1989: 228–229; italics mine)

One significant feature of Daoist opposition is the dissolution of dichotomy between the two contrastive terms. However, the outcome of the dissolution is not the identification of A with B or vice versa, nor is it the obliteration of one of the terms. But we should also note that Graham's analysis does not explicitly address the unequal weighting of the contrastive terms in the text. In the *Daodejing*, terms such as stillness, dark, inferior (chapters 16, 26, 39) are identified as the root of their corresponding terms. We cannot help but notice the preference in the *Daodejing* for the weak, non-assertive and tranquil. In this regard, Schwartz confirms the 'asymmetry' of value in the *Daodejing* raised by D. C. Lau:

> Lau has pointed out the obvious and striking "asymmetry" in the Lao-tzu's [*Laozi's*] view of the female versus the male, the weak versus the strong, the soft versus the hard, and the passive versus the active. In all cases, the first

> term of the dyad is definitely "preferred." It enjoys a higher "ontological" status, just as water is preferred to stone; it seeks lowly places, and it is, in a profounder sense, stronger than stone.[20]

Lau also maintains that the connection between the contrastive opposites may be characterised analogously to a children's slide: 'One climbs laboriously to the top, but once over the edge the downward movement is quick, abrupt, inevitable, and complete' (Lau 1963: 27). The contrast between Lau's and Graham's conceptions of opposition is interesting: Lau presents a simple overturning of conventional values[21] whereas Graham creates a new way of looking at opposition.

There are other interesting ways to explore the applications of Daoist opposition; for example, Antonio Cua elaborates on the notion of *complementation*. He draws on Herman Hesse's characters Narcissus and Goldmund who exemplify two extremes: Narcissus seeks to further develop his scholarly mind and Goldmund pursues sensuous satisfaction.[22] In their close relationship, they each recognise deep differences in their pursuits and commitments. Yet, they do not seek to change the other to become like them: '[i]t is not our purpose to become each other; it is to recognize each other, to learn and see the other and honor him for what he is; each the other's opposite and complement' (cited in Cua 1981: 125). In Cua's analysis, the opposites accentuate contrast but yet do not eliminate the other. The opposites are distinct, contrastive and yet interdependent. The features of complementarity that arise from this analysis include:

(1) *Recognition and acceptance*: Each recognises, and accepts, the other's individuality and integrity. There is no desire to mould or alter the other.
(2) *Embellishment of the other, not duplication*: In their close relationship, the two do not seek to grow like each other. Their individual distinctiveness is highlighted in contrast with the other; in that sense, each is enriched by the other.
(3) *Reciprocity*: It is not the aim of Narcissus and Goldmund simply to establish their relationship on elements of commonality. Their relationship is built upon a reciprocal appreciation of differences in each other.
(4) *Resonance*: This aspect draws upon the concept of *ganying* (mutual resonance), a classical Chinese theory of mutual influence and response.

> According to this theory, entities do not exist in insulated contexts, nor are they detached from other entities. Changes in other individuals and the environment will shape a particular individual, just as that individual's actions will affect others and the environment around them.

This view of non-reductive complementation is significant because it has important practical consequences. According to Cua, the Daoist view of complementation prompts a change in attitude grounded in 'an expansion of intellectual horizon and a restructuring of one's vision of life' (Cua 1981: 127).[23] In practical terms, a person with this attitude does not simply look for similarity, uniformity or conformity. She also does not seek to assimilate, suppress or dominate the other. Cua's interpretation of complementation fits well within the framework of Daoist philosophy as these characteristics are easily aligned with non-assertiveness, quietude and simplicity. In the following section, we explore the philosophical framework of Daoism and the function of these attitudes within it. They are aligned with the Daoist concept *de*, an underemphasised key tenet in Daoist philosophy.

De and the Integrity of the Individual

Until recently, scholarship on the *Daodejing* has focused almost entirely on the concept *dao*, with little attention given to its counterpart, *de*.[24] This seems odd especially as *de* is specifically mentioned in the title of the text, *dao de jing* (treatise). *De* is commonly, and blandly, translated as 'morality', goodness' or 'virtue'.[25] We see this, for instance, in D. C. Lau's introduction to the *Daodejing*. He considers a fascinating interpretation of *de* in early Daoist philosophy but hastily differentiates this from its uses in the *Daodejing*:

> In its Taoist [Daoist] usage, *te* [*de*] refers to the virtue of a thing (which is what it 'gets' from the tao [*dao*]). In other words, *te* is the nature of a thing, because it is in virtue of its *te* that a thing is what it is. But in the *Lao tzu* [*Laozi: Daodejing*] the term is not a particularly important one and is often used in its more conventional senses. (1963: 42)

Lau does not explain why he has excluded the former conception of *de* from its use in the *Daodejing*. The 'conventional sense' of *de* is in fact a retrospective, post-Confucian understanding of the term as moral goodness.[26] This understanding of *de* is problematic also because it overlooks the staunch rejection of contemporary moral values in the *Daodejing*.[27] It does seem that we must at least allow for both interpretations of *de* in the *Daodejing*. If we understand *de* as the 'virtue of a thing' – in Lau's first definition – we see that it pertains to individual entities rather than to the phenomenon or practice of morality. How does this fit in with *dao*, the fundamental, all-encompassing reality? There is a contrastive, yet interdependent relationship between *dao* and *de*: *dao* pertains to the whole (reality) while *de* refers to individuals (that comprise the whole). Wing-tsit Chan describes a derivative relationship between *dao* and *de*: *dao* is the single source from which individual entities each derive their unique characteristics, *de*:

> ...*te* [*de*] is Tao [*Dao*] endowed in the individual things. While Tao is common to all, it is what each thing has obtained from Tao, or its *te*, that makes it different from others. *Te* is then the individualizing factor, the embodiment of definite principles which give things their determinate features or characters (Chan 1963b: 11).[28]

De is a principle of individuation rather than a general virtue or set of virtues. Arthur Waley sheds light on *de* by comparing it with the classical Greek '*virtus*' – 'a latent power, a virtue inherent in something'.[29] This classical conception of virtue is not necessarily correlated with moral goodness. Therefore it may be more constructive to translate *de* into English as 'power', as this does not have the connotation of moral goodness. Both Waley and Max Kaltenmark translate *de* as 'power'. Kaltenmark offers a compelling analysis of *de* as he takes into account various meanings of *de* in its early Daoist usage. His study is also particularly interesting because it explicitly addresses the issue of ethical neutrality:

> [*de*] always implies a notion of efficacy and specificity. Every creature possessing a power of any kind, natural or acquired, is said to have *Te* [*de*]...[*Te*] has varied meanings ranging from magical potency to moral virtue. But the latter is a derived meaning, for originally *Te* was not necessarily good...Nevertheless, *Te* is generally used in the good sense: it is an inner potency that favorably influences those close to its possessor, a virtue that is beneficent and life-giving. (1969: 27–8)

For Kaltenmark, *de* is quintessentially a concept that relates to individual well-being and realisation. His understanding of *de* allows for interesting comparisons to be made between *de* and ideas in early Greek philosophy, including Plato's theory of forms and their instantiations, and Aristotle's notion of essence. In order to exemplify how *de* operates as an individuating principle, and in relation to *dao*, we can investigate *dao* and *de* in *Daodejing* 51:

> *Dao* produces entities,
> *De* fosters them,
> Matter gives them physical form,
> Their functions complete them.
> ...*Dao* produces them but does not take possession of them.
> ...It leads them but does not master them.
> This is called profound *de* (trans. mine; adapted from Chan 1963b: 190).

The complementary roles of *dao* and *de* are important because there is an assurance that focusing on a holistic perspective does not entail neglect of individual interests. *Dao* is not reducible to empty space nor is it merely the sum total of all things and events. It is the environment within which all things and events are necessarily situated. It nourishes the ten thousand things, yet does so impartially (*Daodejing* 23, 5). Chung-ying Cheng effectively contrasts a superficial notion of the term 'environment' with its deeper Daoist sense:

> [According to a superficial sense of the term, environment means] simply "the surroundings," the physical periphery, the material conditions and the transient circumstances...[However, environment] cannot be treated as an object, the material conditions, a machine tool, or a transient feature. Environment is more than the visible, more than the tangible, more than the external, more than a matter of quantified period or time or spread of space. It has a deep structure as well as a deep process, as the concept of Tao [Dao] indicates. (Cheng 1986: 353)

Dao is the conditioning context that in part shapes individuals and events. *De* is that distinctiveness, integrity or excellence of each individual thing that can be realised only in the context of the whole, the ideal *dao*. This means that individuals can only achieve full realisation *in their specific loci* – their places within *dao*. But if we accept this account of *dao* as the conditioning environment, we must also watch that individual interests are not overlooked. In this regard, the correlative concept, *de*, is especially important in maintaining an element of individual self-determination. These two features – integrity of the individual (*de*) and its conditioning locus (*dao*) – are held in a finely tuned balance. If the environing conditions are overly restrictive, the integrity of the individual will be unjustifiably compromised. On the other hand, to refer to individual uniqueness is not also to suggest an independent, separate existence. The individual seeks and attains meaning *within* contextual and relational boundaries and affiliations. Roger Ames describes the complementary tension between *dao* and *de*: while each particular individual 'determines conditions within the range and parameters of its particularity', (1986: 331) it has to do so within the context of the whole, that is, *dao*. The characterisation of *dao–de* by Ames reveals the tension and complementarity between the two concepts:

> ...[*de*] denotes the arising of the particular in a process vision of existence. The particular is the unfolding of a *sui generis* focus of potency that embraces and determines conditions within the range and parameters of its particularity...Just as any one ingredient in the stewpot must be blended with all of the others in order to express most fully its own flavor, so harmonization with other environing particulars is a necessary precondition for the fullest self-disclosure of any given particular...[The particular] can through harmonization and patterns of deference diffuse to become coextensive with other particulars, and absorb an increasingly broader field of "arising" within the sphere of its own particularity. This then is the "getting" or "appropriating" aspect of *te* [de]. (1986: 331)

The use of the analogy of flavours in cooking is even more striking in a fourth-century BCE text, the *Zuo Zhuan*:

> *Genuine harmony is like soup*
>
> The marquis said, "It is only Ju who is in harmony with me!" Yan Zi replied, "Ju is an assenter merely; how can he be considered in harmony with you?" "Are they different," asked the marquis, "harmony and assent?"
>
> Yan Zi said, "They are different. Harmony may be illustrated by soup. You have the water and fire, vinegar, pickle, salt, and plums, with which to cook fish. It is made to boil by the firewood, and then the cook mixes the ingredients, harmoniously equalizing the several flavors, so as to supply whatever is deficient and carry off whatever is in excess..."[30]

In this illuminating analogy a sharp distinction is made between harmony and submission (here referred to as 'assent'). Each individual ingredient contributes to the resulting flavour of the soup and yet does not lose its identity. If vinegar is added to the soup, the taste of vinegar will linger in the soup.

Yet, in a well-made soup the taste of the vinegar integrates with the specific tastes of other ingredients to articulate a pleasing flavour. Paradoxically, the significance of each ingredient lies in its successful release of flavours in order to blend in with others and ultimately to enrich the whole. The correct proportion of each ingredient is necessary to achieve a desired taste.[31] This analogy inspires a view of cooperation that traverses the gap between independent singularity and obliterated self. It also resists the self–other and individual–whole dichotomies. This conceptual framework rests upon and extends the view of contrastive complementation. Contrastive opposites are not necessarily antithetical but may in fact enhance the self. Similarly, the distinctiveness of an individual may be measured not simply in terms of its individual merits but also according to its impact on the whole. This in turn is assessed according to the individual's place within its contextual environment and its relations with other individuals. This theme of interdependence and cooperation was extended in the philosophies especially of the Han period to include all forms of existence as well as cosmic entities and beings.[32] From an ethical point of view, this conceptual framework has a number of important implications, especially in comparison with those frameworks that presume stability and independence of individuals:

(1) Individual entities are shaped by events and processes in their contextual environments. This means that the individual's *place* is an integral part of the self. The polar opposites of self and community are integrated within this schema. The community is not antithetical to the self but is the locus within which the individual expresses and realises itself meaningfully.
(2) There are no independently existing, autonomous entities; the decisions and actions of individuals affect others just as the decisions and actions of others affect the self. In this way, individuals are inevitably participants in their communities. Yet, it is possible to assess the nature of individual participation, control of it and limits to it. The distinctive feature of this Daoist perspective on participation is that it highlights both the vulnerability and responsibility of individuals as participants in a community.
(3) Relations between entities are primary and not reducible to the individuals, events or even processes. In early Confucian philosophy there is emphasis on relationships as well. However, in the early Confucian case, the emphasis is almost entirely on human community and relationships.

Daoist philosophy widens the net to include relations between all entities – the ten thousand things (*wanwu*), so to speak. Such a framework might work particularly well in a contemporary environmental ethic: all species and beings within the natural environment contribute to and extract from their natural environments; they encroach on others, just as they are encroached on; they share the same biosphere; and their existences are deeply intermingled.[33]

(4) Change is a prominent feature of existence. Changes will inevitably occur – whether as a result of individual action, the actions of others, changes in relationships and in events and processes in the social and natural environments. No individuals are immune from change; this is the theory of mutual transformation. It follows from this that causation, events and processes are complex because of the intricate nature of individual, relationship and community.

The account of *dao* in this chapter dwells on its interpretation as a metaphysical concept. As a term denoting a deeper underlying reality, *dao* transcends human perspectives. The perspective of *dao* extends its consideration of issues beyond the human – and in that sense was an important response to the ideas of the Confucians, Mohists and Legalists. We may also draw on its insights in addressing contemporary issues. The conceptual framework generated by the overarching perspective of *dao* also provokes re-examination of contemporary assumptions, attitudes and perspectives. The conception of *dao* in the *Daodejing* lacks clarity; it is partly due to this that the *Daodejing* is often perceived as an immature precursor to more profound philosophies in the Han Dynasty and in particular to the philosophy of the *Zhuangzi*. On the other hand, insights may be drawn from the ideas in the *Daodejing*, as demonstrated in this chapter. In the next chapter, we examine the philosophy of the *Daodejing* and the concept *dao* in the light of the concepts *wuwei* (non-intrusive method) and *ziran* (spontaneity).

Suggestions for Further Reading

The Way of Lao Tzu (Tao-te ching), translated by Wing-tsit Chan (1963), New Jersey: Prentice Hall, Library of Liberal Arts.

Lao Tzu and Taoism, translated by Max Kaltenmark (1969) (translated from the French by Roger Greaves), Stanford: Stanford University Press.

Cua, Antonio (1981) 'Opposites as Complements: Reflections on the Significance of Tao', *Philosophy East and West*, vol. 31, no. 2: 123–40.

Fu, Charles Wei-hsun (1973) 'Lao Tzu's Conception of Tao', *Inquiry*, 16 (1973 Winter): 367–94.

Lau, Dim-cheuk (1958) 'The Treatment of Opposites in Lao-tzu', *Bulletin of the Society for Oriental and African Studies*, 21: 344–60.

Notes

1. For example, the bamboo strips on which the Mawangdui texts are inscribed are arranged in such a way that the final 44 chapters (of 81) of the received text, the *De Jing* (*De* classic), are placed first. This challenges the organisation of the extant version, which had to date been classified by scholars as the *Dao Jing* (*Dao* classic) comprising 37 chapters, and the remaining 44 as the *De Jing* (e.g. Lau 1963). To acknowledge the textual differences in the two versions, a translator of the Mawangdui *Daodejing* has labelled his translation the '*Dedaojing*' (Henricks 1989). The Guodian version incorporates material that is found in 31 of the 81 chapters of the extant version. This version is significantly different from the extant version. Some existing scholarship on the *Daodejing* has been thrown into disarray as new considerations have arisen regarding the issue of originality. Some balance needs to be struck regarding the relative importance of these versions. On the one hand, the positioning of the text in Chinese intellectual history is important in its interpretation. On the other, however, an earlier version does not guarantee authenticity. There would have been a tradition of copying texts for studying and memorisation and both versions could in fact be approximations of the original, if, indeed, there was one 'original' and authentic *Daodejing* (Hansen 1992, Chapter 6, note 7: 400).
2. Wang Bi's commentary on the *Daodejing* dominated scholarship for many years in part because he imposed on it a Confucian reading and did not challenge the dominant Confucian ideology. Furthermore, his interpretation of the *Daodejing*, as compared with others, offered modern scholars a philosophically interesting interpretation of the text (refer to Ariane Rump (1979) for a translation of the text). The other influential commentary was by Heshanggong (a pseudonym or legendary figure depicted as a teacher to the Han Emperor Wen (179–157 BCE)) whose understanding of the *Daodejing* was rooted in the Han intellectual context that fused together elements of cosmological, political and religious thinking. As a result, his commentary on the text was religious and mystical rather than philosophical. Alan Chan

conducts a detailed and authoritative comparison of the two commentaries in *Two Visions of the Way* (1991).

3. Noted by Chan 1963b: 6.
4. *Ibid*.: 3.
5. Angus C. Graham argues it is 'by far the most easily intelligible of the classics of Taoism' (1960: 1). However, one of its chapters, the 'Yangzhu Chapter', pronounces a negative outlook on social life and is suggestive of resignation; this may account for its lack of popularity both in the Chinese imagination and among scholars. Chan (1963a) discusses the features of the philosophy of this text (at pp. 309–13).
6. Schwartz 1985: 186.
7. Hansen 1992: 202.
8. Sima Qian, *Shiji* (*Records of the Grand Historian*), cited in Chan 1963a: 136.
9. This was first suggested in the *Hou Hanshu* (*History of the Later Han Dynasty*), cited in Chan 1963a: 177–9. Chan himself appears to subscribe to this view, suggesting that the Zhuangzi–Laozi philosophical relation is in some ways like the Mencius–Confucius one. Elsewhere (1963b), Chan notes that 'broadly speaking, the differences between Lao Tzu and Chuang Tzu are a matter of degree rather than kind' (p. 22).
10. Kohn 1996: 52. See also Robinet 1997.
11. This view was dominant because it was articulated by the influential historian Sima Qian in the *Shiji* (*Records of the Grand Historian*). Sima presents Laozi as an historian in charge of archives. Confucius meets with Laozi and, following their conversation, describes the latter in reverential terms, as a 'dragon' (Watson 1971: 63).
12. The view that the *Daodejing* may have been composed during the sixth century BCE has also been dispelled, with debates now focusing on whether the text was composed any earlier than the third century BCE.
13. Hansen points out the critical differences between these two interpretations of *dao* (1992: 215f.).
14. D. C. Lau suggests that the use of *dao* to replace *tian* as the ultimate entity is a later, Warring States innovation (1963: p. 22). Lau also notes that in the *Zhuangzi*, Heaven remains the ultimate; this could mean that sections of the *Daodejing* post-date the *Zhuangzi* inner chapters.
15. Charles Fu 1973: 373.
16. We will explore the concept of *qi* in greater detail in the discussion of the philosophy of the *Yijing*, in Chapter Ten.
17. Ames and Hall 2003: 85.
18. See, for instance, Po-Keung Ip (1983) and Peter Marshall (1992).

19. In Andrew Brennan 1995: 239–52.
20. Schwartz 1985: 203, discussing Lau (1958).
21. The mere overturning of existing norms, for instance, to replace preference for the male by a preference for the female, is an unreflective way to handle an enquiry on ethical and social issues (Lai 2000: 139). Hansen argues against this unsophisticated approach, 'Where conventional value assignments favor the upper, the strong, the wise, the dominant, Laozi's sayings help us appreciate the value of the lower, the weak, the ignorant, the submissive. Traditionalists value the male; Laozi emphasizes the female . . . [however] its theoretical point must be more subtle than merely reversing conventional guidance and dogmatically pushing the negative discourse *dao*' (1992: 223).
22. Herman Hesse (1971) *Narcissus and Goldmund*, translated by Ursula Molinaro (New York: Bantam Books) cited in Cua 1981: 123–40.
23. These features are discussed in Lai 2000: 143; see also the discussion on *ganying* at note 23 in the article.
24. Roger Ames discusses this in detail in 'Taoism and the Nature of Nature' (1986), esp. Section IV: *Taoism Misnamed*.
25. See, for instance, Giles (1959), Chan (1963b) and Lau (1963).
26. J. L. Duyvendak (1954), Arthur Waley (1958) and Max Kaltenmark (1969) take care to distinguish *de* from any humanly contrived sense of morality.
27. See chapters 5, 18, 19, 20, 38.
28. This interpretation of *de* also draws upon the traditional meaning of the Chinese character which is linked with its homophone, *de*, meaning to obtain.
29. Waley 1958: 31–2. Waley also suggests that *de* is not unlike the Indian *karma*. See also Duyvendak 1954.
30. Duke Zhao, 20th year – 521 BC; adapted from the translation by James Legge (1991) reprinted from the 1893–5 Oxford University Press copy, Vol. 5: 'The Ch'un ts'ew with the Tso chuen', p. 684, column 3d.
31. I have used the term 'taste' rather than 'outcome' in order to avoid invoking a sense that the final result is determined by some mechanical calculation. In using this term, I intend to suggest that this is an issue relating in part to aesthetic quality. Roger Ames contrasts the Chinese 'aesthetic order' with a 'logical order' that is a significant feature of Anglo-American philosophy (1986: 320–3), though I would be wary of drawing too clear a dichotomy between the two as it may suggest that Chinese philosophy is un-logical or illogical.
32. This is discussed in Chapter Ten.
33. See, for instance, Cheng (1987), Hall (1987), Ames (1986), and Lai (2003a).

6 Early Daoist Philosophy: *Dao*, Language and Society

As we have seen, the concept *dao* may be understood – as it predominantly was – as referring to a deeper, underlying reality. This picture of *dao* is often held in conjunction with the view that *dao* is a monistic reality. This means that reality is ultimately a singular entity, albeit comprised by a multitudinous variety of all things (the ten thousand things). Of course, the correlation is not to be taken as a necessity; one could hold that *dao* refers to a collection of different *truths* or *realities*. However, the philosophy of the *Daodejing* does lend support to the idea of *dao* as the one, singular reality. There are specific references to the 'one': 'Tao produced the One' (chapter 42, trans. Chan 1963b: 176; see also chapters 14, 39). *Dao* has an all-encompassing nature (chapters 16, 21, 25, 34, 35). Furthermore, the themes of return and reversal (chapter 40) suggest a restoration of original unity – the uncarved block (chapter 57) – that is superior to existing ways of life. The discussions in the previous chapter were predicated on the assumption that *dao* is a monistic reality: the complementation of polarities, the concept of nonbeing, the acquiescent virtues in the *Daodejing*, the concept *de* that sustains the individual within the whole, and the transcendence of the mundanely human perspective are aspects of the one *dao*.

But it is also possible to understand the character *dao* as denoting a teaching or a way; hence we have the popular translation of *dao* as 'way'. In its traditional application in the Chinese philosophical context, *dao* was a generic concept that referred to the different doctrines – the Buddhist *dao* (way or teaching), the Confucian *dao* and the Daoist *dao* – each school presenting a different teaching: the *dao* of heaven (*Daodejing* chapters 9, 77; *Analects* 5:13), a father's *dao* (*Analects* 1:11), a sage king's *dao* (*Analects* 1:12), and Confucius' *dao* (*Analects* 6:12; 6:17). If we were to sit 'above' the different claims to truth of each of these doctrines, we would see them as a selection of teachings, each one asserting its own truth. In this case, we would say that there are many *daos* – as many as there are doctrines. The *Daodejing* rejects these other *daos* (doctrines), especially the Confucian one, because it instils conformity through normative concepts and practices. From the point of view of the *Daodejing*, the people who are a product of such a culture act only in formulaic ways. The stance of the *Daodejing* is a meta-ethical one that assesses the objectives and methods of conventional morality. From this point of view, the concepts *dao*, *wuwei* and *ziran* are associated with concerns about conventional norms and expectations and how they constrain thought and behaviour.

Dao, Language and Indoctrination

As with many Chinese characters, the term *dao* has a dual meaning. We have seen in the previous chapter how *dao* may be interpreted as metaphysical reality. However, if we understand *dao* as way or teaching we can see that it is not a universal, singular reality but a doctrine and perhaps even a process or method of attaining that insight. The idea of movement is especially palpable in the Chinese character *dao* as its component on the left, 辶, signifies travel. *Dao* refers not only to the objective but also to the *ways* to achieve the objective. We should also note that this aspect of *dao* is not concerned with the question of monism or pluralism (whether there is one reality or many, or one teaching or many) as the focus is on the nature of the activity itself rather than its number. The translation of *dao* into the English term 'way' is also helpful in understanding the aspect of activity. 'Way' may refer to a particular method, as in 'This is *the way* to do it', or it may refer to the path one needs to take, as in '*The way* to get there is…' Both these applications of 'way' are consistent with its use in the ancient Chinese philosophical context. Each of the philosophical schools advocated particular *ways* of rectifying socio-political unrest. In addition, some of the schools referred to heaven's *dao* in order to justify an all-encompassing or transcendent perspective.

If we understand *dao* to refer to a 'teaching', we would interpret the concepts in Daoist philosophy in part as a response to the ideas of the other schools of thought. According to this view, Daoist philosophy engages with the other schools on issues concerning social organisation, government and ethics. It spurns the proposals of the other schools because they are far too intrusive and regimental. In addition, they are artificial, arbitrary and conventional. Daoist philosophy proposes in their place a non-intrusive, *wuwei* approach. It finds the Confucian values and methods problematic especially in their affirmation and pursuit of status, cultivation and moral authority:

> When the great Tao [*Dao*] declined,
> The doctrine of humanity [*ren*] and righteousness [*yi*] arose.
> When knowledge and wisdom appeared,
> There emerged great hypocrisy.
> When the six family relationships are not in harmony,
> There will be the advocacy of filial piety and deep love to children.
> When a country is in disorder,
> There will be the praise of loyal ministers. . . .
>
> (*Daodejing* 18, trans. Chan 1963b: 131)

> Abandon sageliness and discard wisdom;
> Then the people will benefit a hundredfold.
> Abandon humanity [*ren*] and discard righteousness [*yi*];
> Then the people will return to filial piety and deep love.
> Abandon skill and discard profit;
> Then there will be no thieves or robbers.
> However, these three things are ornaments [*wen*] and are not adequate.
>
> (*Daodejing* 19, trans. Chan 1963b: 132)

Ren and *yi*, two of the core Confucian virtues, are seen as only remedial solutions and not utopian ideals, as the Confucians claim. In fact, they are obstructionist in attaining the aims of filial piety and love. Sageliness and righteousness (or right), two criteria of good Confucian government, do not benefit the country. The *Daodejing* considers these core Confucian aspirations as merely ornamental. What are the reasons for suggesting this, we might ask? From the Daoist point of view, it is because these institutions are unnecessarily restrictive and hence tend to stifle the life of the community. A well-known passage in the *Daodejing* says this explicitly: 'The more taboos and prohibitions there are in the world, the poorer the people will be' (57, trans. Chan 1963b: 201). The reasoning behind this assertion runs like this. When people are taught and expected to behave in particular ways, they will conform to those ways *and not entertain other possible* ways of acting. The dangerous implications of 'taught' norms run even deeper as they are implicitly encoded in language. Hence when someone learns the meaning of the *term* 'beauty', for instance, they also learn the *concept* 'beautiful'. The notion of what constitutes beauty is in most cases internalised by learners and hence shapes their attitudes. Chad Hansen argues this succinctly:

> Learning social distinctions typically involves internalizing society's preferences. Distinguishing between having and lacking, we learn to prefer having. Distinguishing between beautiful and ugly, we learn to prefer beautiful. Learning names shapes our behavioral attitudes, our desires. This is because we learn names by mimicking their use in guiding choices in ordinary contexts. We do not learn them in classes by recitation. Hence we learn to let names guide us to make the same choices that our social models (teachers) do. Our learning consists in daily increasing our mastery of the system of names...Language is a tool in society's project of shaping our behavioral motivations. (Hansen 1992: 212–3)

The use of names to instil attitudes is a central aspect of Confucianism; it is emphasised especially in Xunzi's philosophy of *zhengming* (correct use of names). Xunzi believed that when people were taught terms which encoded normative behavioural proprieties, they would gradually internalise these norms. This is for Xunzi a basic aspect of social regulation. The passage in the *Daodejing* which regards language as an instrument of social control could easily have belonged to Xunzi's arguments about *zhengming*. But there is of course one critical difference: while Xunzi advocates using language as an instrument of socio-political order, *Daodejing* 12 rejects its use:

> The five colors cause one's eyes to be blind.
> The five tones cause one's ears to be deaf.
> The five flavors cause one's palate to be spoiled. ...
>
> (trans. Chan 1963b: 121)

To teach a learner the five colour terms, the five musical tone names or the five flavour terms, is not, as it is commonly assumed, to extend their knowledge. To teach a learner the five colours is also to teach her to see them the way her teacher, or society, does. The same may be said of tone names, colour terms and, by extension, all the terms in a language. The *Daodejing* notes the paradoxically *blinding* nature of education. According to this analysis, to *learn* a language is to be *taught* a particular way of seeing things: one is instilled with a particular *dao*:

When the people of the world all know beauty as beauty,
There arises the recognition of ugliness.
When they all know the good as good,
There arises the recognition of evil. ...

(*Daodejing* 2, trans. Chan 1963b: 101)

There is a strong ethical component in this analysis; language is seen simply as a tool of indoctrination. If we accept this account of Daoist philosophy, we also want to ask whether it proposes any solutions. One might suggest a total disengagement with language, although it seems naïve to think that life is preferable – or even viable – without language. Alternatively, a partial abandonment of language might be suggested though it also appears unlikely that that might eradicate the problem. If the problem lies with the use of language, reduced use will only lessen but not fix the problem. Another suggestion involves looking deeper into why and how language may be used to manipulate people. From this point of view, the use of language as a tool of indoctrination is a symptom of a deeper malaise in society. The problem is a moral one and the Daoist remedy to this lies in a more non-intrusive approach to life.

Wuwei

The concept *wuwei*, literally translated as 'no action', poses many difficulties for interpreters of Daoist philosophy due to its ambiguity. The literal interpretation 'no action' is also uninteresting because it yields unappealing consequences. Is the *Daodejing* advocating taking no action at all, or withdrawing from the life of society? Is this its response to the conventional norms and expectations that stifle individuals and regulate their pursuits? This understanding of *wuwei* suggests passivity and perhaps also a primitivism of the sort described in *Daodejing* 80:

Let there be a small country with a few people.
Let there be ten times and a hundred times as many utensils
But let them not be used.
Let the people value their lives highly and not migrate far.
Even if there are ships and carriages, none will ride in them.
Even if there are arrows and weapons, none will display them.
Let the people again knot cords and use them (in place of writing). ...

(trans. Chan 1963b: 238)

The definition of *wuwei* in terms of passivity, and contrasted with activity, is not helpful. If the *Daodejing* is correct about the sources of disquiet in society, should it not advise its readers to *do* something to rectify these rather than sit back or withdraw from social life? The ideology of passivity – which accounts for a popular translation of *wuwei* as 'going with the flow' – can only be appealing to those with a romantic fascination for acquiescence as a way of life.

If we understand that the *Daodejing* is advocating the eradication of conventional norms and practices, then *wuwei* must also have an active aspect. Angus Graham emphasises the importance of retaining the senses both of refraining from particular types of action and acting to remove conventional boundaries: *wuwei* is, paradoxically, both 'doing nothing' and 'doing but…' (1989: p. 232).[1] According to this view, *wuwei* has two contrastive components, one positive (that censures existing norms and practices) and the other negative (that refrains from manipulating or overpowering others). But although the *Daodejing* is fairly clear on the kinds of actions that ought to be avoided, there is significant ambiguity regarding what is to be done or achieved. Benjamin Schwartz suggests that the positive sense of *wuwei* would involve an overturning of the 'deliberate, analytic, and goal-oriented thought and action in a plural world', a world that espouses a *youwei* (opposite of *wuwei*) consciousness (Schwartz, 1985: 190).[2]

A *youwei* consciousness is one that plans, devises, acts and manipulates. *Youwei* pertains to a particular intentionality directed toward a historically and socially circumscribed notion of achievement and progress. A philosophy that is concerned about the manipulation of the people by language and other tools of social indoctrination should seek to remove or at least reduce the creation of such a consciousness. The idea of *wei* as consciousness, or a particular perspective on the world, is an interesting interpretation as it encompasses an ethical aspect. It is an interpretation that draws from the meaning of the term *wei*: it can mean to *act* (to attempt or bring about socially defined goals) or it can refer to one's judgement (that is, how one *sees* a particular situation). Chad Hansen translates this second sense of *wei* as 'deem' (1992: 212–4). According to this view, to *wei* is to take a certain perspective – interpretive glasses with which one views the world. The stance of the *Daodejing*, according to Hansen, is to reject all forms of 'deem'-ing that are conditioned by conventional values and norms. To *wuwei* is to 'act without deeming' – to act in a manner that is not conditioned by, or restricted to, conventional norms and values:

> *Wei*$^{do:deem}$ is not "purposeful" in the sense of free, rational, conscious, or voluntary action. On the contrary, for Laozi *wei* signals socially induced, learned, patterns of response–the opposite of autonomous or spontaneous response. (1992: 212–3)

This interpretation of *wei* transcends the passive–active characterisation. It allows for an understanding of *wuwei* not only in terms of rejecting conditioned behaviours but also as promoting the more positive effects of unconditioned and spontaneous behaviour.

Edward Slingerland draws together both meanings of *wei*, the behavioural non-action (*wuwei*) and cognitive 'no-regarding' (*wuyiwei*) (2003: 89ff.) in *Daodejing* 38:

> ...The person of highest Virtue is without action (wu-wei) *and* holds nothing in regard [*wuwei er wuyiwei* 無為而無以為]...(Slingerland 2003: 81; italics mine)

Slingerland's translation of *wuwei er wuyiwei* effectively demonstrates how conceptual categories can circumscribe thought and affect action. He also argues that the cognitive *wuyiwei* – what Hansen has translated 'deeming' – is more fundamental than behavioural *wuwei*. In this light, the *rejection* of *youwei* modes and the *advocacy* of *wuwei* modes are not two separate projects. Slingerland's analysis is both interesting and insightful, not least because it successfully avoids the difficulty of translating this phrase, encountered especially by those who translate *wuwei* as 'without action' or 'non-action'. The following two sections examine specific applications of *wuwei* in the areas of government and the pursuit of knowledge.

Wuwei and Government

The concept *wuwei* is most readily and often associated with a Daoist style of government and leadership. It can be understood in a range of ways in relation to government. It may be understood to refer to the style of government, its organisational structures, its objectives and even more broadly, its view of human life in society. It derides conventional markers of success including social status, wealth and economic inequality as these produce conflict, disorder, envy and crime (*Daodejing* 3, 4). But the *Daodejing* does not state how far we are to go in rejecting these conventional valuations of a worthwhile life. The text will have little contemporary relevance if we understand it as a treatise on primitive anarchism, one that advocates a state of affairs described in *Daodejing* 80. Perhaps the *Daodejing* seeks only to reduce to a minimum the projects of civilisation, including technological advances. It may even be a text on statecraft and war strategy, based on its advocacy of a 'stooping to conquer' strategy.[3] The difficulty in understanding the concept *wuwei* seeps into how we might understand Daoist views on government. In the first instance, there seems already to be a mismatch between advocating a government that does nothing, and promoting the idea of (Daoist) leadership. What is the Daoist sage to *do*? Benjamin Schwartz expresses his unease with the idea of Daoist leadership:

> It is true that the behavior of the sage-ruler seems to involve unresolved contradictions. He seems quite deliberately to create a utopia which will turn the world back to the simplicity of the *tao*. The restoration of the primitive must be a conscious project. Here again, we have the problem of the moralistic torque, which introduces a basic inconsistency into the entire vision of the Lao-Tzu. There can be no human morality without preference, without rejection, and without deliberate choice. The civilization-negating "policies" of the sage-ruler seem themselves to be an example of *yu-wei* [*youwei*]. The contradiction remains unresolved. (1985: 213)

At the most fundamental level, *wuwei* involves a rejection of a government style or institutions that oppress the people and threaten them (*Daodejing* 30, 31, 42, 53, 69, 72, 74). Its resentment of corruption is also palpable (*Daodejing* 53, 75). *Wuwei* may also be understood in terms of a government that does not impose unnecessary restrictions on the people (*Daodejing* 57, 58) or one that does not resort to the *wrong* kinds of measures, such as the promotion of sagehood (*Daodejing* 18, 19). We may even detect in the *Daodejing* themes that are consonant with a liberal democratic conception of society. For instance, the Daoist sage has 'no fixed (personal) ideas…he regards the people's ideas as his own' (*Daodejing* 49; trans. Chan 1963b: 186). The *Daodejing* criticises the then contemporary institutions because their intrusiveness and excessive regulation are symptomatic of a lack of trust in the common people: 'It is only when [the ruler] does not have enough faith in others that others will have no faith in him' (*Daodejing* 17 and repeated in 23; trans. Chan 1963b: 130).[4] Furthermore, it appears to advocate equality between the people, especially in its contrast between the way (*dao*) of heaven and the way of humanity:

> Heaven's Way is indeed like the bending of a bow.
> When [...] high, bring it down.
> When it is low, raise it up.
> When it is excessive, reduce it.
> When it is insufficient, supplement it.
> The Way of Heaven reduces whatever is excessive and supplements whatever is insufficient.
> The way of man is different.
> It reduces the insufficient to offer to the excessive...
>
> (*Daodejing* 77; trans. Chan 1963b: 234)

These views of government seem to reflect not only disenchantment with the existing institutions. They are also deeply suspicious of the assumptions about human nature that were correlated with, and which justified the use of, these institutions. At the root of these dissatisfactions, we see a resistance to the conception of human well-being that is endorsed by and promoted in society. This understanding of *wuwei* appears reasonable and appealing in the contemporary context, if we can supply a substantive account of the socio-political goods that the Daoist sage is to promote. There is surely much to gain from standing back, from time to time, from inherited tradition and prevailing expectations in order to reassess one's aspirational goals, or those of society. But we must return to Schwartz's comments on the concept of Daoist political leadership as there is a more intricate reason for his disquiet. Because *wuwei* in the *Daodejing* is undefined, it can yield very different implications. To put this simply, *wuwei* can generate a number of different models of political leadership. Thus far, we have seen how *wuwei* might apply to the actions or commitments of those in power. But *wuwei* may also be employed in political ideology in order to restrict the freedoms of the common people. Passages such as *Daodejing* 3 seem to express the view of government that keeps the people simple:

> ... Therefore in the government of the sage,
> He keeps their hearts vacuous,
> Fills their bellies,
> Weakens their ambitions. ...
>
> (trans. Chan 1963b: 103)

Scholars have had to acknowledge that this application of vacuity is open-ended; this passage may be understood to advocate a manipulative political strategy. However, most scholars have proceeded to defend the notion of vacuity in terms of a simpler, unadulterated lifestyle.[5] But we cannot so quickly brush aside the interpretation of *wuwei* as a dictate to submit to the greater socio-political order (Graham 1989: 289). A *wuwei* government in this case is one according to which the people are to 'go with the flow', to submit to the administration of the government. Shen Dao (c. 350–275 BC), a Legalist thinker who had influenced both Daoism and Legalism, was said to have let 'other things carry him along' (*Zhuangzi* 33, trans. Graham 2001: 279). According to Schwartz, this suggests submission, 'following what cannot be helped': effectively a call for submission 'to the dynamic forces of the larger socio-political order' (Schwartz 1985: 244). Furthermore, the Legalist instruments of reward and punishment to control the people could be justified accordingly: the typical human person is simply mechanistic in his search for reward and avoidance of punishment; the common people are therefore 'predictable instrument[s] of the *tao*' (Schwartz 1985: 246).[6] Here, we see the effects of the ambiguity of *wuwei*; it can be drawn upon to support drastically different models of government. The *Daodejing* gives little guidance on how the concept is employed; is the text itself presenting a *wuwei* approach? Perhaps we may get a better sense of the substantive content of *wuwei* in relation to knowledge.

Wuwei and Learning

A number of passages in the *Daodejing* proudly declare the enigmatic nature of the *dao* (*Daodejing* 1, 14, 21) and the corresponding obscurity of Daoist knowledge (*Daodejing* 16, 25, 41). The passages are emphatic in articulating a paradigmatic Daoist existence associated with ineffability, simplicity, pointlessness and insignificance, all of which contradict the directed and focused pursuits of humanity. In the *Daodejing*, this project involves a rejection of learning. Whereas it is commonly held that learning is at least a conventional good – and perhaps more often understood as a categorical good – the *Daodejing* seeks to overturn the pursuit of learning and its effects:

> The pursuit of learning is to increase day after day.
> The pursuit of Tao is to decrease day after day.
> It is to decrease and further decrease until one reaches the point of taking no action [*wuwei*]. …
>
> (*Daodejing* 48, trans. Chan 1963b: 184)

If we accept the account so far of the Daoist ambivalence – perhaps even rejection – of language, we will also understand why it needs to dismiss the pursuit of knowledge. The two institutions, knowledge and language, are irretrievably intertwined: knowledge is expressed in language and language entrenches received wisdoms: 'When the people of the world all know beauty as beauty, there arises the recognition of ugliness' (*Daodejing* 2, trans. Chan 1963b: 101). The definition of *wei* as 'deem' helps to illuminate this passage: the way of the *dao* is to disencumber oneself from conventional evaluations of the world; hence one should aim to *decrease* in conventional wisdoms. The objective of this exercise to 'decrease' is so that one does not-deem (*wuwei*) the world according to the characterisations shaped through language-use. The Daoist dissatisfaction with knowledge lies partly in the arbitrariness with which distinctions are made in language, and partly in conventional, unthinking acceptance of their legitimacy. From the Daoist point of view, it is ironical that a phenomenon so arbitrarily determined is adhered to so staunchly:

> Abandon learning and there will be no sorrow.
> How much difference is there between "Yes, sir," and "Of course not"?...
> Mine is indeed the mind of an ignorant man,
> Indiscriminate and dull!
> Common folks are indeed brilliant;
> I alone seem to be in the dark.
> Common folks see differences and are clear-cut;
> I alone make no distinctions
> I seem drifiting as the sea;
> Like the wind blowing about, seemingly without destination.
> The multitude all have a purpose;
> I alone seem to be stubborn and rustic. ...
>
> (*Daodejing* 20; trans. Chan 1963b: 134)

The theme of an untutored, indiscriminate mind is also connected to the idea of *dao*, at times described as the uncarved block which is rough, unsophisticated and simple (*Daodejing* 15, 28, 57). Acts of naming and identification, and of attributing function and utility, foster a particular conception of *telos* and value; we learn to value the vessel whereas its real utility lies in its hollowness (*Daodejing* 11; see also 25, 32). Daoist philosophy notes the paradoxicality of conventional values: those which are deemed sophisticated and refined are in fact regurgitated and formulaic projects. Interestingly, understanding this paradox leads us to encounter another: the simplicity (*pu*) advocated in the *Daodejing* is in fact a *sophisticated* meta-philosophical thesis about the deficiencies of conventional beliefs and practices. We may at this point conclude our analysis of the conception of learning in the *Daodejing* and suggest that the value of the text lies in such reflective and critical awareness. In its rejection of Confucian aims and methods, the *Daodejing* demonstrates the importance of critical distance; it helps us to understand the sway of history and the collective on the individual.

Nevertheless, we must not neglect to mention that the rejection of knowledge has also commonly been associated with a heightened awareness of the natural world. According to this view, the appreciation of the world around us, unadulterated by prevailing expectations, comes about only as a result of our personal and direct observations of it. This analysis draws on themes in the *Daodejing* to focus on direct apprehension as opposed to conditioned ways of seeing and interpreting. *Daodejing* 5 articulates the neutrality of the natural world: 'Heaven and Earth are not humane (*ren*). They regard all things as straw dogs' (trans. Chan 1963b: 107). We could ask whether such impartial observation of nature is in some ways similar to detached observation, which is an important part of scientific enquiry. Joseph Needham, the historian of science and civilisation in China, remarks on the 'ataraxy' in Daoism that befits the approach of scientific investigation.[7] Schwartz understands 'ataraxy' to mean 'serene indifference to the vicissitudes and terrors of the world and an aspiration to look at nature without value judgments' (Schwartz 1985: 202).

What is interesting about this understanding of enquiry is that it offers a very different understanding of Daoist epistemology from that previously described. According to the account of learning described earlier, the value of philosophy in the *Daodejing* lies in its *reflective* activity and its critical distance from tradition and custom. But the view described here, of unprejudiced observation, could preclude reflection, perhaps even the pre-philosophical, intuitive grasping that we see in the infant metaphor (*Daodejing* 10, 20)? Schwartz disagrees that the text is promoting objective investigation as there is overwhelming evidence that it has preferences – for the feminine, non-assertive, simple and tranquil – '[t]he nature which appears in the Lao-tzu is the nature of our ordinary experience and nothing more' (1985: 203). There is little to support the view that the *Daodejing* advocates a value-free, scientific approach to understanding the world. This brings us to the question of ethical commitment in the *Daodejing*: does the text offer an alternative approach to human value and meaning? If the prevailing culture fosters unthinking individuals and conventional norms impede human development, what does a *wuwei* approach offer, if anything?

The Ethics of *Ziran* and *Wuwei*

The *Daodejing* aligns a set of metaphors commonly associated with submissiveness and inferiority. It states its preference for characteristics such as ugliness, darkness, submissiveness, tranquillity, femininity and weakness by asserting their primacy over conventionally held values (*Daodejing* 8, 11, 26, 28, 36). But much is also left unsaid regarding how these characteristics are to be realised. This ambiguity is unhelpful especially because it could look as if all the *Daodejing* has to offer is a simplistic overturning of conventional norms. Turning a system of values on its head does not resolve the difficulties associated with the conformist pressures of popular culture and the role of language in reinforcing those conventions. In sum, the structural problems associated with *wei*-conditioned thinking and behaviours are not addressed in an ethic of meekness.[8]

Part of the answer to this issue rests with the interpretation of the concept *ziran*. In the previous chapter, it was noted that *ziran* is often translated 'nature', to designate entities in the natural world and the relations between them. The ethical system derived from this conception of *ziran* models itself on the ways of nature; it is one that defies human control and embodies 'spontaneous patterns, routines, cycles, rhythms, and habits' (Schwartz 1985: 202). The ethical response corresponding to a world of this sort is *wuwei*: non-interference, or letting things be. This is how Chan understands the paradigmatic ethic of the Daoist sage: 'he supports all things in their natural [*ziran*] state but does not take any action [*wuwei*]' (*Daodejing* 64; 1963b: 214). Xiaogan Liu, a contemporary Daoist scholar, identifies *ziran* as the core value in Daoist ethics (Liu 1999). He argues that this is a system in which interpersonal relationships are characterised by naturalness and peace and that, ultimately, the ethic is reducible to the basic relationship between people and naturalness:

> ...although earth, heaven, and the Way are very important concepts in *Laozi*'s philosophy...they are only transitional or intermediate concepts:

> they are necessary for expository and rhetorical purposes, but the emphasis really lies on the two ends of the spectrum – people and naturalness – and the relationship between these two. What this reveals is that people – and particularly the ruler – should emulate naturalness. (Liu 1999: 220–1)

But a shortcoming of Liu's approach – and indeed of all approaches that appeal to an ethic based on 'naturalness' – is that it fails to illuminate what it is about naturalness that should be emulated. There are many contradictory conceptions of the natural world and it is not clear which characteristics we should follow, and how far we should go in instantiating them in human societies. Liu's account assumes that there is an agreed, predetermined conception of naturalness and, furthermore, that life must be conducted according to its specifications. But this of course immediately creates a problem in our understanding of *wuwei*: instead of moving away from conditioned behaviour, adherence to what is 'natural' *circumscribes* what we are to do.

There is, however, another interpretation of *ziran*, not as a noun but as an adjective; both translations are historically accurate. As an adjective, *ziran* designates spontaneity – the way the entity *is*[9] – 'what-is-so-of-itself' (Waley 1958: 174). This understanding of *ziran*, unlike the previous one, does not appeal to the natural world. Instead, it is grounded in a Daoist notion of self, one that is free to articulate itself within its environing conditions. The two interpretations of *ziran*, as 'nature' and 'spontaneity', seem to have opposite implications. To be *ziran* (natural) is to follow a prescribed path of development, that which is 'natural'. In contrast, to be *ziran* (spontaneous) is to be free from undue coercion:

> One important aspect of tzu-jan [*ziran*] is that the movement of things must come from the internal life of things and never results from engineering or conditioning by an external power. (Cheng 1986: 356)

The central focus of *ziran* as spontaneity is the individual in an environment or in a particular state of affairs, rather than in the natural world.[10] The differences between the two interpretations of *ziran* are particularly pronounced when we consider the thesis in *Daodejing* 25 in terms of the natural world:

> ... Man models himself after Earth.
> Earth models itself after Heaven.

> Heaven models itself after Tao.
> And Tao models itself after Nature.
>
> (trans. Chan 1963b: 144)

And alternatively in terms of spontaneity:

> … Humans emulate Earth.
> Earth emulates Heaven.
> Heaven emulates *dao*.
> *Dao* emulates spontaneity.[11]

What is at the core of *ziran* as spontaneity is a principle or a characteristic rather than an entity or organism (the natural world). In this case, what role does *ziran* have in the Daoist rejection of conventional values and practices? How is it action-guiding? As it applies to individuals, self-so-ness depicts the optimum realisation of the individual in context. But spontaneity in the Daoist sense does not mean unfettered freedom. The idea of *ziran* as 'self-so' is not a philosophy promoting complete self-determination. Instead, it should be understood as a concept that incorporates the fundamental relationality of entities and their embeddedness in their contextual environments. In this way, it is not difficult to see how spontaneity can apply both to individuals as well as states of affairs. In relation to the latter, it denotes the relationships between entities, the effects they have on each other and their continuing mutual transformation.

If we accept this analysis of *ziran*, we can also understand *wuwei* as an appreciation of (the) spontaneity (of the other). Within a framework that views individuals as interdependent, recognition of the other's spontaneity, distinctness and separateness entails an ethical response of non-interference or no undue interference – *wuwei*. Non-interference has many significant ethical implications. These include an avoidance of inflexible, absolutist ideals and unilateral and dictatorial methodologies, as well as promotion of those that engender a measure of individual self-determination. *Ziran-wuwei* describes an ethical framework that is grounded in respect for individual spontaneity. It should not be assumed that the practice of *ziran-wuwei* is 'natural' to humanity and therefore comes easily. Indeed, it requires a deep wisdom coupled with particular skills. In *Daodejing* 64, we see the most explicit articulation of the *ziran-wuwei* ethic:

> He who takes conventionally-prescribed action [*wei*] fails
> He who controls things loses them.
> Therefore the sage takes [*wei*] unconditioned and non-controlling action [*wuwei*] and therefore does not fail.
> He seeks not to control anything and therefore he does not lose anything…
> He learns to be divested of conventional norms and their associated conditioned perspectives [*xue buxue*],
> And returns to the original multiplicity and specificity (of individuals)
> Thus he supports all to be spontaneous and not to act according to learned and conditioned responses.
>
> (trans. mine)

This interpretation of *ziran-wuwei* is markedly different from normative ethics as it draws upon self-perception and the appreciation of the other. This approach engenders an attitude of openness toward others rather than an imposition of conventional norms to apply universally, across individuals and situations. It relies on moral sensitivity and responsiveness to the other and sees these as fundamental to morality. This view of what is fundamental stands in stark contrast to those criteria in traditional western moral philosophy including impartiality, objectivity and universality.[12] Moral philosophers in the western tradition are aware of the inadequacies of these criteria of morality, as demonstrated in the vast literature. Nevertheless, we cannot simply abandon them because they are indeed integral to morality and moral reasoning. Perhaps the Daoist ethical considerations in *ziran-wuwei* could enhance the application of these criteria. Dialogue between the two traditions could produce an ethics that is consistent and reliable, that *also* seeks to recognise and encourage spontaneity in human actions and decisions.

Suggestions for Further Reading

Chang, Chung-yuan (1975) *Tao, a New Way of Thinking*, New York: Perennial Library.

Hansen, Chad (1992) 'Laozi: Language and Society', in *A Daoist Theory of Chinese Thought*, New York: Oxford University Press.

Schwartz, Benjamin (1985) 'The Ways of Taoism', in *The World of Thought in Ancient China*, Cambridge: The Belknap Press of Harvard University Press.

Slingerland, Edward (2003) *Effortless Action: Wu-wei as Conceptual Metaphor and Spiritual Ideal in Early China*, Oxford: Oxford University Press.

Notes

1. Regarding the 'paradoxical force' of his translation, Graham writes, "...to call the sage's behaviour at one moment 'doing nothing' and at another 'doing but...' seems...a characteristic Taoist reminder that no word you use will ever fit perfectly" (1989: 232).
2. Schwartz understands the *wuwei–youwei* tension in both the *Laozi* (*Daodejing*) and *Zhuangzi* texts as a reaction to the specifically Mohist goal-directed activity, which is 'based on an accurate analytic knowledge of the factors which bear on the situation at hand and on an accurate "weighing" of such factors' (1985: 190). In response to Mohist aims and method, the Daoist sage exercises non-intrusive or non-interfering action in the government of the empire.
3. Schwartz (1985) discusses these different interpretations of *wuwei* strategy at pp. 210–15.
4. The two passages here stand in contrast to the tone in the Confucian *Analects* 8:9 which does not believe the common people can be made to understand the aims of government and human society: "The Master said, 'The common people can be made to follow a path but not to understand it'" (trans. Lau 1979a: 93).
5. For example, Chan argues that '[l]iterally, empty, *hsü* means absolute peace and purity of mind, freedom from worry and selfish desires' (1963b: 141). Schwartz also defends Daoist simplicity, noting that '[t]he belly refers to the simplest satisfaction of basic biological needs, while the eye refers to the careful discrimination of the outer sensual qualities of things so necessary to "sophisticated" pleasure' (1985: 205).
6. Refer to De Bary and Bloom (eds) 'Syncretic Visions of State, Society and Cosmos', in *Sources of Chinese Tradition*, Vol. 1, pp. 235–82, for a good sample of the Huang-Lao Daoist–Legalist texts.
7. Discussed by Schwartz (1985), pp. 202–5.
8. I have argued elsewhere that we must approach the issue of femininity in the *Daodejing* with much caution, especially if femininity is associated with a set of characteristics including submissiveness. Where Daoist philosophy might be employed in feminist philosophy is in the Daoist notion of complementarity. The latter provides a powerful conceptual scheme within which the notions of both femininity and masculinity may be articulated. Refer to Karyn Lai, (2000) 'The *Daodejing*: Resources for Contemporary Feminist Thinking' in *Journal of Chinese Philosophy* vol. 27(2): 131–53.
9. The idea of self-so-ness derives from a literal combination of its two terms, *zi* referring to 'self' and *ran* referring to 'so'. *Ran* has two meanings, one

associated with fire and the other with a condition of existence, 'as it is so'. The *Shuowen Jiezi* (十篇上, at p. 480) expresses this 'so-ness' as 如此 (*ruci*).

10. Alan Fox argues that such spontaneous individual freedom is a fundamental feature of Daoist philosophy ((1996) 'Reflex and Reflexivity: *Wuwei* in the *Zhuangzi*' in *Asian Philosophy* vol. 6 no. 1: 59–72).
11. Adapted from the translation by Ames and Hall (2003); at p. 115.
12. Bernard Williams's arguments in Bernard Williams and J. J. C. Smart (1973) *Utilitarianism: For and Against*, Cambridge: Cambridge University Press and John Kekes (1981) 'Morality and Impartiality' in *American Philosophical Quarterly* 18: 295–303 give a good snapshot of these concerns.

7 The Mingjia and the Later Mohists

> During the fourth century B.C. it began to occur to the Chinese that words move in a world of their own, a region connected only in the most casual and precarious way with the world of reality... Now there were particular reasons, connected with the history and character not only of the Chinese language, but also of the script, which made this rift between language and actuality not merely a subject of detached philosophic enquiry... but a burning question of the day.
>
> (Waley 1958: 59–60)

Waley calls this phenomenon 'The Language Crisis'. His description suggests it was as though a wave of consciousness had spread among the thinkers in China. They began to question the nature of language and its connection with reality. As Waley rightly points out, there is a peculiarity about the Chinese language that further complicates issues of language–reality correspondence. Each Chinese character (or name: *ming*) has a particular meaning, and how the characters are combined, for instance, to form a compound name or a proposition, is an important matter. It was also critical to understand how these 'names' might accurately reflect reality. Both the Confucian discussion of correcting names (*zhengming*) and the Mohist preoccupation with standards (*fa*) attempt to deal with these issues by determining the correct application of names in order to regulate society. In opposition, thinkers associated with the *Daodejing* advocated greater awareness of the conventionality of language and its manipulative power. The debates about names extended over a range of philosophical areas that we may describe in terms of metaphysics, epistemology and philosophy of language. The discussions of the Mingjia (Terminologists) and the later Mohist thinkers covered areas that were only superficially or tangentially dealt with by other thinkers of the Warring States period.

During the Han dynasty, Sima Tan (d. 110 BCE), who was writing a history of Chinese thought, identified a group of thinkers he collectively dubbed

Mingjia.[1] This set of thinkers are also sometimes referred to as logicians, sophists, dialecticians, terminologists and nominalists because of the variety of their topics of discussion, their style of debate and the openness of the extant texts to interpretation. Their title, Mingjia, is important because it indicates that much of their discussions centred on names (*ming*) and their connection with the actual world. Some of these thinkers were known as Bianzhe (disputers) during the Warring States period. They were known for their expertise in disputation (*bian*), which was intended to resolve disagreements. The Bianzhe believed that disagreements could be resolved if distinctions were clarified. Hence, they took great care to define names, their scope and referents. The Bianzhe were held in low esteem by many of their contemporaries as they were deemed rhetorical and fond of sophistry. Their ideas seemed to lack ethical commitment and practical import. Xunzi complained about them:

> ...they like to deal in strange teachings, and weary people with curious ideas. They are very critical but do not care about its usefulness; they debate but impractically. They make much fuss but accomplish little; their doctrines cannot be the unifying bond of good government. Yet what they support seems reasonable; their teachings are plausible, sufficiently so to deceive and mislead the ignorant multitude – such are Huei Shih [Hui Shi] and Teng Si [Deng Xi]. (*Works of Hsuntze*, chapter 6, trans. Dubs 1966: 79)

Xunzi's comments reflect the concerns many had in relation to the debates of the Bianzhe. However, as we will see in this chapter, these criticisms focus only on the most trivial aspects of the Bianzhe's concerns. There are a number of connected reasons for the underestimation of their ideas both in the history of Chinese thought and in scholarship up to the present time. Their topics of discussion were deemed irrelevant to issues associated with the socio-political unrest of the Warring States period. It was commonly thought that the disputers' discussions strayed from dominant debates on ethical standards, good government and political strategy (the *practical* issues). Although a number of the Bianzhe (such as Deng Xi) were interested in sophistry, others seriously considered methods of argumentation and criteria for justification. In fact, Xunzi himself used some of these methods in his own writings (Graham 1978: 21). In spite of the perception by Confucians and others that discussions of *bian* had little practical import, the Bianzhe believed that disputation would get to the roots of socio-political issues by clarifying the status of names and their connection with the actual world.

Unfortunately, the totalitarian control by the Qin emperor from 221 BCE brought an end to intellectual discussions; the revival of intellectual enquiry in the subsequent Han dynasty focused predominantly on Confucianism. To a large extent, the social and political climate from the Qin to the Han determined the boundaries of philosophical discussion in the periods that followed. The loss of most of the texts associated with the Bianzhe also compounds the difficulty of understanding their doctrines more fully.

Many of the themes discussed by the Mingjia were also taken up by the later Mohists. We do not know these later Mohist personalities and are aware of their ideas primarily through the final six chapters of the *Mozi* text, chapters 40–5. There is a close relation between the later Mohist thinkers and the Mingjia; both sets of thinkers deliberated on similar topics and developed their views using comparable argumentative forms, though their conclusions were different. Hence, we find some traditional texts that categorise later Mohist thought under the School of Names, and, on occasion, others that classify all of them as later Mohist thinkers (Hu Shih [Hu Shi] 1928; cf. Mei 1953: 406). Later Mohist philosophy also suffered a similar fate as it waned in popularity. That the deliberations of both the Mingjia and later Mohists have been eclipsed is a loss of incalculable proportions in the history of Chinese philosophy. In addition to ethical and political issues, the later Mohists also debated a number of areas in what we might call the practical sciences: geometry, mechanics, causality, space, time, optics, and even economics (Fraser 2003: xvii). Their ideas and philosophical methods fill an often-perceived gap in Chinese intellectual thought. The debates of the pre-Qin period are represented predominantly – some would say *overrepresented* – by Confucian and Daoist views on ethics and government. The later Mohists are primarily concerned with questions about knowledge and verification, the adequacy of our understanding of the world and our representations of it in language, and the structure of language in relation to thought and reality. The predominance of Confucianism and Daoism in early Chinese philosophy, and the underestimation of logic, reasoning and argumentation, scientific reasoning, philosophy of language and epistemology, are partly responsible for the deficiencies in these fields in this early period of Chinese thought. A detailed discussion of the ideas of these thinkers reveal elements of philosophical thought much more closely akin to those in western philosophy. Our discussion will also demonstrate the gravity of the oversight of allowing these ideas simply to be cast aside.

The Mingjia Debates

According to the *History of the Former Han Dynasty*,[2] there are seven texts associated with the School of Names, purportedly bearing the names of their authors. Of these seven, two are corrupt and most probably forgeries (*Deng Xi* and *Yin Wen*) and four are no longer extant (*Cheng Gongsheng*, *Huang Gong*, *Mao Gong* and *Hui Zi*) (Makeham 2003: 492–3; Johnston 2004: 271). The ideas of Hui Shi (Hui Zi) are cited in the *Zhuangzi* text and also in the *Works of Hsun Tzu*. The *Gongsun Longzi* is the only text that survives in its original form, though only in part.

The Bianzhe in their time were noted as 'persons who made paradoxical statements, who that were ready to dispute with others, and who purposely affirmed what others denied and denied what others affirmed' (Fung 1948: 81). They seemed to enjoy the effects of their paradoxical assertions that defied common sense and that were disconcerting to others. To their opponents, they gave the impression that they were only interested in winning disputes; Zhuangzi said of Hui Shi (370?–310? BCE) that he 'wished to make a name for himself by winning arguments; that is why he came to be so unpopular' (*Zhuangzi*, chapter 33, trans. Graham 2001: 285). Wing-tsit Chan expresses their preoccupations in more positive terms: 'They were the only group devoted to such problems as existence, relativity, space, time, quality, actuality, and causes…they represent the only tendency in ancient China toward intellectualism for its own sake' (Chan 1963a: 232). Deng Xi (d. 501 BCE) was a senior official in the state of Zheng and is known to have formulated a code of penal laws and engaged in litigation (Makeham 2003: 492). His debates about the interpretation of the laws and definitions of terms are characteristic of the rhetorical style and sophistry that was so despised by others (*ibid.*; Harbsmeier 1998: 287). He was apparently so well versed in sophistry that he could render standards of right and wrong unsustainable, conflating what was regarded possible (*ke*) and not possible (*buke*).

Deng Xi's rhetorical agility may be the most obvious characteristic of the Bianzhe in pre-Qin times. But this is not the most philosophically interesting, or most important, feature of this group of thinkers. In fact, their retrospectively endowed title, Mingjia, identifies the central theme of their debates. Their discussions of names (*ming*), compound terms and the relations between language and actuality, had important connections not only with the topics of later Mohist discussions but also with the views of Xunzi, Laozi and Zhuangzi.

Hui Shi

Hui Shi was a close associate of Zhuangzi, and Zhuangzi seems to have visited his grave (*Zhuangzi*, chapter 24). The *Zhuangzi* text notes that Hui Shi, like the Mohists, advocated broad, universal concern for everyone (*Zhuangzi*, chapter 33). Although Xunzi associates Hui Shi with Deng Xi (*Works of Hsun Tzu*, chapter 6), there is no evidence that Hui Shi encouraged sophistry (Fung 1952, vol. 1: 195). However, Hui Shi was known for his difficult paradoxes and analogies, and a less sophisticated observer might associate paradoxical questions with sophistry, seemingly raised in order to cause perplexity. However, Hui Shi appears to have had a deeper understanding of his method of argumentation, as we see in the following anecdote. The King of Liang criticises Hui Shi for his reliance on analogical reasoning and Hui Shi convincingly defends his method:

> 'When you speak of affairs, sir, I wish you would simply speak directly, with no analogies.'
> 'Let's suppose we have a man who does not know about *tan*', said Hui Shih [Hui Shi]. 'If he says "What are the characteristics of a *tan* like?", and you answer "Like a *tan*", will it be communicated?'
> 'It will not.'
> 'If then you answer instead "A *tan* in its characteristics is like a bow, but with a string made of bamboo", will he know?'
> 'It could be known.'
> 'It is inherent in explanation', continued Hui Shih, 'that by using what he does know to communicate what he does not, you cause the other man to know it. For your Majesty now to say "No analogies" is inadmissible'. (*Shuo Yuan*, cited in Graham 1989: 81)

Hui Shi's answer skirts the issue of straightforward definitions. In fact, his reply is itself an analogy. In the absence of an actual '*tan*', Hui Shi argues, a definition 'by genus' will not do (Graham 1989: 81). Instead, we will have to rely on correspondences and parallels between the known (bow) and the unknown (*tan*) in order to illuminate the unknown.

Short lists of Hui Shi's paradoxes are presented in the *Works of Hsun Tzu* and *Zhuangzi*. Some of the paradoxes in chapter 3 of the *Works of Hsun Tzu* overlap with those in the *Zhuangzi*, some do not appear to be paradoxes at all, and others are difficult to decipher as the text is corrupt. Most of what we can say about Hui Shi is derived from the paradoxes in the *Zhuangzi* text. Here, there is a list of ten paradoxes attributed to Hui Shi, and another twenty-one that the Bianzhe debated on. The ten paradoxes look as if they are conclusions of elaborate arguments although we do not know the arguments. They point to the unreliability of judgements and standards of measurement. The ten paradoxes are:

1. The greatest has nothing beyond itself; it is called the great unit. The smallest has nothing within itself; it is called the little unit.
2. That which has no thickness cannot have any volume, and yet in extent it may cover a thousand *li* [about a third of a mile].
3. Heaven is as low as the earth; mountains and marshes are on the same level.
4. When the sun is at noon, it is setting; when there is life, there is death.
5. A great similarity is different from a small similarity; this is called the lesser similarity-and-difference. All things are similar to one another and different from one another; this is called the great similarity-and-difference.
6. The South has no limit and yet has a limit.
7. One goes to the state of Yüeh [Yue] today and arrives there yesterday.
8. Joint rings can be separated.
9. I know the center of the world: it is north of the state of Yen [Yan] (in the north) and south of the state of Yüeh (in the south).
10. Love all things extensively. Heaven and earth form one body. (Chan 1963a: 233–4)

These paradoxes express scepticism about measurement and may be understood as reactive responses to the attempts especially of Mozi, the Confucians and Legalist thinkers to fix and standardise the referents of names (*ming*) in order to manipulate the common people. They assert the relativity of measurements and standards in size, dimension, height, direction, location and time. A few of them focus on how the measures change in accordance with the position of the observer; Chad Hansen calls these terms 'indexical' (Hansen 1992: 262). Other propositions point to the infinite divisibility of space and time (Graham 1989: 79), not unlike elements in Zeno's paradox. Scholars have attempted to classify these propositions according to a range of categories. These include a recent thesis by Reding that they relate to the political debates of that time.[3] However, we should note with some caution that there are limits to this interpretive task for reasons which Fung Yu Lan expresses with precision:

> These paradoxes represent only the final conclusions arrived at by the Dialecticians, leaving us with no means of knowing the steps of reasoning by which they reached their conclusions. Logically speaking, one and the same conclusion may be arrived at from different premises, so that if we know only the conclusion, it is impossible to know from which of the many possible premises it was reached. Therefore, a strictly historical study of the paradoxes of Hui Shih and the other Dialecticians is impossible, since we are left wholly free to supply our own premises and explanations for these conclusions, quite independent of the ones which were actually used. (Fung 1952, vol. 1: 192)

Notwithstanding Fung's point, it is evident that these propositions indicate at some level the discrepancy between a unified, unchanging reality (propositions 1, 10), on the one hand, and our perceptions of it, on the other. Hu Shih's [Hu Shi] interpretation of the 10 propositions has been influential. He suggests that proposition 10 is in fact the 'moral' of the propositions: it is the conclusion supported by the other nine. The tenth proposition is the only one with ethical implications, built upon the other nine, metaphysical, assertions (Hu Shih 1928: 113). From this point of view, Hui Shi's method is an ingenious one. The nine preceding propositions draw attention to the relativity of measurements (and the names used to describe them); before we take a back flip to affirm, with proposition 10, an absolute and unchanging oneness (cf. Fung 1948: 85). According to this interpretation, Hui Shi's paradoxes may be understood as an argument about the inadequacy of human understanding of a deeper, unified reality. In this light, the author of *Zhuangzi* 33 seems to have grasped Hui Shi's preoccupation with the manifold manifestations of things, though, unfortunately, has not fully understood the point of his words. The text contrasts the erudition of Hui Shi with the lack of resolution in his thought:

> Hui Shih [Hui Shi] answered without hesitation, replied without thinking, had explanations for all the myriad things, never stopped explaining, said more and more, and still thought he hadn't said enough, had some marvel to add…Hui Shih was incapable of satisfying himself with [pursuing a single direction], he never tired of scattering all over the myriad things, and ended with no more than a reputation for being good at disputation. What a pity that Hui Shih's talents were wasted and never came to anything, that he would not turn back from chasing the myriad things! He had as much chance of making his voice

> outlast its echo, his body outrun its shadow. Sad, wasn't it? (trans. Graham 2001: 295)

More of Hui Shi's insights will be discussed in the following chapter, in conjunction with Zhuangzi's philosophy.

Gongsun Long

Gongsun Long (b. 380 BCE?) is recognised as the author of the famous White Horse debate, where it is stated, 'White horse is not horse.' Six chapters of the text associated with Gongsun Long, bearing his name, remain. Of the six chapters (five chapters and a short introduction), it is probable that only the 'White Horse' (chapter 2) and 'Pointing at Things' (chapter 3) discussions are written before the Han period. The introduction provides some detail of Gongsun Long's life, and chapters 4–6 ('Change', 'Hard and White' and 'Names and Actualities') are most likely written later, containing material also covered in the later Mohist texts (Graham 1990a: 125–66).

Like Hui Shi and the Mohists, Gongsun Long was a pacifist (Hu Shih 1928: 110). Although the *Gongsun Longzi*, unlike the Hui Shi snippets, includes extended arguments it is corrupt at many points. It is not easy to decipher the import of Gongsun Long's broader philosophical framework, into which the White Horse and other discussions fit. There are many scholarly interpretations of Gongsun Long's doctrine, which range from metaphysics, philosophy of language, logic, to sophistry. One of the two authentic chapters, 'Pointing and Things', is extremely obscure and the numerous analyses of its themes tend to vary according to the interpreters' perspectives. More recent studies of the *Gongsun Longzi* attempt to understand its philosophy in the light of the existing debates of the period. Chad Hansen situates the Mingjia and later Mohist debates in his discussion of the logic of the Chinese language (1983a); A. C. Graham rearranges the text of the 'White Horse' chapter and establishes that the central task of the *Gongsun Longzi* was to delineate part and whole (1990a)[4]; Ian Johnston presents a translation of the *Gongsun Longzi* as a unified text, notwithstanding the corrupt chapters, in order to illuminate its doctrine in conjunction with later Mohist deliberations (2004).

The White Horse debate is central to Gongsun Longzi's thought and we will explore it in some detail. In the White Horse chapter, Gongsun Long debates (*bian*) with an interlocutor on the topic 'white horse (is) not horse' and provides a number of reasons why he deems it to be admissible (*ke*). For the sake of brevity, I have only reproduced Gongsun Long's responses. There are five connected arguments, some of them overlapping.

> §1: "Horse" denotes form; "white" denotes color. What denotes color does not denote form. Therefore it is said, a white horse is not a horse. (Mei 1953: 421)

Gongsun Long's response seems puzzling because he appears not to have grasped the meanings of identity and class membership (Graham 1989: 82). Surely, the scope of 'white horse' is narrower than the scope of 'horse' – indeed, it is a subset of 'horse' – and hence 'white horse' *is* 'horse'. Instead, Gongsun Long separates colour and shape and seems only to have proved that the colour white is not a horse. He does not seem to have understood that a horse of *any colour* is still a horse. But perhaps more can be said about his attempt to differentiate form from colour. Scholars commonly describe these characteristics, white-ness and horse-ness, in terms of predicates, attributes or abstract universals. This understanding is in part supported by the interpretation of the 'Hard and White' chapter as a treatise on attributes. If Gongsun Long was in fact discussing these features of language, this argument could be about the distinction between white-ness and horse-ness, or it may be an attempt to draw a line between the predicates or concepts white-ness and horse-ness, and horses that actually exist (*shi*).[5]

> §2: When a horse is wanted, yellow or black ones may all be brought. But when a white horse is wanted, yellow or black ones may not be brought. If a white horse be a horse, then what is wanted in the two instances would be the same. If what is wanted were the same, then a white horse would be no different from a horse. If what is wanted were not different, then why is it that yellow and black horses are satisfactory in the one case but not in the other? What is satisfied and what is not satisfied evidently are not the same. Now the yellow and black horses remain the same, and yet they will answer the requirements of a horse, but will not answer the requirements of a white horse. Hence it should be clear that a white horse is not a horse. (Mei 1953: 421–2)

Gongsun Long's second response focuses on the terms 'white horse' and 'horse'. The terms are not co-extensive if their referents are different. This is intuitively correct. However, the argument takes a naïve realist's approach to language: the terms are identical only if the actual horse satisfies both 'white horse' and 'horse'. Of course, it may be that a horse of white colour is brought along that satisfies both terms. But this is only accidental, for there is every chance that a non-white horse is brought. The referents of white horse, or black, or yellow, are different, and the referent of 'horse' does not necessarily fulfil either 'white horse', 'black horse' or 'yellow horse'.

> §3: Horses, of course, have color. Therefore, there are white horses. If horses had no color, there would be merely horses. How could we specify white horses? But a white horse is not a horse. A white horse is horse united with whiteness, or whiteness united with horse. Therefore it is said, a white horse is not a horse. (Mei 1953: 422)

This response hints that white horse is a subset of horse. But of course, that assertion is clearly denied right through the chapter. Here, there is some allusion to the (initial) separateness of horse-ness and white-ness, such that horse-ness is one thing, white-ness another, and white-horse-ness a third.[6]

> §4: To hold that a horse is different from a yellow horse is to differentiate a yellow horse from a horse. To differentiate a yellow horse from a horse is to regard a yellow horse as not a horse. Now to regard a yellow horse as [not] (sic) horse, and yet to hold that a white horse is a horse, would be like flying in a lake or placing the inner and outer coffins in separate places. This would be the most perverse talk and confounded argument in the world. (Mei 1953: 422–3)

This response reiterates the points in the previous two arguments. It relies on an analogy between name–actuality correspondences. To differentiate between yellow horse and horse is also to deem that yellow horses are not horses.

> §5: The whiteness that does not fix itself upon any object may simply be overlooked. But in speaking of the white horse, we refer to a whiteness that is fixed upon its object. Whiteness that is fixed upon an object is not just whiteness as such. The term a "horse" does not involve any choice of color. Therefore yellow and black ones all will answer the requirements. The term "white horse" does involve the choice of color. Yellow and black ones are all rejected owing to their color. White horses alone will do. That which does not exclude any color is not the same as that which excludes certain colors. Therefore, it is said, "a white horse is not a horse." (Mei 1953: 423)

The form 'horse' is separated from its colour, 'white'. In the passage, it is clear that horse-ness does not specify any colour. Furthermore, it appears to conceive of colours not in abstract terms (it does not *fix* itself) but only with respect to particular instantiations of things that are white in colour. Only in 'white-horse-ness' does whiteness manifest itself. Here, again, we can see some connection between philosophy of language and epistemology.

Y. P. Mei's translation of the *Gongsun Longzi*, the one used here, reflects a particular understanding of the themes in Gongsun Long's thought. Mei's interpretation suggests that Gongsun Long was arguing about attributes and how these are expressed in language (Mei 1953; note 7: 436). The discussion considers the attributes of colour and shape and focuses on the relation between attribute and subject, especially in compound names such as 'white horse' or 'yellow horse'. In a variety of analyses, horse-ness and white-ness are explained in terms of universals, predication (e.g. Hu Shih 1928: 127) or logical classes or sets (Chmielewski, cited in Hansen 1983a: 143). These various ways of understanding Gongsun Long's philosophy became the orthodox approaches because they were able to render Gongsun Long's ideas in terms of those in the philosophy of language and metaphysics in western philosophy. Fung Yu-lan's interpretation, that the white horse discussion is to be understood in the light of Platonic universals, has been influential. According to this view, white horse is not horse because white-ness and horse-ness are different from 'white-horse-ness' (Fung 1952, vol. 1: 203; Chan 1963a: 233). The separate universals, white-ness and horse-ness are not co-extensive (that is, they have different scope), just like hard-ness and white-ness ('Hard and White' chapter; Fung 1952, vol. 1: 207). The universals point out (*zhi*) particular, actual things in the world ('Names and Actualities' chapter; Fung 1952, vol. 1: 211).[7] Fung's account of universals and those others that explain Gongsun Long's philosophy in terms of attributes, predication, classes and sets, share a common feature. They hold that white-ness and horse-ness are abstract concepts or categories beyond language and the actual world.

There have been serious challenges to this orthodox approach. The main objection to this interpretive framework is that there is no other evidence in the literature of the period that Chinese thinkers considered abstract universals, mental entities or logical categories. Chad Hansen emphasises that 'there is no role in Chinese philosophical theories like that played by terms such as *meaning*, *concept*, *notion* or *idea* in western philosophy (1983a: 31). Among other things, this means that the early Chinese thinkers assumed a one-to-one relation between names and actuality, a view Hansen calls 'nominalism' (*ibid.*). According to nominalism, the task of epistemology is to distinguish between actually existing things or 'stuffs', one from another (*ibid.*: 32). Hansen's description of Gongsun Long's philosophy as 'nominalism' rests partly on his analysis of the Chinese language. The task of matching names to stuffs may seem rather crude as it does not distinguish between uncountable nouns (as 'sand' or 'water') and countable nouns (as in 'a cat' or 'many cats'). He argues that this is because the *ming* (names) are uncountable nouns – what he calls 'mass nouns' in Chinese. Mass nouns like 'sand' pick out the 'stuff' sand. Likewise, the mass noun 'horse' in Chinese may refer to 'the concrete species, or to some part, specific herd, team or an individual horse, depending on the context' (*ibid.*: 36). According to this view, Gongsun Long's 'white horse' is 'the sum of stuffs [white-stuff and horse-stuff] named by each component term' (*ibid.*: 160).

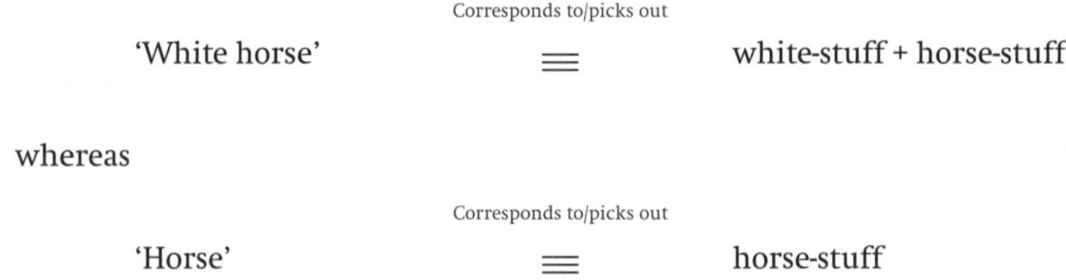

Corresponds to/picks out
'White horse'
≡
white-stuff + horse-stuff
whereas
Corresponds to/picks out
'Horse'
≡
horse-stuff

Hence 'white horse not horse' is admissible.[8]

Although Hansen's hypothesis is not unanimously accepted, his analysis of mass nouns in the Chinese language has generated scholarly attention. Graham draws from this hypothesis and suggests an understanding of the White Horse debate in terms of parts and wholes. The (*whole*) compound term 'white horse' is a combination of a part, horse, with another part, white (Graham 1990a: 198). According to this account, 'horse' and 'white' are not universal ideas that may be instantiated in real, white horses. Rather, we draw on the similarity or difference between terms: in this case, 'horse' is not similar to 'white horse'. In fact, 'horse' is only part of 'white horse' and inadequately stands in for the whole, compound name, 'white horse'. In Graham's words, this is like a synecdoche[9] in English – for instance, to say 'my trusty blade' in place of 'sword', where blade is only a part of sword (*ibid.*). Analogously, to call a white horse a horse is to name only one of its parts; the part 'horse' *cannot adequately stand in* for the whole, 'white horse'.[10]

Hansen's thesis focuses on a particular view of language and its connection with reality. Gongsun Long's nominalism is to be understood in the light of conceptions of language held by other early Chinese thinkers (Hansen 1983a, 1992). Graham's analysis looks to place Gongsun Long's philosophy in Chinese intellectual history. Therefore, it emphasises the applications of compound terms and how those relate to pictures of reality. Given the textual deficiencies, it is difficult to determine which interpretation is to be preferred. And there are other detailed treatments of Gongsun Long's views such as Johnston's (2004). These different interpretations of Gongsun Long's thought are important as they explore different ways in which his ideas can contribute to new understandings of early Chinese philosophy. We must also bear in mind that in spite of the lack of textual material, Gongsun Long's discussions express an awareness of compound terms in the Chinese language. The significance of these reflections should not be underrated as they instigate a series of related and fundamental questions about language and reality.

The Later Mohists

There are only brief references to the later Mohists by name in the *Zhuangzi* and *Han Fei Tzu* (Graham 1978: 22–3). Later Mohist thought is expressed in chapters 40–5 of the *Mozi* text. The six chapters comprise:

Chapters 40–1 (*Canons*): First, 'upper' and second, 'lower'. Each of these *Canons* is a sentence or two in length. They deal with 'procedures of description, ethics, the sciences and logic' (Graham 1978:24).

Chapters 42–3 (*Explanations of the Canons*): 'upper' and 'lower' chapters. These explanations are slightly longer than the *Canons*. They elaborate on, or attempt to provide arguments for, ideas in the *Canons*.

Chapters 44–5 (*Daqu* [*Greater Selection*] and *Xiaoqu* [*Lesser Selection*]): *Daqu* and *Xiaoqu* contain fragments on ethics, semantics and logic. Two titles are included in these fragments, *Expounding the Canons* (*Yu Jing*) and *Names and Objects* (*Ming Shi*), although there does not seem to be much connection between these titles and the topics of discussion in the two chapters. While the *Xiaoqu* is mainly coherent, the *Daqu* contains many fragments.

These last six chapters of the *Mozi* text have undergone considerable twists of fate and it is a wonder they still exist. The entire text disappeared from around 221 BCE, the beginning of the Qin dynasty. However, it resurfaced during the Han dynasty and was then included in the Han Imperial Library collection (*ibid.*: 65). There were some references to the text during the third and fourth century CE by Neo Daoists who were interested in disputation and sophisms. However, some time before the end of the Sui dynasty (581–618 CE), a severely truncated text of the *Mozi* (comprising only chapters 1–13) was circulated, which drove the fuller text out of circulation. Fortuitously, most of the *Mozi* was preserved in the Daoist Patrology; it was recovered during the Ming dynasty (1368–1644) and published whole in 1445 (*ibid.*: 68–9).

The later Mohist chapters were more drastically compromised in two major copying mistakes. In an early version, the characters were written vertically on bamboo strips that had been divided into top and bottom halves. A reader would have read the characters vertically, across the columns of the upper half, then vertically, this time across the columns of the bottom half. At some point in the history of the text, a copyist read the text and copied straight down each column, from the top to the bottom of each strip, unaware that there were two rows (Hansen 1992: 236–7). This rendered the already obscure text impossible to read. There was a second copying mistake. The *Canons* (chapters 40–1) and the *Explanations of the Canons* (chapters 42–3) were cross-referencing texts; the first character of each of the *Canons* was written beside its corresponding strip in the *Explanation* chapters. The mistake in copying occurred when these indexical characters were included as part of the text, hence confounding the grammatical and semantic structure of the statements (Graham believes this happened before the Han period (1978: 65)).[11]

From the eighteenth century, scholars began to read the later Mohist chapters as a treatise with some important insights. They recognised that the chapters were written later than the previous chapters of the *Mozi* text and interpreted them in light of the ideas discussed by the Bianzhe. They reconstructed its sections and attached the *Explanations of the Canons* with the *Canons* (*ibid.*: 70). In an ironical twist, the insertion of the indexical characters into the text by the copyist helped greatly in the unravelling of these mistakes: the characters indicated the beginning of each original fragment and also established the close relation between the *Canons* and the *Explanations* (Hansen 1992: 237). In the early nineteenth century, the later Mohist corpus also came to be valued as a text that covered topics in mathematics, geometry, astronomy, optics and mechanics (Graham 1978: 70–2). A wave of interest in westernisation during this time generated more interest in this text as it was perceived to have many parallels with western thought. A number of modern scholars including Liang Ch'i Ch'ao (Liang Qichao: 1873–1929) and Hu Shih (Hu Shi: 1891–1962) were keen to establish sino-western connections while maintaining a commitment to Chinese philosophical ideas. Hu Shih focused on the Mohist innovations in argumentation as the foundation for his treatise, *The Development of Logical Method in Ancient China*. In this book, Hu Shih appears apologetic for the dominance of Confucian doctrine and promotes Mohist philosophy as a vehicle for progress and cross-cultural understanding:

> I believe that the revival of the non-Confucian schools is absolutely necessary because it is in these schools that we may hope to find the congenial soil in which to transplant the best products of occidental philosophy and science. This is especially true with regard to the problem of methodology. (Hu Shih 1928: 8)

In 1978, Angus Graham published a pioneering volume on the later Mohist texts, comprising analyses and translations. Whereas the large majority of studies of the text had focused on separate sections, Graham made extensive study of it in its entirety. His work includes detailed grammatical and structural analysis of the Chinese language, philological analysis, dating of sections, rearrangement of some sections, and textual emendation. Although scholars disagree with particular claims in the book, there is unanimous agreement that this edition is the best available to date, in terms of its rigour in scholarship and representation of the views in these texts.

Argumentation and Disputation: *Bian*

This most superficial meaning of *bian* refers to argument as a competition. It is argumentation of the sort Deng Xi was known for: arguing to win one's case. Chapter 2 of *Zhuangzi* expresses a sense of despair at the Confucian and Mohist sparring, where both seek to gain the upper hand. A second use of *bian* is more inclusive, referring to debate in general on a range of topics. The *Mozi* text uses *bian* to clarify and articulate knowledge and understanding on a broad range of subject areas, not only in ethics and political philosophy but also in the natural sciences. A third, more distinctive, application of *bian* was a unique characteristic of the Mohists' discussions. Mozi discussed the determination of *fa*, standards, in order to clarify the people's understanding of what was expected. The later Mohists continued and developed this process and sought to distinguish what could be affirmed (*ke*) or not (*buke*), what was similar (*tong*) or different (*yi*), this (*shi*) or not this (*fei*), so (*ran*) or not so (*buran*).[12] This particular usage of *bian* (disputation) draws from its homonym, *bian* (discrimination). The character *bian* (discrimination) helps us to understand the nature of *bian* (disputation 辯). *Bian* (discrimination 辨) includes the character for 'knife' and may be understood as referring to fine, clear distinctions scored by a knife. If we understand *bian* (disputation) also in terms of discrimination, we will grasp its distinctive Mohist applications.

The later Mohists made distinctions on the basis of similarity (*tong*) and difference (*yi*). *Canons* A86–7[13] set out four types of sameness and difference:

> There being two names but one object is the sameness of 'identity'.
> Not being outside the total is sameness 'as units'.
> Both occupying the room is the sameness of being 'together'.
> Being the same in some respect is sameness in being 'of a kind'.
> (A86: Explanation of *tong*, Graham 1978: 334)

> The objects if the names are two necessarily being different is being 'two'.
> Not connected or attached is 'not units'.
> Not in the same place is 'not together'.
> Not the same in a certain respect is 'not of a kind'. (A87: Explanation of *yi*, *ibid.*)

The paragraphs set out criteria for sorting out sameness and difference: identity (for example, of a dog with a whelp), parts belonging to a whole or individuals of a class (for example, different head of oxen being part of the herd), component or constituent parts of a thing (for example, a room filled with different things), and beings of a kind (Graham 1978: 335–6). For the Mohists, these modes of drawing similarities and establishing difference assist in *bian*. The *Canons* set out different types of disputation that vary in generality. In A73, there is a simple application of exclusive 'or' whereby a thing is either ox or non-ox: 'to lack what distinguishes an ox is to be a non-ox' (Graham 1978: 318). A74 is more precise in distinguishing the alternatives: both 'ox' and 'non-ox' cannot fit the fact (*dang*) 'if they do not both fit, necessarily one of them does not fit' (*ibid.*: 318). What fits is described according to the paradigm (*fa*). The criteria for each *fa* to some extent resemble those in early Greek essences or essential properties. But Mohist *fa* is not merely a definitional concept, against which instances or instantiations are checked for accuracy. Interestingly, *fa* may refer to an idea or concept of a thing, or an actual instance of it. The Mohists did not prioritise conceptual knowledge over practical knowledge. When they provide an example for *fa*, the later Mohists refer to a circle, which has three different *fa*: 'the idea, the compasses, a circle, all three may serve as standard' (A70; Graham 1978: 316). Mohist epistemology allows for a broader set of criteria that comprise a thing's defining or essential characteristics. The later Mohists tried to articulate characteristics with respect to *lei*, a particular kind. They wanted to fix the kind, that is, to determine the scope and limits of each *lei*: 'Being the same in some respect is sameness in being "of a kind"' (A86; Graham 1978: 334).

But how do we fix the kinds? The first task, which traverses metaphysical and epistemological issues, is to identify the relevantly similar respects when comparing two or more things. For example, do we select 'four-footed' or 'living' (B2) in our comparisons of natural kinds? 'Four-footed' will not distinguish oxen from horse but will distinguish horse from bird. The problem, of course, is that relevant criteria change depending on what is being compared. The later Mohists and Hui Shi shared concerns about the diversity and variability of standards. However, unlike Hui Shi, they were not happy to accept the lack of clear knowledge about distinctions. They worried about arbitrariness: to say that oxen have horns and horses not, and to apply horns as the distinguishing feature between the two *lei*, will not do (B66). The later Mohists are aware of the acute problems of comparison and classification: how do we 'extend from kind to kind (*tui lei*)' (B2; Graham 1978: 350)? Graham argues convincingly that '*tui*' is a form of analogical argument rather than an inductive one:

> The Mohist is concerned with consistent description, not in inferring from the known to the unknown. Whether the cavities in the creature's head actually contain eyes may not have interested him at all; the point is that if you say of one milu deer that it is four-eyed you must say the same of all. (Graham 1978: 351)

To assert otherwise, that one *milu* deer is four-eyed and another not, while naming four-eyes as the distinguishing feature of *milu* deer, is to commit the sort of arbitrariness deplored in *Canon* B66. The Mohists had accurately diagnosed the root of the problem in making distinctions: when we say, for instance, that oxen have incisors and horses have tails, how are we to *know* that they are in fact *not* distinctive to each of them? Perhaps the simple answer lies in a combination of empirical observations of the world and the application of inductive logic. The more complex answer, of course, requires specification of the criteria for relevant similarities or dissimilarities. But the later Mohists did not supply these; they did not say why it was not fitting to distinguish oxen and horses on the basis of incisors and tails, respectively. In spite of their perceptive surveys of epistemological problems, which was distinctive among the schools of Chinese philosophy, the later Mohists had more questions than answers. Their descriptions of methods of drawing distinctions are haphazard and unmethodical, appearing more as a catalogue of disputation rather than systematic analysis of logic or patterns in argumentation.[14] Graham notes that although they took geometry as paradigmatic of clear and exact thinking, they never developed a discipline of geometric proof. They were content simply to illustrate that certain relationships and regularities obtained by appeal to geometric paradigms (1989: 60). Likewise, *bian* could have been developed into a theory of syllogism, but it did not work out that way either. We see more of the same in their discussions of compound terms and difficulties in language.

Language, Names and Propositions

Canon A80 lists three sources of knowledge: hearsay, personal experience and explanation. We would not normally expect hearsay to be classified together with personal experience. The later Mohists are aware of its tentative nature, yet consider it a source of knowledge. On the other hand, first-person experiences are problematised, the reason being that each person 'may have seen not all but only some [aspect of the thing]' (Graham 1978: 329). Explanation (*shuo*), or demonstration, is the method of illumination used throughout the *Canons* and *Explanations*. *Shuo* is not an argument for the claim made in its corresponding *Canon*. It normally provides examples, or elaborates, in order to present a more substantial claim.

Canon A80 also names four objects of knowledge. These are names (*ming*), things (including entities and events), matching name with thing, and acting. Knowledge of the first two objects, names (*ming*) and things (*shi*), are more theoretical sorts of knowledge as compared with the latter two, which are practical applications of knowledge. To be able to match name with thing is a multi-layered process. One needs to know how to distinguish things, one kind from another, and to apply the appropriate names to them. Matching name with thing (*he*) is an ability (*cai*) (A3; A25). The fourth kind of knowledge, acting (*wei*), is to respond appropriately to things denoted by particular names. The Mohists valued practical knowledge over theoretical or discursive knowledge. They illustrate the importance of 'know-how' in the use of language by referring to the blind man's predicament:

> Now a blind man may say, 'That which shines with brilliancy is white, and that which is like soot is black.' Even those who can see cannot reject those definitions. But if you place both white and black things before the blind man and ask him to choose the one from the other, then he fails. Therefore I say, 'A blind man knows not white from black,' not because he cannot name them, but because he cannot choose them. (*Mo Tse*, chapter 39; in Hu Shih 1928: 66)

The blind man may understand names, but he does not know how to *use names to make distinctions*. This task is more complicated when we consider the issue of compound names: if it is difficult to specify criteria for distinguishing different kinds (*lei*), and difficult to match names with things, how do we match 'white horse' with actual white horses? We have already come across Gongsun Long's struggle with the compound name 'white horse'. The later Mohists extend the discussion to consider more extended strings of names, that is, names that are strung together to form propositions as in 'a white horse is a horse'. Of course, a proposition is something more than a string of names, each independently connected to its own 'bit' of actuality. In this regard, the *Xiaoqu* chapter may be considered the most important in Mohist philosophy of language – indeed, in early Chinese philosophy of language – because it introduces the original idea of a proposition (*Names and Objects*: NO3, Graham 1978: 471). It also sets out a list of similarities and differences between propositions. These include illustrating, drawing parallels, citing the opponent's precedent and analogical reasoning (NO11; 12).[15] The *Xiaoqu* classifies five types of inferences in propositions. These five are 'this (*shi*) and so (*ran*)', 'this and not so', 'not this and so', 'one universal and one not', and 'one this and one not-this'. We will examine the first two types of inferences to get a glimpse of the Mohist understanding of parallelism in propositions.

The first type of inference, 'this and so', allows a straightforward case of predication. The phrase 'a white horse is a horse', when predicated, yields 'to ride a white horse is to ride horses' (NO14; trans. Graham 1978: 485). A parallel proposition in this same passage establishes the Mohist concept of concern for everyone, *jianai*: 'Jack is a person. To love Jack is to love people. / Jill is a person. To love Jill is to love people' (*ibid.*). Jack and Jill (Huo and Zang) are derogatory names for bondsmen and bondswomen. To love the lowly, like Huo and Zang is, surely, to love humanity.

Expressions of the second type, 'this and not so', include: 'Her younger brother is a handsome man, but loving her younger brother is not loving handsome men' (NO15; trans. Graham 1978: 487). Even though her younger brother (*di*) is a handsome man (*meiren*), love for her younger brother (*ai di*) is semantically distinct from loving a handsome man (*ai meiren*). Using this structure, the Mohists draw an analogy to argue that killing robbers is permissible: 'although robbers are people, loving robbers is not loving people...killing robbers is not killing people' (*ibid.*). We can quite readily see the parallel structures of these two sets of inferences. However, the analogy is in fact not required to support the Mohist claim that killing robbers (*shadao*) is not killing people (*sharen*). If we examine the meanings of the two phrases, 'killing robbers' and 'killing people' in Chinese, '*shadao*' means 'executing a robber' while '*sharen*' means 'murder'. The Mohist claim in fact relies on these two *different compound names*, rather than predication. In fact, the argument is a semantic one that turns on the different meanings of the two phrases in ordinary language use. The analogical parallel on its own is insufficient justification for drawing a 'this and not so' conclusion for 'killing robbers is not killing people'.

On first considering the five types of inferences in the *Xiaoqu*, we might come away with the impression that the later Mohists were driving toward syllogistic structures according to which we might be able to categorise different sorts of inferences. There is, however, no evidence of this. The later Mohists do not discuss the criteria for classification into the five types of inferences. We see this in the case of 'killing robbers is not killing people'; as Graham notes, '[t]here is no logical compulsion to put the proposition in the category the Mohist has chosen for it' (Graham 1978: 489). More importantly, whether a particular inference belongs to any one of the five types is determined ultimately by the *meanings, rather than syntax*, of the compound names and propositions. In the phrase 'killing robbers is not killing people', the meanings of *shadao* and *sharen* are determined by convention; disputation involved the settling of these meaning conventions such that only one of them must fit. Xunzi accused the later Mohists of 'disorder[ing] names by confusion in the use of names' (Graham 1978: 43), hence highlighting the unsatisfactoriness of appeal to convention to solve disputes. We might also feel a sense of disappointment in the later Mohists' deliberations on epistemology and language. On the one hand, they are perceptive about the nature of difficulties in language use. Yet, on the other hand, such critical awareness does not lead to systematic analysis. It seems that what could have culminated in more substantial discussions of logic and philosophy of language fell through, merely to conclude with simplistic affirmation of conventional meanings. But it may be that we are expecting the impossible, for the Chinese language, being comprised by characters, does not lend itself easily to systematic grammatical analysis. What the Mohist discussions *do* show is that similarity in grammatical structure does not guarantee analogical or semantic correspondence. Furthermore, the criteria for applying *ming* (matching single characters with reality) are different from those for compound terms and propositions. These particular features of the Chinese language may have impelled the later Mohists to focus on semantic rather than logical analysis.

Scientific Discussions

The *Canons* discuss a selection of topics in the subject areas of geometry, optics and mechanics. Their topics include dimension, alignment, circularity, and measurement (A52–69), space, time and duration (B14–16), light, shadows, mirrors and images (B17–24), and weights, forces, inclination, pulleys and wheels (B25–9). Their discussions demonstrate that they gave significant attention to events and phenomena in the world as, for instance, in the discussion of shadows in B21:

> Canon: The size of the shadow. Explained by: tilt and distance.
>
> Explanation: When the post slants the shadow is shorter and bigger; when the post is upright the shadow is longer and smaller. If the flame is smaller than the post the shadow is bigger than the post. It is not only because it is smaller, but also because of the distance. (trans. Graham 1978: 379)

In their observations of the world, and descriptions of them, the later Mohists identify causes (*gu*) and distinguish between different kinds of causes. *Canon*

A1 specifies the difference between a necessary condition, and a necessary and sufficient condition:

> Canon: "The [*gu*] (reason/cause) of something is what it must get before it will come about.
> Explanation: 'Minor reason': having this, it will not necessarily be so: lacking this, necessarily it will not be so. It is the unit <*which precedes all others* (?)>. (Like having a starting point.)
> 'Major reason': having this, it will necessarily <be so>: lacking <this, necessarily it will not> be so. (Like the appearing bringing about the seeing.) (trans. Graham 1978: 263).[16]

The minor reason is a necessary condition while the major reason is a necessary and sufficient condition. Graham suggests that the later Mohists would have understood causal relations as necessary (*ibid.*: 301). Being interested in the observable world and how it 'works', they look for causal relations in specific phenomena. Their observations of the world also brought them to the point where they were aware of the limits to our understanding of causality: 'Whether the fighter's breakdown is due to drinking wine or to the midday sun cannot be known: "coinciding circumstances"' (B10; trans. Graham 1978: 360). In this case, there is more than one possible cause and this complicates the determination of its actual cause. Graham points out that although the *Canons* made many references to illness (A76, 77, 85; B9, 10, 34), the Mohists, being concerned about certainty, did not dwell on these topics (*ibid.*: 56). He suggests that this is because ongoing discussions on illness and medicine were too fraught with complexity. Hence they relied on examples from optics and mechanics, where they could draw on phenomena that had readily identifiable causes.[17] Bearing in mind these concerns, we also get a glimpse into their views of time, duration and change. The *Canons* also define necessity, *bi*, as 'the unending' (*ibid.*: 299). What is necessary should not change over time:

> For the Mohist, the deepest and most troubling of problems is the relation between knowledge and temporal change... he lives in an age of rapid social transformation in which ancient authority is no longer an adequate guide to conduct. He has developed the moral teaching of Mo-tzu [Mozi] into an elaborate ethical system justified not by authority but by the procedures of disputation; he believes that, alone among the sages, Mo-tzu taught principles which are necessary [*bi*] and therefore invulnerable to

> time. "The judgments of the sages, employ but do not treat as necessary. The 'necessary', accept and do not doubt" (A83). "Even if there were no men at all in the world, what our master Mo-tzu said would still stand" (EC2). (Graham 1978: 33)

Their pursuit of certainty and necessity sits uncomfortably with their observations of the variety and difference in the world. Unlike the Confucians, who could rely on a pre-eminent normative order (articulated in the concept *tian*, heaven), or others who posited a transcendent reality, the Mohists sought to establish stability in a diverse and changing world without reference to a transcendent realm. The later Mohist texts reflect this fundamental difficulty. Their considerations provide enormous amounts of detail, yet they never arrive at more useful generalisations or principles about the way the world is ordered or language may be applied. Their discussions in the sciences seem only to describe a range of observations. That is, they provide a taxonomy of specific phenomena in the observable world without attempting also to work out the general principles that apply to relevantly similar cases. Benjamin Schwartz describes their deliberations in the following terms:

> There are the actual explorations of optics, mechanics and physics. There is the concern with geometric definition and the mathematical treatment of optic phenomena...They are deeply committed to seeking out separate particular causes for separate effects. (1985: 168)

Their explorations in the different scientific fields had an intensely practical focus. This was coupled with a preoccupation with plurality that, to them, seemed to defy abstractions and universals, particularly those encoded in language. In brief, they were worried about the mismatch between the plurality and complexity in the actual world, and the apparent simplicity of language. A question uppermost in their minds was, 'How can names, *ming*, adequately capture reality?' When we understand this anxiety, we also begin to grasp why their discussions of language did not result in the articulation of syllogistic rules, their discussions of propositions did not move toward the development of criteria for inference, and their discussions of scientific phenomena did not result in the formulation of general principles. Unlike Hui Shi, who also dealt with the question of plurality and differences, the later Mohists refused to reduce multiplicity to an ultimate oneness:

> There is no "reductionist" impulse to posit some ultimate "stuff" of minimal properties of mass and motion in terms of which all the variety of the world may be explained . . . they remain resolute pluralists . . .[18] (Schwartz 1985: 168)

In their approach to debates and their resolution of problems, the later Mohists seemed committed to a commonsensical view of reality. In this way, their discussions of scientific phenomena parallel their views of language and disputation: what confirms *shi-fei* in disputation (for example, whether white horse is horse) is conventional language use, just as empirical observation confirms causal connections. They were careful to avoid elusive ideas in the treatment of illness and cosmology, including those of *yin* and *yang*. Their only mention of the theory of five phases (*wuxing*) was to demystify it and explain it in purely causal terms (B43). They remained resolutely committed to the observable world and resisted what others around them were doing: they did not engage in theoretical abstractions nor did they propose cosmological or metaphysical grand theories within which to slot their empirical data. In this sense, their project is primarily scientific (in their observations and descriptions of the world), rather than proto-scientific (in interpreting empirical data according to a cosmological or metaphysical framework) (Graham 1989: 162).

Practising *Jianai*: Utilitarian Morality

The section of the later Mohist writings that focuses on ethics, the *Daqu*, is badly mutilated. However, it is still possible to detect the continuity and development of the concept *jianai*, universal concern, from the earlier sections of the *Mozi* text. In the later writings, there is more consideration of how *jianai* might be realised in practice. There is a distinct shift in the definition of benefit (*li*) that is both more realistic and basic. Whereas the earlier sections of *Mozi* define benefit in terms of aggregate wealth, population numbers and social order, the *Canons* define it in terms of happiness and dislike:

> *Li* (benefit) is what one is pleased to get. (A26; trans. Graham 1978: 282)

> *Hai* (harm) is what one dislikes getting. (A27; *ibid.*)

This appears hedonistic. But if we look carefully, it does not advocate happiness for its own sake but as a component – perhaps a distinguishing feature – of utilitarian good. There is also a more developed sense of how the measures of happiness are worked out. The Mohists interpreted the term *quan* in terms of the 'calculating' process involved in utilitarian practical reasoning. *Quan* is subtler than liking or disliking something directly (A84). More realistically, we may like or dislike something after weighing its benefits and/or harms in the light of alternatives: '[w]eighing light and heavy among the things treated as units [of a whole] is what is meant by "weighing"' (*Expounding the Canons*: EC8; trans. Graham 1978: 46). In this same fragment of *Expounding the Canons*, an example is provided whereby one has to choose between the two alternatives either of losing one's life in refusing to fight, or losing one's arm in fighting. Of course one does not wish to lose one's arm, but in the light of the entire situation, the choice is obvious. This suggests a deeper insight into utilitarianism as it considers not only absolute conceptions of good but also preferences within the constraints of the situation.

Later Mohist discussions also allow for benefit to oneself (EC7). It even suggests a sense of self-worth in the statement 'Love of oneself is not for the sake of making use of oneself. It is not like loving a horse' (A7; trans. Graham 1978: 48). It is not clear, however, whether we can successfully extend this idea to the concept of self-worth in modern thought. Regarding the broader question of 'Whose happiness?' the later Mohists provide a considered response to their critics. They integrate the concepts of *lun lie*, relational proximity, and *fen*, duty to specific others, with the notion of universal concern for all. According to one's duty (*fen*), one is to do more for particular others; these include creditors, rulers, superiors, the aged, elders, and kin. The proportions of duty are allocated according to relational proximity (EC 9–10; Graham 1978: 46). On the other hand, the Mohists maintain concern for others: we are to be as concerned for others' parents as we are for our own (EC12).

The more moderated approach to the utilitarian ethic in the later writings also highlights the major difficulty of *jianai*. It is not only that the demands of *jianai* do not resonate with common practice. The question remains of how we are to balance the two: doing more for particular individuals and concern for all others. The early Confucians were firm in their insistence on the primacy of close relationships. The later Mohists attempted to locate the value of morality in individual contributions to broader social welfare. Graham expresses the Mohist contribution to the early debates on morality: 'A remarkable innovation of the later Mohist ethic is that it conceives morality in terms, not of fixed social relationships between father and son, ruler and subject, but of individuals benefiting themselves, each other and the world' (Graham 1978: 51).

Philosophy of Language in Early China

The Bianzhe had acquired a negative reputation during their time because of some aspects of their debates. Perhaps it was a combination of style (arguing to beat the opponent) and topic (language and its terms of reference) that contributed to the unenthusiastic reception accorded their ruminations and, indeed, the careless handling of their texts. This is unfortunate as the further development of their doctrine would very possibly have taken Chinese intellectual history down a different path. Some of the Bianzhe were not interested in sophistry but were concerned about the philosophical, social and ethical issues of the day. They debated language and its functionality in human society. They worked on issues that were enormously complex and fundamental, and these may have seemed irrelevant to the concerns of the ruling elite of the time, who were keen to instil social order and to see the immediate effects of their measures (Schwartz 1985: 170–1).

Their concerns about *bian*, disputation, were essentially a concern about the real world and how language could adequately capture it. What is the connection between *ming* (names) and *shi* (actuality)? How was the world divided into different kinds (*lei*) and how did language pick them out? For the later Mohists, disputation revolved around drawing correct distinctions: *shi–fei* (this–not this), *tong–yi* (same–different) and *ran–buran* (so–not so). Hui Shi took an extreme position in this debate and posited that there was no basis for drawing distinctions. For him, the selection of names was a purely arbitrary exercise. As we will see in the following chapter, Hui Shi's views are closely connected with those of Zhuangzi's. Gongsun Long remained committed to the world of things (stuff) and focused on how names, including compound terms, could properly pick out things. Our knowledge of Gongsun Long's philosophy is incomplete. Although his discussions appear unnecessarily laborious, it is important to note that he was among those early thinkers who were aware of some of the peculiarities of the Chinese language and who challenged commonsense assumptions about language.

The later Mohists took the discussion further to consider not only compound terms but also propositions. Their discussions on (the Chinese) language are the most developed and detailed in pre-Qin philosophy. Like the other Mingjia, they were concerned about the use of language and the application of names. However, they were not willing to accept the slapdash conclusions of Hui Shi that there was no way to draw distinctions. They searched for ways in which distinctions could be properly drawn, between the so and the not-so. But their detailed investigations throw up significant variances that are difficult to generalise (for instance, similarity in sentence structure does not guarantee similarity in semantic inference). Likewise, their explorations of scientific matters stop short of analysis. Yet, we must appreciate the detail in their observations and the care taken to avoid hasty conclusions about causal connections. Their observational projects also seem untainted by the preconceived cosmological or metaphysical frameworks that were fairly commonly assumed during this time. We might bemoan their failure to develop syllogisms and general principles, or we could appreciate their unyielding commitment to the plurality and complexity of the world. The later Mohist texts allow us glimpses into the difficulty faced by these thinkers. They draw our attention to the difficulty of devising a functional language that facilitates social life but yet does not oversimplify the diversity in the world.

The project of the later Mohists spanned a wide range of disciplines: epistemology, science, economics, philosophy of language, politics and ethics. Their ideas about names, language and the observable world are closely intertwined with their views on society and government. Like the Confucians, they believed that applying names correctly was the key to socio-political order. While the Confucians sought to attain order according to their theory of *zhengming* (rectification of names), the later Mohists emphasised the importance of making correct distinctions; these would in turn function as standards (*fa*). For the later Mohists, disputation and making the right distinctions had implications not only for our observations of the natural world, but also for the ethical and political domains. Xunzi recognised the deep significance of the Mohist debates. He argued that 'confusing the correct nomenclature' was akin to fiddling with measures:

> Distinguishing words, and making unauthorized distinctions, thus confusing the correct nomenclature, causing the people to be in doubt and bringing about much litigation was called great wickedness. It was a crime like that of using false credentials or false measures. (*Works of Hsun Tzu*, chapter 22, trans. Dubs 1966: 282)

To someone who is after quick results, the later Mohist discussions seem circuitous as they take an extended foray into appropriate applications of language before they arrive at recommendations for rectifying the social order. By contrast, the use of *fa* (penal law) by the Legalists, under which people lived in fear, was immediately effective; this may also in part explain the eclipse of Mohist philosophy from the beginning of the Qin (Legalist) dynasty (221–206 BCE) (Schwartz 1985: 170).

The later Mohist discussions on ethics incorporated some of Mozi's concerns, including those about Confucian nepotism. While Mozi did not have any room for Confucian special preference in his concept of *jianai*, the later Mohists went beyond that to integrate concern for particular others with benefit for oneself and others. They upheld a consequentialist theory that understood benefit in a practical and realistic way, not in absolute terms but according to the choices available within particular situations.

What is also remarkable about Mohist ethical theory – and indeed about Mohist philosophy more generally – is an underlying awareness that appeal to authority, whether that of a sage or of heaven, could not serve timelessly and categorically as the ultimate justification for doctrines. The later Mohists skirted prevailing assumptions and sought justification for their views on the basis of their credibility: issues were settled by deciding whether they were cases of 'this or not-this', or 'so or not-so'. It is noteworthy that argumentation in the later Mohist texts refers only to particular doctrines and refrains from mentioning rival philosophers by name; from their point of view, the discredit rests with the doctrine and not with its advocate. Graham notes that these texts are unusual among texts of that period in China, in that the Mohist texts did not promulgate their own, Mohist, ideology. He states,

> Other thinkers, from Confucius down to Han Fei tzŭ [Han Feizi], fail or refuse to detach philosophising from moralising and practical persuasion. But the later Mohist summa never preaches; everything it has to say about morals is pure ethics.... This impersonality is unusual in pre-Han philosophy, where the most interesting examples of disputation tend to be (or to have been dramatised as) actual face-to-face debates between Mencius and Kao-tzŭ [Gaozi], Hui Shih [Hui Shi] and Chuang-tzŭ [Zhuangzi]. (Graham, 1978: 24–5)

It is a loss of incalculable proportions that these debates were stopped short during and long after the Qin dynasty. The dominant social and political forces worked against the Bianzhe's concerns about disputation and the Mingjia's concerns about names appropriately reflecting reality. Perhaps, from the point of view of the status quo, these questions were just too difficult and confronting.

Suggestions for Further Reading

Later Mohist Logic, Ethics, and Science, translation and commentary by Angus C. Graham (1978), Hong Kong: Chinese University Press.

'The Kung-sun Lung Tzu with a Translation into English', translated by Yi-Pao Mei (1953) *Harvard Journal of Asiatic Studies*, vol. 16, no. 3/4: 404–37.

Fraser, Christopher (2003) 'Introduction: Later Mohist Logic, Ethics, and Science After 25 Years', from the reprint edition of Angus C. Graham, (1978) *Later Mohist Logic, Ethics, and Science*, Hong Kong: Chinese University Press.

Graham, Angus C. (1989) 'The Sharpening of Rational Debate: The Sophists', in *Disputers of the Tao*, La Salle: Open Court.

Hansen, Chad (1983) *Language and Logic in Ancient China*, Ann Arbor: University of Michigan Press.

Hu, Shih (1928) *The Development of the Logical Method in Ancient China*, Shanghai: The Oriental Book Company.

Makeham, John (2003) 'School of Names (*Ming Jia, Ming Chia*)', in Antonio Cua (ed.) *Encyclopedia of Chinese Philosophy*, New York: Routledge; pp. 491–7.

Notes

1. Sima Tan had started on the project to compile a chronicle of Chinese history. He did not complete the project although his son, Sima Qian (c. 145–90 BC) did. Entitled *Shiji* (*Historical Records*), the work covers over two thousand years of Chinese history up until the rule of Emperor Wu (156–87 BCE) in the Han dynasty.
2. The *History of the Former Han Dynasty* (*Qian Han Shu*) was begun by Ban Biao (3 CE–54 CE) and completed by his son, Ban Gu (32–92 CE) and his daughter, Ban Zhao (35–100 CE). The text covers the history of the Han dynasty from 206 BCE to 25 CE.
3. Jean-Paul Reding (1985) *Les fondements philosophiques de la rhétorique chez les sophistes grecs et chez les sophistes chinois*, Bern: Peter Lang; cited in Graham 1989: 78.
4. This reading allows for a tighter connection between the discussions of Gongsun Long and Hui Shi as Hui Shi's conclusions may be taken to indicate the multiplicity of parts within a unified whole.

5. The latter interpretation allows us also to draw some connections with the 'Names and Actualities' chapter of the *Gongsun Longzi*, which deals with the connection between names (*ming*) and actuality (*shi*).
6. The line of argument here could also refer to the theme in the 'Hard and White' chapter that hard-ness and white-ness are separate.
7. This explanation also accounts for the concept *zhi* (pointing; designation) in the 'Pointing and Things' chapter, as *zhi* are described as universals that are manifest in actual things in space and time (Fung 1952 vol.1: 205, 211).
8. Hansen argues that 'If a name has two component terms, the compound name should preserve the relation of the names to their stuffs. Compound terms must *always* be more general (or they must be treated as something other than compound terms). All true compound terms name the sum of the stuffs named by each component term' (1983a: 159–60).
9. A synecdoche is a figure of speech in which the word for one part of a thing is used to refer to the whole thing.
10. Graham also applies the part–whole interpretive framework to his discussion of the 'Pointing and Things' chapter of the *Gongsun Longzi* (1990a: 210–5). According to him, there is some ambiguity in the term pointing (*zhi*) in that it could refer either to the act of pointing or the thing that is being pointed at. If we were to take *zhi* as a verb, we may say that to *zhi* is to point out some part of the world. Graham argues that pointing also requires a thing that is being pointed at, a thing that is part of the world. This analysis draws together the concepts of name (*ming*), pointing (*zhi*) and actuality (*shi*).
11. Graham presents a list of scholars in China, from 300 CE, who had contributed to the reconstruction of the text. The prominent thinkers include Lu Sheng (c. 300 CE) and Sun Yirang (1848–1908) (Graham 1978: 67–72).
12. We could suggest that they aimed to set up criteria for making these distinctions. However, as we will see later in the chapter, if they *did* have this aim, they were not successful in attaining it.
13. References to sections of the later Mohist text used in this chapter follow the numbering in Graham's *Later Mohist Logic, Ethics and Science* (1978).
14. Graham contends that the Mohist summa is a manual: "[t]o become a fully educated Mohist I must learn how to apply names consistently, how to choose between courses of action, how to investigate the causes of physical phenomena, how to deduce 'a priori' from the definitions of names" (Graham 1978: 31).

15. Hu Shih (1928) presents a detailed account of these criteria in the light of analogical and other inductive inferences, in his chapter on 'Induction' (pp. 99–108).
16. The insertions are made by Graham as characters and strings of characters in the extant text are illegible.
17. Graham adds, "[t]he explaining of objects which parallels the explaining of names in disputation requires phenomena with causes which are easily isolated and clearly demonstrable" (1978: 56).
18. Graham describes the later Mohist aversion to universals in this way: "The Mohist does not think in terms of a realm of universals in which each name can have its own point-by-point counterpart; he thinks of many names as fitting one mutable object, the name of what it is ('stone'), and names of what is so of it, either throughout its duration ('white') or temporarily ('big' until the stone is broken up) (NO1)" (1978: 35).

8 Zhuangzi's Philosophy

The primary themes and argumentative strategies in Zhuangzi's philosophy bear some resemblance to those in the *Daodejing*. The philosophy of Zhuangzi is expressed in a text bearing his name. However, like the *Daodejing*, sections of the *Zhuangzi* (or *Chuang-Tzu*) were composed by different authors and the compiled text contains writings collected over a period of time. In the case of the *Zhuangzi*, the fragments date from between the fourth to the second centuries BCE (Graham 2003a:58), and debate persists concerning when particular sections might have been written. Traditionally, the two texts, the *Daodejing* and *Zhuangzi*, had been grouped as texts belonging to one tradition, the *Lao-Zhuang* tradition.[1] There was also some consensus that the *Daodejing* was composed earlier than the *Zhuangzi* and, as they stand in that relation, the *Daodejing* is a less sophisticated text while the *Zhuangzi* represents a mature, developed Daoism. For example, Wing-tsit Chan notes:

> The Tao [Dao] in Lao Tzu [*Laozi*] is still wordly, whereas in Chuang Tzu [*Zhuangzi*] it becomes transcendental. While Lao Tzu emphasizes the difference between glory and disgrace, strength and weakness, and so forth, and advocates the tender values, Chuang Tzu identifies them all. Lao Tzu aims at reform, but Chuang Tzu prefers to "Travel beyond the mundane world."...It is not wrong, after all, to link Lao Tzu and Chuang Tzu together, although it must be borne in mind that he [Zhuangzi] certainly carried Taoism [Daoism] to new heights. (Chan 1963a: 178)

There are problems with this traditional classification of the texts, however. At least some sections of the *Daodejing*, especially those that deal with names (*ming*), would have been composed subsequent to the debates on the concept by key figures such as Hui Shi and Gongsun Long. The dating of the two texts impacts on how we can appropriately understand the themes in each text, on the relation between the two texts, and on how they stand in relation to the debates of that particular period. For example, Schwartz suggests that we may understand Daoism in three main, connected 'currents' (1985: 186–254). The first of these is the philosophy of *dao* and its conceptual and practical implications, based primarily on the *Daodejing*. The second, associated essentially with the *Zhuangzi* text, is characterised by the epistemological issues raised in conjunction with the Mingjia debates. The third stream focuses on the political applications of Daoist philosophy, as for instance, of *wuwei* by some of the Legalist thinkers.

There are also textual issues that affect how we read the *Zhuangzi*. The extant text comprises 33 chapters, after a major revision of the 52-chapter text by Guo Xiang (d. 312 CE). Guo Xiang deleted 19 chapters of that text on the basis that they had tenuous connections with the philosophy of Zhuangzi. He also divided the remaining chapters into 3 groups, the Inner Chapters (*neipian*), the Outer Chapters (*waipian*) and the Miscellaneous Chapters (*zapian*). Guo Xiang believed that the Inner Chapters (1–7) primarily reflected the views of Zhuangzi, while the Outer Chapters (8–22) and the Miscellaneous Chapters (23–33) were mainly written by others who were aware of Zhuangzi's discussions. In sections of these chapters, Zhuangzi himself participates in the debates. There are also references to and quotations of passages in the *Daodejing*, as well as to the figure Lao Dan, who was then believed to have been the author of the *Daodejing*; these aspects are absent in the Inner Chapters. The classification and grouping of the 33 chapters of the extant text is still a subject of debate. In 1952, the Chinese scholar Guan Feng published a seminal text suggesting further subdivisions of the chapters based on thematic and stylistic elements that featured in other doctrines of the Warring States period.[2] Following Guan Feng, Graham has published in English an authoritative rearrangement of the *Zhuangzi* based on extensive textual, stylistic and thematic study (2003a). Graham believes that the first 7 chapters of the text, being homogeneous in thought and style, are primarily written by Zhuangzi (this is also the dominant view in modern and contemporary scholarship) (2001:27). He organises the remaining 25 chapters into 4 groups:

(1) The 'School of Zhuangzi' strain (chapters 17–22) comprising sections written by others in the style of Zhuangzi. These chapters discuss the themes in the *neipian* together with other ideas that are also mentioned in the *Daodejing*. They also include stories about Zhuangzi.

(2) The Primitivist strain (chapters 8–10, parts of 11, 12 and 14), which idealises the kind of pristine simplicity expressed in certain passages of the *Daodejing*, as for example in Chapter 80. In a mood similar to that of the *Daodejing*, these sections are critical of the negative effects of conventional norms. They advocate government by non-action (*wuwei*) that helps to encourage spontaneity.
(3) The Yangist strain (chapters 28–31), which attacks worldly (political and moral) ambition because these run against the preservation of the genuine self (*bao zhen*). Yang Zhu's doctrine of nurturing life included a concern for longevity; one way to cultivate longevity was to restrict sensual stimulation. Consequently, a Yangist would never do anything to threaten the prospects of a long life. Although the Yangists, like the Confucians, believed in nurturing the self, in the case of the former, the subject of attention was the individual self. Hence, Mencius was a severe critic of Yangist doctrine. It is interesting therefore to note that in these chapters in the *Zhuangzi*, Confucius is used in the stories as the main advocate of a system that threatens the cultivation of genuineness (*zhen*).
(4) The Syncretist strain (chapters 15, 33 and parts of 11–14), which combines elements of Confucian conventional morality and Legalist administrative practice under a Daoist framework. The early Syncretists believed that government should appropriate the Way of Heaven in order that human society could properly parallel cosmic patterns. This theme was popular especially during the first half of the Han Dynasty (206 BCE–220 CE) and was subsequently dubbed the 'Huang-Lao' doctrine.[3] According to Graham, chapter 33 'Below in the Empire' discusses the different theories – *dao* – '*below* the administrative hierarchy to which it properly belongs' (2003a: 93). Zhuangzi's philosophy is assessed with the competing doctrines and Zhuangzi is criticised for his lack of attention to practical affairs. Graham speculates that this syncretic chapter might have been placed at the end of the text as its conclusion, and that this might mean that these syncretists were the compilers of the *Zhuangzi* text. (2003a: 94, 99–101; 2001: 28)

Graham does not place chapter 16 in this schema. Six other chapters (23–27, 32) contain miscellaneous sections whose badly-mutilated fragments could fit in a number of the groupings; Graham dubs them 'ragbags of odds and ends' (1989:173). Harold Roth has challenged Graham's classification of various fragments of the text on the basis of broader connections, especially between the syncretist sections and other texts of the period, such as the *Guanzi* and *Huainanzi* (Roth 1991a, 2003). Xiaogan Liu has proposed a new framework to group the *Zhuangzi* chapters; he dates the compilation of the text prior to the Qin dynasty (221–206 BCE) and suggests three strains instead of Graham's four (Liu 1994). Both Roth's and Liu's studies are significant additions to the textual studies of the *Zhuangzi*. Similar issues plague the understanding of the *neipian*, the first seven chapters of the *Zhuangzi* text.[4] Although it is not our task to consider these stylistic and textual issues in detail here, it is important to understand that there are different theories about sections of the *Zhuangzi* and that they affect how we might understand Zhuangzi's philosophy in the context of its interactions with other doctrines. As we are examining Zhuangzi's philosophy in this chapter, our primary focus will be on the *neipian* although some doctrinal cross-influences will be discussed where appropriate.

Epistemological Questions in the *Qiwu Lun*

Chapter 2 of the *Zhuangzi*, 'The Sorting which Evens Things Out' (*Qiwu Lun*), is devoted almost entirely to Zhuangzi's epistemological questions. This chapter is the most intensely philosophical and thematically coherent of all the chapters in the *neipian*. Here, Zhuangzi wonders about the basis of assertions made by competing theorists in his day.[5] He scorns the absolutist assumptions of those who promote their theories as a universal and a-historical antidote to the existing socio-political unrest. But, of course, they cannot all be correct, if each theory excludes all others. Zhuangzi evokes such tension when he considers the sparring between the Confucians and the Mohists:

> … we have the 'That's it, that's not' of Confucians and Mohists, by which what is *it* for one of them for the other is not, what is *not* for one of them for the other is. (Chapter 2, trans. Graham 2001: 52)

From Zhuangzi's point of view, the debate is doomed from the start. In a debate, the debater aims to persuade the other to see his point of view. The Mohists and Confucians are adamant that their respective views are the correct one. Their assertions of correctness assume both the objectivity and universality of their views: the Confucians believe that their solution to the unrest is the best – perhaps the only – solution, as do the Mohists of theirs. But of course they cannot both be correct. Their debate is marked by disagreement:

what is and what is not; as Zhuangzi notes, what 'is' for one of them is 'not' for the other. How might we decide which of these theories is actually the correct one? We should re-cast this question into two more specific ones: whom do we ask to adjudicate, and what criteria do we use in the adjudication of such matters? Regarding the first question, Zhuangzi belabours the problems associated with the choice of an impartial judge:

> Suppose you and I argue (*bian*). If you beat me instead of my beating you, are you really right and am I really wrong? If I beat you instead of your beating me, am I really right and are you really wrong? Or are we both partly right and partly wrong? Or are we both wholly right and wholly wrong? Since between us neither you nor I know which is right, others are naturally in the dark. Whom shall we ask to arbitrate? If we ask someone who agrees with you, since he has already agreed with you, how can he arbitrate? If we ask someone who agrees with me, since he has already agreed with me, how can he arbitrate? If we ask someone who disagrees with both you and me to arbitrate, since he has already disagreed with you and me, how can he arbitrate? If we ask someone who agrees with both you and me to arbitrate, since he has already agreed with you and me, how can he arbitrate? (Chapter 2, trans. Chan 1963a: 189–90)

Zhuangzi is not just saying that an impartial judge is a rare find. In fact, he is sceptical about whether such a person exists. His ruminations are sceptical about the *expectation of impartiality* in arbitration. In other words, Zhuangzi reckons that there is no such position as the 'view from nowhere', the angelic view or the God's-eye perspective. He even denounces the all-encompassing 'bird's-eye view' in chapter 1, 'Going Rambling without a Destination' (*Xiaoyao You*). Zhuangzi sets up a striking contrast between a cicada and a dove, on the one hand, and a giant bird, Peng, on the other. The cicada and the little dove laugh at Peng because the giant bird's dimensions and capabilities are incomprehensible to them:

> The cicada and the little dove laugh at this, saying, "When we make an effort and fly up, we can get as far as the elm or the sapanwood tree, but sometimes we don't make it and just fall down on the ground. Now how is anyone going to go ninety thousand *li* to the south!" (Chapter 1, trans. Watson 1964: 24)

Are these little creatures not trivial in their lack of understanding? There is some self-awareness in their caricature of their limitations. But their awareness of the world around them is constrained by their inability to conceive of possibilities beyond the experiences of the self. Does Zhuangzi consider the doctrines of the other thinkers trivial and limited, like those of the cicada and dove? Is he advocating the perspective of Peng?

> "When the P'eng [Peng] journeys to the southern darkness, the waters are roiled for three thousand *li*. He beats the whirlwind and rises ninety thousand *li*, setting off on the sixth month gale." Wavering heat, bits of dust, living things blowing each other about – the sky looks very blue. Is that its real color, or is it because it is so far away and has no end? When the bird looks down, all he sees is blue too...If wind is not piled up deep enough, it won't have the strength to bear up great wings. Therefore when the P'eng rises ninety thousand *li*, he must have the wind under him like that. Only then can he mount on the back of the wind, shoulder the blue sky, and nothing can hinder or block him. (trans. Watson 1964: 23–24)

The giant bird may be large and impressive, and the cicada and dove trivially small, in comparison. But Peng is capable only of a broad view and is unable to discern finer detail. It, too, has only a partial perspective. It likewise suffers from physical limitations: while the small creatures cannot fly far, the giant bird cannot take flight unless the wind conditions are sufficiently strong to carry it. There is neither a privileged observer nor an ideal adjudicator; Zhuangzi is sceptical about the ability of individuals to adopt value-free perspectives. Or, in other words, there are *no* value-free perspectives. Here, Zhuangzi launches a meta-philosophical attack on the expectations associated with disputation (*bian*). In fact, the question of *how* to select the 'correct' theory is misdirected. This is due partly to epistemological complications associated with the selection of an impartial judge. There are also concerns about the abundant richness and diversity of the world and how criteria for adjudication (this relates to the second question posed above) might fail to reflect such diversity. Wang Ni the sceptic evokes a sense of helplessness when we are confronted by the plurality in the world:

> When a human sleeps in the damp his waist hurts and he gets stiff in the joints; is that so of the loach? When he sits in a tree he shivers and shakes; is that so of the ape? Which of these three knows the right place to live? Humans eat the flesh of hay-fed and grain-fed beasts, deer eat the grass, centipedes relish snakes, owls and crows crave mice; which of the four has a proper sense of taste? (Chapter 2, trans. Graham 2001: 58)

Wang Ni's response seems to have been instigated by extreme sceptical doubt: 'How do I know that what I call knowing is not ignorance? How do I know that what I call ignorance is not knowing?' (*ibid.*). At the heart of these analogies is the answer to the question about how we might select the correct theory: there is no 'correct' theory. From this point of view, we sense with Zhuangzi the historicity and circumstantial nature of the competing ideologies. This passage about the different measures of matters both weighty (well-being) and trivial (taste) is not merely about epistemological difficulties in the face of a plural and diverse world. It is also in part a concern about language and its relation to reality, an issue that was a major preoccupation of the later Mohist thinkers and those who debated with them. If we attend to Wang Ni's rhetorical question, we will notice that it is not merely a question about the content of knowledge but really one of language and naming: how do I know that what I *call* (*wei*) knowing is not ignorance? Following his examples of the baffling plurality in the world, Wang Ni turns his attention specifically to the later Mohist project of distinguishing *shi-fei*:

> In my judgment the principles of Goodwill and Duty, the paths of "That's it [*shi*], that's not [*fei*]", are inextricably confused; how could I know how to discriminate [*bian*] between them? (*ibid.*)

The language of the paragraph is familiar, as we have seen, in the Mingjia and later Mohist debates. This may be understood as a direct response to a view resembling that of Gongsun Long's. Gongsun Long subscribed to a theory of one-to-one correspondence between names and reality. Wang Ni demonstrates the simplistic nature of this view. It is likely that Zhuangzi has included Wang Ni's deliberations because he agrees with them at some level. Zhuangzi himself addresses these concerns in Chapter 2:

> Saying is not blowing breath, saying says something; the only trouble is that what it says is never fixed. Do we really say something? Or have we never said anything? If you think it different from the twitter of fledglings, is there proof of the distinction [*bian*]? Or isn't there any proof? . . . By what is saying darkened, that sometimes 'That's it' and sometimes 'That's not' [*shi-fei*]? . . . Whatever the standpoint how can saying be unallowable [*buke*]? (Graham 2001: 52)

Zhuangzi's comparison of speech and the twittering of birds is not mere sophistry; he grants that words mean *something*, but he also has a problem with the assumption regarding the fundamental nature of language. One problem relates to the supposition that language is somehow connected with reality, perhaps on the basis of one-to-one correspondence; we see this for instance in the Confucian programme, especially in Confucius' theory of names (*zhengming*) wherein he advocated that a person's commitment and behaviour must accord with his title (*ming*). To reiterate, such one-to-one correspondence oversimplifies the diversity in the world. It can also mask the issue of how these normative (Confucian) standards might be justified. Secondly, Zhuangzi disagrees with the approach taken by some of the Mingjia thinkers that resort to examination of terms in order to resolve disagreements. This approach assumes some combination of assumptions including that the meanings of names are objective, that they have a fixed relation with the world, and that a more accurate understanding of them will settle disagreements.[6]

There are a number of ways in which Zhuangzi can plausibly respond to this assumption about language. We see a combination of these in the *Zhuangzi*. Hence, they are not mutually exclusive. One approach is to emphasise the diversity in the world, as we see in Wang Ni's description of the different standards for different (types of) individuals. This poses a problem for naming: does language adequately capture the complexity and diversity in the world? This query is also raised in the *Daodejing* (in *Daodejing* 1 and 5, for example). The question about the adequacy of language instigates more fundamental questions about language itself: will clarification of terms *really* provide us with a more accurate or 'truer' picture of reality, and does the clarification – the process of distinguishing (*bian*) – also have sufficient persuasive power to change the views of the debaters? While Zhuangzi himself may not have posed these questions, especially the latter one, it is important to note that these are some questions that arise from an understanding of the Zhuangzi–Mingjia debate.

There is another, related but different, problem associated with the view that names are objective. This response does not venture into ontological questions (about things that exist and the diversity in the world). It is a more direct attack against the assumption of objectivity; it highlights the arbitrariness of the naming process:

> When [people say], "All right," then [things are] all right. When [people say], "Not all right," then [things are] not all right. A road becomes so when people

> walk on it, and things become so-and-so [to people] because people call them so-and-so. How have they become so? They have become so because [people say they are] so. How have they become not so? They have become not so because [people say they are] not so. (Chapter 2, trans. Chan 1963a: 183–4; bracketed phrases inserted by translator)

This passage emphasises the arbitrariness and conventionality of language, a theme that is also prominent in the philosophy of the *Daodejing*. We should also note, from the discussion in the previous chapter, that the terms 'all right' (*ke*) and 'so' (*ran*) are primary concepts in the later Mohist debates: language is meaningful insofar as it captures what is so (*ran*), asserts what is possible (*ke*), and affirms what is the case (*shi*). But these moves attribute far too much objectivity and absoluteness to language. Graham lucidly poses the problem for the later Mohists, as Zhuangzi might see it: 'How can I prove that language is meaningful without using it on the assumption that it is?' (Graham 1989: 200).

A third kind of response evokes plurality of perspectives, as we have seen, in the story of Peng the giant bird and the cicada and dove. Unlike the first kind of response, this third one is not necessarily committed to plurality in the world. While the first is primarily an ontological issue, this is an epistemological issue: its main thrust is that there are different ways of understanding situations and events. From Zhuangzi's point of view, the main reason for such variations is that individuals bring their experiences to bear on their interpretation of events. Imagery of limited perspectives abound in the *Zhuangzi*: the summer cicada or summer insect who does not understand spring or autumn (Chapters 1, 17), the frog in the well whose perspective is cramped by his dwelling-place (Chapter 17), and the giant turtle who had great difficulty trying to fit just one leg into the well (Chapter 17). In all of these examples, characters are limited by their physical conditions and environments. In *Zhuangzi* 17, the limited perspectives of the well-frog and the summer insect represent the narrowness of the views of the debating thinkers:

> You can't discuss the ocean with a well frog – he's limited by the space he lives in. You can't discuss ice with a summer insect – he's bound to a single season. You can't discuss the Way with a cramped scholar – he's shackled by his doctrines. (trans. Watson 1964: 97)

Can we expect agreement among 'cramped scholars'? Disputation about the assertable or not (*ke–buke*), or whether a thing is 'this' or 'not-this' (*shi–fei*) will not resolve disagreements. One gets a sense from Zhuangzi's allegories that each perspective is a 'lodged' perspective; in other words, each individual can only understand the world from within his or her place. According to Graham, Zhuangzi's argument is in effect a method of disputation; Graham calls this 'saying from a lodging place'.[7] To 'say from a lodging place' is to present a view from one's standpoint. In order to understand such a 'saying', a person needs to lodge him or herself in the perspective of the person who proclaims it. In the language of argumentation, we could say that 'saying from a lodging place' is an *ad hominem* argument. In an extreme formulation of this perspectivalist argument, Zhuangzi contends that all views are ultimately indexical:

> There is nothing that is not the "that" and there is nothing that is not the "this." Things do not know that they are the "that" of other things; they only know what they themselves know. (*Zhuangzi* 2, trans. Chan 1963a: 182)

Zhuangzi uses the indexical term 'that' (*bi*) to denote what is external to the self. From an individual's perspective, which is the 'this'-perspective (*shi*), everything else is 'that'. But, of course, no one individual is universally or permanently a 'this' or a 'that' or an 'I' or a 'you'. My 'this' is your 'that', and vice versa. If we follow the reasoning of Zhuangzi's indexicality of perspectives, all claims have an *ad hominem* characteristic; they are ultimately reflections of the self. Indexicality confounds the assumption regarding the objectivity of language. Elsewhere in the *Zhuangzi* (in chapter 23, one that Graham reckons has mixed themes), the indexicality of perspectives is explained with impressive clarity:

> A 'That's it' which deems picks out by a reference *it* as it shifts. Let's see what happens now when you speak about *it* as it shifts. This is to take 'life' as the root of you and the wits as your authority, and use them to go by in charioteering 'That's it, that's not'. They really exist for you, names and substances, and using them to go by you make yourself into a hostage. (trans. Graham 2001: 104)

Does Zhuangzi hold that all assertions by their very nature are *ad hominem*? Or are perspectivally bound arguments only one type of argument, to be contrasted with statements of fact, so to speak? Even if it is the case that only a portion of assertions are perspectivally conditioned, how do we distinguish them, and how might we assess their validity? If Zhuangzi holds that there are many perspectives, and that each perspective can only be assessed in its own reference frame, is he committed to relativism? We will not be able to answer all the questions here, and this is because Zhuangzi rarely presents his conclusions in the affirmative. But an examination of scholarly debate on Zhuangzi's philosophy will illuminate some of these issues to some extent.

Interpretations of Zhuangzi's Scepticism

Where does Zhuangzi's scepticism lead us? Is he a relativist? We will need to consider Zhuangzi's responses to Hui Shi in order to understand Zhuangzi's views. As we have seen in the previous chapter, Hui Shi had acquired a reputation for sophistry as he entertained difficult paradoxes such as 'Heaven is as low as the earth; mountains and marshes are on the same level' (Chan 1963a: 233–4). *Zhuangzi* 33, the syncretist conclusion to the text, notes that Hui Shi had a reputation only for disputation and that he 'chas[ed] the myriad things' (trans. Graham 2001: 295). Many of Hui Shi's paradoxes are relativist in tone. How did Zhuangzi respond to Hui Shi?[8] According to a story in the *Zhuangzi*, when Zhuangzi went past the grave of Hui Shi, he noted the loss of Hui Shi as the loss of a partner in a two-person act: 'Since the Master [Hui Shi] died, I have had no one to use as a partner, no one with whom to talk about things' (*Zhuangzi* 24, trans. Graham 2001: 124). Zhuangzi considered Hui Shi an unparalleled partner, but we need to ask more about the nature of their philosophical affinities. In this regard, a number of scholars have focused on a conversation between Hui Shi and Zhuangzi in *Zhuangzi* 17:

> Chuang Tzu [Zhuangzi] and Hui Tzu [Huizi] were strolling along the dam of the Hao River when Chuang Tzu said, "See how the minnows come out and dart around where they please! That's what fish really enjoy!"
> Hui Tzu said, "You're not a fish – how do you know what fish enjoy?"
> Chuang Tzu said, "You're not I, so how do you know I don't know what fish enjoy?"
> Hui Tzu said, "I'm not you, so I certainly don't know what you know. On the other hand, you're certainly not a fish – so that still proves you don't know what fish enjoy!"

> Chuang Tzu said, "Let's go back to your original question, please. You asked me how I know what fish enjoy – so you already knew I knew it when you asked the question. I know it by standing here beside the Hao." (trans. Watson 1964: 110)

Zhuangzi seems to have had the final say in this debate. But their playful responses to each other gesture toward more profound debate, which scholars have interpreted in various ways. The interpretations include:

(1) Zhuangzi is merely an inept logician who fails to grasp Hui Shi's questions; their interchange marks a futile dialogue between Zhuangzi the mystic and Hui Shi the logician.[9]
(2) Hui Shi is only an accessory to Zhuangzi in this story. The primary aim of it is to demonstrate Zhuangzi's deep wisdom about the experiential, participatory nature of knowledge (Ames 1998b)[10]. An account like this would focus on the idea of knowing-how (*How* does Zhuangzi know that the fish is happy?) rather than on knowing-that (whether the truth-conditions of his claim have been satisfied).
(3) Zhuangzi and Hui Shi both recognise the subjectivity of perspectives. Their argument demonstrates Hui Shi's flawed logic: if he is sceptical about Zhuangzi's claim about fish-happiness, then, according to the same principle of subjectivity of perspectives, Hui Shi cannot himself make claims about Zhuangzi's proclaimed knowledge of fish-happiness. (Hansen 2003)
(4) The dialogue may be understood as a brilliant example of analogical reasoning discussed especially by the later Mohists. (Teng 2006)

These interpretations of the interchange between Zhuangzi and Hui Shi provide us with a deeper understanding of Zhuangzi's philosophy. In his questions to Zhuangzi, Hui Shi implies that experiences are subjective and therefore Zhuangzi does not have access to that particular fish's happiness, and to fish-happiness in general. This conversation can be seen as an extension of Hui Shi's ten paradoxes that express his relativist position. Does Zhuangzi *add* anything to Hui Shi's relativistic view? Perhaps they share a preoccupation with the assortment that the world presents to them. Perhaps, while Hui Shi focuses on the relative nature of terms of comparison, for instance that there is nothing that is absolutely big or little, Zhuangzi gives a reason for relativist comparisons; he suggests that they might be due to variations across perspectives. Hansen's account of the happy fish dialogue is an influential one that understands the dialogue in terms of the different perspectives, of the fish, Zhuangzi and Hui Shi. All these perspectives are individual perspectives and the assertion that Zhuangzi *cannot* know the happiness of the fish effectively contradicts itself because it also asserts that the person making the judgement *can* know what Zhuangzi can or cannot know.

Hansen's interpretation of the happy fish dialogue is an extension of his broader thesis about Zhuangzi's philosophy, that it endorses a multiplicity of perspectives and, in doing so, advocates 'perspectival relativism' (1983b). According to this view, it would be inconsistent for Zhuangzi at the same time to assert that his perspective is the only *legitimate* one: 'Zhuangzi's metaperspective does not lead to nonperspectival knowledge of things. It is not a window on the thing in itself, but on the bewildering range of possibilities' (Hansen 1992: 284–5).[11] The view that Zhuangzi is a relativist is plausible, given that Zhuangzi often begins his inquiry by casting doubt on a particular position, in the form of a rhetorical question: 'Is there any difference?' He then proceeds to detach himself from the debate by presenting the opposite position: 'Or is there no difference?' These questions evoke an aura of non-judgemental detachment that is a characteristic of relativist positions.[12] On the other hand, we should note that the *Zhuangzi neipian* does positively affirm models of knowledge that are more intuitive, such as Cook Ding's butchering skills (*Zhuangzi* 3). Philip Ivanhoe argues persuasively that the characters in the *Zhuangzi*, including Cook Ding and his masterful dexterity, Woodcarver Qing who carves marvellous bell stands, and Wheelwright Bian who 'shapes wheels with an ineffable skill' are Zhuangzi's positive visions of the Way (1993: 643). He notes, 'In his examples of skilful individuals, Zhuangzi completely abandons the perspectivist argument and reveals the foundation of his normative vision' (*ibid.*: 652).

Zhuangzi's questions have a sceptical tone. But it is important to look into the extent of his doubt. Lisa Raphals argues that Zhuangzi in *Qiwu Lun* uses sceptical methods in his argumentation, but that does not imply a denial of knowledge (Raphals 1996). Clearly, Zhuangzi was sceptical about the objectivity of names. In this sense, he is sceptical about meaning, language and its connection with the world (see Ivanhoe 1993). In that same vein, we could argue that he was an epistemological sceptic as he seriously doubted the approach of the Mingjia thinkers to resolve disagreements by disputation (*bian*).

He did not doubt that *all* knowledge was dubitable but rather that some assumptions about it and some particular ways of pursuing it were wrong. He was not a radical sceptic about language as he also recognised its practical importance:

> A road becomes so when people walk on it, and things become so-and-so [to people] because people call them so-and-so. How have they become so? They have become so because [people say they are] so. How have they become not so? They have become not so because [people say they are] not so. (*Zhuangzi* 2; trans. Chan, 1963a: 183–4)

Does Zhuangzi have any views about reality or truth? In our discussion of the philosophy of the *Daodejing*, we have seen that one dominant understanding of *dao* characterises it in terms of a metaphysical concept, as a deeper, underlying primordial reality. Do the *neipian* chapters share this conception of reality? This is a difficult question to answer in relation to Zhuangzi's philosophy because there are few, if any, statements or suggestions to this effect in Zhuangzi's deliberations. Schwartz suggests that the question that underpins Zhuangzi's scepticism is actually an ontological one about the place of humanity within the ten thousand things: what is the 'reality of individual entities' in the face of plurality? (Schwartz 1985: 222).[13] However, if we follow Hansen's line of reasoning, we have to conclude that Zhuangzi *cannot* commit himself to a monistic conception of reality. This makes Zhuangzi a metaphysical sceptic of a particular kind as he holds that there are many perspectives which are equally *valid* rather than *true*: the perspectives of the cicada, the dove and the giant bird, as well as those of the well-frog and the sea-turtle, are equally valid. To express this in contemporary philosophical terms, the validity-conditions for each perspective vary according to a number of factors – perhaps too many to list exhaustively – that shape the perspective. In brief, if we accept Hansen's account of Zhuangzi as a perspectival relativist, we cannot also consistently submit that Zhuangzi advocated a single conception of *dao* as the true or absolute reality (Hansen 1992: 285–92). Zhuangzi must, in other words, be sceptical about a monistic conception of reality.

This leaves us with a final, important type of scepticism, namely ethical scepticism. There is agreement among scholars that Zhuangzi is not an ethical sceptic. This is very clearly the case for those who believe that Zhuangzi upholds the illuminated, intuitive method of the *zhenren*, the cultivated genuine person (see, for instance, Yearley 1996, Roth 1999). The conception of the *zhenren* incorporates important ethical, religious, political, social and psychological qualities. From a different perspective, though also concluding that Zhuangzi is not an ethical sceptic, Graham argues that Zhuangzi has 'no vertigo' in his scepticism (1989: 186). *We* might worry about ethical scepticism because we believe choices must be made, but 'there is anguish in ethical scepticism only if one feels bound to choose without having grounds to choose' (*ibid.*). This may sound implausible – for, of course, choice is a fundamental criterion of moral action – until we realise that Graham is pointing us toward spontaneity in Daoist ethical discourse. In conventional terms, when we make ethical decisions, we *choose*, insofar as we can, to exemplify moral qualities such as honesty, sincerity and compassion. But Zhuangzi's fishermen, cooks, carpenters and suchlike *respond spontaneously and are not constrained by conventional standards of right and wrong*. If Zhuangzi is an ethical sceptic at all, he is sceptical about conventional ethical norms, their corresponding practices and their implementation in human society. In the next section, we move on to examine aspects of the Daoist cultivated person who embodies intuitive skills – knacks – in responding spontaneously.

Cultivating Knack

Chapter Three of the extant *Zhuangzi* text opens with an ominous warning about the limiting nature of conventional knowledge:

> My life flows between confines, but knowledge has no confines. If we use the confined to follow after the unconfined, there is danger that the flow will cease; and when it ceases, to exercise knowledge is purest danger. (trans. Graham 2001: 62)

Conventional knowledge restricts a more genuine 'flow' of life and may even cause its demise. This is a brief chapter – much of it mutilated – concerning 'What Matters in the Nurture of Life' (*Yangshen Zhu*: trans. Graham 2001: 62). As indicated in its opening paragraph, its focus is on shedding conventional norms as they interfere with the proper development of the self. In this regard, it shares the concern of some of the passages in the *Daodejing* regarding language and conventionality (for example, *Daodejing* 2, 12). However, the *Zhuangzi* also advocates a 'nurture of life' theme that is absent in the *Daodejing*. In the *Zhuangzi*, the reason for undoing layers of conventional and cultural conditioning is that they are a hindrance to a more spontaneous and seemingly intuitive expressions of the self; these hindrances threaten the genuine self. These strands of thought resemble those in Yang Zhu's philosophy, and we get a flavour of the latter in the Yangist chapters of the *Zhuangzi* text (chapters 28–31). Yet, where Zhuangzi's philosophy is distinctive is in its depiction of a knack, a know-how in living one's life to the fullest. The focal point of *Zhuangzi* 3 is an analogy of butchering that sheds light on how to nurture such a knack in one's life:

> "A good cook changes his knife once a year – because he cuts. A mediocre cook changes his knife once a month – because he hacks. I've had this knife of mine for nineteen years and I've cut up thousands of oxen with it, and yet the blade is as good as though it had just come from the grindstone. There are spaces between the joints, and the blade of the knife has really no thickness. If you insert what has no thickness into such spaces, then there's plenty of room – more than enough for the blade to play about it. That's why after nineteen years the blade of my knife is still as good as when it first came from the grindstone."
>
> "However, whenever I come to a complicated place, I size up the difficulties, tell myself to watch out and be careful, keep my eyes on what I'm doing, work very slowly, and move the knife with the greatest subtlety, until – flop! the whole thing comes apart like a clod of earth crumbling to the ground. I stand there holding the knife and look all around me, completely satisfied and reluctant to move on, and then I wipe off the knife and put it away." (trans. Watson 1964: 47)

Cook Ding demonstrates a cultivated skill in butchering that is developed, refined and manifest in and through the activity. How fortunate one would be, if he or she had Cook Ding's knack in dealing with situations in life! The choice of butchering as an example of a knack is interesting. Clearly, the knack is very different from the deep wisdoms and intelligence required to rule the nation or to advise the ruler, or to engage in disputes about the best form of government. Perhaps Zhuangzi is attempting to establish a model of (ordinary) life quite distinct from that of political life. But this is where the Yangists and the Syncretists part company. Among the Yangists, there is much debate about whether the cultivated person should engage in political life; but even if they can be interpreted to be advocating political involvement, they held a deep distrust of then-existing ideologies and infrastructure. The Syncretists, on the other hand, not only saw political involvement as a necessary corollary of the cultivated life, they believed that cultivation of the self was a process that culminated in the development of skills and strategies for ruling the people. It is important to understand this fundamental distinction between the two ideologies when reading and interpreting sections of the *Zhuangzi*.

The Cook Ding analogy is the only one about knack in the 'Inner Chapters' of the *Zhuangzi*. Elsewhere in the text, and especially in the Yangist chapter 19, there are many other such examples: the ineffable skill of the wheelwright (chapter 13 – sections of which are Syncretist), the experienced ferryman (chapter 19), the hunchback cicada catcher (chapter 19), and the wood carver and his marvellous bell stands (chapter 19). All these similes overturn conventional images of learned wisdom and power. This intended contrast is explicitly stated in the case of the wheelwright; he questions the status of ancient wisdoms articulated in a book which Duke Huan is reading. The wheelwright, Bian,[14] argues that knack cannot be taught – he failed to teach his skills to his son – and therefore is sceptical that insights can be gained from reading a book. The wheelwright says:

> If I chip at a wheel too slowly, the chisel slides and does not grip; if too fast, it jams and catches in the wood. Not too slow, not too fast; I feel it in the hand and respond from the heart, the mouth cannot put it into words, there is a knack in it somewhere which I cannot convey to my son and which my son cannot learn from me. This is how through my seventy years I have grown old chipping at wheels. The men of old and their untransmittable message are dead. Then what my lord is reading is the dregs of the men of old, isn't it? (trans. Graham 2001: 140)

There is another passage in the 'Inner Chapters' that deals with the inexpressibility of skill in terms of 'words'. In Chapter 6, 'The Teacher who is the Ultimate Ancestor' (trans. Graham 2001: 84–93), a distinction is drawn between understanding the Way (*dao*) and having the ability (*cai*) of a sage; both are necessary for sagehood. Our discussion thus far identifies two aspects of the contrast between conventional knowledge and knack. First, knack is personal, experiential and (therefore) incommunicable, unlike convention, which is shared. Perhaps there is some connection between this idea and the opening stanza of the *Daodejing*, 'the *dao* that can be communicated is not a lasting *dao*' (translation mine). This issue also highlights the doctrinal differences between the Daoists and the Mingjia thinkers. That which *can* be communicated in words – *ming* (names) – cannot be *other than* conventional.

Language is an integral feature of human civilisation; it establishes and propagates dominant attitudes and beliefs. Hence, from Zhuangzi's point of view, the Mingjia thinkers would have seemed particularly naïve to believe that an altercation about names is the fundamental cause of disagreement; there is much that cannot be said.

The second important contrast between conventional knowledge and knack is that the former may inhibit the expression of knack, which is a spontaneous expression of the self. But *what* exactly is spontaneous? Is it inherent human nature (*xing*), or, more specifically, the mind–heart (*xin*)? Zhuangzi in fact makes no references to human nature. He is also suspicious of *xin* due to its exaggerated role in the moral discourse of the time. In 'Essay on Seeing Things as Equal', Zhuangzi expresses incredulity at the suggestion that the heart is the seat of judgements of right and wrong (*shi–fei*):

> Of the hundred joints, nine openings, six viscera all present and complete, which should I recognise as more kin to me than another? Are you people pleased with them all? Rather, you have a favourite organ among them . . . If you go by the completed heart and take it as your authority, who is without such authority? Why should it be only the man who knows how things alternate and whose heart approves its own judgments who has such an authority? The fool has one just as he has. For there to be 'That's it, that's not' before they are formed in the heart would be to 'go to Yüeh [Yue] today and have arrived yesterday'. (trans. Graham 2001: 51)

Zhuangzi launches an argument against those who propose that the mind–heart is the organ which has an inherent capacity for moral discrimination; those who hold such a view include Mencius and Xunzi.[15] The empirical evidence shows otherwise, argues Zhuangzi, as the fool, characterised as one who cannot make such distinctions, also has a mind–heart. The Confucians could of course retort that the fool may have a mind–heart, but has failed to apply or cultivate it. But Zhuangzi's more fundamental point is this: there is no inherent intuitive capacity for decision-making and to assume that there is one – and to *appoint* one – serves only to obscure a more genuine way of life:

> The human heart/mind . . . has the fatal capacity to arrogate to itself the attributes of a fully closed off, fully individualized entity, "the fully completed or individualized heart" (*ch'eng xin*) [*cheng xin*], which by a kind of self-encapsulation is able to establish a self-being of its own cut off from the flow of the *tao*. (Schwartz 1985: 229)

We are left to wonder whether Zhuangzi intends to replace *xin*, the mind–heart, with *dao*.[16] *Dao* is elemental in humanity; for Zhuangzi, feelings (*qing*), rather than knowledge, are expressions of *dao*. 'Joy, anger, grief, delight, worry, regret, fickleness, inflexibility, modesty, willfulness, candor, insolence' (*Zhuangzi* 2; trans. Watson 1964: 32–3). The imagery of these primal feelings is delightfully described in this passage: they are like 'vapour condensing into mushrooms' (trans. Graham 2001: 50). As with the philosophy of the *Daodejing*, we sense here a return to the more basic, pre-civilised and untrained expressions of humanity. The *Zhuangzi* associates the mind–heart with the negative effects of civilisation and therefore advocates the 'fasting the mind–heart'. In *Zhuangzi* 4, Confucius (who in the *Zhuangzi* text is used ironically as a representative of Daoist thought) teaches his disciple Yan Hui how to 'fast his mind–heart'. The first step is to replace listening with ears to listening with his mind–heart. But listening with the mind–heart must in turn be replaced by listening with *qi* ('energies', Graham 2001: 68; 'spirit', Watson 1964: 54).[17] Benjamin Schwartz suggests that for Zhuangzi, *qi* is a 'mystical reality which serves... to connect the world of the manifold, determinate, and discrete to the world of nonbeing' (1985: 218). He also notes that this might have connections with meditation techniques. In view of this comment, we should note that many of the characters in the *Zhuangzi* who have a 'knack' or skill are people who 'forget'. There is a famous image in *Zhuangzi* 6, 'The Teacher who is the Ultimate Ancestor', in which Yan Hui has made such significant progress in 'sitting and forgetting' (*zuowang*) that Confucius begs Yan Hui to take him as his disciple. We can plausibly assume that what these paradigmatic Zhuangzian figures forget is their socio-cultural conditioning – hence they need to 'fast' their mind–heart. What needs to be forgotten is the culture of isolating favourites, of preferential treatment. It engenders trivial inconsistencies and pursuits. The forgetting person, who in *Zhuangzi* 19 is likened to a drunken man[18] – stands in contrast to one who is completely submerged in the norms of the day.[19] Zhuangzi describes the tragic 'hero' of such a culture:

> Sometimes clashing with things, sometimes bending before them, he runs his course like a galloping steed, and nothing can stop him. Is he not pathetic? Sweating and labouring to the end of his days and never seeing his accomplishment, utterly exhausting himself and never knowing where to look for rest – can you help pitying him?... Man's life has always been a muddle like this. (*Zhuangzi* 2; trans. Watson 1964: 33)

The liberation from the need to pursue the goals set up by one's cultural tradition must be energising. Zhuangzi contrasts the moods of great knowledge (*dazhi*) and small knowledge (*xiaozhi*): 'Great understanding is broad and unhurried; little understanding is cramped and busy. Great words are clear and limpid; little words are shrill and quarrelsome' (*Zhuangzi* 3; trans. Watson 1964: 32). Small understanding is limited and restrictive, and preoccupied with trivialities. According to Ivanhoe, Zhuangzi's philosophy of 'perspectivism' enables people to 'free themselves from the grip of tradition and the rational mind' (1993: 646) in order to 'perceive and accord with an ethical scheme inherent in the world' (*ibid.*: 646–7). Presumably, the 'ethical scheme inherent in the world' is different from 'tradition'. What is important in Ivanhoe's interpretation is the spirituality of Zhuangzian liberation (*ibid.*: 646). *Zhuangzi* 6, 'The Teacher who is the Ultimate Ancestor', (trans. Graham 2001: 84–93) describes the characteristics and depth of the daemonic 'true man' (*zhenren*). The spiritual or religious implications of Zhuangzi's philosophy are affirmed by a number of other scholars. Raphals draws on terminology such as 'illumination' and 'awakening' to describe Zhuangzi's 'great knowledge' (1996: 30); Schwartz describes Zhuangzi's philosophy as 'mystic gnosis' at a few points in his analysis (1985: 215–237);[20] Allinson presents a translation of the *Zhuangzi* 'Inner Chapters' according to his thesis that Zhuangzi's philosophy engenders spiritual transformation (1989); Yearley describes the activity and life of the daemonic person in terms of a spiritual state that engages with, yet transcends, many aspects of this-worldly life, including morality (1996); Slingerland understands *wuwei* at the fundamental level as a religious concept (2000);[21] and Roth argues that Zhuangzi recommends a deep mystical tranquillity through meditative contemplation (1999).[22]

We must consider whether spiritual enlightenment for Zhuangzi is an individual pursuit that may involve reclusive detachment from affairs in the world. Zhuangzi's philosophy has been characterised as individualistic for a number of reasons: the distinctive perspectives of different individuals, the subjective, individualised grasp of a knack, and the cultivation of 'great understanding'. It is true that, in the final analysis, each individual must acquire this knack, and transcend 'little understanding', by himself or herself. However, we must emphasise that the aim of Zhuangzi's liberation entails freedom not from life in the world but from its conventions and ideologies. Slingerland argues that this conception of freedom is not about the establishment of individual governance or interests. He notes that 'Whereas spontaneity in the West is typically associated with subjectivity, the opposite may be said of the sort of spontaneity evinced in wu-wei: it represents the highest degree of objectivity, for it is only in wu-wei that one's embodied mind conforms to the something larger than the individual – the will of Heaven or the order represented by the Way' (2000: 311).[23] For Slingerland, Zhuangzi's *wuwei* is a spiritual ideal especially because it promotes harmonisation with the objective, normative order of the cosmos.

We may also justify spiritual transformation as a wider, more inclusive process in terms of the concept *qi*. We have seen previously that Zhuangzi in chapter 4 advocates fasting of the heart–mind in order to abide by *qi*. The concept *qi* occurs in other texts of the Warring States period, especially in the *Guanzi*, a composite text compiled over a period of time, although it takes its name from the Legalist Guan Zhong (683–642 BCE). The 'Inward Training' (*neiye*) chapter of the *Guanzi* deals extensively with the cultivation of *qi*.[24] Graham suggests that its conception of nurturing *qi*, which includes meditation techniques, attention to posture and moderation in diet, is similar to that held by Mencius who also refers to nurturing the 'flood-like' *qi* (*Mencius* 2A:2; in Graham 1989: 100). Graham describes the notion of *qi* in this period as an all-encompassing and unifying 'energetic fluid' (1989: 101). *Qi* vitalises the body, in particular the breath, and circulates outside the body as air; its meaning is similar to "Greek *pneuma* 'wind, air, breath'" (*ibid.*). An interesting development relating to the concept of *qi* was the evolution of the term *shen* (previously denoting a 'spirit' being) as a characteristic that could be manifest in the human sphere. In other words, *shen* was used to refer to the attribute of a particular being or act, rather than to spirit beings. In this sense, *shen* is the daemonic insight that inspires 'numinous awe' (*ibid.*). Such insight involves knowing how to get rid of the shackles which restrict the spontaneous flow of *qi* between the individual and the broader cosmic order. We find a good example of this in *Zhuangzi* 19, a Yangist chapter, in the woodcarver's description of his knack:

> Engraver Ch'ing [Qing] chipped wood to make a bellstand. When the bellstand was finished viewers were amazed, as though it were daemonic, ghostly . . . [The engraver explains his secret:] 'The dexterity for [making the bellstand] concentrates, outside distractions melt away, and only then do I go into the mountain forest and observe the nature of the wood as Heaven makes it grow. The aptitude of the body attains its peak; and only then do I have a complete vision of the bellstand, only then do I put my hand to it. Otherwise I give the

whole thing up. So I join what is Heaven's to what is Heaven's. Would this be the reason why the instrument seems daemonic?' (trans. Graham 2001: 135)

Does a person who has gained such daemonic insight have any lingering interest in the mundane world? The question concerning the involvement of the cultivated person in the affairs of the world was already a lively point of debate during this period. We are concerned here with two connected but different questions; the first relates to general engagement with the world, the second is more specific and deals with involvement with the political affairs of the state. Regarding the first question, we can safely say that Zhuangzi does not advocate *dis*-engagement from the world. The metaphors and examples used throughout the text in fact reveal a deep awareness of the natural world that is obscured or neglected when one is travelling within the safe boundaries set by society and convention. The examples of knack draw from ordinary vocations and actions that sustain and establish life in the world: butchering, swimming, carpentry, fishing and the like. These exemplars are not settled in transcendent awareness, merely going through the motions of men who live in the world; they are *experts* at these activities and engaging with the world in all its imperfections (Schwartz 1985: 235). Where they differ is in their indifference to the vicissitudes of life, and even to death (*Zhuangzi* 7). Such adaptability sustains the individual through different conditions and circumstances and is therefore primarily conceived of in terms of knack: "The Taoist art of living is a supremely intelligent responsiveness which would be undermined by analysing and choosing, and…grasping the Way is an unverbalisable 'knowing how' rather than 'knowing that'" (Graham 2001: 186). Roger Ames draws on the concept *shi* (situation, momentum, manipulation) to express how Zhuangzi's freedom involves unlearning distinctions in order to function efficaciously in different circumstances (1998b: 227). This brings to mind Zhuangzi's rejection of Confucian and Mohist ideology. Zhuangzi rejects them not because they are not at all applicable in any situation but because the Confucians and Mohists assumed that they were universally true or correct and applicable in *every* situation. We could say that, from Zhuangzi's perspective, the Confucians and Mohists were unwilling to adapt their ideologies and perhaps also unable to cultivate a knack for spontaneously adapting them to different circumstances.

The scholar Kuang-Ming Wu (1982) effectively incorporates a sense of playfulness in articulating Zhuangzi's philosophy; he argues that Zhuangzi's philosophy addresses its reader directly to engage in critical self-reflection. Wu contends that such self-reflection has important implications for an individual's engagement with the affairs of the world, not least because it helps to engender spontaneous efficacy in dealing with changing situations. Alan Fox, who argues that Zhuangzi 'affirms [life in the world] as wonderful and enjoyable', is also rather more cautious about Zhuangzi's intended audience (1996: 69). Fox notes that it is not clear in the *Zhuangzi* regarding whether everyone *should* have these skills and insights, or whether they *could* have them, or even whether *anyone* could have them (1996: 70; Fox's emphases).

Regarding the issue of involvement in government, Schwartz expresses the problem tersely, citing the case of Yan Hui's 'sitting and forgetting': 'The problem for all [Zhuangzi's] men of gnosis is how to avoid government' (1985: 232). When Yan Hui has successfully 'fasted his mind', not only is he purged of his ego and forgotten his strategems, he has lost interest in the enterprise of government (*ibid.*: 233). At one level, we might understand Yan Hui's situation as an exaggeration that makes light of Confucius' seriousness about the Confucian enterprise – in this story, Confucius begged to be accepted as Yan Hui's disciple. Alternatively, we can perhaps more correctly understand Yan Hui's illumination in the light of the Yangist philosophy of self-preservation, as it is highly likely that there were Yangist influences even in sections of the *Zhuangzi* that are not specifically defined as Yangist in origin. Mencius (in *Mencius* 3B:9) sets up Yang Zhu as an egoist par excellence. This view of Yang Zhu's ideology has persisted through time, most probably because of the dominance of Confucianism from the Han dynasty onward. But if we examine other texts of the period, such as the *Huainanzi*, Yang Zhu's philosophy appears less trivial.[25] Not only does it incorporate profound spiritual and moral themes, it had an important role among the political debates of the day. Graham articulates the place of Yangism in Chinese social and intellectual history:

> A philosophy entitling members of the ruling class to resist the overwhelming moral pressures to take office remained a permanent necessity in Imperial China. Yangism is the earliest, to be superseded in due course by Taoism and, from the early centuries A.D., by Buddhism ... For the Yangist, *hsing* [*xing*: human nature] is primarily the capacity, which may be injured by excess or by damage from outside, to live out the term of life which Heaven has destined for man. (1989: 56)

Perhaps the *Zhuangzi* has integrated within its ideology a Yangist reticence about engaging in political processes. Perhaps there is also some recognition that power can corrupt the finer elements of humanity. It seems that Yangism, and Zhuangzi's philosophy to some extent, avoids office, though not for the reasons articulated by Mencius. Schwartz notes that, in the *Zhuangzi*, there is awareness that 'The political order can not remedy the human plight, which is rooted in the individual mind itself. The political realm itself reflects this delusive consciousness. It remains part of the furniture of an unredeemed world... Chuang-tzu himself, it would appear, avoids office like the plague' (1985: 233).

In the light of these comments it seems especially ironic that the *Zhuangzi* text includes both Yangist and Syncretist strands, for their views about political office and governmental processes are fundamentally at odds. Whereas Yangist philosophy is at best ambivalent about political society, Syncretist ideology sought to integrate conventional notions of power and authority in Confucian and Legalist philosophy with Daoist conceptions of knack, focusing particularly on *wuwei*. The result of such attempts can be alarming, as for instance, in the case of the notion of *shi*. In Zhuangzi's philosophy the term refers to agility and efficacy in handling different circumstances, while in Legalist thought *shi* refers more narrowly to how the ruler can maintain his authority by handling situations well. Herrlee Creel describes the fine line between the positive and negative pictures of the cultivation of Daoist insight and knack. We will see Daoist philosophy in a positive light if we understand its message in terms of the personal cultivation of insights and skills in order to deal with the contingencies of life. However, the image can change drastically if knack relates to the manipulation of the populace, and the slide from one to the other, what Creel calls 'contemplative' and 'purposive' Daoism, can be too easy:

> ... it is all very well to talk of caring nothing for the world's opinion, of not striving, being perfectly quiescent, remaining content with the lowest position in the world, and so forth. But human beings get tired of that sort of thing. And most of the Taoists were human, not [sic] matter how much they tried not to be. Thus we find in their works repeated statements to the effect that, by doing nothing, the Taoist sage in fact does everything; by being utterly weak, he overcomes the strong, by being utterly humble, he comes to rule the world. This is no longer "contemplative" Taoism. It has moved to the "purposive" aspect. (1953: 110)

In the following chapter we will examine in greater detail developments of Legalist thought that incorporated Daoist themes. Creel's note serves as a chilling reminder that potency that is not properly grounded in ethical commitment can wreak extensive human disaster, of the sort that occurred in China during the Qin Dynasty.[26]

The Implications of the Philosophy of the *Zhuangzi*

The scepticism regarding language in the *Zhuangzi* points to an inescapable feature of human life that is manifest in language. There is a relentless vicious cycle in the propagation of prescriptive norms, coupled with their internalisation by individuals, who in turn teach and require others to abide by them. Zhuangzi is acutely aware of the insufficiencies of language as well as their powerful sway in shaping human consciousness. There is a deep paradox about language that emerges from Zhuangzi's deliberations: the success of language as a tool for communication rests in part in its simplicity. Yet, its simplicity can be a source of despair and frustration because it can foster inaccuracy and over-generalisation. Word meanings are not static but always changing relative to their usage by individuals.

The epistemological questions raised by Zhuangzi are fascinating especially when we understand their place in Chinese intellectual history. Where Confucius takes normative behavioural forms as part of the natural order, Xunzi suggests these are a device – a powerful tool for regulating behaviour. Where the Mingjia thinkers seek to establish certainty through names, the later Mohists demonstrate the deep complexity of names in the structure of the Chinese language. Where the *Daodejing* concerns itself with language as a social phenomenon that misdirects people in their aims and pursuits, the *Zhuangzi* is critical not so much of the use of language but of the assumptions associated with its use. Zhuangzi did not engage in speculative epistemology for its own sake. As these debates progressed it became increasingly obvious that language, being the primary instrument of human communication, was an important political tool. Of the Warring States texts, it is perhaps the *Zhuangzi* that makes this connection most explicit.

From an ethical perspective, we also see a gradual enlightenment that precedes the European Enlightenment which occurred many centuries later. The debating thinkers were progressively more aware that it was difficult to justify a conception of morality that was grounded in some transcendent source that was independent of humankind. The development of such a consciousness in early Chinese philosophy, and the parallels between the themes here and in the European Enlightenment, are important subjects for future research as they will deepen our understanding of philosophical ethics.

While the Warring States thinkers questioned the transcendent basis of morality, they did nevertheless continue to engage with issues concerning spirituality and its broader cosmic implications. Their attention to the cultivation of spirituality incorporates deep concern about the integration of humanity with natural and cosmic phenomena. While there is already a substantial and excellent literature on spirituality and cosmology in early Chinese philosophy,[27] there is scope for interdisciplinary research on the spiritual and psychological benefits to humankind of such an outlook.[28]

We need to consider three philosophical points generated by Zhuangzi's attention to skill. The first point is a focus on a world in which diversity is abundant and irreducible; the later Mohists were also aware of this aspect of the world and hence emphasised the inadequacy of language in capturing such diversity. The second point is that in such a diverse world, the lines of causality are not always fully specificable or predictable (this may account for the lack of development of a systematic, scientific approach to the world in Chinese philosophy). For Zhuangzi, it was important for individuals to know how to deal with the unpredictable and erratic aspects of phenomena in the world: every cicada is different but the good cicada-catcher knows how to catch them all; every ox is different but the good butcher knows how to carve each one at the joints; pieces of wood are different but the good wood-carver knows how to work with each piece to carve an exquisite item out of it. Knack is particularly important in dealing with a changing world, especially to turn a difficult situation to one's advantage. Here, we recall the term *shi*, which encompasses strategic skills in order to manipulate different situations.[29] The third point relates to how individuals are situated in a manifold and constantly-changing world, and how they act and interact with others therein. Zhuangzi's philosophy focuses on how different frames of reference can determine an individual's thought and understanding. This raises important meta-philosophical questions about knowledge and the limits of enquiry and, indeed, about the aim of philosophy itself. Zhuangzi's epistemological questions cast doubt on the picture of knowledge as primarily content-based. In his view, 'knowledge is always a kind of interpretation rather than a copy or a representation'.[30] Zhuangzi's perspectivalism challenges the separation of knowledge *qua* content from understanding, and, as Ames notes, contests 'the independence of the world known, from the knower' (1998b: 220). Future research in epistemology in Chinese and western philosophies can offer interesting insights into comparative cultural assumptions and can also enrich our conception of philosophy and the pursuit of wisdom.

Suggestions for Further Reading

Chuang-Tzu: The Inner Chapters, translated by Angus C. Graham (2001), Indianapolis: Hackett Publishing Co.

Fox, Alan (1996) 'Reflex and Reflectivity: *Wuwei* in the *Zhuangzi*', *Asian Philosophy*, vol. 6:1: 59–72.

Ivanhoe, Philip (1983) 'Zhuangzi on Skepticism, Skill, and the Ineffable *Dao*', *Journal of the American Academy of Religion*, vol. 61, no. 4: 639–54.

Roth, Harold (1991) 'Psychology and Self-Cultivation in Early Taoistic Thought', *Harvard Journal of Asiatic Studies*, vol. 51: 599–650.

Wu, Kuang-ming (1982) *Chuang Tzu: World Philosopher at Play*, American Academy of Religion Studies in Religion, no. 26, New York: Crossroad Publishing Co.

Yearley, Lee (1996) 'Zhuangzi's Understanding of Skillfulness and the Ultimate Spiritual State', in Philip Ivanhoe and Paul Kjellberg (eds.) *Essays on Skepticism, Relativism and Ethics in the Zhuangzi*, Albany: State University of New York Press: pp. 152–82.

Notes

1. Wing-tsit Chan notes that the *Hou Hanshu* (*History of the Later Han Dynasty*) makes this association in a section composed at around the fifth century (1963a: 178). Fung Yu Lan believes that early Daoist philosophy may be characterised in three developmental phases: Yang Zhu's Daoism, Laozi's Daoism and Zhuangzi's Daoism. He argues that each phase is a more sophisticated development of the previous one (Fung 1948: 65–6).
2. Guan Feng (1952) *Zhuangzi Zhexue Taolun Ji* (*Collected Discussions on the Philosophy of Zhuangzi*).
3. Schwartz discusses the elasticity of this phrase, as it was used to refer to a range of different positions (1985: 237–54).
4. Bryan Van Norden (1996) presents a concise summary of the different interpretations of the *neipian* up until the mid-1990s.
5. Graham, who has been influential in promoting the study of Zhuangzi's philosophy in the light of discussions of language by the Mingjia and later

Mohist thinkers, reckons that this is the most important chapter in the book (2003b: 104). His analysis focuses on Zhuangzi's deliberations as responses to these debates, especially those articulated by Hui Shi and Gongsun Long.

6. Fung Yu Lan suggests that Hui Shi and Gongsun Long represent two contrastive versions of Mingjia theory: 'Hui Shih [Hui Shi] and Kung-sun Lung [Gongsun Long] represented two tendencies in the School of Names... Hui Shih emphasized the fact that actual things are changeable and relative, while Kung-sun Lung emphasized the fact that names are permanent and absolute' (1948: 83). We should note here that Fung reckons Hui Shi is a relativist about reality, although another influential view holds that Hui Shi held a monistic conception of reality (Hu Shih 1928). Refer to the discussion on Hui Shi in chapter 7.
7. Graham describes three kinds of strategies in conjunction with chapter 2 of the *Zhuangzi*. The other two are 'weighted saying' and 'spillover saying'. Graham notes that these three strategies are discussed by Zhuangzi in his evaluation of argument strategies (Graham 2001: 25–6).
8. Fung Yu Lan presents an interesting list of similarities between Hui Shi's paradoxes and Zhuangzi's ideas (1952: 196–7).
9. According to Chad Hansen, this is a dominant understanding of the dialogue (2003: 145, 147).
10. Ames does not explicitly state that Hui Shi only has an incidental role, but his discussion focuses almost entirely on Zhuangzi's conception of knowledge.
11. Hansen also argues that his account helps to bridge the gap between interpretations of Zhuangzi's philosophy as mystical, on the one hand, and sceptical, on the other. According to Hansen, 'The skeptic furrows his brow critically and experiences the failure of absolute knowledge as a disappointment. The mystic revels in the very incomprehensibility of it. Put in emotional language, the skeptic *hrmmph* and the mystic *aah* are responses to the same realization of the limits of languages... There is no difference in the substance or amount but a great difference in their emotional reaction' (1992: 284–5). We must wonder, however, whether the difference rests only in the different psychological states of the proponents of each, as Hansen suggests.
12. Other scholars who discuss this issue include Henry Rosemont Jr (1988) and Philip Ivanhoe (1996). Rosemont Jr believes that Zhuangzi is a relativist, while Ivanhoe argues against the position.
13. Schwartz writes, 'One may enjoy the spectacle of the phenomena of nature without raising questions about the "ontological status" of such phenomena in themselves. One suspects that it is precisely Chuang-tzu's concern

with man as one of the ten thousand things which leads him to be most concerned with the question – What indeed is the reality of individual entities?' (1985: 222).

14. There is such playfulness in the Zhuangzi text; note that 'bian' means 'flat', an ironic name for a wheelwright.
15. See Graham 2003b: 115.
16. Graham states that for Zhuangzi, *dao* takes the place of the 'true ruler' (2003b: 115). On the other hand, Hansen argues that Zhuangzi's refutation of Mencius' *xin* is not to replace *xin* with *dao* but rather to reject any assertion of an inherent intuitive capacity (1992: 277–80).
17. We will explore this concept later in the chapter.
18. 'When a drunken man falls from a cart, despite the speed of the fall he does not die. In his bones and joints he is the same as other men, but in encountering harm he is different, because the daemonic is whole in him' (trans. Graham 2001: 137).
19. There would be interesting comparisons between Zhuangzi's tragic hero and Confucius' village worthy in *Analects* 13:24 and *Books of Mencius* 7B:37.
20. Schwartz also states that there is a 'quasi-thesitic' metaphor in the *Zhuangzi*, whereby there are metaphors of a creator of things, a creative principle, and a true ruler (1985: 226–7).
21. In that regard, Slingerland criticises interpretations of Zhuangzi's philosophy that do not properly reflect Zhuangzi's attention to the development of skill. According to Slingerland, Zhuangzi's skill-knowledge is not merely a lifestyle choice. To reduce the philosophy to a discussion of conventional constructs is to strip it of metaphysical significance. Slingerland mentions in particular Robert Eno's and Chad Hansen's accounts of Zhuangzi's thought (2000: 313–4).
22. There is an established tradition of Daoist religious and mystical practice which draws from a range of Daoist textual sources. Studies including Isabelle Robinet's *Taoism: Growth of a Religion* (1997) and Livia Kohn's *The Taoist Experience* (1993) focus centrally on religious aspects of Daoist thought. These investigations play an important role in Daoist research literature, in drawing together religious and philosophical perspectives on Daoism.
23. Slingerland refers to Graham's argument (see Graham 1983: 9–13).
24. Harold Roth provides an excellent scholarly analysis of the *Guanzi* and emphasises key connections between the two texts, the *Guanzi* and the *Zhuangzi* (1991b, 1999).
25. See, for example, Roth 1999.

26. The extent of despotism, manipulation and terror during Qin-dynasty China will be discussed in the following chapter.
27. Refer to the publications of Livia Kohn, Isabelle Robinet, John S. Major, Sarah Allan and Harold Roth.
28. Slingerland (2003), Wu Kuang-Ming (1982, 1990, 1996) and Jullien François (1999, 2004) have presented excellent accounts of the practical implications of *wuwei* (efficacy, spontaneity) in Chinese philosophy. Wu and François also venture into comparisons between western and Chinese philosophies. These inspiring accounts of Chinese philosophy suggest that interdisciplinary research in philosophy, religion and psychology will yield conclusions of considerable magnitude. Stephen Stich and Stephen Laurance *et al.* are involved in a large-scale, cross-disciplinary and cross-cultural project researching the connections between culture, mind and cognition (http://www.philosophy.dept.shef.ac.uk/culture&mind/).
29. *The Art of War* (*Bingfa*), a treatise on military strategy composed during the late Spring and Autumn period and attributed to Sun Zi (c. 544–496 BCE), is well known for strategies that are oriented to and prepared for change in the context of war. That these strategies are applicable beyond wars is attested to by the fact that there are many popular adaptations of them in contemporary business and management scenarios.
30. Zhang Dongsun (1995), *Zhishi yu wenhua: Zhang Dongsun wenhua lunzhu jiyao* (*Knowledge and Culture: A Summary of Zhang Dongsun's Treatise on Culture*), ed. Zhang Huinan, Beijing: Zhongguo Guangbo dianshi chubanshe: 172ff. Cited in Ames 1998b: 221.

9 Legalist Philosophy

To greater or lesser extents, the debates during the Spring and Autumn and Warring States periods challenged the beliefs and practices of the status quo. We have seen the case of Confucianism, which upheld many aspects of traditional life yet raised questions about possibilities for self-directed accomplishments and the basis of political authority. Daoism rejected many more facets of conventional life and practices but retained a vision of the good life for the common people. Legalist thought is singular in its rejection of fundamental tenets of then contemporary life. It rejected the importance of relationships in aspects of life, especially in the public domain, the influence of the bureaucracy, the institutional fostering of ethical awareness, and perhaps most of all the idea of a compassionate government that existed for the sake of the people. Herrlee Creel, a historian of Chinese thought, argues that Legalist philosophy was, 'in considerable degree, a philosophy of counterrevolution' (1953: 135). Creel argues that the Legalists rejected the increasingly popular view that government exists for the people (promoted by most of the other schools, especially by the Confucians) and in its place proposed government for the sake of the ruler.

The classification by Sima Tan, the Han Dynasty historian, of Legalist philosophy as a 'school' (*fa jia*: school of law) is misleading in a number of ways. First, there is no identifiable founder of Legalist thought although Han Fei (c.280–233 BCE) is its most systematic proponent. Secondly, not all of the thinkers considered Legalist actually discussed penal law (*fa*) as a fundamental theme.[1] Third, there is significant disagreement among scholars regarding whose ideas and which themes best characterise the ideology of Legalism. Those who have articulated Legalist ideas, or who have influenced Legalist philosophy in significant ways, include Guan Zhong (d. 645 BCE), Shang Yang (d. 338 BCE), Shen Buhai (d. 337 BCE), Shen Dao (ca. 350–275 BCE) and Han Fei. The impression we get from reading the Legalist texts is that there was lively debate and scrupulous consideration of the idea of penal law and its applications. Existing ideas and themes provided the backdrop against which Legalist philosophy grew: the Confucian emphasis on paradigmatic leadership, the Mohist discussion of standards,[2] debates about language in several of the schools, theories of human nature and the role of government, and debates about political authority and the role of the bureaucracy. There were many cross-currents: for instance, although the Legalists vehemently rejected aspects of Confucianism, Xunzi the Confucianist thinker was the teacher of both Han Fei and Li Si (280?–208? BCE). Li Si was the Prime Minister and political strategist during the Qin period of Legalist rule. We also find in Han Fei's writings attempts to synthesise Legalist strategies with Daoist *wuwei* (non-action) (Nivison 1999: 801). Although these two philosophies are deeply contradictory at points, Huang-Lao thought, as it came to be called, incorporated Daoist *wuwei* into the ruling strategy of the Legalist ruler (De Bary and Bloom 1999: 241–56). For example, Han Fei argued that order would be sustained by laws and ministers carrying out punishments where necessary, while the leader hides behind the system of law and punishments. The Legalist leader was advised to be shadowy and inscrutable, and seemingly without action (*wuwei*) so that he could maintain power and control over his ministers and the people.

An interesting aspect of Legalist philosophy that we rarely see in the other Chinese traditions is that a significant proportion of the thinkers were actually consulted by the government of the day. Shang Yang was a chancellor of the Qin state and Shen Buhai a chancellor of the Han state towards the end of the Warring States period (Bodde 1986: 74). Han Fei was adviser to the Han state just shortly before its annexation by the Qin in 221 BCE. It is unsurprising that these political strategists would have produced written material on government. However, their treatment of subject matter is frequently driven by their political ambitions rather than philosophical reflection. Hence Schwartz, for example, depicts Legalism as 'behavioural science' (1985: 321) and 'science of socio-political organization' (*ibid.*: 335) while Creel describes it as a 'theory of bureaucracy' (in Schwartz *ibid.*: 336). Angus Graham describes Legalism as 'an amoral science of statecraft' (Graham 1989: 267). Among the Legalist texts of that period, Han Fei's writings were the most critically self-aware. Han Fei brought together various components of Legalist philosophy and attempted to articulate his rationale for integrating them in the way he did. It follows that Legalist thought, its applications and eventual failure can be better understood in the light of some events that occurred and measures that were taken by those in power during the Warring States period and the Qin dynasty. For example, the harsh penalties imposed for minor offences, and the atmosphere of fear and oppression, were aspects of Qin rule that were irretrievably connected with Legalist philosophy in the minds of subsequent generations of Chinese people. So, we need to understand the characteristics of Legalist philosophy partly by examining its implications for the Chinese people during the Qin Dynasty and after.

Three Basic Themes: Penal Law, Technique and Power

Han Fei is regarded as the synthesiser of Legalist philosophy (Fung 1948: 157; Chan 1963a: 252; Schwartz 1985: 339–43) as he drew together key concepts articulated in earlier texts and integrated them into a comprehensive philosophy of social order, political authority and bureaucratic efficiency. He is also unanimously identified as the defining thinker of Legalist philosophy, the 'culminating representative', in Fung Yu-Lan's words (Fung 1948: 157). The status of Han Fei's ideas, and the text associated with him, *Han Fei Zi*,[3] are important in determining which other texts and thinkers fall within the ambit of Legalist philosophy. In other words, what constitutes Legalist philosophy is in part determined by the ideas that Han Fei gathered from the range of Legalist doctrines (it is also partly defined by political strategists who were especially concerned to maintain the power of the ruler). This explains the problem alluded to earlier, that the title 'Legalist philosophy' is debatable. The problem is due not only to the retrospective application of the title by historians, but also to vagueness about the nature and characteristics of Legalist philosophy.[4] Nevertheless, it is possible to identify a number of themes that together present a fairly reliable picture of the debates that preoccupied those who proposed the control of people by the state using penal law and comparable institutions for inducing compliance. Han Fei integrated three basic themes, penal law (*fa*), statecraft or technique (*shu*) and power (*shi*) in his proposal for effective government. He drew on Shang Yang's notion of *fa*, Shen Buhai's discussion of *shu*, and Shen Dao's suggestions about *shi*. We discuss these concepts in turn.

Fa: Standards and Penal Law

Two important clarifications must be made regarding the concept *fa* in its Legalist usage. First, *fa* in the discussions among thinkers of the various schools meant 'standard', as we have seen for instance in Mozi's philosophy. Mozi discussed the standards used in craftsmanship and extended their application to paradigmatic behaviour that incorporated *jianai*, impartial concern of each person for everyone else. We find even in the *Analects* reference to the standards: at seventy, Confucius could follow his heart without overstepping the boundaries of the (carpenter's) square (2:4). Han Fei also refers to this broader understanding of *fa* as standard; like Mozi, he extends the application of standards from ordinary life to human behaviour: the magnetic compass, measuring squares, scales, levels, inked string, and right and wrong in human behaviour (*Han Fei Zi*, Chapter 6, 'Having Regulations'). In this section of his essay, Han Fei shifts between two meanings of *fa*: in its broader sense as a method of measurement, and its narrower, Legalist, sense as penal law. Law is the system in which right and wrong are measured: 'to govern the state by law is to praise the right and blame the wrong' (*ibid.*, trans. Liao 1939, vol. 1: 45). One will frequently find shifts between *fa*^{standard} *and fa*$^{\text{penal law}}$ in the texts associated with Legalist thinkers.

Secondly, the idea of penal codes, and their implementation, preceded Legalist discussions about *fa*$^{\text{penal law}}$.[5] Shang Yang was a minister under Duke Xiao (381–338 BCE) of the State of Qin, and is reputed to have instituted numerous reforms that helped advance the state from a minor and backward entity into one with significant military prowess (Duyvendak 1928: 1–40). He is said to have been enthusiastic in his study of penal law (Duyvendak 1928: 8). There are references to the use of punishments as early as 513 BCE in the state of Qin.[6] Guan Zhong (683–642 BCE), who is discussed in the Confucian *Analects* (3:22; 14:9; 14:16; 14:17), advocated measures that were subsequently articulated by other Legalist thinkers, including centralised power, the establishment of bureaucracy, and the imposition of uniform codes on aspects of social and economic life.[7] There are also records of punishments associated with penal codes that were draconian and gruesome; these included severe corporal punishment such as leg-cutting, nose-cutting, branding and castration (Bodde 1963: 379). The Chinese character for punishment, *xing*, included the character for knife and pre-existed the Legalist use of *fa* as a system of penal law (Schwartz 1985: 323).

Shang Yang's doctrine of *fa*$^{\text{penal law}}$ incorporated harsh laws for which the punishments far outweighed the respective crimes. Shang Yang was emphatic that the disproportionate extent of punishment to crime would deter both light and heavy offences, hence securing the ruler's control of the people:

> In applying punishments, light offences should be punished heavily; if light offences do not appear, heavy offences will not come. This is said to be abolishing penalties by means of penalties, and if penalties are abolished, affairs will succeed. (*Book of Lord Shang*, Chapter 3, para. 13; trans. Duyvendak 1928: 258–9)

There is a tendency by scholars to follow Han Fei in amplifying the place of *fa*[penal law] in Shang Yang's system. In fact, we must be mindful that *fa*[penal law] was only a portion of Shang Yang's more complete programme of socio-political change. It is important to understand some details of Shang Yang's programme in order fully to grasp his notion of *fa*[penal law]. The *Book of Lord Shang* (*Shangjun Shu*) is the source of Shang Yang's ideas, although Duyvendak, who has prepared the most thorough translation of the text into English, believes that little, if any, of what Shang Yang might have written remains as part of the translated text (1928: 144–6). Yet Duyvendak values the study of the book because some of its passages address themes in earlier Legalist discussions that were further developed in due course (*ibid.*: 159). On the basis of this text, and from other historical sources,[8] we know that Shang Yang had proposed a complete programme for socio-political reform. His proposals included agricultural and economic reform, strengthening of the military and engagement in war, and political administration and institutional reform.

The *Book of Lord Shang* is extremely thorough in its approach to control of the people. There is a preoccupation with regulating minute aspects of social, economic and political life: crop yields and quality, price of grain, buying and selling grain, merchant activity, and marketplace conduct (Duyvendak 1928: 176–184). Even the setting of the price of food is discussed (*ibid.*: 179). If we consider these aspects of government regulation intrusive, we will be disconcerted by the ruthlessness in dealing with military personnel:

> In battle five men are organized into a squad; if one of them is killed; the other four are beheaded. If a man can capture one head then he is exempted from taxes. (*Book of Lord Shang*, Chapter 5, para. 19, trans. Duyvendak 1928: pp. 295–6)

In the text the determination of affairs is characterised by measurement according to *fa*[standards]. For Shang Yang, for the ruler to be fully in control implies not leaving any room for unexpected turns. To leave anything open to contingency is a weakness. This is the background of Shang Yang's approach to *fa*^penal law^. In the chapter 'Establishing Laws' it is stated that '[W]hen measures and figures have been instituted, law can be followed' (Chapter 3, para. 9, trans. Duyvendak 1928: 243). The determination and application of standards in all areas of life was simply a process of measurement: evaluate an action or state of affairs according to the appropriate standards of measurement. Then punish or reward accordingly.

Han Fei was impressed by the meticulousness of Shang Yang's approach, which he dubbed 'fixing the standards' (*dingfa*).[9] It was necessary for the ruler to set the standards in order to control the people. This was a critical issue because of the population in China, which had reached 57 million by 2 CE.[10] Shang Yang understood this matter a number of centuries prior to the census: 'In administrating a country, the trouble is when the people are scattered and when it is impossible to consolidate them' (*Book of Lord Shang*, Chapter 1, para. 3, trans. Duyvendak 1928: 193). In his major essay advocating rule by *fa* (setting standards and imposing punishments for failure to meet those standards), Han Fei begins with reference to changes in population numbers: 'In the age of remote antiquity, human beings were few while birds and beasts were many…[now] people have become numerous and supplies scanty…people quarrel so much that…disorder is inevitable' (Chapter 49, "Five Vermin", trans. Liao 1939, vol. 2: 273–7). Han Fei argues that the growth in population necessitates government of a different kind from that proposed by the Confucians: large numbers of people could not all be trusted to be virtuous. Han Fei's focus on (population) numbers is not uncharacteristic of political thought of the time, as we shall see later in Shen Buhai's discussion of political strategy.

Shang Yang's programme for standardisation applied not only to behavioural conformity but also at a deeper level to people's thinking. He discussed the indoctrination of the people to pursue only the goods sanctioned by the ruler. Paragraph 9 of the text 'Establishing Laws' is a section that dabbles in the psychological manipulation of the people through the implementation of *fa*^penal law^. This would involve the imposition of rewards and punishments based on disseminated laws[11]. Han Fei praises the use of *fa*^penal law^ to 'unify the folkways of the masses' (*yimin*) (*Han Fei Tzu*, Chapter 6, trans. Liao 1939, vol. 1: 45); nothing could be more effective for political control.

Control of the people is the primary concern in the *Book of Lord Shang*. This ideology places the ruler at odds with the people and thus stands in stark contrast to the Confucian view of benevolent government, especially in Mencius' philosophy. In Han Fei's estimate, Shang Yang's programme was thorough in control of the masses by *fa*[penal law]. However, it was also necessary to complement it with the ruler's control of the bureaucracy. Han Fei drew on the ideas of Shen Buhai to illuminate discussions about the appointment of bureaucrats and control of their power.

Shu: The Technique of Managing the Bureaucracy

Shen Buhai was a successful senior minister (historical records indicate that he was the Chancellor) of Han during the period when Marquis Zhao held power (361?–333 BCE) (Creel 1974: 21–4). According to a number of historical records and as well to Han Fei, political technique was the central feature of Shen Buhai's doctrine:

> ...the means whereby to create posts according to responsibilities, hold actual services accountable according to official titles, exercise the power over life and death, and examine the officials' abilities. It is what the lord of men has in his grip. (*Han Fei Zi*, Chapter 43, "Deciding between Two Legalistic Doctrines," trans. Liao 1939, vol. 2: 212)

Shen believed it was critical for the ruler to have full control of his advisers in the light of the many rulers who had become mere puppets of their advisers during the Spring and Autumn and Warring States periods. He discussed the political techniques that would lead to the desired outcome, not through reverting to the assertion of kingly or sagely power, but in the installation of a system that could objectively measure the abilities and achievements of the officials. Shen's plan was to establish a system of mechanisms to limit the powers of officials. In this way, Shen's ruler resembles Hobbes's ruler who is the guardian of the social contract but who alone is not subject to its statutes. Although simplistic in that it leaves the authority of the ruler unchecked, Shen's ideas are modern in the sense that they have moved away from reliance on interpersonal relationships and patrimonial bureaucracy to the establishment of institutional infrastructure. Hence, Schwartz describes Shen's theory of bureaucracy as 'a most significant event in the world history of social thought' (1985: 336). There are of course many important differences between the administrative structures suggested by Shen and those in contemporary liberal societies. Most notably, Shen's institutional reforms aim only indirectly at socio-political stability and accountability; his ultimate concern is to maintain the power of the ruler. Shen was deeply suspicious of the bureaucrats, perhaps justifiably so (Creel 1974: 61); he highlighted the dangers of the enemy from within:

> The reason why a ruler builds lofty inner walls and outer walls, and looks carefully to the barring of doors and gates, is to prepare against the coming of invaders and bandits. But one who murders the ruler and takes his state does not necessarily force his way in by climbing over difficult walls and battering in barred doors and gates. He may be one of the ruler's own ministers, who gradually limits what the ruler is permitted to see and restricts what he is allowed to hear, until finally the minister seizes his government and monopolizes his power to command, possessing his people and taking his state. (*Shen Pu-hai Fragments*, trans. Creel 1974: 61, 344)

It is believed that Shen Buhai wrote a two-chapter book, although that is now lost. Our access to his ideas is primarily through their citation by other thinkers of the period.[12] When we read these fragments, we begin to grasp the depth of Shen's understanding of political administration. The ruler is dependent on the expertise of his advisers, but to admit or reveal his dependence is dangerous. Shen portrays the ruler's position as an unenviable one. It is a deeply alienating position that is essentially dependent on the bureaucrats but requires a face of independence and superiority. How the ruler maintains his authority over his officers is at the heart of Shen's ideology. Han Fei identifies Shen's core concept as *shu*, technique, although there are no references to the term in the fragments. This is not to say that Shen did not discuss *shu*, given the paucity of the remaining fragments. *Shu*, the ruler's technique, is secret. For, to reveal one's dependence on advisers is simply to intensify and expose one's weaknesses. Yet, in large part, *shu* is not concealed as it is enforced in the system of fixing names (*xing ming*). This theory focuses on the definition of specific tasks and responsibilities that relate to particular offices, that is, the designated titles of the functionaries must be properly matched to their responsibilities. This is in fact not entirely new. The Confucians advocated the normative imposition of titles (*zhengming*); Xunzi in particular emphasised the power of the ruler in devising and imposing standards of behaviour through titles. Daoist philosophy views with suspicion this method of wresting control of the people, in its more general criticism of ordinary language use. So, within the environment of these debates, Shen's use of titles to articulate and establish standards was not new.

However, what was new about *xing ming* was that these were to be applied *objectively* both in the selection of functionaries to office and the assessment of their effectiveness in their respective positions. In practical terms, the articulation of a 'job description' (Schwartz 1985: 338) and the handling of promotions and demotions based on objective criteria upholds the supreme power of the ruler as the sole arbiter of bureaucratic office. This account of political administration does not allow for any inconsistency between, on the one hand, the promulgation of objective criteria and, on the other, the ruler's discretionary authority over the entire system. Of course, such a problem arises only if the primary aim of the institutional infrastructure is to introduce transparency and accountability. By contrast, the aim of the Legalists was to establish and maintain the ruler's authority; from this point of view, it made complete sense that the ruler should not be bound either by the system or its rules.

One interesting feature of *xing ming* is the method of tallying according to the disseminated criteria determined by the ruler. The method of tallying is also present in a way in Shang Yang's *dingfa*, whereby criteria are set up and the acts of particular officials checked against those criteria. To have a set of criteria is to implement an objective assessment method in order to reduce variation due to subjective opinions and points of view. However, the criteria were not in themselves objective as these were determined by the ruler. The Legalist method of tallying was especially important to the Legalist agenda because it was aimed at eradicating difference of opinion among the officials as well as the common people. To implement *fa*^{standards} is an attempt to stamp out difference, just as the purpose of the installation of *fa*$^{penal\ law}$ is to guarantee conformity of behaviour. The imposition of *fa*, in both of its meanings, was the method by which the ruler could control the vast numbers. Creel suggests a connection between *shu*, technique, and its homophone, *shu*, meaning numbers (Creel 1974: 125–8).[13] He suggests that there is a deeper connection between understanding statistics and the application of fixing names: 'It is necessary to know not merely how many, but how many *what*? The answer to the question – what? – is a name, *ming*. These names are *categorisations*' (Creel 1974: 113).

Meticulous deliberations about understanding numbers in order to attain control are characteristic of Legalist thought. However, we should also note that some fragments attributed to Shen Buhai incorporate references to Daoist *wuwei*. In one passage, the merging of ideas is so eloquently expressed it even makes the Legalist–Daoist ruler seem benevolent:

> The ruler is like a mirror, which merely reflects the light that comes to it, itself doing nothing, and yet, because of its mere presence, beauty and ugliness present themselves to view…The ruler's method is that of complete acquiescence. He merges his personal concerns with the public good, so that as an individual he does not act. He does not act, yet as a result of his non-action [*wuwei*] the world brings itself to a state of complete order. (*Shen Pu-hai Fragments*, trans. Creel 1974: 63–4; 351–2)

This passage appears out of character with key elements of Shen's philosophy. The idea that the ruler 'merges his personal concerns with the public good' stands out conspicuously against the techniques of political administration advocated by Shen: the ruler hides his motives and actions (*ibid.*, p. 63). The secretive nature of the ruler's technique is critical to his success in maintaining power. While *xing ming* assists the ruler in his choice and assessment of advisers, maintaining inscrutability keeps him *independent* of the bureaucracy. Shen is canny in his treatment of an important issue in political administration. Creel explains his insight:

> When Shen urged that the ruler should be completely independent, he was taking issue with one of the oldest and most sacred tenets of China's orthodox political philosophy…The idea that rulers should receive the advice of their ministers respectfully, and follow it with care, was present…perhaps even before the Chou dynasty…. Not all rulers did heed the advice of their ministers, but almost all of them found it expedient to pretend to do so. (Creel 1974: 64–5)

We get an even more acute sense of the level of control the Legalist thinkers were keen to achieve when we supplement Shang Yang's *fa* and Shen Buhai's *shu* with Shen Dao's *shi*, power.

Shi: Power

Shen Dao was at Jixia with other thinkers during the Warring States period and it was perhaps when he was there that he was exposed to the ideologies of the different schools. Shen Dao engaged extensively with Daoist philosophy and has been credited as one of the forerunners of 'mature Daoism' (Hansen 1992: 204–10). Because his doctrine integrated Daoist and Legalist thought, he is also believed to have been associated with Huang-Lao ideology. Its doctrine, if there is one, is debated because there is no clarity regarding its texts, thinkers or origins. 'Huang' in the title is thought to refer to the Yellow Emperor, the embodiment of enlightened, detached, 'gnostic' sagehood (Schwartz 1985: 248). The title 'Huang-Lao' has been applied to syntheses of Daoist and Legalist thought and frequently aligned with Legalist preoccupations about maintaining power. However, scholars note the importance of understanding the broader reaches of Huang-Lao thought, as it is closely connected with elements in the *Daodejing*, *Zhuangzi* and other texts of the period (Schwartz 1985: 242–50; Graham 1989: 374, 379).[14]

Only fragments of Shen Dao's writings are still extant,[15] and the most extensive discussions of his ideas in the early canonical texts are in the *Han Fei Zi* and *Zhuangzi*.[16] Han Fei names Shen Dao as the main proponent of *shi*, political power. *Shi*, *fa* and *shu* are often understood as the three foundational components of Legalist doctrine (Fung 1952, vol. 1: 318). The concept *shi* – which overlaps with the meanings of concepts including 'position', 'power-base', 'charisma', 'authority' and 'political purchase' – is what Shen Dao deems necessary to the ruler's control of the nation. It is not easy to grasp what Shen Dao means by *shi*. It seems to refer generally to how the ruler maintains authority, that is, his political sway over the people. It is represented in positive terms as '[support] by the masses', and in negative terms as '[subduing] the masses' (*Han Fei Zi*, chapter 40, trans. Liao 1939, vol. 2: 200). Shen Dao's application of the term may also be influenced by his conception of *dao* and may therefore fluctuate depending on whether we understand his *dao* as a mystical, transcendental reality or an actual, historical reality within which individuals should accept what cannot be changed (Hansen 1992: 206–9). In conjunction with the first conception of *dao*, *shi* could mean the charisma of the elusive ruler to maintain his authority; in accordance with the second, *shi* could refer to the ability of the ruler to deal with social and political reality.

Han Fei was critical of Shen Dao's conception of *shi*. He represents Shen Dao's view as one that upholds *shi* on the basis of its distinction from rule by virtue: 'Position and status are sufficient to rely on, and...virtue and wisdom are not worth going after' (*Han Fei Zi*, chapter 40, trans. Liao 1939, vol. 2: 199). Shen Dao takes the shared Legalist stance that rejects the existing paradigm of virtuous government upheld in most of the other schools – even Mohism, which had strict disciplinary rules for failure to adhere to *jianai*, ultimately looked to secure the common good. Virtue is unreliable, says Shen Dao, only because there can be 'earthworms' (the evil and corrupt) as well as 'dragons' (paragons of virtue). Therefore, the power-base is what sustains order and control, irrespective of the virtue and ability of individual rulers. Although it is not explicitly stated in Han Fei's essay at this point, we can sense an allusion to a standard – this time in the governmental infrastructure – that unwaveringly supports the ruler in his position.

Han Fei launches two criticisms of Shen Dao's *shi*, one from a Confucian point of view and another from his own Legalist perspective. In the first argument, the voice of the Confucian argues that virtuous leadership is more fundamental than political power: is it not preferable if a person of virtue stands on this power-base? Shen Dao may be correct that the power-base is important, but it is not as critical as the *ability and ethical commitment* of individuals who can successfully use the power. Schwartz articulates the problem lucidly:

> Without authority, the ruler cannot be the ultimate source of all the impersonal codes and mechanisms of control which maintain the entire social order. It is, of course, true that when the system is functioning, the system itself enhances the mantle of mystery and the sense of remoteness which surrounds the figure of the ruler, but finally it is the symbolic aura of authority surrounding the figure of the ruler which makes possible the implementation of the system...In a system which would eliminate personal initiative as the source of social behavior, everything comes to depend on a symbolic person. (Schwartz 1985: 340)

Han Fei maintains the importance of authority but points out that it is derivative and not fundamental. In other words, he is unwilling to accept that political power is a phenomenon that ultimately rests on an individual's charisma. Han Fei argues that the power-base is merely an institution and therefore needs to be established:

> The power-base is something with a single name but innumerable variations. If it necessarily derived from the spontaneous there would be no point in talking about the power-base. When I speak of the power-base it is of something instituted by man...the point is that [the power-base is] not something that a single man could institute. (*Han Fei Zi*, chapter 40, cited in Graham 1989: 280)

This leads us to the issue that Han Fei cares more about, and that concerns the role of *shi* within his Legalist agenda. Han Fei argues that *fa* is that critical element that props up the power of the ruler: 'When by embracing the law they occupy the power-base there is order, when by rejecting the law they lose the power-base there is disorder' (*ibid.*, p. 281). Perhaps Han Fei is misrepresenting Shen Dao's conception of *shi*, as *fa* figures prominently in the Shen Dao fragments.[17] Ultimately, though, Han Fei's position is clear: it is important to understand political authority but even more important to understand its source. For Han Fei, *fa* takes priority over *shi*.

Han Fei, the Great Synthesiser

Han Fei belonged to the ruling house of the Han state and is believed to have composed his thoughts for the king of the Han state (King An of Han (238–230 BCE) or King Huan-Hui (272–239 BCE)) (Watson 1964: 2). Ironically, it was the infamous ruler of the rival Qin state, Qin Shihuang (260–210 BCE), who implemented Han Fei's ideas most extensively. Han Fei synthesised the three basic themes, *fa*, *shu* and *shi*, interweaving them into a comprehensive philosophy of political control. His writings stand out as the representative work of Chinese Legalist philosophy. This is due in part to the absence of more substantial sections of texts by other Legalist thinkers. But Fung acknowledges the quality of Han Fei's work on its own merits: '[Han Fei Tzu was] the last and greatest theorizer of the Legalist school' (Fung 1948: 158). Fung is correct, both in terms of Han Fei's philosophy and also if we were to measure the success of his ideas in terms of the achievements of Qin Shihuang during his period of reign. The use of standard (*fa*) weights and measures, currency and script, to name a few innovations, greatly boosted the control the Qin emperor had of the state. These measures also contributed significantly to the social and economic development of the nation.

Yet, in spite of all its outstanding achievements, the period of Qin Shihuang's rule was a dismal failure due to its brutality and lack of humanistic concern. Paradoxically, this deficiency is in effect a success in Legalist terms for, as Han Fei writes:

> [For a ruler t]o shed bitter tears and to dislike penalties, is benevolence; to see the necessity of inflicting penalties, is law. … rewards should not be other than great and certain, thus making the people regard them as profitable; punishments should not be other than severe and definite, thus making the people fear them; and laws should not be other than uniform and steadfast, thus making the people comprehend them. (*Han Fei Zi*, chapter 49, trans. Liao 1939, vol. 2: 281; 283–4)

Han Fei deems law and management of the bureaucracy as key pillars of Legalist thought. When asked to assess the importance of each in his ideology, he says each is indispensable: one like food and the other, clothing (*Han Fei Zi*, chapter 43, 'Deciding Between Two Legalistic Doctrines'). He extends his argument to Shang Yang's and Shen Buhai's views, criticising the incompleteness of each. The third theme, power (*shi*), has a somewhat more dubious position in Han Fei's thought. Although many scholars believe that *shi* is one of the three foundations of Legalism, Han Fei does not insist on its centrality, as he does with the other two themes. If anything, he points out that *shi* is not fundamental; in fact, it must be properly grounded in *fa* in order to be effective (*Han Fei Zi*, chapter 40).

Han Fei also considered Daoist ideas, commenting extensively on a number of passages in the *Daodejing* in order to illuminate his discussion of Legalist doctrine (*Han Fei Zi*, chapters 20, 21). For example, where the *Daodejing* draws an analogy between governing a nation and cooking fish – and the fish are not to be turned over too often – Han Fei argues that the metaphor instructs the ruler not to change laws too frequently (*Han Fei Zi*, chapter 20, trans. Liao 1939, vol. 1: 185). But the chapter that best summarises Han Fei's doctrine of government is chapter 49, 'The Five Vermin'. The chapter deals with five 'moths' – insects that feed on clothes or books – which are a threat to government.[18] The five threats identified by Han Fei, and their effects on government, demonstrate important aspects of his doctrine. They are:

(1) The promotion of *ren* and *yi* (righteousness) by scholars who insist on following the ways of ancient kings. These doctrines are incompatible with *fa* and confuse the ruler.
(2) The frivolous schemes of ministers who have the support of rival countries and who are concerned only to further personal interests. These come at a cost to the nation.
(3) The establishment of bands of swordsmen united by strict codes and discipline. These challenge the control of the state militarily.
(4) Those who offer bribes to influential men in order to avoid military service. They undermine the nation's military prowess.
(5) The merchants and craftsmen who peddle useless merchandise and luxury items. They accumulate private wealth, create desires in the people and exploit farmers (who are an indispensable ingredient of a robust nation).

We can see in these points the preoccupations of a thinker who was gripped by fear of losing control. Two issues seem to lie at the heart of Han Fei's concerns: the sheer size of the population, and the unreliability of the people to act for any other reason than self-interest. Han Fei's response to these two anxieties was to introduce institutions and measures that would ensure conformity and guarantee planned outcomes. But these observable measures, such as *fa*, are not the only distinguishing features of Legalist thought. Above all, Legalist philosophy positioned the ruler at odds with both the people and the bureaucracy.

Debates in Legalist Philosophy

Human Nature

The Confucians debated the nature of humanity because they believed that the ontological question – what human nature originally is – would help resolve the ethical question of human good. We know from Mencius' considerations that there were others who also believed in this approach. Perhaps they were looking in the wrong place, for how is it empirically possible to verify the ethical quality of 'original', pre-socialised human nature, if there is one? In Xunzi's philosophy, we sense a drift from this belief. Although he did proclaim that human nature was originally selfish, he also emphasised *fa* in conjunction with Confucian values. This was an expression of scepticism that the multitude could be relied upon to work toward an orderly realisation of the common good. From Xunzi's point of view, benevolent government on its own was insufficient to curb antisocial behaviours; hence, Mencius was wrong. But Xunzi was nevertheless concerned that people should cultivate propriety in order that a civilised, human society might be established.

Han Fei, his pupil, took the distrust of humanity much further. He was not interested in the question of the original nature of humanity but in controlling human behaviour. Han Fei refuses to engage with ontological questions about human nature, focusing instead on the existential conditions of life:

> ...men of yore made light of goods, not because they were benevolent, but because goods were abundant; while men of today quarrel and pillage, not because they are brutish, but because goods are scarce. (*Han Fei Zi*, chapter 49, trans. Liao 1939, vol. 2: 278)

Unlike Mozi, who identifies plurality of values as the basic cause of disorder, Han Fei nominates conflict of interest resulting from scarcity. He shifts the debate from value theory to social science. In one sense, his focus is more realistic than the evaluative debates of the Confucians and Mohists. Legalism has been compared with Confucianism on those terms:

> The Confucianist ideas are idealistic, while those of the Legalists are realistic. That is the reason why, in Chinese history, the Confucianists have always accused the Legalists of being mean and vulgar, while the Legalists have accused the Confucianists of being bookish and impractical. (Fung 1948: 165)

The Legalist and the Confucian conceptions of human nature are deeply intertwined with their respective views of the nature and aims of government and ultimately, of human life. The two doctrines, Confucian and Legalist, are diametrically opposed.

Citizenry: the Role of the Common People

The Confucians were careful that only those who had the right kinds of abilities and knowledge could lead the people (*Analects* 8:9). So too were the Mohists, in their discussions of standards (*fa*). The cynicism of Legalist thinkers is most prominent in their views of the common people. Han Fei likened the intelligence of people to that of a small child: 'The intelligence of the people can not be depended upon, just like the mind of the baby" (*Han Fei Zi*, chapter 50, trans. Liao 1939, vol. 2: 309). Furthermore, the ruler would be unwise to count on them to have his interests at heart:

> ...the sage, in ruling the state, does not count on people's doing him good, but utilizes their inability to do him wrong. (*Han Fei Zi*, chapter 50, trans. Liao 1939, vol. 2: 306)

We see a similar attitude in Shang Yang, who penned thoughts on 'Elimination of [the people's] Strength' (paragraph 4) and 'Weakening the People' (paragraph 20). He also devised schemes to control them: Shang Yang urged that the ruler should force the people into two primary occupations, agriculture and war ('Agriculture and War', paragraph 3). This being so, the state will be strong. To organise the majority of the people into agricultural production will cause them to be 'simple' (Duyvendak 1928: 186).

Three aspects of the citizenry contributed to Legalist cynicism. The first is the people's perceived lack of ability, the second their unreliability and the third their sheer numbers. For the Legalists, population was – as it still is in present-day China – a formidable force to be reckoned with. The numbers were a threat to political authority of the sort proposed by the Legalist thinkers, especially if the ruler could not trust the people. In the hands of Shang Yang and Han Fei, the use of *fa* embraced and entrenched antagonism between the state and its people. Han Fei in particular even manages to incorporate the non-conformist Daoist philosophy to justify the subjugation of the common people. Commenting on the *Daodejing* 59, Han Fei argues that the ruler should prevent the common people from developing and exercising their skills of critical judgement:

> Therefore, government of the people, as is said in Lao Tzu's text, should suit the degree of motion and repose and *save the trouble of thinking and worry*. The so-called obedience to heaven means not to reach the limits of sharpness and brightness nor to exhaust the functions of wisdom and knowledge. If anybody ventures such extremity and exhaustion, he will have to use too much of his mental energy. If he uses too much of his mental energy, then disasters from blindness, deafness, and insanity will befall him. Hence the need of frugality. (*Han Fei Zi*, chapter 20, trans. Liao 1939, vol. 1: 180; italics mine)

In terms of the participation of the people in political processes and social development, the Legalists ventured much deeper into authoritarianism than did the Confucians. Schwartz expresses this Confucian–Legalist difference in this way:

> In Confucianism we do have a vision in which the agency of living persons (albeit the agency of a vanguard elite) plays a dominant role in shaping society...In legalism we will have a vision of a society in which "objective" mechanisms of "behavioural" control become automatic instruments for achieving well-defined socio-political goals. When viewed from this perspective, the *Analects* can be viewed to some extent as representing an anticipatory, skeptical resistance to a tendency toward what will later be called Legalism – a tendency which was already under way in the Master's lifetime. (1985: 328)

The Confucian political hierarchy – even though it allowed the common people only limited participation – did nevertheless recognise the interdependent nature of government and people in its vision of good government (*Analects* 2:21). That the people *do* matter is noticeably absent in the Legalist theory of government. As noted above, Legalist philosophy has been dubbed 'counter-revolutionary' in that it rejects the prevailing norm that the government exists for the people (Creel 1953: 135). Duyvendak presents a historical perspective on this shift in ideology. The Warring States conflict and turmoil prompted some to seek power; 'Real, concrete power is the thing these rulers are, above all, interested in. Power becomes the new source of their authority' (Duyvendak 1928: 80). In Legalist thought, the good of the state is synonymous with the good for the ruler.

Best Man and Best Laws

Han Fei reckons the time of benevolent sage kings is past. The new situation calls for a break from tradition:

> ...the sage, considering quantity and deliberating upon scarcity and abundance, governs accordingly. So it is no charity to inflict light punishments nor is it any cruelty to enforce severe penalties: the practice is simply in accordance with the custom of the age. Thus, circumstances change with the age and measures change according to circumstances. (*Han Fei Zi*, chapter 49, trans. Liao 1939, vol. 2: 278)

Han Fei could not have been clearer about the calculated, rational approach to the debate about good government. He spurns the inflexibility of those who defend custom and tradition and suggests an a-historical approach to the socio-political crisis. Han Fei uses a parable warning of the consequences of failure to adapt:

> There was in Sung a man, who tilled a field in which there stood the trunk of a tree. Once a hare, while running fast, rushed against the trunk, broke its neck, and died. Thereupon the man cast his plough aside and watched that tree, hoping that he would get another hare. Yet he never caught another hare and was himself ridiculed by the people of Sung. (*Han Fei Zi*, chapter 49, trans. Liao 1939, vol. 2: 276)

A new political infrastructure is necessitated by the changed situation. The most explicit articulation of the nature of political power occurs in Han Fei's discussion of Shen Dao's doctrine (*Han Fei Zi*, chapter 40). As we have seen previously, Shen Dao proposes a political infrastructure – the power-base – upon which the ruler's authority is established. Han Fei draws an analogy in Chapter 40 between the ruler's authority and the clouds upon which the ruler sits. The cloud is the sustaining power-base. Even rulers of limited ability, the 'earthworms', are able to 'ride on the clouds'. Han Fei does not doubt the importance of political power. But he steps in to clarify that what makes the power-base reliable is its grounding in *fa*: Shen Dao is foolish to assume that power provides its own guarantee. What underwrites power is the system and not charisma. Shang Yang and Han Fei have noted the ineffectiveness of charisma as a political method. The strength of their insistence is a response to the Confucian emphasis on paradigmatic men in government. Confucian benevolent government inspires the cultivation of virtue in its people in the realisation of the common good: 'The excellence of the exemplary person is the wind, while that of the petty person is the grass. As the wind blows, the grass is sure to bend' (*Analects* 12:19, trans. Ames and Rosemont Jr 1998a: 158).

Shang Yang responds to the two primary issues associated with Confucian benevolent government, the first being that of personal ability and the second the influence of virtue. He rejects both in a single argument for the establishment of penal law:

> ...it is said, "The benevolent may be benevolent towards others, but cannot cause others to be benevolent; the righteous may love others, but cannot cause others to love." From this I know that benevolence and righteousness are not sufficient for governing the empire...A sage-king does not value righteousness, but he values the law. (*Book of Lord Shang*, Chapter 4, para. 18, trans. Duyvendak 1928: 293–4)

Han Fei's stance against benevolent government is more resolute, as he claims that benevolent rule ultimately undermines the system of penal law and therefore threatens the power of the state (*Han Fei Zi*, chapter 7, 'The Two Handles'; chapter 19, 'On Pretentions and Heresies'). Benevolent rule is fundamentally at odds with rule by *fa*. Han Fei demonstrates this with a story that is now a popular Chinese anecdote (*maodun* [meaning, incompatible; literally, spear and shield]):

> Once there was a man selling halberds and shields. He praised his shields for their solidity as such that nothing could penetrate them. All at once he also praised his halberds, saying, 'My halberds are so sharp that they can

> penetrate anything.' In response to his words people asked, 'How about using your halberds to pierce through your shields?' To this the man could not give any reply. (*Han Fei Zi*, Chapter 40, Liao 1939, vol. 2: 203–4)

This story is, above all, a rejection of his teacher Xunzi's doctrine. Xunzi emphasises *fa* and *li* as complementary instruments in good government. Is Han Fei correct, that the two philosophies, Confucianism and Legalism, are fundamentally incompatible? Does not the dragon ride the clouds better than the earthworm, which would find the task impossible? The system may be essential in maintaining political power, but does it not require know-how to set it up? Schwartz expresses the philosophical problem underlying Han Fei's *maodun*:

> How the people, who are many, are brought to accept the commands of the ruler, who is one, remains the ultimate mystery of authority... In a system which would eliminate personal initiative as the source of social behaviour, everything comes to depend on a symbolic person... Authority in the Legalist system should ultimately be established authority and not "charismatic" authority, since "charisma" leads us back to the pernicious emphasis on the exalted role of individual persons. (1985: 340)

Legalism places emphasis on the system, the political infrastructure. That infrastructure is an integral part of good government was lacking in Confucianism, which seemed to rely only on the dynamism of the paradigmatic sage-ruler. But the Legalist political infrastructure did not go far enough as it did not allow for scrutiny of the ruler – not unlike the case of Hobbes's sovereign who sits above the social contract. In some Legalist texts, especially those whose authors have been influenced by Daoist thought (such as the *Huainanzi*, written in the Han Dynasty), a system of checks was incorporated into the political infrastructure, between the ruler and his bureaucracy. However, this was not true of Legalist rule in the Qin Dynasty. We now turn to the ruler's relation to the bureaucracy.

Bureaucracy

The office of adviser was an important one as it fulfilled two major functions in the Legalist political infrastructure. First, it appointed able men to these positions. The Confucians, of course, insisted that these men also meet another criterion, that of ethical merit. In his discussions on *xing ming*, Shen Buhai added the element of objectivity in the appointment of government advisers and the appraisal of their achievements. Secondly, the advisers had the task of mediating between the ruler and the people. In *Analects* 19:10, we get the impression that this is not an easy task:

> Zixia said, "Only once [*junzi*] have won the confidence of the common people do they work them hard; otherwise, the people would think themselves exploited. Only once they have won the confidence of their lord do they remonstrate with him; otherwise, their lord would think himself maligned." (trans. Ames and Rosemont Jr 1998a: 220)

The Confucians, many of whom belonged to the *shi* (scholar-official) class, and who held advisory positions, were of course concerned about how they could best fulfil their responsibilities. The Legalist thinkers tended to take the perspective of the ruler, according to their belief that government was ultimately to benefit the ruler. We have covered in detail the qualms of Shen Buhai regarding the power of the advisers over the ruler. Duyvendak describes the growing power of the officials during the Warring States period in a way that makes it seem almost necessary for the ruler to assert absolute control:

> ... [the rulers] feel themselves hampered in their career by old customs and immemorial institutions, by privileges of the noble classes, which are almost insurmountable. All these things belonged to the old order which was passing, and inevitably we find strong statesmen, as Shang Yang is said to have been, engaged in curtailing the privileges of the nobles. (1928: 80)

Shang Yang had a practical concern, that support for the privileges of the nobles would lead to a wider perception that the life of nobility is a worthwhile pursuit. This could in turn lead to the undesirable situation whereby farmers abandon their work in order to pursue official life. The officials were, of course, supported by the state and Shang Yang describes them in a derogatory way as 'those who live idly on others' (*Book of Lord Shang*, Chapter 1, para. 3, trans. Duyvendak, 1928: 191). They are one of the 'lice' that threaten the state (*Book of Lord Shang*, paragraphs 3 and 4). Shen Buhai discussed the interdependencies between the ruler and his advisers: the advisers were simply not to know the extent of the ruler's dependence on them. The ruler must juggle the following aspects of his relationships with his advisers: which aspects of their advice to adopt, how to respond to particular advisers when their advice is not adopted, and how to conceal his dependence on them.

Shen Buhai's institution of objective standards in bureaucratic positions is an important element in the development of bureaucracy in China. That one's ability to take on official roles is an objective, quantifiable matter, is a long-lasting legacy of these debates on the roles of advisers. China's Imperial Examinations, a system set up to select high-ranking officials for the bureaucracy, lasted for 1300 years, from 605 to 1905. The departure from patrimonial rule and nepotism marks an important development in Chinese political thought. But the Legalist version of bureaucracy lacked transparency and accountability, elemental components of modern bureaucracy. In bringing together the doctrines of Shang Yang and Shen Buhai, Han Fei characterises the citizenry and the bureaucracy as parallel threats to the ruler's power (*Han Fei Zi*, chapter 43, 'Deciding Between Two Legalistic Doctrines'). The ruler stands at odds with both the people and his advisers. He inflicts severe punishments to keep the latter in line: 'Reward and punishment are the state's sharp tools. If held in the hands of the ruler, they control the ministers. If held in the hands of the ministers, they control the ruler' (*Han Fei Zi*, chapter 20, trans. Liao 1939, vol. 1: 211). The Legalists turn the concept of objectivity on its head by granting the ruler free reign over the bureaucracy. We see in fact the use of objective standards merely as a tool in service of the ruler.

Secrecy, Power and the Control of Knowledge

The ruler's power against the people was sustained by the use of objective, clearly-promulgated penal laws. This strategy was to be kept secret. The ruler's power is most secure when *fa* is publicised as widely as possible while strategy, *shu*, was kept a closely guarded secret. Shang Yang and Shen Buhai also share in the conviction that secrecy is integral to political power. Han Fei articulated the inverse proportions between publicity (of *fa*) and secrecy (of *shu*):

> The law is codified in books, kept in governmental offices, and promulgated among the hundred surnames. The tact is hidden in the bosom and useful in comparing diverse motivating factors of human conduct and in manipulating the body of officials secretly. Therefore, law wants nothing more than

> publicity; tact abhors visibility. (*Han Fei Zi*, chapter 38, trans. Liao 1939, vol. 2: 188)

Han Fei paints a disconcerting picture of the ruler, whose strategy is strengthened by keen observation of the people: 'If the superior's cleverness is visible, people will guard against it; if his stupidity is visible, people will bewilder him... Only by not doing anything I can watch them' (*Han Fei Zi*, chapter 34, trans. Liao 1939, vol. 2: 99). The suppression of information available to the people was coupled with strict controls on learning. For Shang Yang, learning and discussion, especially debate about *fa*, must be prohibited:

> What I mean by the unification of education is that all those partisans of wide scholarship, sophistry, cleverness, good faith, integrity, rites and music, and moral culture, whether their reputations are unsullied or foul, should for these reasons not become rich or honoured, should not discuss punishments, and should not compose their private views independently and memorialize their superiors. (*Book of Lord Shang*, Chapter 4, para. 17, trans. Duyvendak 1928: 282)

To allow the people an independent vantage point from which to judge the affairs of the state was simply to weaken the state. Customs or traditions that competed with allegiance to the ruler were forbidden: 'the dutiful son of the father was a rebellious subject of the ruler' (*Han Fei Zi*, chapter 49, trans. Liao, vol. 2: 286). The most thorough method of eliminating knowledge was to restrict learning. Han Fei's chilling message calls this to attention:

> ... in the state of the enlightened sovereign there is no literature written on bamboo slips, but the law is the only teaching; there are no quoted sayings of the early kings, but the magistrates are the only instructors... (*Han Fei Zi*, chapter 49, trans. Liao, vol. 2: 291)

According to Duyvendak, there are records to the effect that Qin Shihuang read this chapter of Han Fei's and expressed a wish to meet him. Duyvendak lays part of the blame for Qin's book-burning exercise on Legalist philosophy:

> This leaves no doubt but that it was the anti-cultural teaching of the School of Law, which had prepared the mind of [Qin Shihuang] for the deed by which he incurred the hatred of all later generations: the Burning of the Books in 213 [BCE]. (1928: 126)

Government and Human Development

Legalist ideology was reductive in many ways. In limiting its fundamental concern to the issue of political power, it simultaneously reduced its vision of humanity and potential human achievement. According to this view, the people were instruments of state power; they had two primary functions: food production, on the one hand, and defence and military expansion, on the other. Other pursuits that ran contrary to these two basic functions were prohibited. The accumulation of private wealth primarily by merchants was prohibited. So were aspects of culture, tradition, learning and virtue. The Confucian virtues which greatly valued relationships were a prime target of Legalist philosophy.

The ruthless punishments that accompanied penal law were devised to ensure that people lived in fear. The gruesome punishments included cutting a person into two (Duyvendak 1928: 14). Ironically, grisly deaths seem to be a feature of the Legalist thinkers' lives: Shang Yang's body was tied to four chariots and torn apart, Han Fei fell for a scheme by Li Si, his fellow-pupil who was prime minister in Qin Shihuang's service, and committed suicide while in prison, and Li Si was himself cut into two in public upon the instigation of a eunuch, Zhao Gao (?–207 BCE), during the reign of Qin Er Shi (229–207 BCE).

Perhaps the worst aspect of Legalist philosophy was the fact that many of its doctrines were actually implemented, in the Qin state, especially during the reign of Qin Shihuang. When Xunzi visited Qin some time after 300 BCE he reported that:

> ...he found its people simple and rustic, standing in fear of the officials and quite obedient. As for the officials, they too attended strictly to business, going from their homes to their offices and from their offices straight home, having no personal concerns. Both people and officials, Hsun Tzu [Xunzi] said, were of "antique type," having no modern foolishness about them." (Creel 1953: 137)

The people were 'deeply afraid of the officials, and obedient'.[19] The measure of brutality inflicted on the common people simply to maintain the power of the ruling authority is unspeakable. The diversity and quality of intellectual debate up until the Qin period had been ruthlessly reduced in the pursuit of that one goal. Perhaps the sensibilities of future generations of Chinese impelled them to rid their civilisation of the texts written by these thinkers.

This might account for the paucity of Legalist texts: our study of them being often limited to the mention of Legalist doctrine in other canonical works. The valuable insights of Legalist philosophy have also been discarded when scholars distanced themselves, psychologically and intellectually, from it. For example, the Huang-Lao proposal, for the sage to maintain his *wuwei* quietude while his officials are assigned *youwei* tasks of political administration, is a plausible system of delegation (Schwartz 1985: 249–50). Furthermore, in contemporary China, use of the same term '*fa*' persists in reference to its legal system. Unfortunately, this may mean that the vestiges of Legalist *fa*, as the symbol of antagonism between the government and the people, are difficult to erase. Finally, the bleakness associated with Legalist rule in China might have been instrumental in convincing its people that Confucian ideology – offering a vision of civilisation that engendered the common good – was utopian. As we will see in the following chapter, in the Han Dynasty that followed the Qin, Confucianism was instituted as the state ideology.

Suggestions for Further Reading

Basic Writings of Han Fei Tzu, translated by Burton Watson (1964), New York: Columbia University Press.

Book of Lord Shang, translated by J. J. L. Duyvendak (1928), London: Arthur Probsthain.

Creel, Herrlee (1974) *Shen Pu-hai: A Chinese Political Philosopher of the Fourth Century B.C.*, Chicago: University of Chicago Press.

Schwartz, Benjamin (1985) 'Legalism: The Behavioral Science', in *The World of Thought in Ancient China*, Cambridge: The Belknap Press of Harvard University Press, pp. 321–49.

Notes

1. For instance, Shen Buhai is widely thought of as a key proponent of Legalist thought, although Creel, who studies Shen's philosophy in extensive detail, argues that 'Shen Pu-hai [Shen Buhai] was not a legalist [because]...it is unlikely that anyone who has been seriously concerned with administration could doubt [the place of] law in the administration of government.' (Creel 1974: 135)
2. Schwartz (1985) notes that elements in Mohist thought (rejection of *li* and inner motivation, emphasis on utility, role of rewards and punishments)

may have prepared the ground for Legalist philosophy, although the differences between the two traditions should not be underestimated (at p. 329).

3. The most comprehensive translation of Han Fei's works into English is by W.K. Liao, *The Complete Works of Han Fei Tzu: A Classic of Chinese Political Science*, vols. 1 and 2, 1939, London: Arthur Probsthain.
4. J. J. L. Duyvendak discusses how different historians have categorised different thinkers and texts as belonging to the School of Law (*fajia*) (1928: 66–71).
5. Schwartz discusses early textual sources that anticipate *fa* ('Anticipations of Legalism' 1985: 323ff.).
6. There is a passage in the *Zuo Zhuan* of 513 BCE where Confucius is meant to have expressed dismay at the institution of penal codes and punishments (James Legge, trans. (1893–5) vol. 5: *Tso Chuan Chu-su*, 53, 6b–7a: 732).
7. Schwartz 1985: 324–5.
8. Sima Qian's *Shiji* (trans. Burton Watson (1961)) describes Shang Yang's life and achievements in some detail. Duyvendak (1928: 1–40) refers to the mention of Shang Yang in other historical texts.
9. Chapter 43 of the *Han Fei Zi* is entitled 'Ding Fa' (fixing the standards).
10. These were the earliest complete census figures, discussed by Hans Bielenstein (1947) 'The Census of China during the Period 2–742 A.D.', in *Bulletin of the Museum of Far Eastern Antiquities*, Stockholm, XIX: 125–63, cited in Herrlee Creel, 1974: 116.
11. Punishment and reward were the two 'handles' of government. Han Fei discussed these complementary tools of instilling political order (in *Han Fei Zi*, Chapter 7, 'The Two Handles'). Punishments and rewards were used, accordingly, to discourage or encourage certain behaviours and actions. Rewards were to be used promote actions that demonstrated loyalty to the ruler.
12. Herrlee Creel has written the most comprehensive discussion of Shen's ideas which includes an analysis of fragments that are associated with Shen: (1974) *Shen Pu-hai: A Chinese Political Philosopher of the Fourth Century B.C.*
13. Apparently, *shu* (numbers) was commonly used during the Chunqiu period, 'with meanings such as "number", "figure", "several", "frequent", "to enumerate", and "to reprimand" (that is, to enumerate faults)' (Creel 1974: 126). The same character was also used in the Warring States period to refer to technique. But by the Zhanguo period, the use of the character *shu* (technique) became significantly more frequent and referred exclusively to political strategy.

14. Graham (1989) also discusses those esoteric and mystical aspects of Huang-Lao doctrine that focus on 'Inward Training', in the *Guanzi* text (pp. 100–3). The complexity of scholarship has increased since a number of texts associated with the Yellow Emperor were unearthed at Mawangdui in China in 1973 (at p. 374).
15. The fragments have been collated by P.M. Thompson in *The Shen Tzu Fragments* (1979), a major exercise that involved the collation of ideas from ancient texts and serious considerations about authorship, including whether Shen Dao did himself write a book.
16. Xunzi also discusses Shen Dao's doctrine, although he appears to have confused the doctrines of Shen Buhai and Shen Dao, crediting the former as the key proponent of *shi* (Graham 1989: 268).
17. This may have been because he felt he had to take sides with his teacher, Xunzi, as Shen Dao was one of Xunzi's rivals (Graham 1989: 268; 279).
18. Shang Yang also discusses threats to governmental control using the term 'lice' (*shi*). Duyvendak translates the term as 'parasites'; Shang Yang nominates a range of these: benevolence, literature, ritual, music, virtue, sophistry, righteousness, and unwillingness to fight for one's country (Duyvendak 1928:85).
19. Wang Hsien-ch'ien, *Hsun Tzu Chi-Chieh*, Taipei: Shih-chieh, 1961, 19.12b, cited in Creel 1953: 133.

10 The *Yijing* and its Place in Chinese Philosophy

The *Yijing* (*The Book of Changes*) is an old text incorporating sections that date from around the ninth century BCE. The older section of the text includes symbols comprised by six lines each, called 'hexagrams'. It also includes interpretations of each hexagram (*guaci*: hexagram statement) and statements on each of a hexagram's six lines (*yaoci*: line statement). The six lines of a hexagram are either broken (– –), signifying *yin*, or unbroken (—), signifying *yang*. The concept *yin* represents a set of characteristics associated with receptiveness, while *yang* a set of characteristics associated with firmness. Each line statement provided an individual prognosis as well as recommendations for action (Cheng 2003: 517). The hexagram and line statements are attributed to King Wen of Zhou (1099–1050 BCE), the founder of the Zhou Dynasty. Together with the hexagrams, sixty-four in total, these statements are the earliest layer of the *Yijing*. There are two other layers which are later additions to the text. The idea of using hexagrams for representing clusters of concepts and in divination precedes the composition of the *Yijing*. The two previous dynasties, the Xia (c. 2070–1600 BCE) and the Shang (c. 1600–1046 BCE), had their respective divination manuals called *Yi* of Xia and the *Yi* of Shang (Cheng 2003: 517). The hexagrams are each a compilation of two trigrams, symbols which consist of some combination of three broken and unbroken lines. The 8 trigrams are attributed to the (Confucian) culture hero, the sage Fu Xi (c. 2800 BCE) (Legge 1899: 32):

☰	☱	☲	☳	☴	☵	☶	☷
qian	*dui*	*li*	*zhen*	*xun*	*kan*	*gen*	*kun*
heaven	body of water	fire, sun	thunder	wind, wood	moon, clouds, streams	hills	earth

The sixty-four hexagrams in the *Yijing* are made up of all the combinations and permutations of the 8 trigrams, one set of three lines stacked on another. During the early Zhou period, the *Yijing* was used as a manual for divination. Divining sticks of yarrow stalks were used to identify the correct hexagram pertaining to a particular issue. While divination, in the Shang period, was a system for consulting with and influencing dead ancestors, it evolved during the Zhou into a system for deciphering cosmic processes and interpreting their correlations for the human world, individual people and particular events (Lynn 1994: 1).

There were additions to the *Yijing* in the later part of the Zhou Dynasty (known to historians as the 'Eastern Zhou', *Dong Zhou* from 770–256 BCE). These additions were called the ten 'appendices' or 'wings' (*Shi Yi*), which were commentaries on the first, existing layer of hexagrams, judgements on the hexagrams and line statements. All 'Ten Wings' were believed to have been composed by Confucius, although modern scholarship is not convinced this is the case. Around the early Han period (c. 200 BCE), the 'Ten Wings' were often called *Yi Zhuan* (*Commentaries on the Yijing*) and the whole text comprising the hexagrams, the first layer of commentary on the hexagrams and the later Zhou additions was known as *Zhou Yi*. During this same period, the *Yijing*, together with another four texts, the *Book of Poetry* (*Shi Jing*), *Book of History* (*Shu Jing*), *Book of Rites* (*Li Ji*) and *Spring and Autumn Annals* (*Chunqiu*), were endorsed as the 'Five Classics' (*Wu Jing*) of Confucianism. This collection of texts expressed, and further entrenched, Confucianism in Han society.

The philosophical significance of the *Yijing* lies not in its early usage as a divination manual. The later commentaries – its appendices – played an especially important role in the development of Chinese philosophy from the Warring States period. The spirit of the *Yijing*, which expressed an outlook of interdependency, transformation and resonance, was given articulation in a variety of ways by different thinkers. During the Han Dynasty, when the dominant intellectual method was to synthesise concepts and themes from different doctrines and schools, these themes which underlined the views of the *Yijing* were applied to a wide range of issues including in cosmology, astronomy, politics, society and its institutions, ethics, health and personal well-being. Ideas about resonances between the cosmic realm and the human realm in its different manifestations continued to develop through time; these developments were influential in shaping Neo-Confucianism, the dominant philosophical force right through to Qing Dynasty (1644–1912) China.

The Text and Commentaries

Each hexagram has a name which expresses its core meaning and which actually denotes an entire set of associated concepts. The terms include, for example, *qian* (heaven), *kun* (earth), *pi* (obstruction), *gu* (corrupted or decayed), *fu* (return), *heng* (permanence), *huan* (dispersion) and *sheng* (ascendancy). Each of these terms is not strictly linked with a singular concept for two important reasons. The first is that each hexagram signifies a transitional state rather than a static concept. Entities undergoing any of the states may change at any point in time. The second reason is that each term or hexagram carries with it a group of meanings associated in some way. For instance, the *qian* (乾) hexagram denotes the power of heaven, which is firm, active, creative and light-giving; it can therefore have any or all of these meanings. In its associations with the human realm, it refers to the masculine sage-ruler whose rule parallels heaven's rule. It is thus also associated with *yang*, the core set of characteristics of firmness, as opposed to *yin*, the core of receptiveness. In divination, the interpreter must understand the set of features associated with each of the hexagrams. The *Yijing* provides descriptions of the hexagrams, called statements or judgements (*tuan*), which are often terse and cryptic. For example, in the interpretation of the hexagram termed '*heng*' (恆), the judgement is as follows:

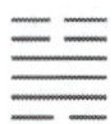

> Perseverance is such that prevalence is had, and that means that there will be no blame and that it is fitting to practice constancy here. It would be fitting should one set out to do something here. (Hexagram 32, trans. Lynn 1994: 335)

Interpretation is required to apply the relevant characteristic or set of characteristics, in this case, of *heng*, to the particular issue in question. Needless to say, these divinatory judgements would have been fraught with randomness and superstition, even if we allow that an experienced interpreter is carefully observant about the world and makes informed guesses (Cheng 2003: 518–9).

The classification of the *Yijing* into layers (three in total) suggests partly the method and content of the chapters and partly their chronological development. As discussed previously, the first layer is comprised by the hexagram symbols, the hexagram statements and the line statements. The second layer is believed to have been written either by Confucius himself or a disciple well acquainted with his ideas. It consists of two parts which are further sub-divided into four chapters. These two parts are the *Commentary on the Judgments* (*Tuan Zhuan*), and the *Commentary on the Images* (*Xiang Zhuan*). The first part focuses on the meanings of hexagrams while the second on the meanings of individual lines. The material of these two parts is essentially Confucian in spirit (Lynn 1994: 2–3). Its passages uphold the Confucian ideal of a tripartite partnership between heaven, earth and humanity, and emphasise the importance of the *Yijing* to effective government and political order.

The six chapters that comprise the third layer are later additions, some of which have been dated at around the third century BCE (Lynn 1994: 3). Together, the chapters of the second layer (four chapters) and those of the third, comprise the 'Ten Wings' or *Yi Zhuan* (Commentaries on the *Yi*). The first chapter in the third layer of the *Yijing* is the *Commentary on the Words of the Text* (*Wenyan*). It consists of two fragments, one focusing on the concept *qian* (pure *yang*) and the other on *kun* (pure *yin*); the commentary on the other sixty-two hexagrams is no longer extant. The *Wenyan* discusses a number of Confucian virtues in terms of *yang* and *yin*.

The second and third chapters of the third layer, which are also the sixth and seventh chapters of the 'Ten Wings', are the most philosophically profound of the entire text. These two chapters are sections of one work, known by two names, either as the *Great Commentary* (*Dazhuan*) or *Commentary on the Appended Phrases* (*Xici Zhuan*). There are two kinds of material covered in the *Great Commentary*; one dealing with the nature and meaning of the *Yijing*, and the other with specific remarks on the judgements and lines statements of individual hexagrams (Lynn 1994: 3). These two chapters are philosophically influential because they explain the place of the *Yijing* not primarily in terms of its use in divination but in articulating some of its assumptions and rationale, focusing especially on the integrated nature of the human and cosmic realms.

The final three chapters of the 'Ten Wings' are later additions to the *Yijing*. They are the *Commentary on the Trigrams* (*Shuogua Zhuan*), *Commentary on the Sequencing of the Hexagrams* (*Xugua Zhuan*) and the *Commentary on the Hexagrams in Irregular Order* (*Zagua Zhuan*). The *Commentary on the Trigrams* includes remarks on the eight trigrams, explaining their meanings in terms of the *yin-yang* and *wuxing* (five phases) concepts. This was probably a composition of the early Han period. The *Commentary on the Sequencing of the Hexagrams* justifies the order of the hexagrams. The *Commentary on the Hexagrams in Irregular Order* is a brief chapter that includes remarks on the meanings of individual hexagrams, not in the order that they appear in the older portion of the text but most frequently in terms of contrastive pairs (for instance, *qian* and *kun* are discussed together). Although the appendices of the *Yijing* had been written prior to the Han Dynasty, more reflective focus on the hexagrams and their use in divination were properly Han period developments.[1] In addition, discussions in the appendices focused on cosmological interpretations of the text, meaning that they took into account phenomena such as stars, seasons, waters and mountains, and correlated these with events in the human world. Hence, it is important to understand the appendices of the *Yijing*, which are its most interesting and philosophical sections, against some of the major characteristics of Han intellectual debates.

Comprehensive Synthesis and Correlative Thinking during the Han

The downfall of the Qin Dynasty was brought about by a revolt organised by the common people (De Bary and Bloom 1999: 228). These people were the victims of Qin Legalist rule and, as such, acted immediately, upon its downfall, to eliminate *fa* (penal law) and its institutions. However, it was also the task of the Han ruling house to devise social, intellectual and political structures in order to maintain their hold on the vast empire set up by Qin. Many of the intellectual debates during the Han period focused on government, drawing such analogies as those between the divine rule of heaven in the cosmological sphere and the inspired statesmanship of the king. The rulers who were interested in legitimising their rule and the measures they took were keen to encourage these debates and to adopt means to prolong their rule as well as their own longevity. As a result, there was a peculiar mix of sources these rulers drew on, including doctrines from the early philosophical traditions as well as Daoist alchemic practices and life-prolonging elixirs. With regard to the former, the rulers encouraged the consolidation of the early texts. Lau and Ames describe the impressive activity associated with the coordinated compilation of materials:

> The contribution of the Han dynasty in setting the formal structures of intellectual growth is enormous: the proliferation of official institutions such as imperial libraries and court bureaucracies, the first attempts to compile comprehensive histories, the editing and designation of a literary canon and the beginnings of the commentarial tradition in "the study of the classics" *jingxue* 經學, the establishment of the long-lived examination system that provided China with its government officials until its final abolition in 1905, the ascendancy of Confucianism as a state ideology which would shape the content of the examination curriculum throughout the life of the empire, and so on. (1998: 9)

These developments have had a lasting influence on the Chinese intellectual tradition. Han China had emerged from a period of rule by fear and was determined to learn from the mistakes of the past. In the early Han period, texts were written that outlined the faults of Qin; these include 'The Faults of Qin' ('*Guo Qin Lun*') by Jia Yi (201–168? BCE), the *Records of the Grand Historian* (*Shiji*) by Sima Tan, and the *History of the Former Han Dynasty* (*Qian Hanshu*), a project begun by Ban Biao (DeBary and Bloom, 1999: 228–32). The two significant histories of the period, the *Shiji* and the *Qian Hanshu*, set out to tell and re-create a sense of the past in order to learn from it. These histories articulated a sense of respect for the past and its traditions; they also established the purpose and style of historical writing in ancient China. They were partly historical and partly didactic, as they not only recounted events of the past but also used them to point out difficult issues, ethical paradigms and cases of moral decrepitude. Burton Watson expresses this twofold function of historical writing, of which the *Shiji* and *Hanshu* are paradigmatic examples:

> The function of history . . . is twofold: to impart tradition and to provide edifying moral examples as embodied in the classics. These two traditions, one recording the words and deeds of history, the other illustrating moral principles through historical incidents, run through all Chinese historiography. (1999: 368)

Like the other texts of the Han period, these accounts of history synthesised elements from different doctrines in order to arrive at particular points of view. In the *Shiji*, Sima Tan classified existing philosophical doctrines into six schools (*jia*) of thought. The doctrines of five of these 'schools' (that is, the Yin-Yang jia, Ru-jia (Confucians), Mo-jia (Mohists), Fa-jia (Legalists), and

Ming-jia (Terminologists)) are deficient in one way or another. The sixth, the Daoist (Dao-jia), is the culminating comprehensive vision, in Sima Tan's view. Sima Tan argues that this view 'is grounded in the overall harmonies of the Yin-Yang school, selects the best from the Ju [Ru: Confucians] and Mohists, picks out the essentials of the Schools of Names and Law' (Sima Tan, *Shiji*, chapter 130, cited in Graham 1989: 379). Sima Tan was at ease borrowing elements from different strands and doctrines; this method was used widely by thinkers of the period. Another example of this method is in chapter 33 of the *Zhuangzi* text. We have seen in our discussion of Zhuangzi's philosophy that sections of the *Zhuangzi*, including chapter 33, may be attributed to the syncretists of the late Warring States period.[2] In this chapter, there is a survey and ranking of a number of theories, including that of Mozi and the Later Mohists, Shen Dao, Hui Shi and even Laozi and Zhuangzi. According to the author of *Zhuangzi* 33, all of these views are one-sided and fall short of 'the Way of Heaven and Earth' (*tian di zi dao*). If Graham is correct about the syncretist author of chapter 33 of the *Zhuangzi*, it seems that the syncretist, as the term implies, had no hesitation about integrating elements from different doctrines to formulate his view. In fact, at the start of chapter 33, the author laments that the different doctrines only have sections of the true, larger picture: '...below in the empire there are many who find a single point to scrutinise and delight in as their own...However, they are not inclusive, not comprehensive; these are men each of whom has his own little corner' (trans. Graham 2001: 275). Syntheses such as those by Sima Tan and the author of *Zhuangzi* 33 exemplify a particular style of argumentation which presents an overview of existing doctrines, all of which (in the assessment of the author) are inadequate, and build up to a climactic articulation of the view of the author.

In the early part of the Han, the syncretic doctrines tended to favour Daoism as the doctrine that provided a framework for a comprehensive philosophy. The preference for Daoism over Confucianism had carried over from the Qin Dynasty. We have seen, for instance, the attempts of Legalist thinkers such as Shen Buhai and Han Fei to synthesise elements of Daoist philosophy in their discussions of the ruler's strategy for dealing with his officers and the people. On the other hand, the Confucian theme of benevolent government was vehemently rejected by the Legalists. The synthesis of Daoist and Legalist philosophies is frequently labelled 'Huang-Lao' thought. 'Huang' refers to the mythical Yellow Emperor, while 'Lao' to the philosophy of Laozi.[3] There are problems with understanding the scope of Huang-Lao thought in part because of the lack of texts that specifically discuss this ideology. The theory also seems to encompass a range of elements including the doctrines associated with Laozi's views, Legalism, checking name (*ming*) against 'shape' (*xing*, performance or form), the ruler's *wuwei*, *yin-yang* dualism, the mutual flourishing of the ruler and his subjects, and even Confucian terminology such as *ren*, *yi* and *junzi* (Graham 1989: 374).[4] Huang-Lao ideology was most influential in court during the second century BCE. The success of Daoism was ensured in large part by those in positions of power. For example, Emperor Jing (reigned 157–141 BCE) and Emperor Wu (reigned 141–87 BCE) were captivated by what Huang-Lao ideology had to offer, including especially the apparent super-human powers of doctors, diviners and magicians. The practitioners of magical feats, *fangshi* (masters of technical methods), also promoted immortality elixirs (De Bary and Bloom 1999: 293).

Toward the latter half of the Han, however, thinkers of a Confucian persuasion began to have some sway over those in power. Dong Zhongshu (195?–115? BCE) was especially successful in his endeavours to end Emperor Wu's support for Daoist ideology. In the *Chunqiu fanlu* (*Luxuriant Gems of the Spring and Autumn Annals*), Dong and his disciples interpreted the *Spring and Autumn Annals*, drawing out concordances between the moral order of heaven and the transformative, 'pivotal' rule of the sage.[5] The *Chunqiu fanlu* outlines detailed correspondences of a numerological, anatomical and psychological nature, between heaven and humanity. Dong maintained the fundamental Confucian triad of heaven, earth and humanity,[6] and the superiority of humankind. He also drew upon a range of doctrines and explicated this trinity in terms of *yin-yang*, *qi* (vital essence), and Daoist passivity (Queen, in De Bary and Bloom 1999: 295–310). Dong's political and intellectual influence was remarkable and had a lasting legacy, for his efforts led directly to the establishment of a 'text-based ideology represented in the first Confucian canon' (De Bary and Bloom 1999: 294). This canon was called the *Wu Jing* (Five Confucian Classics) and consisted of the *Yijing*, the *Book of Poetry*, the *Book of Rites*, the *Shu Jing*, and the *Chun Qiu*. The endorsement of the Confucian canon by the Emperor was only one indication of the success of Confucianism during the later Han. In 136 BCE, official posts were created for literati known as the 'Erudites of the Five Classics', and in 124 BCE an Imperial College was set up to train future officials in these classics (*ibid.*). Indeed, the Han Confucian literati became 'the teachers and guardians of the ancient literature, originally not exclusively Confucian but embracing the best in China's literary heritage...once established as the state teaching, with the examination system and the imperial college to ensure its continuance, it became almost a fixture of the imperial system itself' (De Bary and Bloom 1999: 317–8).

Apart from the tendency to synthesise elements from different ideologies, thinkers of the Han sought to understand phenomena in the human world in terms of their concordances and connections with cosmic processes and phenomena, including those of heaven and earth, other planetary bodies, the weather and climate, and even heavenly and spiritual beings. In this respect, the historical records, the *Shiji* and the *Hanshu*, are like other texts of the period. The historians interpreted history as part of the process of the unfolding world: 'Han scholars, influenced by yin-yang and Five Phases theories, conceived of history as a cyclical succession of eras proceeding in a fixed order. Not only this succession but all of history was a manifestation of the universal process of birth, growth, decay, and rebirth, constantly coming to realization in the course of human events' (Watson 1999: 368). Although the phrase '*yin-yang*' occurs earlier in texts like the *Book of Poetry* and the *Zuo Zhuan*, it was used only to express complementarity rather than embody the concept of change. For example, in the *Book of Poetry*, dated at around the tenth century BCE, *yin* is used in conjunction with rain (*Guofeng* section, *Beifeng* (Book 3, Ode 10), trans. Legge 1935: 55) while *yang* with the sun that dries the dew (*Xiao Ya* section, *Baihua* (Book 2, Ode 10), *ibid*: 276). In Poem 250 (*Da Ya* section, *Sheng Min* (Book 2, Ode 6), *ibid.*: 488), *yin* and *yang* are again used in complementary fashion, to denote the shady and sunny sides of a mountain and to capture the regular succession of shade and sunlight according to the position of the sun. Even in the *Daodejing*, where *yin-yang* is mentioned (Chapter 42), there is no explicit suggestion of correlation, or cosmological focus (Schwartz 1985: 355). Yet, these early uses of *yin-yang* are important because the two poles, *yin* and *yang*, are non-antagonistic (Major 1993: 28). In that sense they reinforce an important feature of the conceptual framework in Chinese philosophy, one that emphasises interdependencies and correlations. In its uses in the Han, *yin-yang* was conceived of as an alternating pattern which explained change. It was frequently associated with *wuxing* (five elements or five phases) for this purpose.

Like *yin-yang*, the concept and applications of *wuxing* were developed during the Han. Prior to the Han, there were discussions about numerological categories which sought to explain analogies or simple correspondences across different realms of existence. However, there was no particular mention of *wuxing*. For example, the *Zuo Zhuan* mentions four seasons, five tastes, five colours, five tones, six illnesses, and six *qi* (weather conditions).[7] It may be that the five materials (*wucai*) mentioned twice in the *Zuo Zhuan*[8] are among the earliest references to the concept of five materials or elements. These five materials are 'the resources provided by Earth for human labour' (Graham 1986: 77). By the Han period, the *wuxing* – Wood, Fire, Earth, Metal and Water – referred to the peculiar qualities of a particular element rather than the element itself (Henderson 2003:191). During the earlier part of the Han, there were quite clearly defined distinctions between materials, powers and processes. For example, there were distinctions between the properties of water (its powers) and its capacity to quench the flaming fire (processes). It was only later, for instance in the *Huainanzi* (a text written in the second century BCE), that *wuxing* is conceived of in phases, each of the elemental phases proceeding to the next in cyclic fashion; this sense of *wuxing* is most aptly captured by the translation 'five phases' rather than 'five elements' (Graham 1986: 77). Zou Yan (305?–240? BCE) is widely regarded as the originator of *yin-yang* and *wuxing* theory in a framework of cosmological concordances (Fung 1952: 159–63). Sima Tan in the *Shiji* names him as the founder of the Yin-Yang school.[9] Sima Tan also attributes to Zou Yan a treatise on the five virtues or powers (*wude*): 'Now among his books there is an Ends and Beginnings of the Five Virtues (or there are 'Ends and Beginnings' and 'The Five Virtues', *Wu te chung shih* 五德終始)' (cited in Sivin 1995b: 11)). Unfortunately, the treatise is no longer extant.

Yin-yang and *wuxing* were correlated in a range of different ways by the Han thinkers. The *Lüshi Chunqiu* (*Spring and Autumn Annals of Mr Lü*), completed in 241 BCE, is among the earliest texts, if not the earliest, that sets out correspondences between various realms, including the cosmological realm.[10] The text is named after Lü Buwei (291?–35? BCE), who wrote parts of it as a guide for the emperor of Qin, Qin Shihuang; the other parts were presumably completed by his disciples by 241 BCE. The views in the text are eclectic, drawing primarily on ideas in the Huang-Lao tradition.[11] In the *Lüshi Chunqiu*, although the ruler is the ultimate authority, administration is the task of his officials. The ruler is dependent upon the bureaucracy as it is through this body that he acts. What is particularly important, however, is that the ruler is morally cultivated and does not rule over his officials arbitrarily; he is the embodiment of the standard of 'all-under-Heaven'

(Sivin, in De Bary and Bloom 1999: 237–8). The *Lüshi Chunqiu* adapts the theme of 'heaven is round and earth is square', a familiar theme during the third century BCE that is also discussed in the *Yijing*, to its notion of ideal kingship.

According to Sivin, this theme probably had naturalistic origins, derived from measurements in astronomy.[12] But interpretations of this naturalistic theme – of which the *Lüshi Chunqiu* is an example – extended it metaphorically and related it to discussions about good government. The interdependence between heaven and earth, one being round and the other square, was expressed in terms of *yang* (of heaven) and *yin* (of earth). *Yang* and *yin* in turn were associated with complementary opposites such as creative and receptive, comprehensive and bounded, ruler and official. 'The Round Way' in the *Lüshi Chunqiu* connects the paradigmatic way (*dao*) of heaven with the ideal leadership of the sage which is interdependent with the administration of his bureaucracy:

> The Way of Heaven is round; the way of Earth is square. The sage kings took this as their model, basing on it [the distinction between] above and below. How do we explain the roundness of Heaven? The essential *qi* alternately moves up and down, completing a cycle and beginning again, delayed by nothing; that is why we speak of the way of Heaven as round. How do we explain the squareness of Earth? The ten thousand things are distinct in category and shape. Each has its separate responsibility [as an official does], and cannot carry out that of another; that is why one speaks of the way of Earth as square. When the ruler grasps the round and his ministers keep to the square, so that round and square are not interchanged, his state prospers. (trans. Sivin, in De Bary and Bloom 1999: 239)

Other prominent texts of the period were similarly creative in their approaches. The *Guanzi*, a text named after the statesman Guan Zhong, was actually compiled and edited over two centuries, reaching its final form in the first century BCE (De Bary and Bloom 1999: 256–7). It had at various points been classified as Legalist, and then as Daoist, although it is best known for its chapter on 'Inner Enterprise' (*neiye*), which contains descriptions of Daoist meditation techniques.

The *Huainanzi*, attributed to Liu An (180?–122? BCE), the erudite king of Huainan, was composed around the middle of the second century BCE (Major 1993: 3–5). The text quotes extensively, from the *Zhuangzi*, *Laozi*, *Hanfeizi* and the *Lüshi Chunqiu*, and comments on passages from them. In the *Huainanzi*, conflicting views, for instance, of Zhuangzi and Han Fei, are integrated so as to complement each other. The text examines the nature and practice of sage rulership, drawing on the Daoist themes of quiescence (*jing*) and *wuwei*, and on the Confucian theme of human nature (*xing*) that is grounded in heaven's way. The cultivated sage is quiescent yet responsive when he needs to be (Chapter 1, '*Yuan Dao*', trans. Lau and Ames 1998: 71). In Chapter 3, '*Tian Wen*', there are numerological and calendrical details including, for instance, planetary movements, solstices, seasons and equinoxes, lunar lodges and omens (Major 1993: 55–139). The chapter also emphasises the reciprocity of humanity and heaven and lists correspondences between cosmic phenomena and human life.[13] As a text, the 21 chapters of the *Huainanzi* embody the spirit of Chinese philosophy in the Han, especially in its method of synthesis that draws on a number of existing doctrines. Its cosmological discussions bring together topics in astronomy, the empirical sciences, mythology, ethics and politics.

The inclusion of aspects of the cosmos into correlative schema was also a particular development of Han intellectual debates. A key concept in cosmological resonance is *qi*, which has been used in numerous ways in early Chinese philosophy and which has a number of meanings including energy, spirit, temperature, (a person's) temperament and essence. In its earliest usage, *qi* referred to 'the mists, the fogs, and moving forms of clouds that are what we see of the atmosphere' (Sivin, in Henderson 2003: 190). In the *Zuo Zhuan*, a pre-Han text, *qi* refers to aspects of the climate: shade (*yin*), sunshine (*yang*), wind, rain, dark and light are the six *qi* of heaven.[14] As a fundamental concept in correlative cosmology during the Han, *qi* denoted the medium by which resonances were conducted, between correlative entities in different realms. In later cosmological theory, *qi* became an even more complex concept in that it could transform into various states; for instance, congealing to form solids or dispersing to make up fogs and mists. Hence, 'action at a distance between two resonating entities might be facilitated not only by vibrations emitted through the medium of the *qi* connecting them, but also because they are composed of the same general type of *qi*' (Major, in Henderson 2003: 190).

Correspondences between the cosmic and human realms were also extended to more defined concerns, as for instance in discussions of human health. The *Lüshi Chunqiu* (in the chapter 'The Round Way') applies *qi* to the human body: 'Human beings have nine orifices. If [the *qi*] abides in a single one, eight will be depleted. If eight are depleted for a very long time, the body will die…stagnation results in failure. That is the Round Way' (trans. Sivin, in De Bary and Bloom 1999: 239–40). The *Chunqiu fanlu* outlines the analogies between the 'health' of the state and that of the human body:

> The purest vital force (*qi*) is vital essence.
> The purest men are worthies.
> Those who regulate their bodies consider the accumulation of vital essence to be a treasure.
> Those who regulate the state consider the accumulation of worthy men to be the Way.
> The body takes the mind-and-heart as the foundation.
> The state takes the ruler as the master…
> Only when the body is free from pain can it achieve tranquillity.
> Only when the numerous offices each obtain their proper place can the state achieve security.
>
> (trans. Queen, in De Bary and Bloom 1999: 297)

These themes are extended in a set of three texts comprising the *Huangdi Neijing*.[15] These three texts bring together the disciplines of philosophy, medicine and politics, drawing correspondences between cosmic order and individual well-being. In some sections of these texts, the Yellow Emperor, Huangdi, is asking questions, and his minister provides the answers. The minister takes on both the roles of a master instructing his disciple, and a minister advising his sovereign (Sivin, in De Bary and Bloom 1999: 274).[16] Although the texts deal primarily with the human body and its correspondences, they draw on concepts that were available, such as *yin-yang* and *wuxing*, like other texts of the Han. Sivin suggests that a full appreciation of Han philosophy must include consideration of the *Huangdi Neijing* (*ibid.*: 275).

Confucian texts of the Han period that were prominent include *Chunqiu fanlu*, discussed previously. In its discussion of the moral cultivation of the sage, attention turns to correlations between the emotions of the king with the seasons and temperatures: 'The master's love, hate, happiness, and anger are tantamount to Heaven's spring, summer, autumn and winter, which, possessing warmth, coolness, cold, and heat, thereby develop, transform, and complete their tasks' (11: 9a–12a; trans. Queen, in De Bary and Bloom 1999: 301). Ban Gu, who wrote sections of the historical text the *Qian Hanshu*, also recorded a set of discussions entitled *Bohu Tong* (*Discourses of the White Tiger Hall*). These discussions were held at the court of the emperor Zhang (reigned

75–88 CE) (De Bary and Bloom 1999: 344) and there were elaborate accounts of correspondences between heaven and earth, court protocols, human nature, human relationships, and the five phases. There were other significant defining texts of Confucianism, such as the *Xiao Jing* (*Book of Filial Piety*) and the *Li Ji* (*Book of Rites*), which were revised and completed during the later Han (25–220 CE). The *Book of Filial Piety* emphasised the primacy of filial piety in all strata of life, from the emperor to the common people, and the emperor's responsibilities to the people.[17] The *Book of Rites* articulates the moral significance of rites (*li*: ritual) in spiritual, courtly and ordinary dimensions of life. The book provides a comprehensive vision of a unified world order brought about by the inner moral transformations of the sage and the people. Two of its sections, the *Great Learning* (*Daxue*) and the *Doctrine of the Mean* (*Zhong Yong*), received more prominence when they were classified during the Song period by Zhu Xi (1130–1200), the Neo-Confucian thinker, as two of the Confucian *Four Books* (*Si Shu*). These two short treatises embody a distinctively Confucian vision of benevolent government whose leadership has far-reaching effects, transforming the people and realising the Way of Heaven.

The *Yijing*, one of the Confucian Five Classics of the Han, was part of the canon that defined Han Confucianism, and which shaped Neo-Confucian thought. In texts like the *Yijing*, Han Confucianism reinforced the Confucian optimism in the ability of humankind to effect positive changes in the world. However, it also expanded the Confucian vision (of Confucius, Mencius and Xunzi) in two significant ways. First, it absorbed elements from other doctrines, thus enriching in particular its notions of self cultivation and government. Secondly, it broadened its humanistic vision to incorporate correlations between the human, natural and cosmic realms. The belief that the natural world was implicated in human affairs would have generated a heightened sense of responsibility on the part of humankind. In the following section, we turn our attention to the features of correlative thinking that define the philosophical character of the *Yijing*.

Correlative Thinking: the Spirit of the *Yijing*

The appendices of the *Yijing* are deliberative in the sense that they reflect on a number of issues associated with the text and its use as a manual for divination. These issues include the rationale for divination, the composition of the symbols, the interpretation of the symbols, the cosmological underpinnings of divination and the place of human action, and the implications of divination for individual action and the transformation of society. In the *Yijing*, both the older, divination sections, and the appendices, are not systematic philosophical treatises. However, the reflections in the appendices are built upon deeper philosophical assumptions. The analysis in this section will focus on the more philosophically significant treatises in the appendices, the *Xici zhuan* (or the *Great Commentary*), and the *Shuogua* (*Commentary on the Trigrams*). Seven key elements of correlative thinking in the *Yijing* are explored in this section. They include (1) the primacy of observation, (2) a holistic, all-encompassing perspective, (3) a dialectical and complementary approach to dualisms, (4) correlative thinking and resonance, (5) an interpretive approach to the meanings of the hexagrams and correspondences, (6) constant movement marked by the inevitability of change, and (7) the action-guiding nature of the judgements.

(1) The Primacy of Observation

Chinese thought places emphasis on observations of the concrete, phenomenal world as the basis of reflection. Careful observation of one's world was prominent, as we have seen, in the pre-Qin debates. The Confucian, Mohist, Daoist and Legalist questions about organising the human world, and the Daoist, Mohist and Mingjia preoccupations with language and its associations with reality, are expressions of concern about how to deal with situations and vicissitudes in life. The solutions to these questions require observation (*guan*) and understanding of the natural, political and social environments as well as the relations between entities. In the *Yijing*, we find explicit acknowledgement of the observational processes upon which its symbols are constructed:

> When in ancient times Lord Bao Xi ruled the world as sovereign, he looked upward and observed [*guan*] the images in heaven and looked onward and observed [*guan*] the models that the earth provided. He observed the patterns on birds and beasts and what things were suitable for the land. Nearby, adopting them from his own person, and afar, adopting them from other things, he thereupon made the eight trigrams in order to become thoroughly conversant with the virtues inherent in the numinous[18] and the bright and to classify the myriad things in terms of their true, innate natures. (*Xici zhuan* 2.2, trans. Lynn 1994: 77)

Lord Bao Xi's observations are comprehensive, covering both cosmic and human realms and their correspondences. Chung-ying Cheng states that observation is a fundamental aspect of the *Yijing*, marking it with the phrase 'the observational origins of the *Yijing*' (2003: 517–24). The passage above on the origin of the trigrams reveals another important feature of the philosophical commitment of the *Yijing*, that one should be deeply aware of the sources of imminent change that are external to the self, but that may nevertheless have a significant impact on it. What underlies this belief is a broad cosmic vision of all things that may impact on one entity, and of how one entity may impact on others in turn. Given this conception of self, it is critical for a person to understand his or her place in an environment that has many interconnected dimensions, and, within them, a rich diversity of beings and entities.

(2) A Holistic, All-encompassing Perspective

The tendency of Chinese philosophy to take a holistic perspective is articulated in different conceptions of the 'whole'. The early Confucians focused on human society; Mohists on a utilitarian concern for the benefit of all; and Daoists in the overarching perspective of *dao*. The *Yijing* similarly has a holistic focus, and it describes *dao* in terms of an encompassing whole that also includes the evolution of events and processes through time:

> The *Changes* deals with the way things start up and how matters reach completion and represents the Dao that envelops the entire world. If one puts it like this, nothing more can be said about it. Therefore the sages use it to penetrate the aspirations of all the people in the world, to settle the great affairs of the world, and to resolve all doubtful matters in the world. (*Xici zhuan* 1.11; trans. Lynn 1994: 63–4)

The notion of *dao* in this passage closely resembles the concept *qi*[19] as the conveying medium of resonating influences. Resonance across different realms, and integration between different entities, are important aspects of holism in the *Yijing*. In line with other Confucian texts of the period, it draws together the Confucian trinity of heaven, earth and humanity:

> As a book, the *Changes* is something which is broad and great, complete in every way. There is the Dao of Heaven in it, the Dao of Man in it, and the Dao of Earth in it. It brings these three powers together and then doubles

> them. This is the reason for there being six lines. What these six embody are nothing other than the Dao of the three powers. (*Xici zhuan* 2.10; trans. Lynn 1994: 92)

Heaven, earth and humanity are integrated and their interactions are fully captured, altogether, in the lines of the sixty-four hexagrams. In the *Yijing*, the broader, holistic context is not viewed in transcendent or exclusive terms; although the *Dao* of Heaven is the larger, cosmic vantage point, it is not detached from the human world. Indeed, the wisdom of the *Yijing* is a resource also for the 'ordinary folk' (*Xici zhuan* 2.12; trans. Lynn 1994: 94). The emphasis is on resonances between a cosmic macrocosm (for example, movements of stars and planets) and a microcosm (for example, the state) rather than a power hierarchy wherein the microcosm is controlled by the macrocosm. Due to the suggestive nature of the *Yijing* and the later additions to the text through time, the nature of the 'whole' in the *Yijing* is a debatable matter. We may understand it literally, as an ontological account of all existence, or we may understand it metaphorically, as an image designed to encourage a spirit of cooperation.

(3) A Dialectical and Complementary Approach to Dualisms

The interdependence between *qian* (powers of heaven) and *kun* (powers of earth) is part of the conceptual framework of the *Yijing*. The opening passage of the *Xici zhuan* sets out the complementarity between *qian* and *kun*, and their associated characteristics:

> As Heaven is high and noble and Earth is low and humble, so it is that *Qian* [Pure Yang, Hexagram 1] and *Kun* [Pure Yin, Hexagram 2] are defined. The high and the low being thereby set out, the exalted and the mean have their places accordingly. There are norms for action and repose, which are determined by whether hardness or softness is involved... The Dao of *Qian* forms the male; the Dao of *Kun* forms the female. *Qian* has mastery over the great beginning of things, and *Kun* acts to bring things to completion. (1.1, trans. Lynn 1994: 47)

These binary pairs are not oppositional but are interdependent. There is a dialectical complementarity between each set of polarities: high and low, noble and humble, exalted and mean, action and repose, hardness and softness, male and female, beginning and completion. Although there is a hierarchy in some of the binary pairs, for instance in the contrast between noble and humble, the hierarchy is nevertheless a complementary one. The meaning of each term, say of humility, is not a matter of absolute definition. Rather, the meanings of the terms in each binary set are relative, each being defined in terms of the other depending on the situation at hand. Henderson explains how the interdependent, complementary relationship between each binary set is captured in relative rather than absolute terms:

> Even at the height of the *yang* there exists the germ of *yin*, and vice versa. *Yin* and *yang*, moreover, are not absolutes but relational ideas: an old man may be *yang* with respect to a woman but is *yin* with respect to a young man. (Henderson 2003: 191)

This was a feature of *yin-yang* theory that had developed during the Han. It is important to note that although the female element, *yin*, is associated with the lowly, humble, mean, and the quality of softness, it is not degraded by its association with these qualities, in part because each is conceived in relative terms to the other, and in part because *yin* and *yang* were cyclical phases rather than static definitions.[20] In Han thought, the notions of *yin* and *yang* are not defined in terms of their intrinsic qualities but by their relative positions (Wilhelm 1977: 195). The *Xici zhuan* maintains the place and necessity of both *yin* and *yang* in the originating and continuing processes of the cosmic and human worlds. The dualistic schema of *yin-yang* was used to explain a range of phenomena including seasonal change, the human life cycle, and the rise and fall of dynasties. The conceptual binary framework of *yin-yang* as reciprocal, interdependent and dynamic dominated Chinese thinking, so much as to eclipse earlier conceptions of dualism in China (Henderson 2003: 191). The dynamic waxing and waning of *yin-yang* is also captured in the *Xici zhuan* (1.5), where *dao* is described in terms of the reciprocal process of *yin* and *yang*. In this same passage, *dao* is pictured as a provident source of renewal: 'As replete virtue and great enterprise', the Dao is indeed perfect! It is because the Dao exists in such rich abundance that we refer to it as the "great enterprise", it is because the Dao brings renewal day after day that we refer to it here as "replete virtue"' (*ibid.*, trans. Lynn 1994: 54). The dialectical relation between binary terms is symptomatic of philosophy in the Han period, which emphasises correlations between entities such that a change in one of them may produce resonant effects in others.

(4) Correlative Thinking and Resonance

Correlative thinking, especially in terms of correlations between cosmic and human realms, was a particular feature of philosophy during the Han. Correlations, or correspondences, must be distinguished from analogies. The latter emphasises significantly similar aspects of two items or topics in comparison while correlations dwell on parallel events or chains of events in different spheres. Elaboration of correlative thought was the major subject of many Han texts. The approach of correlative thinking is to extend correspondences between changes or movements across different realms. John Henderson describes the dynamics of correlative thinking:

> Correlative thinking draws systematic correspondences among various orders of reality or realms of the cosmos, such as the human body, the body politic, and the heavenly bodies. It assumes that these related orders are homologous, that they correspond with one another in number, in structure, in kind, or in some other basic respect. (Henderson 2003: 187)

Correspondences included those between planetary movements, affairs of heaven and earth, meteorological conditions, political affairs, agricultural yields, the welfare of humankind, and also individual human health, especially in relation to dietary considerations. More specifically, these correlations included correspondences between aspects of the cosmos with the imperial bureaucracy of the Han, ritual acts and attitudes of the ruler with the cycle of seasons[21] and natural disasters, cosmic structures with the nine orifices and the 366 joints of humans, and seasonal changes with medical conditions and even moods[22] (Henderson 1984).

The origins of correlative thinking are debatable. However, there were probably earlier and simpler correlations, perhaps in a farmer's almanac, describing plants, animals and climactic conditions of each month (Henderson 1984: 21). In the early Han, cosmic changes were used to legitimise the structure and functions of the newly established imperial authority. For example, the text *Bohu Tong* (*Discourses of the White Tiger Hall*), draws an analogy between the relation of the sun and moon with that of the proper relationship between ruler and minister. In some cases, the correlations were conceptualised in terms of the macrocosm of the cosmic realm and the microcosm of the state, with events in one correlated to events in the other. For example, the *Shiji* identifies particular constellations with the positions at the imperial court (Henderson 2003: 188–9). The concepts of *qi*, *yin-yang* and *wuxing* were used to define various correspondences. For example, *wuxing* was correlated with other sets of five such as the five colours, smells, tastes, tones, directions, seasons, planets, winds, animals, grains, mountains, reservoirs, sage-rulers, social classes, viscera and emotions (*ibid.*: 191). The correlations were explained in practical ways. For instance, it was important for a physician to understand the phase correlate of a particular disease in a patient so that he could suggest the appropriate medical remedy. Likewise, for the ruler to understand the correct five-phase correlate of the Han dynasty would enable him to determine appropriate rituals and policies. The texts that debated political cosmology include the *Chunqiu fanlu*, *Huainanzi* and *Shiji*.

It is important to note that resonance is not a defining characteristic of correlations.[23] In other words, two items may be correlated without necessarily being resonant each to the other.[24] However, resonance is an integral feature of the macrocosm–microcosm relation because it signifies the mutuality of the two realms, rather than the overarching governance of the cosmic realm over all others. For instance, macrocosmic events such as natural disasters were in some cases read as portents of disasters in the microcosmic, socio-political realm. Equally, misgovernment could impact on aspects of the natural order, including stars and planets, winds and rains, and birds and insects (*ibid.*: 190). Resonance may be described in terms of the concept *ganying*, a theory that asserts that 'Things of the same category but in different cosmic realms [are] supposed to affect one another by virtue of a mutual sympathy, to resonate like properly attuned pitchpipes' (Henderson 1984: 20). Henderson suggests that this concept of resonance is associated with the experience of music and musical instruments where, for instance, a vibrating lute string will generate a response from a sympathetic string on another lute that is nearby.[25] An underlying assumption of the concept of resonance, which is also present in the *Yijing*, is that one should *attune* oneself to others, or aspects of the environment, in order to respond appropriately. The passage below from the *Xici zhuan* communicates the idea of attunement and resonance in terms of synchronising oneself with change and movement:

> The *Changes* manifests the Dao and shows how its virtuous activity is infused with the numinous. Thus one can through it synchronize himself with things and with it render service to the numinous. (1.9, trans. Lynn 1994: 62)

There is a metaphor in this passage that is not articulated in its translation, although it is spelled out in a note. In the phrase to 'synchronise himself with things', what has been translated as 'things' is a phrase, *chouzuo*, which means 'host toasts guest (*chou*) and guest returns toast (*zuo*)' (Lynn 1994: note 43 at p. 73). The imagery of toasting and returning a toast effectively illustrates the concept of resonance in correlative thinking. However, we must also note that the 'toasting' metaphor is an isolated incident, whereas in correlative thinking responses to change can in turn proceed to effect other changes.

Benjamin Schwartz suggests that the divination origins of the *Yijing*, that is, the tasks of correlating sign with situation, is itself a type of correlative thinking (1985: 393). The eight hexagrams and their associations, multiplied to sixty-four, allow for many more correlations than those according to the *yin-yang* and *wuxing* schema. The early divination sections of the *Yijing* do not explicitly mention correlations, although the *Xici zhuan* asserts that the text is itself a microcosm that corresponds to the macrocosmic heaven and earth:

> The *Changes* is a paradigm of Heaven and Earth, and so it shows how one can fill in and pull together the Dao of Heaven and Earth. Looking up, we use it [the *Changes*] to observe the configurations of Heaven, and, looking down, we use it to examine the patterns of Earth. Thus we understand the reasons underlying what is hidden and what is clear. (1.4, trans. Lynn 1994: 51; translator's annotation)

There is also explicit mention of correspondences, where the concept and characteristics of change are compared with different phenomena:

> In capaciousness and greatness, change corresponds to Heaven and Earth; in the way change achieves complete fulfilment, change corresponds to the four seasons; in terms of the concepts of yin and yang, change corresponds to the sun and moon; and in the efficacy of its ease and simplicity, change corresponds to perfect virtue. (1.6, trans. Lynn 1994: 56)

The correlations in the *Yijing* and other Han period texts were extended over numerous fields including alchemy, music, geomancy, astronomy, medicine and religion. An important underlying assumption is that one *can* – from the images, their respective associations and references to the past – work out the fitting or correct response. In the following section, we examine the interpretive approach associated with understanding the *Yijing*.

(5) An Interpretive Approach to the Meanings of the Hexagrams and Correspondences

We have seen how the *Xici zhuan* affirms the importance of reflecting on the hexagram symbols and the judgements to inform one's decision-making. That the symbols are central to the ideas of the *Yijing* is demonstrated in the extensive discussion of these symbols in the appendices, as well as in the explicit statement that '[t]o plumb the mysteries of the world to the utmost is dependent on the hexagrams' (*Xici zhuan* 1.12, trans. Lynn 1994: 68). In fact, the origination of the text and its use in divination is couched primarily in terms of the origination and development of the symbols. The symbols are grounded in experiences of the observable world, as we have seen, in the description of Lord Bao Xi (*Xici zhuan* 2.2). Each hexagram is given a name and attributed with a set of associated characteristics; these subsequent developments of the symbols are more abstract than the derivation of symbols from images in the experiential world.

There is yet more reflection in formulating the judgements associated with each hexagram and with each of the six lines of the hexagrams, though it is clear on the other hand that these readings of the symbols rely on ideas drawn from the social realities of the time. For example, the commentary on the judgement of hexagram 37, 'the Family' (*jiaren*), states that 'As far as the Family is concerned the woman's proper place is inside it, and the man's proper place is outside it' (Hexagram 37, trans. Lynn 1994: 363). The commentary is primarily Confucian in spirit, setting the boundaries of family life (Wilhelm 1977: 217–9). It is not only in the derivation of the symbols and their associated concepts where interpretation plays a key role. In the use of the *Yijing* as a divination manual, interpretation is also a major issue. The *Xici zhuan* notes both the importance and difficulty of interpreting the hexagrams and their implications in particular cases:

> The way they [the hexagrams] are named involves insignificant things, but the analogies so derived concern matters of great importance. The meanings are far-reaching, and the phrasing elegant. The language twists and turns but hits the mark. (2.6, trans. Lynn 1994: 87).

Each hexagram in the *Yijing* has a list of associated meanings; this means that the enquirer needs to relate his or her situation to a particular symbol. Let us take, for instance, the Judgment (*Duan*), Commentary on the Judgment

(*Duan Zhuan*), and Commentary on the Image (*Xiang Zhuan*) of the hexagram associated with *dui*, joy:

> Judgment: *Dui* [Joy] is such that prevalence is had. It is fitting to practice constancy here.
>
> Commentary on the Judgments: *Dui* means "to give joy." It is by being hard inside and yet soft outside that one manages to give Joy and still fittingly practice constancy. This is how one can be obedient to Heaven and yet responsive to mankind. If one leads the common folk with Joy, they will forget their toil, and if one has them risk danger and difficulty with Joy, they will forget about dying. Great is Joy, for it is the motivating force of the common folk!
>
> Commentary on the Images: Lake clinking to Lake: this constitutes the image of Joy. In the same way, the noble man engages in talk and study with friends. *Clinging* [*li*] means "linked" [*lian*]. No more flourishing application of Joy can be found than this.[26] (Hexagram 58, trans. Lynn 1994: 505)

There is little in these judgements and in the *Yijing* more generally to guide interpretation or understanding of the hexagram. How might this *translate*, for example, if an enquirer was concerned about the condition of his health? The mystery surrounding the interpretation of the hexagrams is symptomatic of the vagueness surrounding the understanding of correspondences. There were disagreements about what were proper correlates. For instance, 'The imperial Han dynasty changed its patron phase no less than four times. On two of these occasions, the dynasty adopted a different color of ritual paraphernalia, including court vestments of a different color, and a calendar beginning in a different month, both of which had to correspond to the newly inaugurated phase' (Henderson 2003: 192). In many cases, cosmologists needed to make significant compromises to fit with numerological schemes.[27] For instance, the four seasons had to fit in with the five phases (*wuxing*), or, more generally, two (of *yin-yang*) had to fit with five (of *wuxing*). In the *Huangdi neijing ling shu* (*Divine Pivot of the Inner Canon of the Yellow Emperor*), the Yellow Emperor is attempting to work out the relation between *yin-yang* and *wuxing* as it is applied to human health:

> The Yellow Emperor said, "According to the Five Phases, the eastern quarter, the first two of the ten stems [used to count days in the week], and the phase Wood rule over spring. Spring [is associated with] the color of the blue sky and governs the liver functions. The liver functions are those of the attenuated yin tracts connected with the feet. But now you claim that the

> first stem [corresponds to] the immature yang tract connected with the left hand, which does not tally with these regular relationships. Why is that?"
>
> Qibo said, "These are the yin and yang [correspondences] of Heaven and Earth, not the sequential changes of the four seasons and the Five Phases. Now yin and yang are names without physical form [i.e. abstractions, not concrete things]. 'They can be enumerated ten ways, separated a hundred ways, distributed a thousand ways, deduced a myriad ways' refers to this." (7:2, 41, trans. Sivin, in De Bary and Bloom 1999: 277–8; translator's annotations)

The issue of correspondences was a tricky one for cosmologists of the Han period, for they had to strike a balance between mechanical mapping of the correlations, on the one hand, and scope for interpretation, on the other. This was especially important for the *Yijing* as a divination manual because each hexagram reading had multiple applications in all sorts of different situations. Graham discusses this tension in the application of *yin-yang* as a cosmological scheme. When the correlates of *yin* and *yang* are clearly specified (e.g. *yin* with female, cold, water, square, goes down, and *yang* with male, hot, fire, round, goes up), *yin-yang* loses its significance as a spontaneous, mutually resonant conceptual framework within which to interpret events (1986: 33–4). Graham's discussion is insightful:

> With the specifying of the respects [of *yin* and *yang*] correlative thinking becomes explicit; it is no longer just the spontaneous formation of a *Gestalt*...The great interest of such system-building...is that it is the only kind of thinking which makes this try at bringing everything submerged to the surface. The result is a coherent but of course very simplified scheme...But once imprisoned in formulae correlative thinking loses its capacity for fine discriminations and assimilations. (1986: 34)

It takes no stretch of imagination to see that the complex balance between specification and interpretive scope is vastly magnified in the multivalent cosmology of the *Yijing*. This issue gives cause for concern especially if one is preoccupied with the pre-Socratic question, 'What are the ultimate constituent material elements of the world?' (Schwartz 1985: 357). The worldview of the *Yijing* and its openness to interpretation simply do not sit well with a scientific account of the world. For instance, the kind of systematisation and standardisation of cause–effect relationships in post-Galilean science (Graham 1986: 34) are not a possibility in the view of the *Yijing*. The *Yijing* is grounded in a world that is diverse and irreducibly so, with unlimited relations between the different entities (*ibid.*). This is not to explain away the problems associated with the interpretive aspect of the *Yijing*. Rather, it brings to the surface the assumptions of a manifold and interconnected world that underlies the thought of the *Yijing*. Lau and Ames discuss the haphazard and unsupervised world of early Daoism, a feature that is also present in the *Yijing*. Their remarks capture the commitment of the *Yijing*, which focuses on coordinating or resolving situations in the constantly transforming world:

> The *Book of Changes* is not a systematic cosmology that seeks to explain the sum of all possible situations we might encounter in order to provide insight into what to do, but is a resource providing a vocabulary of images that enable us to think through and articulate an appropriate response to the changing conditions of our lives...Rather than a vocabulary of truth and falsity, right and wrong, good and evil – terms that speak to the 'whatness' of things – we find pervasively the language of harmony and disorder, genuineness and hypocrisy, trust and dissimulation, adeptness and ineptness – terms which reflect the priority of the continuity that obtains among things: "how well" things hang together. (Lau and Ames 1998: 34)

(6) Constant Movement Marked by the Inevitability of Change

Change is a primary idea in the *Yijing*, expressed specifically in its title, *The Book of Changes* ('*yi*' meaning 'change'). The *Xici zhuan* and the *Shuogua* deal explicitly with the nature of change and issues associated with it, including the anticipation of and responses to change, understanding occurrences of change in the past in order to deal with changes in the present, and knowing when to act. The sense of movement in time, like the seasonal alternation of *yin* and *yang*, is repeated in this and many other passages of the appendices to the *Yijing*:

> When the sun goes, then the moon comes, and when the moon goes, then the sun comes. The sun and the moon drive each other on, and brightness is generated in this process. When the cold goes, then the heat comes, and when the heat goes, then the cold comes. The cold and the heat drive each other on, and the yearly seasons come into being in this process. What has gone is a contraction, and what is to come is an expansion. Contraction and expansion impel each other on, and benefits are generated in this process. (2.5, trans. Lynn 1994: 81)

The cycles of seasonal change are described in terms of a generative metaphor; the opposites 'impel each other on'. Although the *Yijing* does not specifically mention *wuxing*, the five phases, either in its older sections or the appendices, the philosophy underlying change is similar to a particular formulation of *wuxing* theory. The two significant ways of conceptualising the five phases were in terms of generation and conquest. In the generation cycle, each phase drives toward the following phase according to this pattern: wood impels fire, fire impels earth, earth impels metal, metal impels water, and water impels wood, and the cycle continues. In the conquest cycle, wood conquers earth, metal conquers wood, fire conquers metal, water conquers fire, earth conquers water, and the cycle continues (Henderson 2003: 191). The *Yijing* seems to support a generative rather than conquest cycle, as we see both in this passage above and in another of the appendices, the *Shuogua*. In section 6 of the *Shuogua*, *Commentary on the Trigrams*, there is a list of the defining characteristics of each of the eight trigrams. At the end of the list, there is an argument for the necessity of change: because each triad is associated with a specific set of characteristics, change is necessary to allow 'the myriad things to become all that they can be' (trans. Lynn 1994: 122). The replacement of one phase with the next is inevitable; change is unstoppable (*Xici zhuan* 1.6). As it was the case with *yin-yang*, *wuxing* was not merely a classificatory scheme. It was a conceptual framework for predicting and explaining change.

The primary task of the *Yijing* from ancient times was to predict change such that the ruler would be able to anticipate and deal with it. Underlying divination practice is an expectation and anticipation of change. Both the *Xici zhuan* and the *Shuogua* articulate the rationale for the continued use of the *Yijing* as a divination manual, drawing on the experiences of enlightened sages in the past who used it:

> By virtue of its numinous power, it lets one know what is going to come, and by virtue of its wisdom, it becomes a repository of what has happened...[The intelligent and perspicacious ones of antiquity] used the *Changes* to cast light on the Dao of Heaven and to probe into the conditions of the common folk. This is the numinous thing that they inaugurated in order to provide beforehand for the needs of the common folk. (1.11, trans. Lynn 1994: 64–5)

> ...the eight trigrams combine with one another in such a way that, to reckon the past, one follows the order of their progress, and, to know the future,

> one works backward through them. Therefore, the *Changes* allow us to work backward [from the future] and reckon forward [from the past]. ("*Shuogua*" 3, trans. Lynn 1994: 121)

The inductive argument in the first passage implies that these sages were successful in Confucian terms – in implementing a benevolent government – as they provided for the common people. One is encouraged to learn from the applications of the oracles. The *Shuogua* passage spells out how we adapt wisdoms from the past, to our experiences in the present. The concept of time is fundamental to the practice of divination. This concerns, centrally, how one reflects on one's experience, draws from the past, then applies that to the present case. Hellmut Wilhelm explains the process of divination in terms of a synchronic conception of time:

> ...each situation can be apprehended in two ways: through direct experience as a consequence of the dynamism of existence, and through theoretical speculation as a consequence of the continuousness of existence and its government by laws...The questioner thus obtains access to the theoretically established aspect of his own situation, and by reference to the texts set forth under this aspect in the Book of Changes he obtains counsel and guidance from the experience of former generations and the insights of the great masters. Thus the synchronicity disclosed by the oracle is merely the apprehension of two different modes of experiencing the same state of affairs. (1977: 12)[28]

There is another conception of time that seems in the first instance to conflict with its synchronous bringing-together of past and present, and to some extent, of the future. This is the view that time proceeds and, with it, frequent shifts and changes occur: 'Change and action never stand still but keep flowing all through the six vacancies [the six line positions]' (2.8, trans. Lynn 1994: 89). The shifts in the line diagrams are symbolic of changes in the world. As one line changes into *its* other (*yin* into *yang* or *vice-versa*), the hexagram changes. The *Shuogua* discusses how the line changes – changes at the most fundamental level – effect shifts in the trigrams; movement from trigram to trigram represents changes in phase. This picture of continuous change that 'flows' is compatible with a synchronic understanding of time in divination because the former relates to the urgency of anticipating and responding to change while the latter is a concept of time that underlies *each* process of divination. In the light of constant shifts and changes, it is important to respond appropriately. Here, again, time is a critical issue, for timeliness in large part determines the appropriateness and success of a particular response. Not only should one acquire appropriate resources but he or she should also be aware of the right time to act:

> The noble man lays up a store of instruments in his own person and waits for the proper moment and then acts, so how could there ever be anything to his disadvantage! Here one acts without impediment; it is due to this that when one goes out, he obtains his catch. (2.5, trans. Lynn 1994: 83)

Wilhelm explains how the concept of *timeliness* relates to the original meaning of the term. In its original meaning, time (*shi*) was related to awareness of seasonal changes, which was critical to timeliness in agricultural activities:

> ...the Book of Changes eschews such theoretical concepts of time, operating with the word *shih* [*shi*], "time," in a manner that is much closer to its derivation. The word meant originally "sowing time," then "season" in general...In its early form it was composed of the character for "sole of the foot" (Latin, *planta*) above that for a unit of measurement. In China, too, the sole of the foot is related semantically to planting; thus, the word means a section of time set apart for a certain activity. Thence its meaning was extended to the four seasons, all of which are correspondingly filled with certain activities, and only then to time in general. The word is often used in the Book of Changes in the meaning of "season," and many of the characteristic attributes of time can be traced to this heritage. (1977: 17–18)

There is a distinct sense here of waiting for the right moment, of seizing an opportunity, which is associated with divination practices. Wilhelm suggests that the conception of time that underlies the reasoning in the divination sections of the *Yijing* is a 'concrete' one, in that it is filled with possibilities that change in different moments (1977: 17).[29] In understanding these changes, and how people in the past dealt with them, one is equipped to respond to situations. In the following section we discuss the action-guiding aspect of the *Yijing*.

(7) The Action-guiding Nature of the Judgements

A fundamental assumption of divination is that one can discover aspects of the future and is able to influence its course. This outlook expects that events occurring in the human realm will effect changes in other realms, and vice-versa. The *Xici zhuan* articulates the process of divination in terms of understanding correlations and affirms the action-guiding nature of divination: 'The means to know the future through the mastery of numbers is referred to as "prognostication", and to keep in step freely with change is referred to as "the way one should act"' (1.5, trans. Lynn 1994: 54).

According to Chung-ying Cheng, the process or act of divination is not itself a philosophy, although its assumptions reveal significant underlying philosophical commitments (Cheng 2003). The philosophical framework is one that indicates both the limitations of the human condition and its freedom of decision and action. This standpoint emphasises the importance of knowing what to do in particular situations, within environing contexts. Lau and Ames express the centrality of knowing what to do in the Chinese philosophical traditions: 'In China, the pursuit of wisdom has perennially centered on finding a way to stabilize, to discipline, and to shape productively and elegantly the unstoppable stream of change in which the human experience is played out' (1998: 38). We have seen in our previous discussion the importance of timeliness in action, which Lau and Ames call 'seizing the moment' (*ibid.*). The *Xici zhuan* also acknowledges how it is important to turn a situation to advantage (*li*: benefit, advantage) (2.12). In this passage, advantage is discussed in conjunction with good fortune and misfortune, emphasising the importance of working with the situation to achieve the best outcome. In the popular imagination, ideas about good and bad fortune were interwoven with superstitious beliefs about natural and cosmic events interpreted as portents for humankind;[30] the absence of criteria regarding how correspondences were drawn contributed to the looseness of interpretations about correlations.

More profoundly, in Chinese philosophy, knowledge is construed in practical terms. Lau and Ames emphasise the focus on efficacy and pragmatism implicit in the Chinese conception of knowledge; they note its 'meliorative' intent (1998: 26). Applying the distinction articulated by Gilbert Ryle, knowing in the Chinese tradition is 'knowing how' rather than 'knowing that'.[31] Zhang Dongsun makes a similar distinction in his characterisation of western and Chinese philosophies:

> These two kinds of thinking not only differ in terms of categories and the value of their terms, but also differ markedly in their attitudes. If we take inquiry, for example, Western thinking, in respect of any particular thing or

> event, is inclined to ask "What is it?" before asking "How do we deal with it?" Chinese thinking, on the other hand, is inclined to do the opposite: "How do we deal with it?" takes precedence. Thus I would say that the West has a "*what* priority attitude" while China has a "how priority attitude."[32]

It is important not to dichotomise the two approaches, western and Chinese. Zhang is careful to note that the difference is one of emphasis rather than a categorisation of two types of approaches that are antithetical. We are aware, from our examination of the Chinese philosophical traditions, that what was important in early Chinese thought was not to specify the general characteristics of cause–effect relations or universal laws of nature. Rather, the focus is on a critical reflection that concentrates on dealing with the particular issue at hand and how to achieve resolution. In the light of this feature of Chinese philosophy, it is important for a person both to focus on particular situations and to understand how these unfold and change through the course of time. In other words, one should have an attitude that is expectant of change:

> The Master said: "To get into danger is a matter of thinking one's position secure; to become ruined is a matter of thinking one's continuance protected; to fall into disorder is a matter of thinking one's order enduring. Therefore the noble man when secure does not forget danger, when enjoying continuance does not forget ruin, when maintaining order does not forget disorder. This is the way his person is kept secure and his state remains protected. The *Changes* say: 'This might be lost, this might be lost, so tie it to a healthy, flourishing mulberry.'" (2.5, trans. Lynn 1994: 83)

Complacency is an apt term for describing the potential pitfalls described here. There is contempt, articulated through the voice of Confucius, for shortsightedness that isolates the self from its relationships and contexts. This passage presents the importance of understanding resonances and expecting change in terms of individual benefit. But there are also important moral implications when we understand that many if not most of our decisions and actions impact on others. Belief in the potency of resonating effects is expressive of an outlook that understands causality in complex ways. This belief is also connected with a view of individuals not as isolated entities but as situated within a broader, manifold environment.

The Impact of the *Yijing*

During the Han period, the main application of correlative thinking was in government and political administration. Proposals of correspondences between events of the cosmos and those of the state arose in response to the establishment and justification of empire in the Qin and Han. However, aspects of correlative thinking permeated different spheres of life and continue to persist in different forms in Chinese society today. For example, in Chinese approaches to health, the human body is considered a microcosm, that is, a small-scale universe. Health and disease are explained in terms of *qi* and blood. Correlations also extend to poetry, philosophy, religion and aspects of popular culture. The practice of geomancy in contemporary architecture, which considers *qi* in astrological, geographical, physiological, psychological and aesthetic terms, is still pervasive. The concept of food and its classification in terms of nutritional value (for example in *yin* (cooling) foods and *yang* (heating) foods) and flavour (the five tastes) is an integral part of Chinese popular belief (Henderson 1984: 46–8).

The appendices of the *Yijing* are a product of the worldview that understands correlations between individual entities across different realms. They absorbed the philosophical mood of the time and integrated that with Confucian themes. They endorsed key aspects of Confucianism including the heightened role of the ruler, the providence of heaven and earth, the capacity of human beings to improve their situation, and the hope in a socio-political utopia wherein individual and social ends coincide. Hence, the *Yijing* became involved with and was part of the development of Neo-Confucianism. But the influence of correlative thinking was not confined to the Confucian tradition. The worldview that sees integration and correspondences between different entities is pervasive in Chinese philosophy. The description by Lau and Ames of a Daoist view of the world is familiar; although it draws on the language of Daoism, the *wanwu* (ten thousand things), the conceptual framework of 'collaborative unfolding' is an integral part of the philosophy of the Han period:

> There is no principle (*archē* > *principium*) of order – no superordinate One standing independent of the world to order it as an efficient cause. Rather, there is only the collaborative unfolding of the myriad things or events – the *wanwu* 萬物 or *wanyou* 萬有. Within this collaboration, there is an ever-changing processional regularity that can be discerned in the world around

> us, making experience *in some degree* coherent and determinate and, given its inherent indeterminacy, in some degree novel and unpredictable. (1998: 19)

The *Yijing* is itself a seedbed of concomitant beliefs grounded in the idea of a correlated and ceaselessly transforming world. This conception of the world is one of the fundamental features of Chinese thought. It is a metaphysical account of the world, but not one that articulates a determinate and static ontology. It is an orientation to processes and change rather than events and substances. The conception of passing time that is 'filled' with processes underlies the conception of individual life that is continually affected by changes in its environment. Yet, on the other hand, an individual's actions and responses also impact on others. The picture of related individuals in a ceaselessly transforming world is a feature of Chinese thought that shaped, and continues to shape, the intellectual and institutional traditions of China until modern times.

Suggestions for Further Reading

Cheng, Chung-ying (2003) 'Philosophy of Change', in Antonio Cua (ed.) *Encyclopedia of Chinese Philosophy*, New York: Routledge: pp. 517–24.

Henderson, John B. (1984) 'Correlative Thought in Early China', in *The Development and Decline of Chinese Cosmology*, New York: Columbia University Press: pp. 1–58.

Henderson, John B. (2003) 'Cosmology', in Antonio Cua (ed.) *Encyclopedia of Chinese Philosophy*, New York: Routledge: pp. 187–94.

Lynn, Richard John (1994) *The Classic of Changes: A New Translation of the I Ching as Interpreted by Wang Bi*, New York: Columbia University Press.

Graham, Angus C. (1986) *Yin-Yang and the Nature of Correlative Thinking*, IEAP Occasional Paper and Monograph Series no. 6, Singapore: Institute of East Asian Philosophies.

Lau, D. C. and Ames, Roger (1998) *Yuan Dao: Tracing Dao to its Source*, New York: Ballantine Books.

Major, John S. (1993) 'A General Introduction to Early Han Cosmology', in *Heaven and Earth in Early Han Thought*, SUNY Series in Chinese Philosophy and Culture, Albany: State University of New York Press.

Sivin, Nathan (1995) 'The Myth of the Naturalists', in *Medicine, Philosophy and Religion in Ancient China: Researches and Reflections*, Aldershot: Variorum (Ashgate Publishing), Section IV, pp. 1–33.

Notes

1. Graham believes that the later commentaries would have been written at the very latest by the early Han Dynasty (1986: 13). Yet, prior to the Han Dynasty, references to the *Yijing* and its ideas were sparse: the reference in the Confucian *Analects* (7:17) to the 'Changes', *yi*, is questionable; Xunzi ignores the *Yijing* when he lists the five classics; the concepts *yin* and *yang* were discussed but not within correlative frameworks; *wuxing* (five phases) was mentioned in the Mohist *Canons*, the *Sunzi* and *Han Fei Tzu* in a derogatory manner (Graham 1986: 9).
2. Graham suggests that this chapter was written prior to the *Shiji* as it seems unaware that there was a Daoist 'school'. The author of this chapter deals with (the shortcomings of) Laozi's and Zhuangzi's doctrines separately, with a clear preference for the former (2001: 282).
3. We should interpret this phrase with caution because to describe Huang-Lao ideology in terms of Daoism and Legalism is reductionistic (refer to Schwartz 1985: 237; Graham 1989: 374). Schwartz is cautious about the label 'Huang-Lao' and how it is defined (1985: 237–54), while Graham emphasises the possible extent of its influence as he considers its connection with other doctrines (1989: 374–6; 379–410).
4. In 1973, two silk manuscripts of the *Lao-tzu* (the received version is called the *Daodejing*) were discovered in a Former Han tomb in Mawangdui. One of the silk manuscripts had four appended documents, called the *Huang-Lao Boshu* (Graham 1989: 374).
5. In *Chunqiu fanlu*, 6:11a–16a, trans. Sarah Queen, presented in De Bary and Bloom (1999), at pp. 298–9. The *Chunqiu fanlu* had traditionally been ascribed to Dong Zhongshu although it is now believed that the text is a compilation of pieces written by Dong Zhongshu, his disciples and critics (De Bary and Bloom: 294).
6. The triadic relationship between heaven, earth and humanity is a fundamental idea in a number of Confucian texts of the Warring States period such as the *Xiao Jing* (*Book of Filial Piety*) and the *Daxue* (*Great Learning*). It became a central theme in the Neo-Confucianism doctrine of Wang Yangming (1472–1529).
7. *Zhao Gong* (1.8), in Graham 1986: 71.
8. *Xiang Gong* (27.2), *Zhao Gong* (11.4), in Graham 1986: 74, note 52.
9. The issue of Zou Yan's status as a thinker of some capacity is debated. Graham argues that Zou Yan's fame rides on his ability to persuade the powers that be to accept his views; Graham also intimates that Zou Yan is not to be considered a thinker of one of the debating schools (1986: 11–13).

Graham's view runs against the commonly held estimate of Zou Yan. Sivin argues that Zou Yan's ideas had an important impact on Chinese intellectual history (Sivin 1995b: 8).

10. Graham argues that this is the 'earliest firmly dated philosophical text to lay out schemes of correspondences' (1986: 13).
11. Apparently, they drew from 'practically every other philosophic tradition of its time, but scantily on Legalist writings' (Sivin, in De Bary and Bloom 1999: 237).
12. Sivin writes, '[i]t probably originated in the astronomer's difference between measuring locations in the sky in degrees radiating from the North Pole and those on Earth in linear distances north and south, east and west' (in De Bary and Bloom 1999: 238). See also Major 1993: 32–35.
13. For example, section XLI of the same chapter states that 'Heaven has twelve months, to regulate the 360 days, Man also has twelve joints, to regulate the 360 bones' (trans. Major 1993: 135). Some of the numerological correspondences seem simplistic.
14. *Zuo Zhuan* 1.8, in Graham 1986: 71. Graham notes that, outside of cosmological discussions, *qi* featured in discussions of human health, relating to the breath and energies of the body, and frequently paired with blood (the circulatory system) (1986: 71–2).
15. The three texts are the *Basic Questions* (*Huangdi neijing suwen*), the *Divine Pivot* (*Huangdi neijing ling shu*), and the *Grand Basis* (*Huangdi neijing taisu*) (Sivin, in De Bary and Bloom 1999: 273–8).
16. Sivin also notes that this form of dialogue between the emperor and his minister 'mirrors the political ideals of the elite in its master image of the emperor as a man of knowledge concerned not with running a government but with embodying the link between the cosmic order and the individual' (*ibid.*: 284).
17. The *Book of Filial Piety* was popular right through to pre-modern East Asia, especially during the Tokugawa period (1603–1868) in Japan (De Bary and Bloom: 325–6).
18. The 'numinous' is Lynn's translation of the term *shen*, which has a sense of the transcendental. The *Yijing* emphasises a person's ability to understand the numinous realm. In some cases, sages are said to have numinous power to apply the wisdom of the *Yijing* in alignment with the numinous realm of heaven and earth (refer to Lynn 1994: note 11 at p. 70).
19. In his comments on the *Xici zhuan*, Wang Bi presents a (materially-productive) interpretation of *kun* (powers of earth), stating that 'When it is at rest, it condenses its *qi* [material force], and when it becomes active, it opens up and so brings things into existence' (trans. Lynn 1994: 56).

20. For a more detailed discussion of the dimension of *yin-yang* theory and its associations with a degraded sense of the feminine, refer to Rosenlee 2006: 45–68.
21. The *Yueling*, a chapter of the *Liji* (*Book of Rites*), prescribes activities and rituals, and provides prohibitions, for the emperor on a monthly basis.
22. The *Chunqiu fanlu* asserted a direct connection between human moods and emotions, on the one hand, and particular cosmic units (such as seasons of the year), on the other (in 11.186, in Henderson 1984: 4).
23. Henderson makes this point persuasively in 'Correlative Thought in Early China' (1984: 22–28).
24. Henderson argues that the correlation between 366 days and 366 joints of man in the *Huainanzi* were simple correlations without resonance (*ibid.*).
25. In addition, there are musical 'numbers', such as the five tones, eight voices and twelve pitchpipes, that are applied to health and weather changes (Henderson 2003: 189–90).
26. Wilhelm discusses a selection of symbols, focusing in particular on the *Commentary on the Images* (*Xiang Zhuan*), sections relating to the symbols (or images).
27. Henderson believes that such compromises reflect the importance of some of these categories, such as *wuxing*, in the thinking of the Han cosmologists (2003: 191–2).
28. Wilhelm argues, persuasively, that synchronicity of answer and question would be possible (without collapsing into chance) only if a system (of how a question becomes coordinated with the correct answer from the *Yijing*) is presupposed (1977: 11).
29. Wilhelm writes, 'The conception of time that we encounter in these quotations is very concrete. Here time is immediately experienced and perceived. It does not represent merely a principle of abstract progression but is fulfilled in each of its segments; an effective agent not only in which reality is enacted but which in turn acts on reality and brings it to completion. Just as space appears to the concrete mind not merely as a schema of extension but as something filled with hills, lakes, and plains – in each of its parts open to different possibilities – so time is here taken as something filled, pregnant with possibilities, which vary with its different moments and which, magically as it were, induce and confirm events. Time here is provided with attributes to which events stand in a relation of right or wrong, favorable or unfavourable' (1977: 17).
30. Xunzi was keen to establish the legitimacy of political institutions (especially in his formulation of the Confucian theory of rectification of

names) without reference to a transcendent heaven. In chapter 17 of the *Works of Xunzi*, 'Discourse on Heaven', he limits the jurisdiction of heaven and dispels superstitions. Refer to the discussion in chapter 3, pp. 43–4.

31. In 'Knowing How and Knowing That', Ryle argues against the prevailing doctrine, which holds '(1) that Intelligence is a special faculty, the exercise of which are those specific internal acts which are called acts of thinking . . . and (2) that practical activities merit their titles "intelligent", "clever", and the rest only because they are accompanied by some such internal acts of considering propositions . . .' (p. 1). Ryle transcends the theory–practice gap and contends that (1) knowledge-how cannot be defined in terms of knowledge-that; and (2) knowledge-how is a concept logically prior to the concept of knowledge-that (pp. 4–5).
32. Zhang, Dongsun (1995) *Zhishi yu wenhua: Zhang Dongsun wenhua lunzhu jiyao*, [*Knowledge and Culture: an Anthology of Zhong Dongsun's Works on Culture*] ed. Zhang Yaonan, Beijing: Zhongguo guanbo dianshi chubanshe: 375; cited in Lau and Ames (1998: 29).

11 Chinese Buddhism

Buddhism was first introduced into China during the first century CE, during the Han Dynasty. At the time of its introduction, it would have had influence only as the practising faith of a small community of foreign traders. As Confucianism was the dominant ideology during the Han period, Buddhism did not have much influence on the lives of the majority people in China, nor was it given serious consideration by Chinese scholars and officials. However, the period during the third and fourth centuries CE,[1] when China was once again divided by ethnic and territorial wars and Confucianism lost its footing as the state-sponsored ideology, was also a time when Buddhist religious and philosophical notions were considered, in the first instance by non-Han Chinese tribes.[2] The tenets of Buddhist thought underwent intensive scrutiny and those who sought to promote this 'foreign' ideology primarily articulated its ideas in terms of existing concepts in Chinese philosophies, especially those of religious Daoism. It was not until the sixth century that doctrinal differences in strands of Chinese Buddhism began to take shape, establishing Chinese Buddhist doctrine as both separate from Indian Buddhism, and distinct from Confucianism and Daoism.

Given this long period of development of Chinese Buddhism and its eventual division and definition into different strands, the discussion in this chapter will be necessarily brief and to some extent disjointed. It is important first to understand the fundamental tenets of Buddhist thought including some examination of its origins in Indian philosophy. The second section of this chapter explores the early stages of the introduction of Buddhism into China, focusing especially on its parallels and interactions with the indigenous philosophies of China. Finally, there will be a summary of doctrinal differences between the strands of Chinese Buddhism.

Basic Tenets of Buddhist Thought

Introductions to Buddhist thought typically provide a systematic account of its key concepts including suffering, non-permanence, the fourfold noble truth, the eightfold noble path, Nirvana (cessation of the ego self), interdependent causality, karma (effects and consequences) and rebirth. However, it is unsatisfactory simply to explain Chinese Buddhist thought in terms of its concepts alone without some understanding of both the Indian philosophical background against which it arose, and its subsequent development into different Buddhist doctrines in China. This problem is more pronounced in Chinese Buddhism because we need to be aware of the transmission of particular notions from India to China, and further modification in the hands of Chinese thinkers. Hence, the account offered here will identify certain core notions in Buddhist thought and, where relevant, note its origins and subsequent developments. The discussion of core notions in this section leans heavily on the account of Buddhist philosophy outlined by David Kalupahana in *Buddhist Philosophy*. Kalupahana offers an account of Buddhist philosophy set against the backdrop of pre-Buddhist Indian thought.[3] Even though Kalupahana's concern was not to investigate Chinese Buddhist philosophy, his philosophically sensitive account of the origins of key elements in Buddhist philosophy is important to the discussion here.

The founder of Buddhism, Siddhartha Gautama, is believed to have been contemporaneous with Confucius around the sixth century BCE, though his exact dates are not known. Many aspects of Buddhist philosophy, including asceticism, meditation, belief in extra-sensory perception and yogic intuition, questions about self, consciousness and continuity, and a conception of ultimate reality, were already present in the Upanishadic and Jainist traditions (Kalupahana 1976: 3–15). In philosophical terms, the thought of Gautama Buddha is characterised by empirical observations of human life coupled with belief in extra-sensory phenomena, the realm within which rebirth and de-individualised consciousness are possible. There is little attention in his system to metaphysical questions concerning the existence of supernatural beings or domains, including that of gods, hell, or heaven. In the early texts, such concepts had a purely regulative role in guiding moral action and did not reflect ontological commitment to their existence (Kalupahana 1976: 66). This is not to say, however, that later developments in Buddhist thought were similarly devoid of these metaphysical considerations.

In epistemological terms, Buddhism emphasised the limitations of all sources of knowledge. This was at the same time a criticism of the then current epistemological theories that relied on some combination of reason, perception or extra-sensory perception for insight into truth. Gautama Buddha was not sceptical about sensory or extra-sensory perception, as he affirmed six senses as the primary sources of knowledge: eye, ear, nose, tongue, body and mind. However, he was concerned with how the objects of such forms of perception were misconstrued because subjective prejudices tainted one's interpretation of experiences. In this sense, there are two possible sources of ignorance (*avidya*; in Pali), absence or lack of knowledge, and the imposition of a false view on the object in question (Kalupahana 1976: 19–24). The implications of ignorance are far-reaching as they can lead to misconceptions about the nature of self which in turn lead to the human predicament of unsatisfactoriness. A core element of Buddhist thought concerns the nature of suffering and its elimination. The fourfold noble truth, a core doctrine of Buddhism, sets out the nature of suffering:

> (1) all life is inevitably sorrowful; (2) sorrow is due to craving; (3) sorrow can only be stopped by the stopping of craving; (4) this can be done by a course of carefully disciplined conduct, culminating in the life of concentration and meditation led by the Buddhist monk. (Hurvitz and Tsai 1999: 416)

At the most basic level of moral concern, craving is associated with sensory pleasures. Suffering arises from such craving because these objects, and their associated pleasures, are transient. The pursuit of these pleasures is also associated with a temperament of selfishness, greed and insatiable desire that looks only to the here and now. There is at the root of the human predicament a deep-seated craving for permanent happiness of the sort defined by social norms. Suffering, *dukkha* (in Pali), covers both physical and mental distress. It can vary in extent, from acute pain and agony to an underlying and persistent feeling of unsatisfactoriness. Apart from the association of suffering with unmet sensory desires, there are more profound reasons for the suffering associated with craving. The most significant object of an individual's craving is not external, sensory pleasures but a deeper yearning for permanent selfhood. Permanent selfhood is the most fundamental object of craving because it is after all the self who enjoys the pleasures of life. Freedom from suffering can only be attained if one stops this basic form of craving. Such freedom emancipates one from a desirous, though false, belief that the self be permanent. Without grasping this fourfold truth, no individual has any chance of being relieved of suffering. This theory of emancipation has a cognitivist tone in that it comes about only after an intellectual realisation of one's impermanence. Hence, Hurvitz and Tsai suggest that the 'fundamental truths on which Buddhism is founded are not metaphysical or theological but, rather, psychological' (1999: 413).

In practical terms, the fourfold noble truth also advocates a life of quiet discipline expressed in the eightfold noble path. The eightfold path consists of stages of incorporating right view, right thought, right speech, right action, right livelihood, right effort, right mindfulness, and right concentration. These stages may be understood in developmental terms, where each stage builds upon the previous one. However, all of these characteristics must be present in the person who is considered to have attained the Buddhist goal in life, the *arahant* (in Pali). The *arahant* lives a paradigmatically contemplative life and is always mindful of Buddhist doctrine. As in the case of the fourfold noble truth, we may understand the eight characteristics in a more superficial sense, in terms of normative moral guidance, whereby one develops the right kinds of behaviours and attitudes. Alternatively, embodiment of the eightfold path can reflect a deeper understanding of life as expressed in Buddhist doctrine. The phenomenal self – the thinking, volitional and conscious self that acts and interacts in the everyday world – is not a unified or unchanging entity in Buddhist thought. This is because it is constituted by five components, or processes:

(1) Form and matter (*rupa*; in Pali): matter, material processes, corporeality.
(2) Sensations (*vedana*; in Pali): sense reactions arising as a result of contact with the world through the exercise of the six senses.
(3) Perceptions (*samjna*; in Sanskrit): cognition of material and mental objects through the six senses.
(4) Psychic dispositions or constructions (*samskara*; in Sanskrit): psychological emotions, impressions and volitional processes that influence behaviour.
(5) Consciousness or conscious thought (*vjnana*; in Sanskrit): awareness of self and awareness of the phenomenal world.

An individual – the phenomenal self – is made up of a combination of these five components, which are in a state of constant flux. Hence, the physical self as we know it is impermanent, composite and not correlated with an eternal self or soul.

The Buddhist conception of existence has three fundamental characteristics:

(1) Impermanence (*anicca/anittya*; in Pali/Sanskrit): this is an empirically grounded theory that focuses on arising (generation) and passing away.
(2) Unsatisfactoriness (*dukkha/duhkha*; in Pali/Sanskrit).
(3) Nonsubstantiality (*anatta/anatman*; in Pali/Sanskrit): non-ego, non-self theory; there is no enduring individual personhood.

These three characteristics encapsulate the Buddhist rejection of notions of the self in the Indian religious and philosophical context. The Upanishadic tradition upheld a conception of the enduring and immutable self (Kalupahana 1976: 38–9). In its place, Buddhism proposed a conception of self as impermanent and ever-changing, according to the five components; this phenomenal self is effectively a 'bundle' whose continuity is comprised by a series of causal events. Failure to grasp these three aspects of existence leads to sorrow. Hurvitz and Tsai explain how the five processes may come into play, in the case of one who misunderstands self and existence, to generate more suffering:

> The root cause of the process of birth and death and rebirth is ignorance, the fundamental illusion that individuality and permanence exist, when, in fact, they do not. Hence there arise in the organism various psychic phenomena, including desire, followed by an attempt to appropriate things to itself...each act, word, or thought leaves its traces on the collection of the five constituents that make up the phenomenal individual, and their character alters correspondingly. This process goes on throughout life, and when the immaterial and material parts of the being are separated in death, the immaterial constituents, which make up what in other systems would be called soul, carry over the consequential effects of the deeds of the past life and obtain another form in one of the ten realms of existence...(1999: 416–7).

Misapprehension about the self, that it is an individual being separate from others, is intertwined with an incorrect view of causality. According to the view that each self is an individual and independent entity, the lines of causation are reasonably straightforward. However, Buddhist philosophy holds that there is a chain of *interdependent* causality that underlies processes and events. According to this view, existence is an ever-changing process in which interrelated entities are implicated by changes in others. Complex causal relations and caused phenomena pertain not only to the world of physical existence, but also to psychic and mental phenomena. The Buddhist doctrine of causality is distinctive in the following ways:

(1) Causal events are real and not merely perceived.
(2) There is a certain necessity about it in that all existence is entwined in interdependent causality.
(3) Interdependent causality admits of regularity; it has certain patterns. When we say that events are 'accidental', that only reflects our ignorance of the actual causal processes that were in play in that situation.
(4) Interdependent causality is conditional; this means that events or consequences are not strictly determined, nor are they simply arbitrary.

These features of Buddhist doctrine arose in response to a number of existing theories about causality. That causal events are *real* (point 1) was a response to the idealism held by some Upanishadic thinkers; Upanishadic thinkers believed that causations are mental fabrications and have no objective reality. The emphases on an element of *necessity* (point 2) and *regularity* (point 3) were attempts to address indeterminism, a view that was expressed in Gautama Buddha's time. The suggestion that causality is *conditioned* (point 4) marks a focus on processes rather than (individual) agents or events. All these elements, necessity, regularity and conditionality, work together in any one event. Thus, the causal patterns provide part of the overall picture of an event, but it is also essential to understand the circumstances that were conditioned, the effects, and the objects and entities that were involved in the event. But it is important to remember that it is not entirely appropriate to discuss *an* event in these terms as if one could circumscribe its limits, for the effects arising from a situation will in turn condition other future 'events'. Events in time are only snapshots, like a photograph, frozen in time. This account of interdependent causality was a middle-path position – or middle-way, that is, an approach that avoids two extremes and tries to incorporate both – between two theories, one of eternal self and the other of annihilation upon bodily death (Kalupahana 1976: 27–9).

There are many metaphysical questions that arise within this conceptual framework. These include questions about the nature of causal interactions between sensory and extra-sensory phenomena; the origination of phenomenal entities (such as the animated human body); feelings of pain and happiness by the phenomenal self given that there is no 'individual' as such; the survival of the human personality; the knowledge of the past and other issues based on inductive inference; the nature of mind; as well as metaphysical and epistemological bases for ongoing processes after cessation of bodily form (Kalupahana 1976: 29–31, 84, 153–162). Many of these questions were not covered in early Buddhist thought although they were, subsequently, and debate on these topics continues in contemporary scholarly work.

The doctrine of interdependent causality has important moral implications. Because the self is both acting and acted upon in situations that are conditioned, the conclusions of autonomy (based on an independent self) and fatalism (based on a self determined by external factors) are avoided. The phenomenal self *qua* agent is conditioned by causes and in turn generates consequences that condition other, future events. Every action (*karma*; in Sanskrit), whether physical or mental, is followed by correlated consequences (*vipaka*; in Sanskrit). Even thoughts and thought-processes are considered *active* from the point of view of *karma*; hence it is important to cultivate right mindfulness and right concentration as articulated in the eightfold path. The doctrine of *karma* was already present in the early mainstream Brahmanic and ascetic traditions (Kalupahana 1976: 44). In the Upanishadic tradition, the phenomenal self is in control of *karma*. In the Jainist tradition, once *karma* is performed, it is out of the individual's hands. Buddhism rejected the conception of *karma* in such a-temporal, deterministic terms and instead views *karma* in causal terms. The Buddhist doctrine of *karma* included a consideration of external stimuli, conscious motives and unconscious motives. It also examines consequences within a dynamic time frame of situations that are partly determined by circumstances, but also arising as a result of a particular cause. On this view, the implications of each individual act or thought, undertaken by the self, are profound and complex as their impacts will condition any number of future events.

The doctrine of *karma* is correlated with the concept of self. In Buddhism, the true self is a psycho-physical self (Kalupahana 1976: 51–2), which is defined essentially in terms of a stream of consciousness that continues in spite of the demise of the physical body it is associated with. On the other hand, the physically-instantiated self is caught up in a cycle of birth (*jati*; in Pali and Sanskrit) and consequent decay and death (*jaramarama*; in Pali and Sanskrit). Buddhism rejects the dominant view that identifies physical existence with continuity of self. It holds instead that the self and physical existence are separate and therefore, cessation of bodily existence does not imply the cessation of self. Continuity of self is what underlies the cycle of rebirth, *samsara* (in Sanskrit). According to a more trivial and punitive version of the ethics of *samsara* and *karma*, to have a short and miserable life (Kalupahana 1976: 49) or to be reborn as a being belonging to a less-than-human species is punishment of sorts for the negative consequences accumulated by a particular stream of consciousness. Such a theory is of course a self-sealer but it also raises more general and important questions about *karma* and rebirth and how we are to understand the connections between particular acts and their implications for streams of consciousness. It is also unclear whether different streams of consciousness might merge or re-form such that an 'individual' person, say, might experience any number of different streams. Treatment of such issues is unclear and unsatisfactory in early Buddhist thought, although they were explored in later Buddhist thought.

The issues relating to the concept of interdependent causality are also integral to the concept of *nirvana* (in Sanskrit), which literally means 'to extinguish', that is, a halt to the process of rebirth. It is not to be understood negatively, as annihilation of the self, but rather, in terms of enlightened detachment from craving and its attendant disappointments. In its broadest sense, *nirvana* refers to the removal of all craving, especially that for an independent and unchanging individual self. The craving for such a self is, in itself, not different from enslavement. The individual who attains such emancipation, the *arahant*, may continue to experience all the aspects of conditioned life, but he or she remains unmoved by them (Kalupahana 1976: 77). The *arahant* has acquired a level of understanding that transcends the illusion of separate and permanent selfhood.

When Gautama Buddha passed away, adherents of Buddhism believed that he had attained *nirvana*. As we would expect, many questions were raised about his doctrines as well as his whereabouts after death. These questions instigated a host of different responses, some of which through time became the defining doctrines of different schools of Buddhist thought in India and, subsequently, in parts of east and south-east Asia. Questions about Gautama Buddha and Buddhahood were instrumental in the creation of a major rift in Buddhist doctrine, between the Mahayana (in Sanskrit) and Hinayana (in Sanskrit) strands. Soon after the passing away of Gautama Buddha, the First Council of Buddhism was held to collate, consolidate and affirm his doctrine. This council may be considered the beginning of the scholasticism that was a key characteristic of the Hinayanist tradition (Kalupahana 1976: 94). Meanwhile, issues were raised regarding whether there was some direction for ordinary followers of Buddha, who were in need of religious edification (*ibid*.: 95–6). The concerns about ordinary and religious ethical life gradually developed into the doctrine of *bodhisattvas* (in Sanskrit), a theory of beings who have attained Buddhahood but yet choose to re-enter the cycle of rebirth in order to assist others to attain the same condition. The *bodhisattva*, 'being of wisdom', was first used to refer to a previous incarnation of Gautama Buddha. According to this view, for many years before his life as Gautama, the *Bodhisattva* did mighty deeds of compassion and self-sacrifice. These stories about Gautama Buddha were evoked to inspire lay Buddhists (Hurvitz and Tsai 1999: 418).

Through time, this intensely altruistic doctrine developed as the defining characteristic of Mahayana (literally 'Great Vehicle') Buddhism. The Great Vehicle to salvation claimed to offer salvation for all, as opposed to the older Buddhism, which it referred to disparagingly as Hinayana, or the 'Lesser Vehicle'. It is commonly held that the 'older' Buddhism refers to Theravada (in Pali, meaning 'The Way of the Elders') Buddhism, which the Mahayanists christened Hinayana; therefore the terms Theravada and Hinayana are synonymous. However, while Theravada Buddhism spread to Sri Lanka and is the oldest surviving school of Buddhist doctrine, the phrase Hinayana Buddhism existed only as a pejorative term; it was only an appellation for the non-Mahayanist approach to Buddhism.

The form of Buddhism that spread to China from north-western India was primarily of the Mahayana type. Its introduction brought a range of benefits, especially in literature, philosophy and the arts. Philosophically, it introduced elements as yet not considered by the Chinese thinkers, including especially the concept of mind, ideas of space and time, psychological phenomena and conscious self-awareness. Its theme of interdependent causality was not entirely alien to Chinese thought, as some Chinese thinkers from the early Han were deeply preoccupied with connections between the human and cosmic realms. Likewise, the Mahayana Buddhist view of *bodhisattvas* putting aside *nirvana* for altruistic reasons would have resounded with the Confucian concept of benevolent government that serves the good of humankind.

The Introduction of Buddhism into China

There is evidence that aspects of Buddhist culture had been introduced into China by the first century CE (Wright 1959: 21–2), although its presence was noted only sporadically in extant texts. This is a fair indication that during this time, the influence of Buddhism in Chinese society was fairly minimal. From around the third century CE there were more attempts to understand and explain Buddhist thought. Buddhist doctrine was endorsed by the non-Han Chinese rulers of northern China from around 317 CE by the Tuoba people, who subsequently established the northern Wei dynasty (386–534 CE). There was significant racial hostility and conflict between the Tuoba and the Han Chinese (Wright 1959: 55). The Tuoba, who were keen to maintain their ethnic differentiation from the Han Chinese, held Confucian ideology at bay. To them, Buddhism seemed an attractive alternative for a number of reasons. It was not of Chinese origin, it offered possibilities of magical and superhuman feats, and its teachers were foreigners, which meant that the Tuoba leaders did not have to rely on the Chinese for political ideology and strategy (*ibid.*: 56–7). Through time, some of these leaders developed close relationships with Buddhist teachers and monks as they believed that kings who supported Buddhist teaching would be protected by it. Nevertheless, such strong state patronage of Buddhism was neither continuous nor pervasive. Some rulers were wary of the power accumulated by the monks and persecuted them. Furthermore, in Southern China, where the Han Chinese had their stronghold, the relationship between Buddhist monks and rulers was much more ambiguous (*ibid.*: 42–64).

More broadly in Chinese society, as interest in Daoist religious practices, elixirs and methods of attaining immortality developed during and after the Han dynasty, many looked to Buddhism for additional clues to superhuman achievements (Hurvitz and Tsai 1999: 421). At one point, it even became common to regard Daoist and Buddhist scholars as belonging to a single intellectual trend (Fung 1953: 240). The issues surrounding the introduction of Buddhism to China affect the subsequent development of both Chinese Buddhism and Chinese philosophy. In addition, the early responses to Buddhism – suspicion, translation, reception, scrutiny and adoption – reveal significant aspects of philosophical method used by Chinese thinkers to translate and understand Buddhist ideas.

Early efforts to translate Buddhist scriptures were carried on under much difficulty as Indian Buddhist missionaries knew little Chinese and their Chinese collaborators likewise knew little Indian or central Asian languages (Wright 1959: 35). During this early period, around the third and fourth centuries, simplistic translations were made using the terms that were available in the Chinese language and, it seems, without much scrutiny or assessment of Buddhist thought on its own terms. Wright describes the superficiality in such translations:

> ...for example, the ancient and honoured word *tao*, the key term of philosophical Taoism, was sometimes used to render the Buddhist term *dharma*, "the teaching"; in other cases it was used to translate *bodhi*, "enlightenment," or again *yoga*. The Taoist term for immortals, *chen-jen* [*chengren*], served as a translation of the Buddhist word *Arhat*, "the fully enlightened one." *Wu-wei*, "non-action," was used to render the Buddhist term for ultimate release, *nirvana*. The Confucian expression *hsiao-hsün* [*xiaoshun*], "filial submission and obedience," was used to translate the more general and abstract Sanskrit word *śīla*, "morality." (1959: 36).

This method of concept-matching (*geyi*) reflected a failure to attend to the underlying assumptions and conceptual frameworks of Buddhist philosophy. It basically ruled out anything new or interesting Buddhism had to offer to China. From what we know about the Chinese concepts such as *dao*, *wuwei* and *xiao*, and our understanding of Buddhism thus far, it is clear that this involved gross misinterpretations of concepts in both Buddhist and Chinese philosophies. Gradually, a more sophisticated version of this method was used – perhaps reflecting the understanding of *geyi* as 'method of analogy' by some scholars (Fung 1953: 241–2). In the application of this more developed method, Buddhist ideas were given more consideration on their own terms, rather than reduced to concepts in Chinese philosophy. In other words, the method used was analogy rather than simplistic translation. For instance, the five precepts for the behaviour of Buddhist lay adherents were analogised with the five virtues of Confucianism (Wright 1959: 37). A biography of Buddhist monks of that period describes the effectiveness of this method of analogy used by the monk Hui Yuan (334–416 CE):

> In his twenty-fourth year he began to give lectures, the attendants of which, however, on one occasion raised objections against his theory of reality.

> Though the discussion continued for some time, they became increasingly doubtful and bewildered. Thereupon Yüan [Yuan] quoted ideas of Chuang Tzŭ [Zhuangzi] that belonged to the same category, and in this way the skeptics came to understand.[4]

The benefits of the method of *geyi* were mixed, however. Although it rendered Buddhist ideas more accessible to Chinese thinkers, a good number of the analogies were forced, leading to much inaccuracy and distortion (Fung 1948: 242). By the fifth century, following much debate about this method of analogy, its use was abandoned. While many texts translated during this time continued to use Chinese philosophical terminology, especially those of Daoism, translators were now more careful to examine the meanings of concepts in Buddhism on its own terms, hence producing more faithful translations of texts (Fung 1948: 242).

Another source of confirmation that Buddhism was gaining a foothold in Chinese society is the apologetic texts, wherein authors attempted to defend Buddhism to a Chinese audience by articulating its resonance with indigenous Chinese views, or even promoting its merits. The existence of these texts indicates that more people in China had come to know about Buddhism and were demanding justification for its views. There were many features in Buddhist thought that were alien to Chinese culture and tradition, and these needed to be adequately explained before people would accept them. Some major differences include conceptions of family and family responsibility, ritual behavioural prescriptions, prudential economics, and finite human existence in the Chinese worldview, as contrasted with monasticism, generosity, and transmigration in Buddhism (Wright 1959: 38–9). Arthur Wright notes that an apologetic has a special place in the study of the interaction of two traditions because 'the points at which defense is felt to be necessary are invariably the points of greatest conflict between the two systems of ideas' (*ibid.*: 38). Some of the topics covered in an early apologetic text, *Disposing of Error*, dealt with questions including why Buddhist ideas are not mentioned in the Chinese classics, head-shaving of Buddhist monks, celibacy of Buddhist monks, Buddhist conceptions of death and rebirth, and the foreign nature of Buddhist thought.[5] Celibacy was an idea alien to the Chinese mind, and Mouzi, the author of the text, attempts to argue that there are other things more important than familial life:

> Mouzi said…“Wives, children, and property are the luxuries of the world, but simple living and doing nothing (*wuwei*) are the wonders of the Way. Laozi has said, ‘Of reputation and life, which is dearer? Of life and property, which is worth more?’…Xu You and Chaofu dwelt in a tree. Boyi and Shuqi starved in Shouyang, but Confucius praised their worth, saying, ‘They sought to act in accordance with humanity and they succeeded in acting so.’ One does not hear of their being ill-spoken of because they were childless and propertyless. The monk practices the Way and substitutes that for the pleasures of disporting himself in the world. He accumulates goodness and wisdom in exchange for the joys of wife and children.” (De Bary and Bloom 1999: 424)

A more significant indication of the acceptance of Buddhism was the establishment of seven schools or sects (*zong*) of Buddhist thought during the third and fourth centuries, six of which had developed in the south and one, the School of Original Non-Being, in the north.[6] The features of the seven schools are summarised as follows:

> (1) School of Original Non-Being (*benwu*)
> This doctrine was propagated by the monk Dao-an (312–85 CE). It asserts that all the elements of existence, including physical matter, mental sensations, thoughts and the five *skandhas*[7] are in their original nature void and empty (*kong*). Dao-an also claimed that the other six schools, relying on the method of *geyi*, misinterpreted the truth of Buddhist thought. He argued that the method of matching did not adequately capture the Buddhist doctrine of emptiness, which is at the basis of all existence. (Chan 1963b: 338)
>
> (2) Variant School of Original Non-Being (*benwu yi*)
> This doctrine is essentially similar to that proposed by the School of Original Non-Being, as it also focuses on the precedence and significance of emptiness, *kong*. Where it seems to be different from the first is that it relies on the *Daodejing* (e.g. “Being is the product of Non-being…” *Daodejing* 40) to explain *kong*. (Fung 1953: 248)
>
> (3) School of Matter As Such (*jise*)
> The matter of our experience, that is, matter that is “right here,” does not have an innate nature but exists only as a result of external causes and conditions. Hence, we say that it is empty. This doctrine was further developed in two different ways. In the first view, it was held that the matter underlying the things of our immediate experience was *not* empty. This distinction was sustained by distinguishing between “coarse matter” – matter

of our experience – and its opposite, "fine matter." The second view was critical of the first, asserting that both forms of matter, coarse and invisible, were both empty. (Fung 1953: 248–52)

(4) School of Non-being of Mind (*xinwu*)
This school focuses on the epistemological distinction between what we might in contemporary philosophy call "mind and world." It contends that non-being pertains not to the myriad things of the world, but rather to the mind of the sage. In fact, it expressly affirms that matter is genuine, that is, that material existence is real. The phrase "non-being," when applied to the mind of the sage, means that he lacks any deliberate mind toward the ten thousand things, the *wanwu* of the external universe. This is the state of perfect understanding – one of omniscience – whereby the sage's mind is free from erroneous clinging to things. The doctrine of this school skilfully moves between metaphysics and epistemology, and suggests that metaphysical statements – that matter is empty – are effectively psychological-epistemological ones, about watching one's mind.

(5) School of Stored Impressions (*shihan*)
All the phenomena of existence are apparitions, as if one was in a great dream. Continuing with the metaphor of the dream, when one awakens from it, the consciousness which gives rise to illusion is extinguished. At this point, the mind is empty and is no longer a part of production. (Fung 1953: 256–7)

(6) School of Phenomenal Illusion (*huanhua*)
All the things of ordinary "truth" are all illusory. However, the spirit of the mind (*shen*) is not empty as there must be a receptacle or capacity to understand and embody Buddhist truth and teaching. The genuine mind attains the highest truth. (Fung 1953: 257)

(7) School of Causal Combination (*yuanhui*)
Being results from the combination of causes, and as such is called worldly truth. With the dissipation of these causes, however, non-being results, which constitutes the highest truth. (Fung 1953: 257)

Chinese Buddhism had become popular among thinkers during the Eastern Jin period (317–420) and the main topic of discussion in these seven schools, that of being and non-being, shaped future philosophical discussions in Buddhist philosophy. Although the records of these schools are scanty, and although the doctrines did not remain intact, the records mark important turning points in Chinese intellectual history. The indigenous Chinese philosophies, particularly Daoism, greatly influenced Buddhist thought in China. In this phenomenon, we see the beginning of the development of Chinese Buddhism, as distinct from Indian Buddhism.

Another significant development in the history of Buddhism in China began with the arrival of the Buddhist monk, Kumarajiva (*Jiumoluoshi*) (344–413), in Chang'an in 401. Kumarajiva had the support of a royal patron to translate Buddhist texts into Chinese. There were apparently numerous specialists who worked on this project with Kumarajiva. This was not merely a translation exercise, for the project sparked many doctrinal discussions, with comparisons of the new translations against the old and imperfect ones (Wright 1959: 62–3). According to Wright, the project was instrumental in defining the future development of Buddhism in China because:

> ...the ideas of Mahayana Buddhism were presented in Chinese with far greater clarity and precision than ever before. [For example,] Śūnyatā – Nāgārjuna's concept of the void – was disentangled from the Taoist terminology which had obscured and distorted it, and this and other key doctrines of Buddhism were made comprehensible enough to lay the intellectual foundations of the great age of independent Chinese Buddhism that was to follow. (1959: 63)

This project had a lasting impact not only because the quality and quantity of Buddhist scriptures had been greatly increased, allowing for a more substantial consideration of Buddhist thought by Chinese thinkers. It also benefited many of the monks and thinkers who had come to work with Kumarajiva on the project, who went on to articulate important Buddhist doctrines with distinctive Chinese influences that were not oversimplified by simple assimilations. Two disciples of Kumarajiva's were especially prominent in this regard. The first was Sengzhao (394–414), who had studied the philosophies of Laozi and Zhuangzi. He proposed a distinctive, middle-path resolution to a number of topics including the immutability of things, and the emptiness of the unreal. In his discussion of the emptiness of things, he criticised the doctrines of a number of the seven schools, including the School of the Non-being of Mind, School of Matter As Such, and School of Original Non-being. He argued that their respective doctrines were one-sided, emphasising only the empty or non-being. Sengzhao adopted an approach – reminiscent of that in Daoist philosophy – that brought together in dialectical interplay paired notions such as motion and rest, cause and effect, action and non-action, permanence and impermanence, past and present, stability and change, existence and non-existence, finite and infinite, and actuality and name (Fung 1953: 258–70).

Kumarajiva's other prominent disciple was Dao Sheng (c. 360–434). He discussed topics with a more practical orientation, including retribution and enlightenment. His most distinctive contribution was perhaps his discussion of instruction, words and religious illumination: once one has attained illumination, symbols (words) should be forgotten. This view has a Daoist tone as it shares Daoist concerns about the inadequacy of language and the ineffable nature of wisdom. Dao Sheng also uses the kind of imagery that we see especially in the *Zhuangzi*; he likens words to fishtraps, that are to be cast aside once the fish is caught. For Dao Sheng, this theory of learning was consistent with his argument that, if truth is determinate and unified, then the enlightened realisation of this '*one* vehicle' must be sudden and total. This doctrine was held suspect because it effectively discounted the learning processes and disciplinary practices associated with gradual enlightenment. Others, including Sengzhao, opposed it. Dao Sheng's deprecation of language coupled with an emphasis on intuitive understanding expresses an outlook not unlike that in the doctrine of Chan (Zen) Buddhism that was to develop later.

Chinese Buddhist Doctrines during the fifth and sixth centuries CE

As Buddhist philosophy became increasingly popular in China, doctrinal divisions developed on the basis of different scriptures that were read and interpreted by different thinkers. If the numerous Buddhist texts were the word of Buddha, they all had to be consistent and unified.[8] As Chinese thinkers showed more interest in Mahayana rather than Hinayana Buddhism, this task was even more difficult because of the nature of the Mahayanist texts. Unlike the case with the Theravadin scriptures, which had been consolidated at a number of councils of Buddhism in India, the Mahayanist scriptures did not receive collective or official endorsement. The Mahayanist writings contradicted the Theravadin scriptures and each other as well (Hurvitz *et al.* 1999a: 434). Chinese Buddhist thinkers dealt with inconsistencies and contradictions by claiming that a text, or a set of them, was the final or culminating word of Buddha among the range of Buddhist texts. One method of dealing with this problem was called the 'classification of teachings' (*pan jiao*). This method was:

> ...motivated by the need to resolve a basic contradiction: that between the theory that the Buddhist scriptures were all utterances of the Buddha himself, and therefore represented a single unified teaching; and the actual fact that, having really been written by many different persons at different times they were therefore often quite inconsistent with one another. The Chinese solution was to develop the theory that the scriptures were indeed all utterances of the Buddha, but that he had often deliberately varied his teachings to suit the particular occasion and audience for which they were intended. (Fung 1953: 284)

During the Sui Dynasty (581–619) which followed the Southern and Northern Dynasties, scholarship on Buddhism flourished. By the Tang dynasty (618–907), distinctive doctrinal characteristics had developed, which helped to distinguish different Buddhist sects. There were some that focused on doctrine and others on practice. As we are primarily concerned with Buddhist philosophy, we will focus centrally on the doctrinal sects. It should however be noted that Pure Land (*Jingtu*) Buddhism, which focuses on religious practice, is possibly the most popular form of Buddhism in China and other parts of Asia, even in the present day. Pure Land Buddhism is a Mahayanist movement that believes in a sphere, the Pure Land, which is free from temptations and defilements in the human world (Hurvitz *et al.* 1999b: 482). The dogma of Pure Land Buddhism was that the Buddhist world was in decline, hence rendering it almost impossible for people to attain nirvana. In response to this problem, it proposed a doctrine of salvation based on the belief that Amita, a *bodhisattva* on his way to Buddhahood, had taken forty-eight vows, one of which allowed beings who invoked his name, 'Amituo Fo', to attain salvation by being reborn in the Pure Land.

We turn now to the Buddhist doctrines that had developed during the fifth and sixth centuries in China, all of which had been influenced to greater or lesser extents by themes and concepts in Chinese philosophy.

Three Treatise (*San Lun*) Buddhism

This sect advocated the Madhyamaka (Middle Doctrine) school of Nagarjuna (ca. 100–200 CE) and was introduced to China by Kumarajiva. The doctrine of this sect derives its name from three key texts of the Madhyamaka tradition. The three texts are *The Treatise on the Middle Way*, *The Treatise on the Twelve Gates*, and *The One-Hundred-Verse Treatise*. Madhyamaka doctrine holds that the phenomenal world as perceived through our senses is not real. An analogy is made between illusion (that the phenomenal world is real) and poor eyesight: a monk with defective eyesight 'sees' all things inaccurately, he understands things to be real when they are in fact not (Hurvitz *et al.* 1999a: 436). Reality, that is, the void (*sunyata* in Sanskrit; *kong* in Chinese), is also nirvana or Buddha-essence. Unlike the phenomena of our ordinary world, the void is absolute and unchanging.

Ji Zang (540–623) was the major proponent of Three Treatise philosophy. His philosophy is also sometimes known as 'Double Truth' theory because he proposes two levels of truth, Common Truth (*shi*) and Absolute Truth (*zhen*). Common Truth pertains to this world while Absolute Truth is associated with the noumenal world, the underlying reality. These two types of truth are comparable with the modern metaphysical distinction between appearance and reality. According to Ji Zang, there are three levels of Common and Absolute Truth. At the first, simplistic level, Common Truth affirms 'being', that is, the existence of the phenomenal world. Absolute Truth by contrast affirms 'non-being'. At the second level, non-being and being are both considered, although Common Truth affirms either being or non-being while Absolute Truth transcends the dichotomy. At the third, most sophisticated, level, affirmations and negations are under scrutiny as both reveal attachment to the phenomenal world. Common Truth either affirms or denies being and non-being while Absolute Truth neither affirms nor denies being and non-being. Derk Bodde expresses the two types of truth, in three levels, schematically:

[THREE LEVELS OF DOUBLE TRUTH]

Mundane [Common Truth]	*Absolute*
(1) Affirmation of being	(1) Affirmation of non-being
(2) Affirmation of either being or non-being	(2) Denial of both being and non-being
(3) Either affirmation or denial of both being and non-being	(3) Neither affirmation nor denial of both being and non-being[9]

A person progresses along these levels of truth in a dialectical manner: from Common Truth (1) to Absolute Truth (1), then to Level Two. At Level Two, the person progresses from Common Truth (2) to Absolute Truth (2), then to Level Three, and so on. Bodde writes, 'The highest level of truth is to be reached through a series of successive negations of negation, until nothing remains to be either affirmed or denied' (in Fung 1953: 295). Yet, Three Treatise doctrine maintains that nirvana is to be found in the Higher Truth, but without one having to extract oneself from the (dependent) life of Common Truth. Meditation is the path to attain insight into the truth. Three Treatise Buddhism declined in the ninth century, although Ji Zang's ideas were assimilated into later Buddhist philosophy. Many of his writings have survived and have influenced other Chinese Buddhist doctrines.

Consciousness-only (*Wei Shi*) Buddhism

Consciousness-only Buddhism derives from the Yogacara (Sanskrit: Yoga practice) strain in India. Yogacara and Madhyamaka are the two main branches of Mahayanist philosophy. Xuan Zang (596–664) played a significant role in developing Consciousness-only doctrine. He journeyed to central Asia to study Buddhism, learning from Vasubandhu (ca. 4th–5th century), one of two brothers who founded Yogacara Buddhism based on Mahayanist texts. Xuan Zang's most significant work was *A Treatise in the Establishment of Consciousness-only* (*Cheng Weishi Lun*), in 10 volumes. Yogacara doctrine held that everything is empty because it is (only a product) of the mind. Adopting this philosophy, Xuan Zang proposed that all perceived objects are merely experiences, hence denying the substantial reality of matter. He referred to dream experiences to support his claim that it is impossible to find definite proof for the veridical nature of sense experience. Objects possess no reality apart from mind. While we might believe that 'objects' such as gardens and villages exist, Xuan Zang argues that they exist only insofar as they are seen at a particular time and place, not at all times and places (Fung 1953: 321–3). We may express Xuan Zang's views in terms of perception, that is, our perception of things in the world '…is no proof of the independent existence of any entity, and all perceptions may be explained as projections of the percipient mind' (Hurvitz *et al.* 1999a: 441).

In epistemological terms this doctrine holds that nothing can be established independently of mind. The world as we know it is created by the transformations of consciousness. Objects are empty (without innate substance) and, as they are the creations of consciousness, are dependent on consciousness. Xuan Zang proposes eight levels of consciousness, the eighth, most mature level of consciousness, being called 'storehouse consciousness' (*alaya-vijnana* in Sanskrit). The storehouse consciousness is a store of perceptions accumulated through time. Every deed, good or bad, leaves a trace in the storehouse consciousness. Storehouse consciousness is also sometimes called 'seed' consciousness as it contains, as it were, the seeds of all things in and outside the phenomenal world. Each individual being has its own storehouse consciousness that does not begin at birth. There were different views among proponents of Consciousness-only Buddhism regarding how storehouse consciousness is influenced (or 'perfumed') by experience. There were also debates about transmigration processes given that storehouse consciousness is not identified with an individual's bodily existence but can precede an individual's bodily existence and survive its bodily death (Fung 1953: 305–6). The theory of storehouse consciousness was also riddled with the problem of extreme idealism. In other words, if there are storehouse consciousnesses, is everything ultimately subjective? These problems are comparable to the ones associated with Descartes' idealism, one of them being solipsism, that is, that a person cannot know anything beyond his or her own mind. An attempt was made to address the problem of subjectivity by positing a universal storehouse consciousness that includes all of the individual storehouse consciousnesses. However, the concept of universal storehouse consciousness brought problems as well because there needed to be an adequate explanation for the interactions and causal connections between universal and non-universal storehouse consciousness. Some notion of intersubjectivity was suggested, but its details were far from clear (Fung 1953: 308–9).

The Consciousness-only doctrine of idealism, which Fung describes as 'Mere Ideation', attempts a middle-path solution to consciousness and the phenomenal world of ordinary experiences (1953: 319). While it maintains that only consciousness exists and that there are no real things apart from consciousness, it also on the other hand asserts that the phenomenal world, a product of and inseparable from consciousness, does exist. Yet, there are limits to the middle-path theory of Consciousness-only Buddhism. Although it upholds the existence of the phenomenal world (albeit as a product of consciousness), it is clear that phenomena must ultimately be eliminated so as to reduce and abolish impressions on storehouse consciousness. There are unresolved problems in a theory that upholds such an extreme form of idealism. It does not seem to have adequate answers to a number of questions including the role of the human sensory faculties in relation to storehouse consciousness, the distinction between storehouse consciousness in its universal and non-universal (that is, individual, embodied) forms, and the problem of other minds (Fung 1953: 309–10; 326). The practical implications of Consciousness-only Buddhism rest in exhausting the store of consciousness until it becomes empty. At this stage, we say that a being has attained a state of 'thusness' (*tathata* in Sanskrit). The means of achieving this state is through yogic activity; the texts prescribe a range of such activities. Consciousness-only Buddhism declined in the eighth century, perhaps because its idealism was too far-fetched to capture the imagination of the Chinese.[10]

Tian Tai Buddhism

Tian Tai Buddhism remains influential especially in parts of modern-day East Asia. It takes its name after the Tian Tai Mountain in China, where its founder, Zhi Yi (538–97), spent many years learning and teaching. The origin of the name is noteworthy because, in pointing to its location in China, the name signifies its non-Indian origin. Yet, its philosophy is grounded in the *Lotus Sutra* (*Fahua Jing*).[11] The *Lotus Sutra* was a popular Mahayanist Sutra and its focus was primarily on religious practice; it was not a systematic treatise. Zhi Yi interpreted the Lotus Sutra and wrote three major texts, *Profound Meaning of the Lotus Sutra* (*Fahua xuan yi*), *Words and Phrases of the Lotus Sutra* (*Fahua wenju*), and *The Great Calming and Contemplation* (*Mohe zhiguan*).

Tian Tai doctrine emphasised a philosophy that harmonised a three-in-one approach whereby the following three themes worked as a unit:

(1) all things or *dharmas* are empty because they are produced through causes and conditions and therefore have no self-nature, but
(2) they do have tentative or provisional existence, and
(3) being both empty and tentative is the nature of *dharmas* and is the Mean. (Hurvitz *et al.* 1999a: 444)

As there is only one reality, these three, emptiness, tentativeness and the Mean, must be taken as one. The three-in-one harmony has no starting point or, in other words, it does not matter where one starts because the three-in-one is in fact a circular (*yuan*) interplay of empty, real and neither. Unlike the doctrine of the Consciousness-only sect, Tian Tai doctrine emphasises the interconnectedness of consciousness and phenomena: the phenomenal world provides content for the consciousness while on the other hand, it also relies on the mind's cognition in order to interpret it according to the deeper, underlying reality (*dharmas* in Sanskrit). This middle-way doctrine advocates non-duality of consciousness and phenomena. In this sense, it differs from the doctrine of the Consciousness-only school, which understands phenomena entirely as a product of consciousness. Zhi Yi also bridged the gap between contemplative faith and analytical wisdom using the dialectical middle-way approach. In Zhi Yi's time, Buddhist thought in south China was primarily philosophical in character, while those in the north were keen to develop Buddhism as a religion of faith and discipline. Because Zhi Yi was himself from the south, and because he had a teacher from the north, he combined both aspects of Buddhist doctrine. He developed a view that saw the contemplative and philosophical aspects of Buddhism in terms of the two wings of a bird (Hurvitz *et al.* 1999a: 444).

In its religious and contemplative aspects, Tian Tai doctrine posited a rich phenomenal world of one thousand levels, including the existence of hell beings, heavenly beings, animals, hungry ghosts, humans, Buddhas and Bodhisattvas. It also claimed, according to the *Lotus Sutra*, that there are many Buddhas and that Buddhahood is open to all people. Like Mencius' philosophy of human nature, Tian Tai doctrine holds that all humans have the inherent capacity to develop Buddhahood. However, unlike Mencius' theory, Tian Tai believes in essential evil, which even Buddha has, as an element of his nature. Zhi Yi proposes a doctrine of repentance as well as a range of purification processes in rectifying evil (Hurvitz *et al.* 1999a: 462–71).

Zhi Yi explained differences in Buddhist doctrines by reference to the fact that different individuals have different capabilities and, therefore, that the doctrines needed to accommodate different levels of understanding. Yet, in the final analysis, he proposed One Great Vehicle that embraces all humanity in spite of their differences. In a conversation the Buddha is meant to have had with one of his disciples, Sariputra, emphasis is placed on different argumentative techniques such as empirical examples (various causes and conditions), analogies (words of simile and parable), and doctrinal exposition (expounding the Law):

> ... Śāriputra, the Buddhas preach the Law in accordance with what is appropriate, but the meaning is difficult to understand. Why is this? Because we employ countless expedient means, discussing causes and conditions and using words of simile and parable to expound the teachings. This Law is not

> something that can be understood through pondering or analysis. Only those who are Buddhas can understand it…
>
> …Śāriputra, I know that living beings have various desires, attachments that are deeply implanted in their minds. Taking cognizance of this basic nature of theirs, I will therefore use various causes and conditions, words of simile and parable, and the power of expedient means and expound the Law for them. Śāriputra, I do this so that all of them may attain the one Buddha vehicle and wisdom embracing all species…" (Kumarajiva's translation of the *Lotus Sutra*, cited in Hurvitz *et al.* 1999a: 447)

The doctrine of the universality of Buddha nature rejected the assumptions of the Indian caste system. But more importantly, it affirmed the widely held optimism in Chinese philosophy that self cultivation was available for all. In its use of the term 'Buddha' as a generic term, allowing for many Buddhas, the doctrine emphasises the availability of Buddhahood for all.

Flower Garland (*Hua Yan*) Buddhism

The teachings of Flower Garland Buddhism are based on the *Flower Garland Sutra* (*Huayan jing*), a text known for its ornate and obscure language, which describes a Buddhistic vision of the universe. Within the Mahayana tradition, the *Flower Garland Sutra* is sometimes reputed to have been the first sermon of Buddha, composed when he had attained enlightenment (Hurvitz *et al.* 1999a: 471). It is also believed that the Buddha, recognising the profundity of the text and its language for most ordinary people, subsequently preached other Sutras that were easier for them to understand. Many of the basic tenets of the *Flower Garland Sutra* are similar to those in other branches of Mayahana Buddhism, including its focus on the compassion of *bodhisattvas* and ethically correct conduct. It also agrees with other sects that objects are empty (*kong*) as they are devoid of an inherent nature and independent existence. Objects as such are unreal and illusory, being creations of the mind; nothing on this plane of existence endures through time.

Flower Garland Buddhism in China was established by five patriarchs. Among them, the monk Du Shun (557–640) is regarded as its founder because he assisted in its definition as a distinct sect. Fa Zang (643–712) is considered its greatest proponent because he systematised the doctrine for greater acceptance by lay followers. In his *Essay on the Gold Lion* (*Jin Shizi Zhang*), Fa Zang uses the example of a gold lion to explain Buddhist doctrine. He refers to the gold(-ness) of the gold lion, and the lion *qua* perceived object, to demonstrate a range of Buddhist ideas. Fa Zang is said to have written this essay at the emperor's palace because the emperor was having difficulty understanding Buddhist insights (Fung 1953: 340). In the *Essay on the Gold Lion*, Fa Zang uses the 'classification of teachings' method to explain different Buddhist doctrines; he places them in a sequence of stages, all of the one truth (in Fung 1953: 346–7). Flower Garland Buddhism, for him, tops the list, while Hinayana Buddhism is presented in a derogatory way.

At the first level, one realises the impermanence and insubstantiality of objects: 'The lion is a product of causation, and undergoes generation and destruction from moment to moment, there is really no quality to the lion that may be grasped' (Fung 1953: 346). This is the most elementary Buddhist teaching, meant for the followers of Hinayana Buddhism. At the second level one recognises that 'In the final analysis there is only emptiness' (*ibid.*). This is basic Mahayana teaching. The third level, the final teaching of Mahayana, recognises that emptiness (of the real, noumena) is not inconsistent with the illusory appearance of phenomena. Being and non-being are both maintained. At the fourth level, emptiness and being are mutually annulled and the false impressions of the senses are cast aside. Word and speech are abandoned. This is the instantaneous teaching of Mahayana. At the fifth level, 'All things of the senses are revealed in their true essence, and become merged into one great mass . . . every one of which represents the Absolute' (*ibid.*). The myriad are one as all things equally have the nature of non-being. This is the perfect teaching of the One Vehicle.

In terms of its philosophical commitments, Flower Garland Buddhism appears remarkably similar to Zhuangzi's Daoism. It emphasises the diversity in the world, the interdependence of all things, non-duality and scepticism about language. Unlike the view in Consciousness-only Buddhism that tries unsuccessfully to account for the overlap between universal and non-universal (individual) consciousness, Flower Garland Buddhism denies that there is commonality among different mental constructions. Many 'worlds' are created by mental acts and are all different. The individual minds that produce them are likewise different. There is only one real Mind, and that is eternal, absolute and embraces individual minds. Fa Zang employed the Mahayanist text, the *Awakening of Faith in Mahayana*, to articulate the idea of 'suchness', that is, a true consciousness at the heart of all realities. However, he avoids dualism between the realm of 'suchness' and the phenomenal world by including the manifold as part of his totalistic doctrine. He replaced Tian Tai's 'Three are One' with 'All are One', claiming that every part of the universe embodies or reflects the whole: in and through each being, we see all the others as well.[12] He extended this 'All are One' dogma in a number of ways, as for instance, to assert that all Buddhas are 'one'. Although Fa Zang believed that objects are unreal and illusory, he also incorporated them within his theory of enlightenment by positing four *dharma* realms:

(1) realm of principle (*li fa jie*)
(2) realm of things (*shi*)
(3) realm of non-interference between principle and things
(4) realm of non-interference of all things

According to Fa Zang, the realm of principle is the realm of noumenon, the underlying reality. His concept of principle is philosophically noteworthy as later Chinese thinkers, such as Wang Yang Ming (1472–1529), the Neo-Confucian idealist, drew extensively from this concept in Buddhist doctrine. Fa Zang emphasised the integrated nature of principle and things (objects and events), which inter-penetrate and inter-identify the other, yet without interference. He draws from the example of the gold lion to illustrate that objects do not have an inherent nature of their own and are therefore empty. The lion does not have its own being; its existence is dependent on others. This is the theory of integrated dependency (Fung 1953: 342). While the lion does not have an inherent nature, it gives the illusion of having particular qualities and it is on such a basis that it exists. In this way, emptiness is not annihilatory; it is also not external to matter (Fung 1953: 343). Fa Zang's endorsement of both principle and things is markedly different from Indian Buddhist thought in general, which tends to identify the phenomenal world as the source of illusion to be shunned. Fa Zang brought the two realms, principle and things, together in his theory of non-interference. To exemplify his theory of non-interference and the integrated and interdependent nature of all things, Fa Zang appeals to the various faculties of the gold lion to demonstrate interdependence between parts of a whole:

> ...if the eyes of the lion are taken to include the whole lion, the all is the eyes. But if the ears are taken to include the whole lion, the all is the ears. And if all the organs are simultaneously taken to include the whole lion, everyone of them is the perfect whole. (in Fung 1953: 349)

We might find this analogy not entirely plausible. Fa Zang's intention is to demonstrate that all phenomena (the many) are each complete manifestations of the one (absolute) mind in its totality. A more stimulating metaphor is that of 'Indra's Net', found in the text *Calming and Contemplation in the Five Teachings of Huayan*:

> The jeweled net of Śakra is also called Indra's Net, and is made up of jewels. The jewels are shiny and reflect each other successively, their images permeating each other over and over. In a single jewel they all appear at the same time, and this can be seen in each and every jewel. There is really no coming or going.
>
> Now if we turn to the southwest direction and pick up one of the jewels to examine it, we will see that this one jewel can immediately reflect the images of all the other jewels. Each of the other jewels will do the same. Each jewel will simultaneously reflect the images of all the jewels in this manner, as will all of the other jewels. The images are repeated and multiplied in each other in a manner that is unbounded. Within the boundaries of a single jewel are contained the unbounded repetition and profusion of the images of all the jewels. The reflections are exceedingly clear and are completely unhindered. (in Hurvitz *et al.* 1999a: 473)

The jewels of the net are separate yet bound together. Each single jewel contains reflections of all the others. The concepts of non-interference together with interdependence play an important role in a doctrine that embraces a manifold reality. In other words, a holistic and pluralistic theory is plausible only insofar as it also includes an ordering principle, so to speak, of how the many can co-exist. The danger lies in two extremes: in the first, the plurality is so chaotic that there is no semblance of integration or interdependence. In the second, the (total) whole could dominate its parts such that the myriad things lose their distinctive qualities. In this light, the doctrine of One Vehicle, translated as 'All are One', could be misleading as it may imply homogeneous rather than pluralistic unity. Perhaps an alternative dictum, 'One but many', is a better reflection of how the concept of non-interference properly functions in an atmosphere of interdependence. Fa Zang notes explicitly the importance of recognising and maintaining the many: the five organs of the lion are different from the lion as a whole and hence each is unique. They are similar in that they all arise from a cause. But inasmuch as they combine to make the lion, they are integrated. He concludes by drawing out the implications of his analogy:

> ...the object [in the phenomenal world] as a whole has the quality of generalness, whereas each of its parts has the quality of speciality. Inasmuch as the object as a whole, as well as its separate parts, are all products of causation, this is their quality of similarity. Yet inasmuch as each part remains distinct from the other parts, this is their quality of diversity. Inasmuch, however, as the combination of the parts results in the formation of the object as a whole, this is their quality of integration (trans. Fung 1953: 355).

In both doctrine and practice, Fa Zang remained committed to the phenomenal world in its plurality. There is an interesting anecdote of how he demonstrated to students the essence of the integrated and interdependent nature of everything:

> He took ten mirrors, arranging them, one each, at the eight compass points and above and below, in such a way that they were a little over ten feet apart from each other, all facing one another. He then placed a Buddhist figure in the center and illuminated it with a torch so that its image was reflected from one to another. His students thus came to understand the theory of passing from 'land and sea' (the finite world) into infinity. (*Song Gaoseng Juan*, cited in Fung 1953: 353)

In the final analysis, Fa Zang emphasises that the understanding of Buddhist truth is intuitive and instantaneous. Such attainment is beyond words and concepts, resists analysis and is at its core anti-language. That Buddhist enlightenment is instantaneous was an issue that sparked much debate for, if correct, it would imply the pointlessness of gradual cultivation toward a goal. Furthermore, that enlightenment is primarily intuitive seems to nullify the practice of good acts and living according to moral and disciplinary codes. These issues, as well as the view of enlightenment as an essentially mental process, influenced debates in Chan Buddhism.

Chan Buddhism

Chan Buddhism is better known by its Japanese name, Zen, as it was introduced to the western world early in the twentieth century by the notable Japanese scholar and translator, Daisetz Teitaro Suzuki (1870–1966). The name 'Chan' is a shortened version of 'Chan-na', a phonetic translation of the Sanskrit 'dhyana'. *Dhyana* is popularly though loosely translated as 'meditation', although it more accurately refers to contemplative rather than theoretical or detached thinking. There are stories about the origins of Chan Buddhism including its direct line of transmission from Buddha, method of transmission and Indian origins. According to a popular account, Buddha transmitted his teaching to a disciple and this teaching was different from what he preached in public. Subsequent transmission of this doctrine relied primarily on oral transmission, passed from one patriarch to another. The twenty-eighth patriarch, Bodhidharma (470–543), is said to have brought the teaching into China. Hence he was considered the first patriarch of Chan Buddhism. The sect split after the fifth patriarch, Hong Ren (601–74), into the Northern and Southern Chan sects, each of which claimed its leader as the genuine sixth patriarch. Shen Xiu (ca. 605–706) was the patriarch of the northern sect and Hui Neng (638–713) that of the southern. After about a century of rivalry, Shen Hui (670–762), a disciple of Hui Neng, managed to gain acceptance by the Tang court as the genuine Chan strain.

Contemporary scholars regard the Indian origins of the sect as untrue and doubt whether there was a person named Bodhidharma who transmitted Chan Buddhism during the said period (Fung 1953: 386–8; De Bary and Bloom 1999: 492–3). However, that there were two sects, led by Shen Xiu and Hui Neng, is historically accurate (Fung 1953: 388). The differences between Shen Xiu and Hui Neng's ideas are philosophically interesting as their debates replay and capture many doctrinal divisions in Chinese Buddhism. Many of Hui Neng's ideas, including his responses to Shen Xiu, are described in the text, the *Platform Sutra of the Sixth Patriarch* (*Liu Zu Tan Jing*). It includes a biography of Hui Neng and a collection of his sermons, although its authorship is questionable.[13] While its information about Hui Neng and other historical details may not be accurate, the text is a foundational one in Chan Buddhist philosophy. Many aspects of Hui Neng's philosophy are revealed in the text. In our exposition of his ideas, we will use the five characteristics of Chan Buddhism set out by Fung (1953), as they are effective in summarising the philosophy of the sect. Furthermore, they will be useful in elucidating the disagreements between the northern and southern sects.[14] These five characteristics are: (1) the Highest Truth or First Principle is inexpressible; (2) spiritual attainment cannot be cultivated; (3) in the last resort nothing is gained; (4) "there is nothing much in the Buddhist teaching"; (5) "in carrying water and chopping wood: therein lies the wonderful *Tao*" (1953: 390).

(1) 'The Highest Truth or First Principle is inexpressible because what it attempts to express is actually "Beyond the realm of causation and the (conscious) mind"' (Fung 390). The first principle is important in both setting out Hui Neng's philosophy and distinguishing it from that of the northern sect. There are two verses relating to the first principle:

> The body is the *bodhi* tree,
> The mind is like a clear mirror.
> At all times we must strive to polish it,
> And must not let the dust collect.
>
> (*Platform Sutra*, trans. Yampolsky, in De Bary and Bloom 1999: 496)

> The *bodhi* tree is originally not a tree,
> The mirror also has no stand.
> Buddha-nature is always clean and pure;
> Where can it be stained by dust?
>
> (*ibid.*: 498)

The first verse, attributed to Shen Xiu of the northern sect, upholds the enlightened person whose mind is clear like a mirror. Based on this first principle, it advocates constant and gradual cleaning of the mirror. Watchful diligence is required in this process as the mirror could be clouded over by dust. The second verse opposes the first and is attributed to Hui Neng. According to this verse, there was nothing originally, neither *bodhi* tree nor mirror. The verse recognises the paradox involved in this assertion, that to suggest there is nothing is to identify it, and therefore, to express the inexpressible. From Hui Neng's first principle that there is originally nothing, he claims that there is no dust either. In addition, to say there is no dust is a metaphorical way of saying that cleaning the mirror, that is, self cultivation, is pointless. The disagreement between the two verses sets out dramatically different views of enlightenment, the first (of the northern sect) understood as a (gradual) *process* and the second as an (instantaneous) *state*.[15] The former is more closely aligned with theories of cultivation in China then, especially in Confucianism. Cultivation theories typically involved arduous physical and mental exertion and also self-restraint. The doctrine of instant enlightenment does not accept that there is a developmental path toward enlightenment but holds that it is immediate and in that sense timeless. Instantaneous enlightenment looks neither to (improve) the past nor to (positively influence) the future but to embrace the moment of the enlightenment, that very present.

(2) *Spiritual attainment cannot be cultivated.* From the point of view of the northern sect, spiritual cultivation is a purposive activity. It centres on the concept *jian* (to see), that is, to see the truth, which is non-being or empty (*kong*). By contrast, the point of cultivation in the southern sect, if we may call it 'cultivation', is *guan*, beholding, which is more passive than seeing. *Guan* is more closely aligned with contemplative awareness while *jian* with perceptive and interpretive processes. Hui Neng argues that even to affirm not one, not many, non-being, is to make a judgement and therefore to act. This in turn will generate more *karma*, as mental acts cause *karma* as well. One must cease even in the affirmation of nothingness, for in cultivating and abiding in emptiness, one is bound by that emptiness. To avoid creating more *karma* involves non-practice of spiritual cultivation. Non-practice is itself cultivation (Fung 1953: 393–4).

(3) *In the last resort nothing is gained.* The instantaneous enlightenment championed by Hui Neng does not have an object, whereas the enlightened mind of the northern sect seeks mind as ultimate reality. In the views of the northern sect, ultimate reality is sought, the goal of which is the real, undefiled mind. In the *Platform Sutra*, a text of the southern sect, this method of seeking the mind, 'sitting in meditation', is held up for ridicule because it is associated with the search for reality by the pure mind (in De Bary and Bloom 1999: 501). In this text, there is an explicit rejection of reality as object, stated in remarkably precise philosophical terms: 'Purity has no form, but nonetheless, some people try to postulate the form of purity and consider this to be Chan practice' (*ibid.*). In Hui Neng's philosophy, the proper objects of knowledge are not external things – or even emptiness or void – but one's own mind. Unlike in the doctrine of the northern sect, where mind is a device for attaining enlightenment, mind here is viewed as the foundation of self. There is no distinction between the mind as subject and the mind as object. Such sudden enlightenment does not have an object. We can perceive here some inkling of a distinction between consciousness (mind as subject) and mind (mind as object) that is otherwise non-existent in early Chinese philosophy. The elimination of the subject–object distinction avoids the difficulties of Flower Garland Buddhism because there is no problem of other minds. In Hui Neng's philosophy, all minds are similar and equal because all humans have the same mind that can at any point be enlightened. An enlightened person

has direct access (not through thought) to his or her own mind, and as mind is the same in all persons, one can speak reasonably of another's enlightened mind. This, however, is not a positive kind of knowledge. Hence, it is not a gain of any kind at all.

(4) *There is nothing much in the Buddhist teaching*. This tenet asserts that the life of the sage is no different from that of ordinary men. Northern Chan Buddhism, which advocates that only the undefiled mind is real, would also require detachment from the phenomenal world. It is in that sense akin to the philosophy of extreme idealism in Consciousness-only Buddhism. Furthermore, the cultivation of the mind according to this sect is a difficult and gradual process. The assertion that there is nothing much in Chan Buddhist teaching appears to insult and trivialise the emphasis the northern sect places on cultivation. In contrast, Hui Neng's doctrine suggests that there is really no secret; the only secret is that people do not understand that enlightenment is this simple.

(5) *In carrying water and chopping wood: therein lies the wonderful* Tao [*dao*]. This tenet follows from the previous one. In his consideration of enlightenment, Hui Neng claims that enlightenment does not require detachment from this-worldly activities. From this perspective, the phrase 'Pure Land' does not relate to any 'real' entity or location as such, but is only a referent for mental purity. The southern sect does away with metaphysical speculation about ultimate reality and instead focuses on mental illumination. The *Platform Sutra* argues:

> ...people of the East [China], just by making the mind pure, are without crime; people of the West [the Pure Land of the West], if their minds are not pure, are guilty of a crime. The deluded person wishes to be born in the East or West; [for the enlightened person] any land is just the same...Why should you seek rebirth [in the Western Land]? (translator's additions; in De Bary and Bloom 1999: 502).

It also denies the pure mind-phenomenal world dualism maintained by many Buddhist sects. Like the Buddhism of the Tian Tai sect, southern Chan Buddhism does not shun the phenomenal world. For Hui Neng and followers of his sect, it is inconsequential where mental illumination happens. A person could be chopping wood or drinking tea when illumination comes upon him or her. The enlightened person engages in ordinary daily activities, just like everyone else, but her acts have a different significance from those of ordinary people. Activities in themselves are not good or bad, for to label them as such, even in an anti-conventional way, is to be bound by those values. The dangers of making judgements and discriminating are described in terms of duality. 'If within [the mind] and without [in the activities of the phenomenal world] you are not deluded, then you are apart from duality. If on the outside you are deluded, you attach to form; if on the inside you are deluded, you attach to emptiness' (*Platform Sutra*, in De Bary and Bloom 1999: 503).

The influence of southern Chan Buddhism gradually surpassed that of the northern sect. The tenets of Southern Chan Buddhism are more closely aligned with Daoist themes, especially in Zhuangzi's philosophy, not only in terms of the wordless realisation of vacuous non-being but also in its continuing engagement with the affairs of this world. (In response to a question about the whereabouts of *dao*, Zhuangzi is reputed to have said that it was in the urine and excrement; *Zhuangzi* 22.) As with Zhuangzi's Daoism, Chan Buddhism needs to address the paradoxes associated with communication that focuses on mental illumination but which in the final analysis rejects language. In the Tang Dynasty, Chan Buddhism continued to develop further and, because it focused on instantaneous mental illumination, developed paradoxes known as *gongan* (Japanese and more recently English: *koan*). These paradoxes had a 'shock value' and were supposedly designed to challenge everyday logic. Famous *gongans* include puzzles such as 'Does a dog have Buddha-nature or not?', stories of a monk who attained enlightenment when he was asked to wash his bowl after his meal (alluding to the simplicity of the Chan message), and queries about whether the flag, or the wind, moves (to which Hui Neng's answer was that it was the mind that was moving).[16] These *gongans* are suggestive rather than informative and engage their readers or listeners in reflective thinking. Their use for illumination raises the paradox about language mentioned earlier: if there is an irreconcilable mismatch between language and truth, then why bother reading the *Sutras*, or contemplating the *gongan*?[17] As Chan Buddhism developed, series of *gongan* were developed as planned programs of instruction – which seems inconsistent with Hui Neng's emphasis on non-cultivation. Furthermore there were other methods that were incorporated to 'shock' a person into instantaneous enlightenment. Some of these methods were violent, including beatings and whippings:

> Frequently these *gongan* could not be answered verbally, which accounts in part for the beatings, shouts and gestures so often described in the stories. Often the Master would find his disciple's mind so sensitized and receptive,

that a scream, a blow of the stick, or a blasphemous word would be the cause of his awakening to Truth. (De Bary and Bloom 1999: 492)

It is interesting, though disappointing, to note that Chan Buddhism could have developed much more extensively in its philosophical meanderings, but instead is now better known for its practices. Contemporary scholarship is divided on the issue of whether Chan Buddhism is properly considered a philosophical doctrine or a practice.[18] Hui Neng avoided consideration about a metaphysical reality that is external to the self, and this is a fundamental issue in philosophy. In focusing on mental illumination through *gongan*, Chan Buddhism in the modern context has developed some semblance of a self-help thesis that assists individuals to attain equanimity by being detached from the concerns of ordinary life. Yet, on the other hand, if these puzzles instigate reflective thinking in the layperson – whether or not Chan enlightenment is reached – they are in fact promoting one of the central aims of philosophical thinking.

Chinese Buddhism

By the Tang Dynasty, Buddhism had established itself as a religious, ethical and doctrinal field quite distinct from its Indian origins. Chinese Buddhism developed its distinctive character by incorporating a number of ideas that were integral aspects of Chinese philosophies. For example, in Pure Land Buddhism, which is popular in modern-day China, human relations are thought to continue in the Pure Land. The Chinese were much more interested in Mahayana Buddhism, which advocates a returning *bodhisattva* who suspends *nirvana* in order to assist others to attain enlightenment. This reflects that, in the Chinese consciousness, what was most significant about *nirvana* was the ethico-social leadership of the enlightened person, akin to that of the Confucian paradigmatic person and the Daoist sage.[19] Another important example of how Chinese Buddhism developed its distinctive character is exemplified in the notions and methods of self cultivation, polarities of being and non-being, concerns about continuing existence of the person, and dialectical approaches of the different sects, as we have seen above. This is not to say that these themes were not existent in Indian Buddhism but rather that, in the way they were articulated in Chinese Buddhist doctrine, there were many borrowings from concepts and approaches in Chinese philosophy.

Yet, on the other hand, Chinese Buddhism began to take its distinctive shape in the synthesis of elements in Indian and Chinese philosophies. We see the extent of this synthesis when we consider how the different Chinese Buddhist sects deal with a major issue, that of duality. A fundamental conceptual issue in Buddhist philosophy is that of dualism. This is articulated in a wide range of Buddhist doctrines, between pure mind and phenomenal world, reality and unreality, equanimity and dissatisfaction, non-being and being, non-existence and existence, consciousness and bodily existence, permanence and impermanence, good and evil, and independent and caused. One distinctive feature of Chinese Buddhism is how, in general, the different doctrines take a middle-path solution to the issue of duality. Three Treatise Buddhism, which maintains a clear preference for Absolute Truth, is the only school that asserts a dichotomy between the two notions of truth, Common and Absolute. The other sects take a middle-path strategy that embraces both aspects of the duality. Consciousness-only Buddhism marginally embraces the middle-path approach. It sees the phenomenal world as undesirable but it also acknowledges its place in human life. Tian Tai Buddhism proposes an integration between consciousness and the phenomenal world and is in that sense more obviously a middle-path doctrine. Flower Garland Buddhism not only takes a middle-path approach to consciousness and the phenomenal world but also emphasises the interdependence of everything in a way that is similar to Zhuangzi's perspectivalism. There is a general tendency in Chinese Buddhist doctrine to adopt a dialectical and middle-path approach that does not seek to abandon this-worldly life. Chinese Buddhism has established itself within the Chinese intellectual tradition as a distinct field in terms of its influences in later developments in Chinese philosophy. Many Buddhist themes appear in the development of Neo-Confucianism during the Song Dynasty, in the philosophies of Han Yu (768–824) and Li Ao (died ca. 844) (Lai 2003: 18). In turn, these views were instrumental in shaping cosmological theories that dominated debates during the ninth to the eleventh centuries (Fung 1953: 407–33) and even after that, to the establishment of Neo-Confucian philosophy.

Suggestions for Further Reading

Chan, Wing-tsit (1957–58) 'Transformation of Buddhism in China', *Philosophy East and West*, vol. 7, no. 3/4: 107–16.

Fung, Yu-Lan (1953) 'Buddhism and Its Critics During the Period of Disunity', in *A History of Chinese Philosophy* (translated by Derk Bodde), vol 2. Princeton: Princeton University Press: pp. 237–92.

Hurvitz, Leon and Tsai, Heng-Ting (1999) 'The Introduction of Buddhism' in Wm Theodore De Bary and Irene Bloom (eds.) *Sources of Chinese Tradition: From Earliest Times to 1600*, vol. 1, 2nd edn. New York: Columbia University Press: pp. 415–32.

Hurvitz, Leon *et al.* (1999) 'Schools of Buddhist Doctrine', in Wm Theodore De Bary and Irene Bloom (eds.) *Sources of Chinese Tradition: From Earliest Times to 1600*, vol. 1, 2nd edn. New York: Columbia University Press: pp. 433–80.

Lai, Whalen (2003) 'Buddhism in China: A Historical Survey', in Antonio Cua (ed.) *Encyclopedia of Chinese Philosophy*, New York: Routledge: pp. 7–19.

Notes

1. The period of the Three Kingdoms (*Sanguo*: 220–80 CE) brought some measure of stability after the war which ended the Han Dynasty. In 184 CE a secret Daoist society led a peasant rebellion against the then Han emperor. The rebellion was called the 'Yellow Turban Rebellion' (*Huangjin zhi luan*), after the headscarves worn by the rebels. Following the demise of the Han dynasty, each of the three kingdoms was ruled by an emperor, each of whom claimed to be the legitimate successor of the Han ruling house. Nevertheless, there was an agreement between the three kingdoms to ensure a level of military stability. The Three Kingdoms period is often grouped together with two successive periods, the Jin Dynasty (265–420 CE) and the Southern and Northern Dynasties (420–589 CE), and collectively termed the period of the 'Six Dynasties'.
2. During the Southern and Northern Dynasties, the powerful non-Han Xianbei tribe invaded the Jin capital, Loyang. This forced members of the ruling Jin family to flee and re-establish their capital in the south, in Jiankang (modern-day Nanjing). In the north, where the Xianbei people established their stronghold, Buddhist ideas were embraced partly because the Xianbei people were hostile to Confucianism and other characteristics of Chinese culture, and partly because they were attracted to the apparent magical powers of the monks (Wright 1959: 42–64; esp. at 56).
3. Kalupahana examines Buddhist philosophy according to a number of modern philosophical categories including epistemology, causality and ethics. There may be some concern about superimposing modern western philosophical categories on to a subject matter that was not constructed according to the dictates of western philosophical frameworks. Nevertheless,

the task of this book is to understand Chinese philosophy first and foremost on its own terms, and where appropriate in comparison with categories in western philosophy. It is from this same vantage point that we consider Buddhist philosophy; hence Kalupahana's method is well suited to our purposes here.

4. The *Biographies of Eminent Buddhist Monks* (*Gaoseng Juan*) by Hui-chiao (d. 554 CE), cited in Fung 1953: 241.
5. The text *Disposing of Error* (*Lihuo lun*) features a person, *Mouzi*, as the defender of Buddhist doctrine. The date and authorship of the text are unknown; sections of it are reproduced in De Bary and Bloom 1999: 421–426.
6. These records, recapitulated by Fung Yu-Lan in *A History of Chinese Philosophy* (1953), were written by Ji Zang (549–623) in his *Commentary on the Madhyamika Sastra* (*Zhongguanlun shu*), and by the Japanese monk, Ancho, who wrote a commentary on the same *Sastra* (Fung 1953: 244).
7. These are the five components or processes that are in constant interplay, which the Chinese labelled '*yin*' as opposed to '*yang*'.
8. According to Hurvitz *et al.*, Chinese thinkers did not realise that the texts from India were divided along sectarian lines, and their attempts to create some coherence among them were often fraught (1999a: 433).
9. From Derk Bodde, included as part of translator's notes in Fung 1953: 295.
10. Fung Yu-Lan states that the doctrine of the Consciousness-only sect completely contradicted common sense (1953: 339).
11. The long name of this text is *Sutra on the White Lotus of the Sublime Dharma*. Its long name in Chinese is *Miaofa Lianhua Jing*.
12. This religious–philosophical outlook would have been appealing in a political climate that sought unification and stability (Hurvitz *et al.* 1999a: 475).
13. It was said to have been composed by an obscure disciple but recent scholarship attributes the work to a monk from a different strain of Buddhism who had come into contact with Chan ideas. Moreover there have been additions to the *Platform Sutra* over the years. In 1967, Philip Yampolsky published an authoritative translation of a version of the *Platform Sutra* located in Dunhuang; that version turned out to be the earliest extant version of the work. However, the copy contains numerous errors and is believed to have been a copy made by a semi-literate scribe (De Bary and Bloom 1999: 494).
14. Fung notes that his five points hold true of Chan Buddhists, 'irrespective of which interpretation they accept' (1953: 390). However, this assertion is doubtful because in Fung's ensuing discussion a number of these tenets would not have been endorsed by those of the northern sect.

15. Fung traces the idea of instantaneous enlightenment back to Dao Sheng (1953: 388).
16. These examples are from the text *The Gateless Gate* (*Wumenguan* in Chinese; *Mumonkan* in Japanese), published in 1228 by the Chinese monk Wumen. Another famous collection is the *Blue Cliff Records* (Biyan Lu), which were compiled during the Song dynasty in 1125 and subsequently expanded into its present form by the Chan master Yuanwu Keqin (1063–1135).
17. Chung-ying Cheng in 'On Zen (Ch'an) Language and Zen Paradoxes' raises the paradox of the *gongan* in Chan enlightenment (1973). His discussion has instigated many responses to the paradox.
18. See, for example, Henry Rosemont, Jr's discussion on 'Is Zen Buddhism a Philosophy?'. In the compilation of source materials by De Bary and Bloom (1999), Chan Buddhism is classified under the 'Schools of Buddhist Practice' rather than with the 'Schools of Buddhist Doctrine'.
19. Wing-tsit Chan discusses the distinctive features of Chinese Buddhism in 'Transformation of Buddhism in China' (1957–8).

Postscript

In this book, we have assumed that 'Chinese philosophy' is an identifiable field of study. However, the meaning of 'Chinese philosophy' is debated by contemporary scholars.[1] There are a few reasons why the phrase 'Chinese philosophy' is controversial and three of them are discussed here. First, the Chinese phrase denoting philosophy, *zhexue*, was coined only in the nineteenth century by a Japanese scholar.[2] Thus the phrase 'Chinese philosophy' is applied retrospectively to a field of enquiries and debates that arose in China around 500 BCE among thinkers who did not know the term. Secondly, the term 'philosophy' is a distinct disciplinary field with ancient Greek origins and as such is characterised, partly in historical terms, by particular topics and modes of enquiry, methods of argumentation and reasoning styles. The term 'philosophy' is unlike the term 'religion', for instance, whose conception is not necessarily associated with particular aspects of one civilisation. 'Philosophy' both in its origin and as it is conceived is a more restricted term of reference. The third reason is a historical one and relates to how the phrase 'Chinese philosophy' was used by Chinese intellectuals of the modern period such as Hu Shih (1891–1962) and Fung Yu-Lan (1895–1990), who had studied western philosophy and who were eager to present the intellectual traditions of China as 'philosophy'. They wrote accounts of the history of Chinese philosophy in terms of the ideas, categories and methods of the western philosophies they had studied. However, these histories in different ways neglected aspects of Chinese philosophy that did not fit into their framework (Cua 2005: 317–47). Both these accounts are pioneering and influential works, and they helped to define Chinese philosophy as a discipline and shaped its present form.

There are important lessons from these points above. If we wish to consider Chinese philosophy as a legitimate field of study, we need perhaps to tread a middle path. This involves, on the one hand, not overextending the term 'philosophy' in order that any semblance of reflection qualifies as part of the discipline and, on the other, not misrepresenting Chinese intellectual debates due to one's earnestness to fit them into existing western conceptions of philosophy. A plausible basis for suggesting that early Chinese thought qualifies as 'philosophy' is to consider parallels between its reflective activities and those of western philosophy, rather than to look for similarity in content and style. The discussions in this book explore the assembly of ideas associated with the different schools of thought that arose in ancient China, their roots, divergences and cross-influences, the effect some of these ideas may have had in shaping Chinese society, its institutions and practices, and their contemporary significance. They demonstrate that the early Chinese thinkers, to different extents, engaged in systematic, reflective enquiry. The thinkers considered ethical questions, the nature of government, conceptions of social good, meta-ethical issues, metaphysical visions, the role of language, and strategies for persuasion and argumentation, all of which are core philosophical activities. On the basis of these reflective activities, we can reasonably say that Chinese philosophy is a 'philosophy'. Furthermore, as in the cases of Anglo-American philosophy and contemporary European philosophy, the content and methods of enquiry in Chinese philosophy are in some ways unique; these help to establish it as a distinctive disciplinary field.

The distinctive features of Chinese philosophy are spread across the standard areas in traditional western philosophy: ethics and political philosophy, metaphysics, epistemology and logic. However, the dominant paradigms in Chinese and western philosophy – conceptions of self, common good, existence, causality, language and its connection with reality, knowledge and wisdom – are not always similar. In some cases, the concepts and conceptual frameworks in Chinese philosophy challenge the boundaries in traditional western philosophy. Here, I discuss a number of significant examples that demonstrate the value of Chinese philosophy.

Chinese philosophy presents a dynamic and realistic picture of the self at the centre of ethical decisions. The conception of self in Chinese philosophy, as a relationally constituted and culturally and historically situated person, is complicated and profound. There is much in the literature that draws on insights in the Chinese philosophical traditions to illuminate contemporary discussions of ethics. Here, I discuss briefly a number of interesting points that can be drawn from an engagement between Chinese and western ethics. According to the view that understands relationships and contexts as essential aspects of personhood, ethical decisions, actions and behaviours are not isolated events. Ethical situations are not frozen in time and independent of lived realities, and therefore cannot be assessed in abstraction, as if they were discontinuous with other aspects of a person's life. Therefore, in thinking about ethics, we should take into account the relevant causal aspects of a particular event, the moral agent's role in it and her responses to it. These are considerations in addition to those we might typically see as morally significant, namely, a person's character, attitudes and emotions as well as her relations with significant others, obligations, duties, loyalties and consequences. That a person is in part a product of a particular history and culture also adds to the complexity of ethics. The Chinese conception of ethics discussed here suggests that there are limits to systematisation or universalisation across ethical situations. This is not to say that ethics in Chinese philosophy is entirely *ad hoc* and situational; indeed, situational factors are only one among the many factors involved.

From this brief outline of the features of ethics in Chinese philosophy, we can draw three important insights. First, a proper understanding of ethics must correspond with ethical decision-making in real life. Ethical issues must be understood in context, in terms of the concrete realities of moral agents. Norms and standards are important in guiding ethical decision-making, but the circumstantial aspects of a situation help to determine how we might appropriately apply these norms. Secondly, there is a need to understand ethics more broadly, not in terms of pre-determined transcendent ideals but as the products of particular cultural and historical traditions. The early Chinese thinkers were consciously aware that when aspects of society change – for instance, in population, through social mobility, accumulation of wealth by individuals, family and other group structures – norms, values, beliefs and ideals change as well. This means that, in our discussions of ethics, we should also consider a person's assumptions, such as their conceptions of society, government, selfhood and identity, individual well-being, relations between individual and collective goods, and meaningful pursuits in life. The third point focuses on the self at the centre of ethical decision-making. In Chinese philosophy, a person's character is more important than his correct practice of moral standards. For example, to be sensitive to another person's feelings might be more important than taking the correct action. Furthermore, moral norms are considered secondary to a person's character and development such that ethical requirements for one person may be different from ethical requirements for another. According to this view, ethics is a dynamic process; the important question in ethics is not, *what* the norms are, but *which* are the appropriate considerations to apply, and *how* they might be applied. In brief, the conception of ethics in Chinese philosophy takes into account a broad range of factors that affect ethical decision-making. Although it is complicated, it presents a realistic picture of the person who is at the centre of the ethical decisions.

The epistemological reflections of Zhuangzi embody the thoughts of one who is captivated by the diversity in the world and is concerned about how to deal with it. We have seen how Zhuangzi is exasperated at those who claim to hold the truth. His despair at absolute or universalistic conceptions of truth was also shared by the Daoists more generally, as well as by the Dialecticians and the later Mohists. The early Chinese thinkers were engaged in debates from very early on, since the inception of reflective thinking in China during the Spring and Autumn period. Perhaps, in being exposed to many different views, the early Chinese thinkers also saw the merits in the views of other doctrines. The profusion of different views may have engendered in the Chinese thinkers a disposition toward compromise and synthesis rather than analysis and definition. In broad terms, the method of synthesis looks for concordances and is comfortable with drawing elements from different, sometimes incompatible, doctrines. The analytic approach (an important method in western philosophy), by contrast, seeks to understand the constitutive elements of each doctrine as well as how these are combined in argumentation. This approach also focuses on systematisation, which is an integral element of modern science that the Chinese intellectual traditions seemed to lack. However, the method of synthesis, which continues to be a dominant method in scholarship in modern-day China, appreciates different perspectives and pragmatically seeks to draw from the range of available views, and to build a coherent view with the different elements. Both the analytic and synthetic methods are important approaches to knowledge. It is particularly important in an increasingly global context that we learn not only to scrutinise the ideas of different civilisations and cultures, but also to draw from their insights.

The early Chinese thinkers were concerned about the inadequacy of language to capture the complexity and diversity of life and thought. Yet, they also realised that language was a potent force in society as it could be used as an instrument of political control. The Confucians in particular were keen to incorporate language into their ethico-political agenda. In their theory of the rectification of names, they proposed that a normative use of titles (such as father or brother) should help to shape the behaviour of the people. The later Mohists and the Mingjia attempted to systematise aspects of language. However, they were confounded by the mismatches between language and reality. Their discussions prompt further questions about the nature of the Chinese language. In the Chinese language, each character has a defined meaning. Because this is the case, it is not particularly important how the characters are placed in order to convey meaning. This contrasts with a language that is based on syntax, such as English. In English, meaning is partly determined by grammatical structure (for instance, in the two statements 'Jane, I am' and 'I am Jane'). Do these different ways of expressing meaning affect the way users of these different languages think? The early Chinese thinkers were insightful about the features of the Chinese language and we should extend their investigations more generally to compare the connections between language and thought. In the field of comparative philosophy, some scholars have argued that there is an important connection between language and logic: the thoughts that particular language-users have are shaped by the different 'structures' in their language. In other words, different language-speakers 'see' the world differently. It is important to appreciate this point especially in cross-cultural communication, and particularly because language is a central aspect of human life.

These three examples provide a sense of the distinctiveness of Chinese philosophy as well as the breadth and depth of its insights. They also establish its relevance in the contemporary world. The worldview in Chinese philosophy is one that, on the whole, is guided by observations of the world rather than theoretical schemes. Therefore, it tends to be more empirical and concrete, focusing on plurality and how the manifold things in the world are interdependent. This is in turn connected with its views of change and complex causalities, and its focus on processes rather than events. This means that although early Chinese philosophy is at times frustratingly unsystematic, it also affords a more inclusive picture of life, one that refuses to simplify diversity. The discussions in this book point to a need for more extensive comparative studies, including those of an interdisciplinary nature. Perhaps these studies will enlighten our understanding of Chinese philosophy as it stands in comparison with other systems of thought, as well as our visions of human well-being.

Notes

1. See, for instance, Defoort 2001 and Cua 2005: 317–47.
2. Nishi Amane (1829–87) coined the phrase in Japanese as a combination of two characters: *tetsugaku* (*zhexue* in Chinese). See Defoort 2001: 394.

Glossary

Texts

Bingfa	*Art of War*	兵法
Biyan Lu	*Blue Cliff Record*	碧巖錄
Bohu Tong (or *Baihu Tong*)	*Discourses in the White Tiger Hall*	白虎通
Cheng Gongsheng	Mingjia text, no longer extant	成公生
Cheng Weishi Lun	*A Treatise in the Establishment of Consciousness-Only*	成唯識論
Chun Qiu	*The Spring and Autumn Annals*	春秋
Chunqiu fanlu	*Luxuriant Gems of the Spring and Autumn Annals*	春秋繁露
Daodejing	or *Lao Tzu*	道德經
Daqu	*Greater Selection*; Mohist Canons	大取
Daxue	*Great Learning*	大學
Dazhuan	*Great Commentary*, of the *Yijing*	大傳
Fahua Jing	*Lotus Sutra*	法華經
Fahua wenju	*Words and Phrases of the Lotus Sutra*	法華文句
Fahua xuan yi	*Profound Meaning of the Lotus Sutra*	法華玄義
Gongsun Longzi	or *Kung-sun Lung-tzu*	公孫龍子
Guanzi	*Kuan-tzu*	管子
Guo Qin Lun	*The Faults of Qin*	過秦論
Han Feizi	*Han Fei-tzu*	韓非子
Hou Hanshu	*History of the Later Han Dynasty*	後漢書
Huainanzi	*Huainan-tzu*	淮南子
Huang Gong	Mingjia text, no longer extant	黃公
Huangdi neijing ling shu	*Divine Pivot of the Huangdi neijing*	黃帝內經靈樞
Huangdi neijing suwen	*Basic Questions of the Huangdi neijing*	黃帝內經素問
Huangdi neijing taisu	*Grand Basis of the Huangdi neijing*	黃帝內經太素
Huangdi Neijing	*Inner Canon of the Yellow Emperor*	黃帝內經
Huang-Lao Boshu	Huang-Lao Silk Manuscripts	黃老帛書
Huayan jing	*Flower Garland Sutra*	華嚴經

Huizi	Mingjia text, no longer extant	惠子
Jin Shizi Zhang	*Essay on the Gold Lion*	金獅子章
Laozi	or *Daodejing*	老子
Li Ji	*Book of Rites*	禮記
Liezi	*Lieh-tzu*	列子
Lihuo Lun	*Disposing of Error*	理惑論
Liu Zu Tan Jing	*Platform Sutra of the Sixth Patriarch*	六祖壇經
Lunyu	*Analects of Confucius*	論語
Lüshi Chunqiu	*Spring and Autumn Annals of Mr Lü*	呂氏春秋
Mao Gong	Mingjia text, no longer extant	毛公
Mengzi		孟子
Miaofa Lianhua Jing	*Sutra on the White Lotus of the Sublime Dharma*	妙法蓮華經
Ming Shi	*Names and Objects*	名實
Mo Tzu	*Mo-tzu*	墨子
Mohe zhiguan	*The Great Calming and Contemplation*	摩訶止觀
Neipian	Inner Chapters of *Zhuangzi*	內篇
Neiye	'Inner Enterprise/Training'; chapter of Guanzi	內業
Qian Hanshu	*History of the Former Han Dynasty*	前漢書
Qiwu lun	Chapter 2 of *Zhuangzi*	齊物論
Shang Shu	also known as *Book of History*; see *Shu Jing*	尚書
Shangjun Shu	*Book of Lord Shang*	商君書
Shi Jing	*Book of Poetry* or *Book of Odes*	詩經
Shi Yi	*Ten Appendices*	十翼
Shiji	*Records of the Grand Historian*	史記
Shu Jing	*Book of History; Classic of History or Documents*	書經
Shuogua Zhuan	*Commentary on the Trigrams*	說卦傳
Shuowen Jiezi	*Shuowen* Lexicon	說文解字
Si Shu	(Confucian) *Four Books*	四書
Tian Wen	Chapter 3 of the *Huainanzi*	天文
Tianlun (from *Xunzi*)	*Discourse on Heaven*	天論
Tuan Zhuan	*Commentary on the Judgements*	彖傳
Waipian	Outer Chapters of *Zhuangzi*	外篇
Wenyan	*Commentary on the Words of the Text*	文言
Wu Jing	(Confucian) *Five Classics*	五經
Wumenguan	*Gateless Gate* (Collection of Chan *gong-an*)	無門關
Xiang Gong	(section of *Zuo Zhuan*)	襄公
Xiang Zhuan	*Commentary on the Images*	象傳

Xiao Jing	*Book of Filial Piety*	孝經
Xiaoqu	*Smaller Selection*; Mohist Canons	小取
Xiaoyao you	Chapter 1 of *Zhuangzi*	逍遙遊
Xici Zhuan	*Commentary on the Appended Phrases*	繫辭傳
Xugua Zhuan	*Commentary on the Sequencing of the Hexagrams*	序卦傳
Xunzi	*Hsun-tzu*	荀子
Yangsheng Zhu	Chapter 3 of *Zhuangzi*	養生主
Yueling	Chapter of the *Liji*	月令
Yi Zhuan	*Commentaries on the Yijing*	易傳
Yijing	*Book of Changes*	易經
Yin Wen		尹文
Yu Jing	*Expounding the Canons*; Mohist Canons	語經
Yuan Dao	Chapter 1 of the *Huainanzi*	原道
Zagua Zhuan	*Commentary on the Hexagrams in Irregular Order*	雜卦傳
Zapian	*Miscellaneous Chapters*; in *Zhuangzi*	雜篇
Zhao Gong	(section of *Zuo Zhuan*)	昭公
Zhong Yong	*Doctrine of the Mean*	中庸
Zhongguanlun shu	*Commentary on the Madhyamika Sastra*	中觀論疏
Zhou Yi	*Changes of Zhou*; see *Yijing*	周易
Zhuangzi	*Chuang-tzu*	莊子
Zuo Zhuan	*Tso Chuan*	左傳

Names

Amituo Fo	Amitabha	阿彌陀佛
Baijia zhi xue	Hundred Schools of Learning	百家之學
Ban Biao	(3–54 CE)	班彪
Ban Gu	(32–92 CE)	班固
Ban Zhao	(1st century CE)	班昭
Ben Wu Yi	Variant School of Original Non-Being	本無異
Ben Wu	School of Original Non-Being	本無
Bianzhe	Disputers	辯者
Chang'an		長安
Chan-na	Chan Buddhism	禪那
Chunqiu	Spring and Autumn Period (722–476 BCE)	春秋
Dao-an	(312–85 CE)	道安
Dao Sheng	(ca. 360–434 CE)	道生
Daojia	Daoists	道家

Daojiao	Daoist religion	道教
Deng Xi	(d. 501 BCE)	鄧析
Dong Zhongshu	(ca. 195–ca. 115 BCE)	董仲舒
Dong Zhou	Eastern Zhou	東周
Du Shun	(557–640 CE)	杜順
Fa Zang	(643–712 CE)	法藏
Fajia	Legalist thinkers	法家
Fangshi	masters of technical methods	方士
Fu Xi	(ca. 2800 BCE); mythical?	伏羲
Gaozi	or Kao Tzu (ca. 420–350 BCE)	告子
Gongsun Long	(b. 380 BCE?)	公孫龍
Guan Zhong	(d. 645 BCE)	管仲
Guo Xiang	(d. 312)	郭象
Guodian		郭店
Han Chao	Han Dynasty (206 BCE–220 CE)	漢朝
Han Fei	(ca. 280–233 BCE)	韓非
Han Huanhui Wang	King Huanhui of Han (272–239 BCE)	韩桓惠王
Han Wang An	King An of Han (238–230 BCE)	韩王安
Heshanggong		河上公
Hu Shi	Hu Shih (1891–1962 CE)	胡適
Hua Yan	Flower Garland (Buddhism)	華嚴
Huan Hua	School of Phenomenal Illusion	幻化
Huangjin zhi luan	Yellow Turban Rebellion	黃巾之亂
Huang-Lao	(Daoist doctrine)	黃老
Hui Neng	(638–713 CE)	慧能
Hui Shi	(370?–310? BCE)	惠施
Hui Yuan	(334–416 CE)	慧遠
Huo	common name, in later Mohist text	獲
Ji Se	School of Matter as such	即色
Ji Zang	(540–623 CE)	吉藏
Jia Yi	(200–168 BCE)	賈誼
Jin Chao	Jin Dynasty (265–420 CE)	晉朝
Jing Tu	Pure Land (Buddhism)	淨土
Jingdi	Emperor Jing of Han (reign 157–41 BCE)	景帝
Jiumoluoshi	Kumarajiva	鳩摩羅什
Jixia		稷下
Kongzi	Confucius (551–479 BCE)	孔子
Lao Dan	or Laozi	老聃
Laozi	Lao Tzu	老子
Li Si	(ca. 280–208 BCE)	李斯
Liang Qichao	(1873–1929 CE)	梁啟超

Liu An	(ca. 180–122 BCE)	劉安
Liu Chao	Six Kingdoms period	六朝
Lü Buwei	(ca. 291–235 BCE)	吕不韋
Mawangdui		馬王堆
Mengzi	Mencius (385?–312? BCE)	孟子
Mingjia	Terminologists (thinkers belonging to the School of Names)	名家
Mouzi	Master Mou	牟子
Mozi	Mo Tzu (480 BCE?–390 BCE?)	墨子
Nanbei Chao	Southern and Northern Dynasties (420–589 CE)	南北朝
Qin Chao	Chin Dynasty (221–206 BCE)	秦朝
Qin Er Shi	(229–207 BCE)	秦二世
Qin Shihuangdi	(260–210 BCE)	秦始皇帝
Ru	Confucianism	儒
Ru-Mo	Confucian-Mohist	儒墨
San Lun	Three Treatise (Buddhism)	三論
Sanguo	Three Kingdoms period (222–63 CE)	三國
Seng Zhao	(394–414 CE)	僧肇
Shang Yang	(d. 338 BCE)	商鞅
Shen Buhai	(d. 337 BCE)	申不害
Shen Dao	(ca. 350–275 BCE)	慎到
Shen Hui	(670–762 CE)	神會
Shen Xiu	(ca. 605–706 CE)	神秀
Shi Han	School of Stored Impressions	識含
Shijiazhuang		石家莊
Sima Qian	(ca. 145–86 BCE)	司馬遷
Sima Tan	(d. 110 BCE)	司馬談
Sui Chao	Sui Dynasty (581–618 CE)	隋朝
Sun Zi	Sun Tzu (ca. 544–496 BCE)	孫子
Tang Chao	Tang Dynasty (618–907 CE)	唐朝
Tian Tai	Tian Tai (Buddhism)	天台
Tuoba		拓拔
Wang Bi	(226–49 CE)	王弼
Wang Ni	Figure in *Zhuangzi*	王倪
Wang Yangming	(1472–1529 CE)	王陽明
Wudi	Emperor Wu of Han (reigned 141–87 BCE)	武帝
Xianbei	nomadic tribe in Han China	鮮卑
Xin Wu	School of Non-being of Mind	心無
Xuan Zang	(596–664 CE)	玄奘
Xunzi	Hsun Tzu (310?–219? BCE)	荀子

Yang Zhu	Yang Chu (370–319 BCE)	楊朱
Yanhui	Yen Hui (Confucius' disciple)	顏回
Yuan Hui	Causal Combination	緣會
Yuanwu Keqin	Chan Buddhist master (1063–1135 CE)	圜悟克勤
Zang	common name, in later Mohist text	臧
Zengzi	(505–436 BCE)	曾子
Zhanguo	Warring States period (475–221 BCE)	戰國
Zhao Gao	(d. 207 BCE)	趙高
Zhou Chao	Zhou Dynasty (1122–221 BCE)	周朝
Zhou Wen Wang	King Wen of Zhou (1099–50 BCE)	周文王
Zhu Xi	Chu Hsi (1130–1200 CE)	朱熹
Zhuangzi	Chuang Tzu (ca. 4th century BCE)	莊子
Zigong	Tzu-kung	子貢
Zilu	Tzu-lu	子路
Zisi	Tzu-lu (ca. 483–402 BCE)	子思
Zixia	Tzu-hsia	子夏
Ziyou	Tzu-yu	子游
Zizhang	Tzu-chang	子張
Zou Yan	(ca. 305–240 BCE)	鄒衍

Concepts and Themes

ai	love	愛
ai ren ruo ai qishen	valuing others as one values oneself	爱人若爱其身
aidi	love for a (younger) brother	愛弟
bao zhen	preservation of the genuine self	保真
bi	necessary/necessity	必
bi	that	彼
bian	debate, disputation	辯
bian	discriminate, distinguish	辨
bian	flat	扁
bie	(drawing) a sharp distinction	別
buke	not possible	不可
buran	not-so	不然
cai	ability	才
chang dao	enduring *dao*	常道
chouzuo	toast	酬酢
chi	guilt/shame	恥
ci	phrase	辭
dang	fit the fact	當
dao	way, path	道

dazhi	great(er) wisdom	大知
de	power, virtue	德
de	to obtain	得
di	younger brother; respect for an older brother	弟
dingfa	fixing the standards	定法
dui	body of water	兌
e (or 'wu')	evil, aversion to evil	惡
fa	punishment, standard, penal law	法
fan	return, reversion	反
fei	negative, is not the case that	非
fen	portion, duty	分
fu	reunion	復
ganying	resonance	感應
gen	hills	艮
geyi	concept-matching	格義
gongan	Zen Buddhist *koan*	公案
gu	ill, corrupted or decayed	蠱
gua	symbol, of trigram or hexagram	卦
guaci	trigram or hexagram statement in *Yijing*	卦辭
guan	observe	觀
heng	perseverance, permanence	恆
huan	dispersion	渙
huang	yellow	黃
jia	family, school	家
jiaren	family (members)	家人
jian	see	見
jian	whole, unit	兼
jianai	Mohist universal concern	兼愛
jing	well	井
jingxue	study of classics	經學
ju	carpenter's square	矩
junzi	paradigmatic man	君子
kan	moon, clouds, streams	坎
ke	possible	可
kong	empty	空
kun	earth	坤
lei	category, type	類
li fa jie	realm of principle (in Buddhism)	理法界
li	benefit, advantage, profit	利

li	clinging, fire, sun (one of the eight trigrams)	離
li	principle	理
li	propriety	禮
lun lie	relational proximity	倫列
maodun	contradiction (lit.: spear and shield)	矛盾
meiren	beautiful/handsome person	美人
milu	(deer)	麋鹿
ming	illumination	明
ming	name, term	名
mu	mother	母
nei	inner	內
nei-wai	inner-outer (debate)	內外
pan jiao	classification of teachings	判教
pi	obstruction	否
pu	simplicity	樸, 朴
qi	energy, spirit	氣
qian	heaven	乾
qing	emotions	情
ran	so	然
ren	human-heartedness, compassion	仁
ren	person	人
renzheng	benevolent government	仁政
rong	honour	榮
shadao	to kill a robber	殺盜
sharen	to kill a person	殺人
shen	spirit, numinous (realm)	神
sheng	ascend	升
sheng	birth, growth	生
shi	actuality	實
shi	time	時
shi	affirmative, is the case that	是
shi	power, momentum	勢
shi	scholar official	士
shi	world	世
shifei	this/not this	是非
shu	count	數
shu	method	術
shu	mutuality	恕
shuo	speak, say	說

siduan	four roots (Mencius)	四端
taiji	Supreme Ultimate	太極
ti	part/body	體
tian	heaven	天
tian di zi dao	way of heaven and earth	天地之道
tianzi	son of heaven	天子
tong	sameness	同
tongyi	sameness/difference	同異
tuan	judgement (in the *Yijing*)	彖
tui	extension, analogy	推
tui lei	extend from kind to kind	推類
wai	outer	外
wanwu	manifold reality (lit.: ten thousand things)	萬物
wei	act, deem	為
wei	regard, deem	謂
weiwo	each for himself or herself	為我
wen	script, culture	文
wu	nothing, non-being	無
wu (or 'e')	evil, aversion to evil	惡
wu ming	nameless	無名
wucai	five materials	五材
wude	five powers	五德
wulun	five relationships	五倫
wuwei	non-action; without conditioned action	無為
wuwei er wuyiwei	without action and holding nothing in regard	無為而無以為
wuxing	five phases	五行
xiao	filial piety	孝
xiaozhi	small(er) wisdom	小知
xin	mind-heart	心
xin	sincerity, trustworthiness, doing one's word	信
xing	ancestral name	姓
xing	form	形
xing	(human) nature	性
xing	punishment	刑
xing e	human nature (is) evil	性惡
xing ming	fixing names	刑名
xing shan	human nature (is) good	性善
xiu	shame, disgrace	羞

xiushen	cultivation of self	修身
xu	emptiness	虛
xuan	mystery	玄
xun	wind, wood	巽
yang	male, sun	陽
yao	line on a trigram or hexagram	爻
yaoci	line statement	爻辭
yi	easy, change	易
yi	different/difference	異
yi	right, righteousness	義
yiguan	one thread	一貫
yimin	unify the masses	一民
yin	female, dark	陰
yin yang	shady/sunny; female/male	陰陽
you	have, possess	有
yuan	round	圓
yue	music	樂
zhen	genuine, real	真
zhen	thunder, shake	震
zheng	govern, government	政
zhengming	rectification of names	正名
zhexue	philosophy	哲學
zhi	innate quality, substance	質
zhi	knowledge, wisdom	知, 智
zhi	point	指
zhong	conscientiousness, being one's best	忠
zhongguo zhexue	Chinese philosophy	中國哲學
ziran	spontaneous, natural	自然
zong	ancestor, sect	宗
zuowang	sitting and forgetting	坐忘

Bibliography

Primary Texts

Analects of Confucius, trans. Dim-cheuk Lau (1979a), Harmondsworth: Penguin Books.

Analects of Confucius: A Philosophical Translation, trans. Roger Ames and Henry Rosemont Jr (1998a), New York: Ballantine Publishing Group.

Basic Writings of Han Fei Tzu, trans. Burton Watson (1964), New York: Columbia University Press.

Book of Lieh Tzu, trans. Angus C. Graham (1960), London: John Murray.

Book of Lord Shang: A Classic of the Chinese School of Law, trans. J. J. L. Duyvendak (1928), London: Arthur Probsthain.

Chinese Classics: with a Translation, Critical and Exegetical Notes, Prolegomena, and Copious Indexes, trans. James Legge (1893–5), Taipei: SMC Publishing Inc.; reprinted from the last edition by Oxford University Press in 1991; vol. 1: *Confucian Analects, The Great Learning, The Doctrine of the Mean* (3rd edn), with a Biographical Note by L. T. Ride; vol. V, *The Ch'un ts'ew, with the Tso chuen*, 2nd edn, with minor text corrections.

Chuang Tzu: Basic Writings, trans. Burton Watson (1964), New York: Columbia University Press.

Chuang-Tzu: The Inner Chapters, trans. Angus C. Graham (2001), Indianapolis: Hackett Publishing Co.

Classic of Changes: A New Translation of the I Ching as Interpreted by Wang Bi, trans. Richard J. Lynn (1994), New York: Columbia University Press.

Commentary on the Lao Tzu by Wang Pi, trans. Ariane Rump in collaboration with Wing-tsit Chan (1979); monograph no. 6 of the Society for Asian and Comparative Philosophy; Honolulu: University of Hawai'i Press.

Complete Works of Han Fei Tzu: A Classic of Chinese Political Science, trans. W. K. Liao (1939), vols. I and II, London: Arthur Probsthain.

Daodejing: "Making This Life Significant", trans. Roger Ames and David Hall (2003), New York: Ballantine Books.

Ethical and Political Works of Mo Tzu, trans. Yi-pao Mei (1929), London: Arthur Probsthain.

Ho-Shang-Kung's Commentary on Lao-Tse, trans. Eduard Erkes (1950), Ascona, Switzerland: Artibus Asiæ.

Hsün Tzu: Basic Writings, trans. Burton Watson (1963), New York: Columbia University Press.

Hsüntze: The Moulder of Ancient Confucianism, trans. Homer H. Dubs (1966), Taipei: Ch'eng-Wen Publishing Co.; originally published in 1927 by Arthur Probsthain, London.

Lao Tzu and Taoism (translated from the French by Roger Greaves), trans. Max Kaltenmark (1969), Stanford: Stanford University Press.

Lao Tzu Tao Te Ching, trans. Dim-cheuk Lau (1963), Harmondsworth: Penguin Books.

Mencius, trans. Dim-cheuk Lau (1979b), revised edition, Hong Kong: Chinese University Press.

Mo Tzu: Basic Writings, trans. Burton Watson (1963), New York: Columbia University Press.

Platform Sutra of the Sixth Patriarch, trans. Philip B. Yampolsky (1978) 6th edn., New York: Columbia University Press.

Records of the Grand Historian of China (Shiji), trans. Burton Watson (1971), 2 vols., New York: Columbia University Press.

Sacred Books of China: The Texts of Confucianism, trans. James Legge (1879), vol. 3, *The Shu King (Shujing);* reprinted 1970, Delhi: Motilal Banarsidass.

Sayings of Lao Tzu, trans. Lionel Giles (1959), London: John Murray.

Shen Tzu Fragments, trans. Paul M. Thompson (1979), London Oriental Series, vol. 29, Oxford: Oxford University Press.

Shiji (Records of the Historian: Sima Qian), trans. Burton Watson (1961), New York: Columbia University Press.

Shuowen Jiezi Zhu / Xu Shen zhuan; Duan Yucai zhu (Shuowen Lexicon by Duan, Yucai (1735–1815)), Shanghai: *Shanghai gu ji chu ban she: Xin hua shu dian, 1981;* reprinted from the original (1815), China: Jing yun lou.

A Source Book in Chinese Philosophy, trans. Wing-tsit Chan (1963a), Princeton: Princeton University Press.

Sources of Chinese Tradition: From Earliest Times to 1600, compiled by Wm Theodore De Bary and Irene Bloom (1999) vol. 1, 2nd edn., New York: Columbia University Press.

Tao Te Ching: The Book of the Way and Its Virtue, trans. J. J. L. Duyvendak (1954), London: John Murray.

'The *Gongsun Longzi:* A Translation and an Analysis of its Relationship to Later Mohist Writings', trans. Ian Johnston (2004), *Journal of Chinese Philosophy,* vol. 31, no. 2: 271–95.

'The *Kung-sun Lung Tzu* with a Translation into English', trans. Yi-pao Mei (1953), *Harvard Journal of Asiatic Studies*, vol. 16, no. 3/4, December: 404–37.

The Original Analects: Sayings of Confucius and His Successors, trans. Brooks, E. Bruce and Brooks, A. Taeko (1998), New York: Columbia University Press.

The *She King* (Book of Poetry), trans. James Legge, *The Chinese Classics*, vol. IV, 2nd edn. (1935), with minor text correctins, Taipei: SMC Publishing Inc.

The Way and Its Power: A Study of the Tao Te Ching and Its Place in Chinese Thought, trans. Arthur Waley (1958), New York: Grove Press.

The Way of Lao Tzu (Tao-te ching), trans. Wing-tsit Chan (1963b), New Jersey: Prentice Hall, Library of Liberal Arts.

Xunzi: A Translation and Study of the Complete Works, trans. John Knoblock, Stanford: Stanford University Press, vols 1–3; vol 1 (1988), books 1–6; vol 2 (1990), books 7–16; vol 3 (1994) books 17–32.

Yî King (Yijing), trans. James Legge (1899), *The Sacred Books of the East,* vol. 16, Oxford: The Clarendon Press.

Yuan Dao: Tracing Dao to its Source, trans. D. C. Lau and Roger Ames (1998) New York: Ballantine Books.

Secondary Sources

Ahern, Dennis (1980) 'An Equivocation in Confucian Philosophy', *in Journal of Chinese Philosophy*, vol. 7: 175–86.

Allan, Sarah (1997) *The Way of Water and Sprouts of Virtue;* SUNY Series in Chinese Philosophy and Culture; Albany: State University of New York Press.

Allinson, Robert E. (1985) 'The Confucian Golden Rule: A Negative Formulation', *Journal of Chinese Philosophy,* vol. 12: 305–15.

– (1989) *Chuang-tzu For Spiritual Transformation,* Albany: State University of New York Press.

Ames, Roger (1986) 'Taoism and the Nature of Nature', *Environmental Ethics,* vol. 8: 317–50.

– (1998b) 'Knowing in the *Zhuangzi:* "From Here, on the Bridge, over the River Hao"', in Roger Ames (ed.) *Wandering at East in the Zhuangzi,* Albany: State University of New York Press: pp. 219–30.

Ames, Roger and Hall, David (2001) *Focusing the Familiar: A Translation and Philosophical Interpretation of the Zhongyong,* Honolulu: University of Hawai'i Press.

Bodde, Derk (1963) 'Basic Concepts of Chinese Law: The Genesis and Evolution of Legal Thought in Traditional China', *Proceedings of the American Philosophical Society,* vol 107, no. 5: 375–98.

– (1986) 'The State and Empire of Ch'in', in Denis Twitchett, and Michael Loewe (eds.) *The Cambridge History of China,* vol. 1: The Ch'in and Han

Empires, 221 B.C.–A.D. 220, Cambridge: Cambridge University Press, pp. 21–102.

Chan, Alan (1991) *Two Visions of the Way: A Study of the Wang Pi and Ho-shang Kung Commentaries on the Lao-tzu*, Albany: State University of New York Press.

– (ed.) (2002) *Mencius: Contexts and Interpretations*, Honolulu: University of Hawai'i Press.

Chan, Wing-tsit (1955) 'The Evolution of the Confucian Concept *Jen*', *Philosophy East and West*, vol. 4: 295–319.

– (1957–58) 'Transformation of Buddhism in China', *Philosophy East and West*, vol. 7, no. 3/4: 107–16.

– (1975) 'Chinese and Western Interpretations of *Jen* (Humanity)', *Journal of Chinese Philosophy*, vol. 2: 107–29.

Ch'en, Ta-chi (1953) *Mengzi xingshan shuo yu Xunzi xinge shuo de bijiao yaniiu (A Comparative Study of Mencius' Theory that the Nature of Man is Good and Hsun Tzu's Theory that the Nature of Man is Evil)*, Taipei: *Zhongyang wenwu gong yin she.*

Cheng, Chung-ying (1973) 'On Zen (Ch'an) Language and Zen Paradoxes', *Journal of Chinese Philosophy*, vol. 1: 77–102.

– (1977) 'Toward Constructing a Dialectics of Harmonization: Harmony and Conflict in Chinese Philosophy', *Journal of Chinese Philosophy* vol. 4: 209–45.

– (1986) 'On the Environmental Ethics of the Tao and the Ch'i', *Environmental Ethics*, vol. 8, Winter: 351–70.

– (2003) 'Philosophy of Change', in Antonio Cua (ed.) *Encyclopedia of Chinese Philosophy*, New York: Routledge: pp. 517–24.

Chong, Kim-chong (1998) 'Confucius's Virtue Ethics: *Li, Yi, Wen* and *Chih* in the *Analects*', *Journal of Chinese Philosophy*, vol. 25: 101–30.

Ch'u T'ung Tsu (1965) *Law and Society in Traditional China*, The Hague: Mouton and Co.

Clarke, J. J. (2000) *The Tao of the West: Western Transformations of Taoist Thought*, London and New York: Routledge.

Creel, Herlee (1953) *Chinese Thought from Confucius to Mao Tse-Tung*, Chicago: University of Chicago Press.

– (1974) *Shen Pu-hai: A Chinese Political Philosopher of the Fourth Century B.C.*, Chicago and London: University of Chicago Press.

Cua, Antonio S. (1971) 'The Concept of Paradigmatic Individuals in the Ethics of Confucius', *Inquiry*, vol. 14: 41–55.

– (1973) 'Reasonable Action and Confucian Argumentation', *Journal of Chinese Philosophy*, vol. 1: 57–75.

– (1978) *Dimensions of Moral Creativity*, University Park: Pennsylvania State University Press.

– (1979) 'Tasks of Confucian Ethics', *Journal of Chinese Philosophy,* vol. 6: 55–67.

– (1981) 'Opposites as Complements: Reflections on the Significance of Tao', *Philosophy East and West,* vol. 31, no. 2: 123–40.

– (1984) 'Confucian Vision and Human Community', *Journal of Chinese Philosophy,* vol. 11: 227–38.

– (1988) 'Reflections on Moral Theory and Understanding Moral Traditions', in Gerald James Larson and Eliot Deutsch (eds.) *Interpreting Across Boundaries,* Princeton: Princeton University Press.

– (1989) 'The Status of Principles in Confucian Ethics', *Journal of Chinese Philosophy,* vol 16: 273–96.

– (1996a) 'The Conceptual Framework of Confucian Ethical Thought', *Journal of Chinese Philosophy* vol. 23: 153–74.

– (1996b) 'The Nature of Confucian, Ethical Tradition', *Journal of Chinese Philosophy,* vol. 23: 133–51.

– (1998) *Moral Vision and Tradition: Essays in Chinese Ethics,* Washington, D.C.: Catholic University of America Press.

– (ed.) (2003) *Encyclopedia of Chinese Philosophy*, New York: Routledge.

– (2005) *Human Nature, Ritual, and History: Studies in Xunzi and Chinese Philosophy* (Studies in Philosophy and the History of Philosophy), Washington, D.C.: Catholic University of America Press.

De Bary, Wm Theodore (1991) *The Trouble With Confucianism,* Cambridge: Harvard University Press.

– (1998) *Asian Values and Human Rights: A Confucian Communitarian Perspective,* Cambridge: Harvard University Press.

– and Tu, Weiming (eds.) (1998) *Confucianism and Human Rights,* New York: Columbia University Press.

Defoort, Carine (2001) 'Is There Such a Thing as Chinese Philosophy? Arguments of an Implicit Debate', *Philosophy East and West*, vol. 51, no. 3, July: 393–413.

Fang, Thomé H. (1981) *Chinese Philosophy: Its Spirit and Its Development,* 2nd edn., Taipei: Linking Publishing.

Fingarette, Herbert (1972) *Confucius: The Secular as Sacred*, New York: Harper and Row.

– (1979) 'The Problem of the Self in the Analects', *Philosophy East and West,* vol. 29, no. 2: 129–40.

– (1983) 'The Music of Humanity in the *Conversations* of Confucius', *Journal of Chinese Philosophy*, vol. 10: 331–56.

Fox, Alan (1996) 'Reflex and Reflectivity: *Wuwei* in the *Zhuangzi*', *Asian Philosophy,* vol. 6:1: 59–72.

Fraser, Christopher (2003) 'Introduction: Later Mohist Logic, Ethics, and Science After 25 Years', from the reprint edition of Angus C. Graham (1978) *Later Mohist Logic, Ethics, and Science,* Hong Kong: Chinese University Press.

Fu, Charles Wei-hsun (1973) 'Lao Tzu's Conception of Tao', *Inquiry*, 16 (1973 Winter): 367–94.

Fung, Yu-Lan (1947) *The Spirit of Chinese Philosophy* (trans. E. R. Hughes), London: Routledge and Kegan Paul.

— (1948) *A Short History of Chinese Philosophy* (ed. Derk Bodde), New York: Free Press.

— (1952) *A History of Chinese Philosophy*, vol. 1 (trans. Derk Bodde), Princeton: Princeton University Press.

— (1953) *A History of Chinese Philosophy*, vol. 2 (trans. Derk Bodde), Princeton: Princeton University Press.

Graham, Angus C. (1967) 'The Background of the Mencian Theory of Human Nature', reprinted (2002) in Xiusheng Liu (ed.) *Essays on the Moral Philosophy of Mengzi*, Indianapolis: Hackett Publishing, pp. 1–63.

— (1978) *Later Mohist Logic, Ethics and Science*, Hong Kong: Chinese University Press.

— (1983) 'Taoist Spontaneity and the Dichotomy of 'Is' and 'Ought', in Victor Mair (ed.) *Experimental Essays on the Chuang-tzu*, Honolulu: University of Hawai'i Press: pp. 3–23.

— (1986) *Yin-Yang and the Nature of Correlative Thinking*, IEAP Occasional Paper and Monograph Series no. 6, Singapore: Institute of East Asian Philosophies.

— (1989) *Disputers of the Tao: Philosophical Argument in Ancient China* La Salle: Open Court Press.

— (1990a) 'Three Studies of Kung-sun Lung', in Angus C. Graham (ed.) *Studies in Chinese Philosophy and Philosophical Literature*, Albany: State University of New York Press: pp. 125–215.

— (1990b) *Studies in Chinese Philosophy and Philosophical Literature*, Albany: State University of New York Press (first published in 1986 by Institute of East Asian Philosophies, Singapore).

— (2003a) 'How much of *Chuang Tzu* did Chuang Tzu Write?', in Harold Roth (ed.) *A Companion to Angus C. Graham's Chuang Tzu*, Monograph no. 20, Society for Asian and Comparative Philosophy, Honolulu: University of Hawai'i Press, pp. 58–103. Originally published in 1980, in Henry Rosemont, Jr and Benjamin Schwartz (eds.) *Studies in Classical Chinese Thought*, Journal of the American Academy of Religion Thematic Studies, Chico: Scholars Press.

— (2003b) "Chuang Tzu's Essay on Seeing Things as Equal," in Harold Roth (ed.) *A Companion to Angus C. Graham's Chuang Tzu*, Monograph no. 20, Society for Asian and Comparative Philosophy, Honolulu: University of Hawai'i Press (pp. 104–129). Originally published in 1969, in *History of Religions*, vol. 9, no. 2/3: pp. 137–159.

Grange, Joseph (2004) *John Dewey, Confucius and Global Philosophy*, SUNY Series in Chinese Philosophy and Culture, Albany: State University of New York Press.

Guan Feng (1952) *Zhuangzi Zhexue Taolun Ji (Collected Discussions on the Philosophy of Zhuangzi)*, Beijing: Zhonghua shu ji.

Guha, Ramachandra (1995) 'Radical American Environmentalism and Wilderness Preservation: A Third World Critique', in Andrew Brennan (ed.) *The Ethics of the Environment*, International Research Library of Philosophy series, London: Dartmouth Publishing: pp. 239–52.

Hall, David (1987) 'On Seeking a Change of Environment: A Quasi-Taoist Proposal', *Philosophy East and West* 37, no. 2: 160–71.

Hall, David and Ames, Roger (1997) *Thinking Through Confucius*, Albany: State University of New York Press.

– (1998) *Thinking from the Han: Self, Truth, and Transcendence in Chinese and Western Culture*, Albany: State University of New York Press.

– (1999) *The Democracy of the Dead: Dewey, Confucius, and the Hope for Democracy in China*, La Salle: Open Court Publishing Company.

Hansen, Chad (1983a) *Language and Logic in Ancient China*, Ann Arbor: University of Michigan Press.

– (1983b) 'A *Tao* of *Tao* in Chuang-tzu', in Victor Mair (ed.) *Experimental Essays on Chuang-tzu*, Asian Studies at Hawai'i no. 29, Center for Asian and Pacific Studies, Honolulu: University of Hawai'i Press: pp. 24–55.

– (1992) *A Daoist Theory of Chinese Thought*, New York: Oxford University Press.

– (2003) 'The Relatively Happy Fish', *Asian Philosophy*, vol. 13, nos. 2/3: 145–64.

Harbsmeier, Christoph (1998) *Science and Civilization in China*, vol. 7, part 1, *Language and Logic*, Cambridge: Cambridge University Press.

Henderson, John B. (1984) *The Development and Decline of Chinese Cosmology*, New York: Columbia University Press.

– (2003) 'Cosmology', in Antonio Cua (ed.) *Encyclopedia of Chinese Philosophy*, New York: Routledge: pp. 187–94.

Henricks, Robert (1989) *Lao-tze Te-tao ching: A New Translation Based on the Recently Discovered Ma-Wang-Tui Texts*, New York: Ballantine Books.

Ho Hwang, Philip (1979) 'What is Mencius' Theory of Human Nature?', *Philosophy East and West*, vol. 29, no. 2: 201–9.

Hsu, Cho-Yun (1965) *Ancient China in Transition: An Analysis of Social Mobility 722–222 B.C.*, Stanford: Stanford University Press.

– (1999) 'The Spring and Autumn Period', in Michael Loewe and Edward Shaughnessy (eds.) *The Cambridge History of Ancient China: From the Origins of Civilization to 221 B.C.*, Cambridge: Cambridge University Press.

Hu, Shih (1928) *The Development of the Logical Method in Ancient China*, Shanghai: The Oriental Book Company.

Hurvitz, Leon and Tsai, Heng-Ting (1999) 'The Introduction of Buddhism', in W. T. De Bary and Irene Bloom (eds.) *Sources of Chinese Tradition: From Earliest*

Times to 1600, vol. 1, 2nd edn., New York: Columbia University Press: pp. 415–32.

Hurvitz, Leon *et al.* (1999a) 'Schools of Buddhist Doctrine', in W. T. De Bary and Irene Bloom (eds.) *Sources of Chinese Tradition: From Earliest Times to 1600*, vol. 1, 2nd edn. New York: Columbia University Press: pp. 433–80.

Hurvitz, Leon *et al.* (1999b) 'Schools of Buddhist Practice', in W. T. De Bary and Irene Bloom (eds.) *Sources of Chinese Tradition: From Earliest Times to 1600*, vol. 1, 2nd edn. New York: Columbia University Press: pp. 481–536.

Ip, Po-Keung (1983) 'Taoism and the Foundations of Environmental Ethics', *Environmental Ethics* 5, 335–43.

Ivanhoe, Philip (1990) 'Thinking and Learning in Early Confucianism', *Journal of Chinese Philosophy*, vol. 17, no. 4: 473–93.

– (1993) 'Zhuangzi on Skepticism, Skill, and the Ineffable Dao', *Journal of the American Academy of Religion*, vol. 61, no. 4: 639–54.

– (1996) 'Was Zhuangzi a Relativist?', in Philip Ivanhoe and Paul Kjellberg (eds.) *Essays on Skepticism, Relativism and Ethics in the Zhuangzi*, Albany: State University of New York Press: pp. 196–214.

Ivanhoe, Philip and Kjellberg, Paul (eds.) (1996) *Essays on Skepticism, Relativism and Ethics in the Zhuangzi*, Albany: State University of New York Press.

Johnston, Ian (2004) 'The *Gongsun Longzi:* A Translation and An Analysis of Its Relationship to Later Mohist Writings', *Journal of Chinese Philosophy*, vol. 31, no. 2: 271–95.

Jullien, François (1999) *The Propensity of Things: Toward a History of Efficacy in China*, trans. Janet Lloyd, New York: Zone Books.

– (2004) *Treatise on Efficacy: Between Western and Chinese Thinking*, Honolulu: University of Hawai'i Press.

Kalupahana, David J. (1976) *Buddhist Philosophy: A Historical Analysis*, Honolulu: University of Hawai'i Press.

Kohn, Livia (1993) *The Taoist Experience: An Anthology*, SUNY Series in Chinese Philosophy and Culture, Albany: State University of New York Press.

– (1996) '*Laozi:* Ancient Philosopher, Master of Immortality, and God', in Donald S. Lopez, Jr (ed.) *Religions of China in Practice*, Princeton, Princeton University Press.

Lai, Karyn (1995) 'Confucian Moral Thinking', *Philosophy East and West*, vol. 45, no. 2: 249–72.

– (2000) 'The Daodejing: Resources for Contemporary Feminist Thinking', *Journal of Chinese Philosophy*, 27:2, June: 131–53.

– (2003a) 'Conceptual Foundations for Environmental Ethics: A Daoist Perspective', *Environmental Ethics*, vol. 25: 247–66.

– (2003b) 'Confucian Moral Cultivation: Some Parallels with Musical Training', in Kim-Chong Chong, Sor-Hoon Tan and C. L. Ten (eds.) *The Moral*

Circle and the Self: Chinese and Western Perspectives, La Salle: Open Court Press: pp. 107–39.

– (2006) *Learning from Chinese Philosophies: Ethics of Interdependent and Contextualised Self*, Aldershot: Ashgate Publishing.

Lai, Whalen (2003) 'Buddhism in China: A Historical Survey', in Antonio Cua (ed.) *Encyclopedia of Chinese Philosophy*, New York: Routledge: pp. 7–19.

Lau, Dim-cheuk (1958) 'The Treatment of Opposites in Lao-tzu', *Bulletin of the School of Oriental and African Studies*, 21: 344–60.

Li, Chenyang (ed.) (2000) *The Sage and the Second Sex*, La Salle: Open Court Press.

Liu, Xiaogan (1994) *Classifying the Zhuangzi Chapters*, trans. William E. Savage, Ann Arbor: University of Michigan, Center for Chinese Studies.

– (1999) 'An Inquiry into the Core Value of Laozi's Philosophy', in Mark Csikszentmihalyi and Philip Ivanhoe (eds.) *Religious and Philosophical Aspects of the Laozi*, Albany: State University of New York Press.

Mair, Victor (ed.) (1983) *Experimental Essays on the Chuang-tzu*, Honolulu: University of Hawai'i Press.

Major, John S. (1993) *Heaven and Earth in Early Han Thought: Chapters Three, Four and Five of the Huainanzi*, SUNY Series in Chinese Philosophy and Culture, Albany: State University of New York Press.

Makeham, John (2003) 'School of Names *(Ming Jia, Ming Chia)*', in Antonio Cua (ed.) *Encyclopedia of Chinese Philosophy*, New York: Routledge: pp. 491–7.

Marshall, Peter (1992) *Nature's Web: Rethinking Our Place on Earth*, New York: Paragon House.

Munro, Donald J. (1969) *The Concept of Man in Early China*, Stanford: Stanford University Press.

Neville, Robert C. (1986) 'The Scholar-Official as a Model for Ethics', *Journal of Chinese Philosophy*, vol. 13: 185–201.

Nivison, David (1980) 'Two Roots or One?', *Proceedings and Addresses of the American Philosophical Association*, 53:6 (August 1980): 739–61.

– (1999) 'The Classical Philosophical Writings', in Michael Loewe and Edward Shaughnessy (eds.) *The Cambridge History of Ancient China: From the Origins of Civilization to 221 B.C.*, Cambridge: Cambridge University Press.

Nylan, Michael (2001) *The Five "Confucian" Classics*, New Haven: Yale University Press.

Peerenboom, Randall P. (1991) 'Beyond Naturalism: A Reconstruction of Daoist Environmental Ethics', *Environmental Ethics* 13: 3–22.

Raphals, Lisa (1996) 'Skeptical Strategies in the *Zhuangzi* and *Theaetetus*', in Philip Ivanhoe and Paul Kjellberg (eds.) *Essays on Skepticism, Relativism and Ethics in the Zhuangzi*, Albany: State University of New York Press: 26–49. Reprinted, with minor revisions, from *Philosophy East and West*, vol. 44, no. 3 (1994): 501–26.

Robinet, Isabelle (1997) *Taoism: Growth of a Religion* (trans. Phyllis Brooks): Stanford: Stanford University Press.

Rosemont, Jr, Henry (1970) 'Is Zen Buddhism a Philosophy?', *Philosophy East and West,* vol. 20, no. 1: 63–72.

— (1988) 'Against Relativism?', in Gerald James Larson and Eliot Deutsch (eds.) *Interpreting Across Boundaries,* Princeton: Princeton University Press: pp. 36–70.

Rosenlee, Li-Hsiang Lisa (2006) *Confucianism and Women: A Philosophical Interpretation,* SUNY Series in Chinese Philosophy and Culture, Albany: State University of New York Press.

Roth, Harold D. (1991a) 'Who Compiled the Chuang Tzu?', in Henry Rosemont, Jr (ed.) *Chinese Texts and Philosophical Contexts,* La Salle: Open Court Press.

— (1991b) 'Psychology and Self-Cultivation in Early Taoistic Thought', *Harvard Journal of Asiatic Studies* vol. 51: 599–650.

— (1999) *Original Tao: Inward Training (Nei-yeh) and the Foundations of Taoist Mysticism,* New York: Columbia University Press.

— (2003) 'An Appraisal of Angus Graham's Textual Scholarship on the *Chuang Tzu*'; in Harold D. Roth (ed.) *A Companion to Angus C. Graham's Chuang Tzu,* Society for Asian and Comparative Philosophy Monograph, Honolulu: University of Hawai'i Press.

Ryle, Gilbert (1946) 'Knowing How and Knowing That', *Proceedings of the Aristotelian Society,* XLVI: 1–16.

Sartwell, Crispin (1993) 'Confucius and Country Music', *Philosophy East and West,* vol. 43: 243–54.

Schwartz, Benjamin (1985) *The World of Thought in Ancient China,* Cambridge: Belknap Press of Harvard University Press.

Shaughnessy, Edward (1997) *Before Confucius: Studies in the Creation of the Chinese Classics;* SUNY Series in Chinese Philosophy and Culture; Albany: State University of New York Press.

Shun, Kwong-loi (1993) '*Jen* and *Li* in the *Analects*', *Philosophy East and West,* vol. 43, no. 3: 457–79.

— (1997) *Mencius and Early Chinese Thought,* Stanford: Stanford University Press.

Sivin, Nathan (1999) 'The Springs and Autums of Mr. Lü (Lüshi chunqiu)', in Wm Theodore De Bary and Irene Bloom (eds.) *Sources of Chinese Tradition: From Earliest Times to 1600,* vol. 1, 2nd edn. New York: Columbia University Press: pp. 236–41.

— (1995a) *Medicine, Philosophy and Religion in Ancient China: Researches and Reflections,* Aldershot: Variorum (Ashgate Publishing).

— (1995b) 'The Myth of the Naturalists', *in Medicine, Philosophy and Religion in Ancient China: Researches and Reflections,* Aldershot: Variorum (Ashgate Publishing); Section IV, pp. 1–33.

Skaja, Henry G. (1984) 'Li (Ceremonial) as a Primal Concept in Confucian Spiritual-Humanism', in Chang Chi Yun *et al.* (eds.), *Chinese Philosophy*, vol. 3, *Confucianism and Other Schools*, Taiwan: Chinese Culture University Press: pp. 47–71.

Slingerland, Edward (2000) 'Effortless Action: The Chinese Spiritual Ideal of Wu-wei', *Journal of the American Academy of Religion*, vol. 68, no. 2: 293–328.

— (2003) *Effortless Action: Wu-wei as Conceptual Metaphor and Spiritual Ideal in Early China*, New York: Oxford University Press.

Tan, Sor Hoon (2004) *Confucian Democracy: A Deweyan Reconstruction*, SUNY Series in Chinese Philosophy and Culture, Albany: State University of New York Press.

Teng, Norman Y. (2006) 'The Relatively Happy Fish Revisited', *in Asian Philosophy*, vol. 16, no. 1: 39–47.

Tu, Weiming (1968) 'The Creative Tension Between *Jen* and *Li*', *Philosophy East and West*, vol. 18, no. 1–2: 29–40.

— (1972) '*Li* as Process of Humanisation', *Philosophy East and West*, vol. 22: 187–201.

— (1976) *Centrality and Commonality: An Essay on Chung-yung*, Monograph of the Society for Asian and Comparative Philosophy, no. 3, Honolulu: University of Hawai'i Press.

— (1985) *Confucian Thought: Selfhood as Creative Transformation*, Albany: State University of New York Press.

Tucker, Mary Evelyn and Berthrong, John H. (eds.) (1998) *Confucianism and Ecology: The Interrelation of Heaven, Earth, and Humans*, Cambridge: Harvard University Press.

Twitchett, Denis and Loewe, Michael (eds.) (1986) *The Cambridge History of China*, vol. 1: The Ch'in and Han Empires, 221 B.C.–A.D. 220, Cambridge: Cambridge University Press.

Van Norden, Bryan (1996) 'Competing Interpretations of the Inner Chapters of the *Zhuangzi*', *Philosophy East and West*, vol. 46, no. 2: 247–68.

Watson, Burton (1999) 'The Great Han Historians', in Wm Theodore De Bary and Irene Bloom (eds.) *Sources of Chinese Tradition: From Earliest Times to 1600*, vol. 1, 2nd edn. New York: Columbia University Press: pp. 367–74.

Wilhelm, Hellmut (1977) *Heaven, Earth, and Man in the Book of Changes*, Seven Eranos Lectures, Publications on Asia of the Institute for Comparative and Foreign Area Studies, no. 28, Seattle and London: University of Washington Press.

Wright, Arthur (1959) *Buddhism in Chinese History*, Stanford: Stanford University Press.

Wu, Kuang-ming (1982) *Chuang Tzu: World Philosopher at Play*, American Academy of Religion Studies in Religion, no. 26, New York: Crossroad Publishing Co.

– (1990) *The Butterfly as Companion: Meditations on the First Three Chapters of the Chuang Tzu*, SUNY Series in Religion and Philosophy, Albany: State University of New York Press.

– (1996) *On Chinese Body Thinking: A Cultural Hermeneutic*, Leiden: Brill Academic Publishers.

Yearley, Lee (1996) 'Zhuangzi's Understanding of Skillfulness and the Ultimate Spiritual State', in Philip Ivanhoe and Paul Kjellberg (eds.) *Essays on Skepticism, Relativism and Ethics in the Zhuangzi*, Albany: State University of New York Press: 152–82.

Index